ISLAND TECHNOLOGY

*Technology for Development
in the South Pacific*

The publication of this book was
generously assisted by UNESCO

ISLAND TECHNOLOGY

*Technology for Development
in the South Pacific*

edited by
Tony Marjoram

Intermediate Technology Publications
in association with
Australian Scholarly Publishing
1994

© Tony Marjoram 1994, with the copyright in each contribution held by its author

First published 1994 by Intermediate Technology Publications Ltd
103–105 Southampton Row, London WC1B 4HH, UK

British Library data

A CIP catalogue record for this book is
available from the British Library

ISBN 1 85339 223 5

Cover designed by Louise Roy

Typset by Aristoc Press Pty Ltd, Melbourne, Australia, printed by SRP, Exeter, UK

CONTENTS

Preface   vii

Contributors   xii

Introduction   xv

Part One   Technology, Development and the South Pacific
1.1   Technology, Development and the South Pacific   1
    Tony Marjoram
1.2   Technology Transfer   16
    Tony Marjoram
1.3   Technology and Economic Development   29
    Ben Higgins
1.4   Balancing Technology, Development and Culture   39
    Stephen Hill
1.5   Technology, Development and the Environment   49
    Suliana Siwatibau
1.6   Fifty Years of Science and Technology in the Cook Islands   62
    Stewart Kingan and Tony Utanga

Part Two   Perspectives On Technology And Development
2.1   Appropriate Technology: An Overview   75
    Don Mansell
2.2   If it's Not Appropriate for Women, it's Not Appropriate   82
    Ruth E. Lechte
2.3   Technology Information and Communication:
    Message and Media   93
    Tony Marjoram
2.4   Communication Technology: In Whose Interests?   104
    Helen Molnar
2.5   Technology and Marine Resource Development   118
    Phillip Muller and Andrew Wright
2.6   Social and Political Constraints on Appropriate Technology
    in Papua New Guinea   128
    Elizabeth Cox
2.7   Education and Training for Technology and Development   139
    Tony Marjoram

Part Three Technology for Development
3.1   Technology in Agriculture: An Overview   147
    R. Keith Leonard
3.2   Agricultural Mechanisation: Tractors and Technology
    Choice in Tonga   157
    Tevita H. Moengangongo

3.3 Technology, Food and Food Processing   165
Susan Parkinson and Bill Aalbersberg

3.4 Affordable Housing and Development Training in Kiribati   176
Clive Stewart

3.5 Telecommunications: Potential and Problems for
New Technology   185
Jim Wilkinson

3.6 Pipes and Pits: Water Supply and Sanitation   191
Tony Marjoram

3.7 Inter-Island Shipping and Marine Transport   203
Tony Finch

3.8 Land Transport: On Wheel and Foot   214
Tony Marjoram

3.9 Aviation   226
Tony Marjoram

3.10 Mining: El Dorado or Fool's Gold?   235
Don Stewart

Part Four   Technology Projects and Management

4.1 Technology Management and Development of
Small Industries   246
Lukis Romaso

4.2 LikLik Buk Revisited: Technology, Information and
Village Development   256
B. David Williams

4.3 The Development of Appropriate Technology in
Papua New Guinea   263
Dick Burton

4.4 Energy Supply and Management   271
Tony Marjoram

4.5 Technology and Development Banking   283
Lisiate 'A. 'Akolo

4.6 Women Can Do: Technology and Training for Women   300
Sue Fleming

Part Five   Technology Policy and Planning

5.1 Technology and Development Planning   309
David F. Abbott

5.2 Technology and Development Aid   328
Rodney C. Hills

5.3 Technology Policy and Management   336
Stephen Hill

5.4 Technology Policy Initiatives in the South Pacific   347
Tony Marjoram

5.5 Technology, Development and Island Futures   360
Tony Marjoram

Notes and References   371

Bibliography   392

Index of Names   405

Index of Subjects   407

PREFACE

Development is seen by many as synonymous with industrialisation and the application of modern technology. Little attention, however, has been directed at the particular problems of technology and development in small island states such as those of the South Pacific.

This book emerged as the indirect result of years of conversation with friends and colleagues on the subjects of technology and development in 'developed' and less-developed countries. My own interest in technology and development began to develop while I was an undergraduate engineer, and it prompted post-graduate study in the social and policy aspects of science and technology at Manchester University. A special interest in the Pacific grew with an involvement in a policy research project on the potential and policy implications for new marine resources, particularly manganese nodules and ocean thermal energy — primarily Pacific resources. The offer of a position on a programme of outreach support to member countries of the University of the South Pacific, with one focus on technology and development, led me to Suva and the Centre for Applied Studies in Development in 1980. I was subsequently appointed to organise the technology programme of the new Rural Development Centre (later the Institute of Rural Development) of USP in 1982.

The idea for the book occurred in 1987, when I had just left USP to take up the Dyason Senior Research Fellowship at the Development Technologies Unit (now the International Development Technologies Centre) at the University of Melbourne. While reflecting on the need for information and its provision to policy-makers, planners, bankers and others working with technology in the South Pacific, and thinking of the many specialists in technology and development I knew in and around the region, it struck me that a book of essays on the subject would be a worthwhile effort and useful source of information. The idea met with unanimous support and, subject to the usual constraints of time, offers of contributions.

Possible sponsors and publishers were approached. UNESCO agreed to offer financial assistance, and Intermediate Technology Publications agreed to publish the book, in association with Australian

Scholarly Publishing. Now all that was required was to brief the contributors, write and edit contributions and give the manuscript to the publisher. If only plans translated so easily into reality, however, as every development planner should know. The production of a book, like 'development', involves more than 'just add water', in the words of Na'a Fiefia of USP.

Many Pacific islanders, like Archimedes, have a historic interest in and experience of hydrostatics, dynamics, floating bodies and displacement. The traditional technology or material culture of the Pacific, especially marine technology, illustrates real technological ingenuity and resourcefulness in conditions of limited resources. Much of this technology, and its associated skills and wisdom, has been displaced by Western technology. This book has been produced in the hope that traditional, indigenous and Western technology may be better and more innovatively and resourcefully integrated, for the best of both worlds, and that some of the myths relating to technology and development in the island context are displaced.

The book is divided into five interconnected parts, each containing contributions on related topics. Topics are discussed from different perspectives. Contributors include engineers, scientists, economists, sociologists, planners and policy specialists who work in education, development planning, banking, management, technical research and development, extension and community work. All have a close interest in work involving technology and development in the Pacific. Contributions vary in depth and breadth, perception and perspective. Some have a technical focus whilst others take a broader view. They are concise and intended to be read either as a set of collective readings or as stand-alone chapters for reference or consultation. The book is intended primarily for people with backgrounds similar to those of the contributors, working in development and technology in the South Pacific, and it takes a practical rather than academic approach. In the field of technology and development, work at community level needs better integration and coordination with policy and planning — linking the grass-roots with the tree-tops.

In the production of the book, editorial intervention has been kept to a minimum and exercised mainly to limit the size of the book and to maintain style and continuity. Size restrictions have limited discussion, examples, the repetition of common themes and qualifying statements. Some variation in presentation, style and language has been retained to maintain the individual feeling and flavour of the contributions. This will hopefully allow the reader to appreciate the differences in perception and perspective between specialists, and to see, for example, how development planners, economists or community development workers approach, examine and prioritise areas of technology and development regarding such issues as project design, appraisal and management and the 'viability' of island development.

Many people have been directly and indirectly involved with this book. I would first like to note my sincere thanks to the contributors, whose writing and friendship sustained productions. Writing concise, informative, accessible pieces on technical subjects for a wide audience is not an easy task, especially for busy people. Many contributors would have liked to spend more time on research, writing and receiving feedback on their contributions, but distance and time meant that most were unable to see and comment on the edited versions of their manuscripts. A big *malo aupito* and *tangio tumas* to you all for efforts and support under such circumstances.

One contributors expressed concern that their contribution was partly anecdotal, with limited referencing due to constraints of time, and another that information and examples were becoming outdated. Personal reflection and anecdote, however, are the essence of a book intended for and written by practitioners, reflecting their experience of technology and development activity. Obsolescence in information and technology is a perennial problem in the South Pacific, where changes that took two hundred years in the West have been compressed into the last thirty years — a technological revolution within living memory. The number of TV stations in the region, for example, has increased from 3, two or three years ago, to around 15 today. Examples were chosen mainly to be illustrative, and some outdatedness is inevitable given the pace of change.

I would like to offer special thanks to Sue Fleming, a close friend and colleague before, during and since my time in the Pacific. Harry Rothman helped me get to the Pacific in this first place, and Stephen Hill stimulated the grey matter when I got there. Both represent the 'human' side of science and technology policy. Thanks to friends and colleagues from the South Pacific go to David Abbott, Lisiate 'Akolo, Paula Bloomfield, Lawnin Crawford, Simione Durutalo, Garaio Gafiye, Chris Harwood, Epeli Hau'ofa, Ben Higgins, Lance Hill, Peter Johnston, Stuart Kingan, Jim Lamont, Mana Latu, Jeff Liew, George Moengangongo, Soane Ramanlal, Jim Rizer, Lukis Romaso, Reg Sanday, Suliana and Siwa Siwatibau, Claire Slatter, Ankim Swamy, Anote Tong, Monalisa Tuku'afu and Tony Utanga. It is sad that I will not be able to discuss the finished book with Andrew Kauleni, Kevin Makin and Greg Stutzman, as past discussions infuse many pages.

Friends and colleagues in Australia I would like to thank include Don Mansell, Don Stewart, Bob Fuller, Hector Malano, Jill Allen and

Fiorella Chiodo of the International Development Technologies Centre, and Bill Charters, Hugh Turral, Keith Barnard, Liz Ampt and David Curry, at the University of Melbourne. I would also like to express my gratitude to the Dyason Fellowship and Committee at the University of Melbourne for the support of my work. Other friends and colleagues who commented on ideas in the manuscript, or whose brains were otherwise picked (often without knowing it), include Helen Hill, Karin von Strokirch, Deborah Rhodes and Nic McLellan. Discussions with Elizabeth Cox, Glennys Romanes and Margaret Clausen at Community Aid Abroad, and members of the CAA Pacific Advisory Committee, were always most stimulating. Ian Bevege and Rod Hills from the Australian International Development Assistance Bureau (AIDAB) provided friendly support and advice. For their support of a distant son downunder, I would also like to thank my mother and my father — who introduced me to technology and knew of 'the book', but sadly is another with whom I will not be able to discuss it.

The book would not have appeared without the support and assistance of several people and organisations. In addition to the financial input of UNESCO, the personal support of Marc Chapdelaine in Paris was particularly valuable, as was the subsequent help of Vladislav Kotchetkov. The Australian National Commission for UNESCO, and Grattan Wilson, John Elsom and Ian Anderson, were helpful and supportive. Peter Higginson at the UNESCO Pacific office in Apia also helped organise the very useful UNESCO–SPEC High Level Regional Meeting of Policy and Management of Science and Technology for Development in the South Pacific Region, held in Apia in March 1987. The ever-jovial and friendly Nick Walker became involved with the book soon after its conception, and performed an essential midwife role as Australian Scholarly was also born, and has maintained this cheery involvement in the face of overly optimistic timelines and other editorial excesses. Also on the publishing side, I would like to thank Neal Burton for the support and valuable input of IT Publications. I would like to thank other people who expressed interest and support for the book, and potential contributors who were too constrained by time and other commitments to contribute.

I apologise for any omissions in acknowledgement. Needless to say, whilst all the opinions expressed by authors are their own, any remaining errors and omissions in the book are entirely the responsibility of the editor.

Finally, I would like to observe that writing can often be limited by the ability of words to convey image and feeling. This is why examples and stories are of great value. The Pacific islands are famous for their oral traditions. Oratory and story-telling remain esteemed skills, although their status has declined, as in the West, with the expansion of the electronic media. The effects of Western technology were graphically impressed upon me when talking to villagers in a remote part of the Solomon Islands about the potential effects of a proposed fish cannery. Villagers had little detailed knowledge of the proposal, and were keen to discuss the project and 'development' in general. In one village, as we thanked villagers for their hospitality, the village chief asked if we could explain the context of the troubles in Ireland, of which villagers had heard on Solomon Islands radio news, re-broadcast from the BBC. It is to such people that this book is ultimately, respectfully and kindly dedicated.

Tony Marjoram
Jakarta 1994

Contributors

DAVID F. ABBOTT   David Abbott is a development economist with more than fifteen years experience, mostly in the South Pacific. He has worked in Tuvalu, Tonga, the Solomon Islands and Fiji, with responsibility for the preparation of national development plans and the formulation and appraisal of a wide range of development projects and training.

LISIATE 'A. 'AKOLO   Lisiate 'A. 'Akolo was the managing director of the Tonga Development Bank until 1990, when he became the managing director of the Tonga Commodities Board.

RICHARD BURTON   Dick Burton was the director of the Appropriate Technology Development Institute (ATDI) of the University of Technology, Papua New Guinea, before becoming a director of Biomass Energy Services and Technology in Australia. He is now at the Botswana Technology Centre.

ELIZABETH COX   Elizabeth Cox is a project officer with Community Aid Abroad and Freedom From Hunger, and is a specialist on community development and wider development issues in Papua New Guinea.

TONY FINCH   Tony Finch worked with the International Maritime Organisation, and is a specialist on South Pacific shipping and marine safety.

SUE FLEMING   Sue Fleming established and coordinated the Women's Development Training Program at the Institute of Rural Development, University of the South Pacific (USP). She is now an honorary research fellow at the International Development Centre, University of Manchester, and a consultant, research and adviser to various bilateral and multilateral agencies and NGOs.

BEN HIGGINS   Ben Higgins was a pioneer development economist and former director of the Centre for Applied Studies in Development, USP. He was a professor and is currently an honorary professor of the University of Ottawa and an honorary fellow of the National Centre for Development Studies, Australian National University.

STEPHEN HILL   Stephen Hill is the director of the Centre for Research Policy at the University of Wollongong, and was a co-director of the Centre for Technology and Social Change at the University of Wollongong.

RODNEY C. HILLS   Rodney Hills is the director of the Australian International Development Assistance Bureau (AIDAB) Centre for Pacific Development and Training (ACPAC), and was a deputy director of the National Centre for Development Studies at the Australian National University and an Australian High Commissioner to Tonga.

STUART KINGAN AND TONY UTANGA   Stuart Kingan went to Raratonga to conduct ionospheric research in 1944, stayed, and has since acted in many roles, including that of science advisor to Cook Islands Government — a unique position in the Pacific. Tony Utanga was a long-standing secretary for internal affairs in the Ministry of Internal Affairs of the Cook Islands Government.

RUTH E. LECHTE   Ruth Lechte is the energy and environment specialist at the World YWCA in Geneva, partly based at the YWCA South Pacific office in Fiji, with wide interests in women and appropriate technology.

R. KEITH LEONARD   Keith Leonard is a senior consultant with ANZDEC Ltd, agricultural and rural development consultants in Auckland. He worked on the Tonga Banana Export Revitalisation Scheme at the Ministry of Agriculture in Tonga in the mid-1980s.

DON MANSELL   Don Mansell is the director of the International Development Technologies Centre at the University of Melbourne, and former professor of civil engineering at the University of Technology in Lae, PNG.

TONY MARJORAM   Tony Marjoram is the programme specialist in engineering, technology and informatics at the UNESCO Regional Office for Science and Technology in Southeast Asia and the Pacific, based in Jakarta.

TEVITA H. MOENGANGONGO   Tevita H. Moengangongo is an agriculture consultant based in Tonga, and the former head of the machinery pool at the Ministry of Agriculture, Fisheries and Forests in Tonga, and of Agricultural Engineering at the USP School of Agriculture in Alafua.

HELEN MOLNAR   Helen Molnar is a senior lecturer in Media Studies at Swinburne University of Technology, Melbourne, and also a member of the Australian National Commission for UNESCO, with interests in the media and communications and the South Pacific.

PHILIPP MULLER AND ANDREW WRIGHT   Philipp Muller was the director of the Forum Fisheries Agency in Honiara, and is now the director of the

South Pacific Applied Geoscience Commission. Andrew Wright was the research co-ordinator at the Forum Fisheries Agency.

Susan Parkinson and Bill Aalbersberg   Susan Parkinson and Bill Aalbersberg are both specialists on food and nutrition in the South Pacific, based in Fiji.

Lukis Romaso   Lukis Romaso is a senior consultant with Kum Gie Consult, a PNG consultancy in technology and industrial development, and was the deputy vice chancellor of the University of Technology, PNG, and deputy director of the Appropriate Technology Development Institute (ATDI) of UniTec.

Suliana Siwatibau   Suliana Siwatibau is a freelance consultant with interests in environment and resource utilisation. He was the director of energy at the Ministry of Lands, Minerals and Energy in Fiji, and a lecturer in biology at the University of the South Pacific.

Clive Stewart   Clive Stewart works in the field of technology and development, and is a former manager of the Rural Training and Development Centre of the Tarawa Technical Institute in Kiribati.

Don Stewart   Don Stewart is the deputy director of the International Development Technologies Centre at the University of Melbourne, and former professor of Chemical Engineering at the University of Technology in Lae, PNG.

B. David Williams   David Williams now lives in Portland, Oregon, USA. He was the agricultural secretary for the Melanesian Council of Churches from 1974–77. He edited the first two editions of 'Liklik Buk' and organized numerous rural development seminars throughout Papua New Guinea.

Jim Wilkinson   Jim Wilkinson is a consultant in the field of telecommunications, and former manager of the South Pacific Telecommunications Development Programme of the South Pacific Bureau for Economic Cooperation (now the Forum Secretariat).

INTRODUCTION

There is increasing concern in the independent island Pacific regarding the 'external' impacts of Western technology, such as the disposal of poison gas and toxic waste at Johnston Atoll, the transportation of nuclear materials, nuclear testing at Mururoa and the overwhelming prospect of global warming and sea-level rise — which could destroy many islands. There is also cause for concern regarding the 'internal' effects of Western technology, including problems associated with unsustainable fishing, forestry and mining — as at Bougainville and elsewhere in the region. Away from the headlines, whilst the increasing transfer of technology, via imports and aid, brings undoubted benefits, it is also accompanied by difficulties of assimilation, technological and economic dependence, and social, cultural, economic, environmental and other effects and problems. Although Pacific island countries have been actively united at the international and regional levels regarding the negative external impacts of Western technology, they have been less active regarding significant but often more subtle internal effects of technology transfer and dependence.

Technology is pervasive, people everywhere live in increasingly 'technological' cultures — 'technocultures' — supported by technological infrastructures. Technology is arguably the single most powerful agent of change. Technology includes smaller products and the skills and knowledge of individual people — 'microtechnology', and larger products, processes, collective skills and infrastructure — 'macrotechnology'. Technology derives increasingly from and is 'shaped' in Western industrialised countries, in line with Western needs and interests. These needs and interests are not necessarily the same as those of developing countries.

Technology consists of 'hardware' products, tools and equipment and 'software' processes, skills, operating and management knowledge. Hardware and software are of equal importance — both are required for technology to work properly. This is often overlooked, however, leading to various unanticipated effects and impacts in the transfer of Western technology to developing countries. These primarily arise because hardware and software may be inappropriate and incomplete. Modern motor cars, for example, require increasingly sophisticated diagnostic and maintenance equipment beyond the reach of most third world garages.

As technology becomes more pervasive and powerful, the potential for positive benefit and negative impact increases, particularly in small island communities sensitive to change. Although technology creates a 'comparative advantage' in Western companies and countries, limited technological resources can also create a comparative disadvantage, especially for smaller less-industrialised countries. The role of and need to plan for technology in development has long been recognised in the West. The main aim of this book is to direct similar attention to the management, policy and planning of technology for development in small island states.

In the South Pacific, technology includes traditional, indigenous (introduced but adopted or otherwise 'established' technology) and newly introduced technology. Traditional and indigenous technology is important, but often overlooked. It now appears likely, for example, that agriculture was first practiced nearly 30,000 years ago in Melanesia — 20,000 years before Mesopotamia, the supposed 'cradle of civilisation'.

Over 50% of the increasing amount of imports and aid to the Pacific consists of technology — technology is a central point of contact between the island Pacific and the West. The increasing transfer of Western technology has two major overall effects. Hardware and software may be inapparopriate and incomplete. Traditional and indigenous technology also tends to be displaced or replaced. This leads to increasing dependence on the West — from highly resourceful people with limited physical resources, Pacific islanders have become technology takers rather than makers.

It is important, however, to recognise that not only does Western technology impact upon and displace indigenous society, culture and technology, but also that indigenous society, culture and technology 'persist' and 'articulate' with technology as a leading agent of change.[1] Whilst there is often contradiction between indigenous and introduced technology, there may also be complementarity — modern agriculturalists now recognise the importance and appropriateness of traditional systems of small farming, for example. In the process of articulation, Western cultural forms, values and technologies may be transformed or 'transvalued' to fit with local knowledge and technology.

This discussion illustrates the need to link modern with indigenous practice, and to adapt Western technology to better suit island needs and conditions. Because the rate of change in the Pacific is so rapid, however, traditional and indigenous society and culture are less able to articulate and persist, and are increasingly displaced by Western cultural forms and technology.

The South Pacific

The 23 island countries and territories in the South Pacific range from single islands to vast archipelagoes, with populations from 1600 (Tuvalu) to over 3 million (Papua New Guinea). Island communities are generally small and isolated by sea or land — around 70% of islanders live in communities of less than 200 people. Although there are similarities — a unity in diversity — there are also distinct differences between islands and islanders. Islands vary enormously in size, appearance and available physical and human resources. Social systems and cultures differ markedly, even at the national level — there are over 700 languages in Papua New Guinea, for example. Most countries were colonised, becoming independent within the present generation, although some remain the overseas territories of metropolitan powers.

The focus of the book is the thirteen politically independent or self-governing island nation members of the South Pacific Forum — the Cook Islands, Fiji, Kiribati, Marshall Islands, Federated States of Micronesia, Nauru, Niue, Papua New Guinea, Solomon Islands, Tonga, Tuvalu, Vanuatu and Western Samoa (Australia and New Zealand are also Forum members). The larger 27-member South Pacific Commission (SPC) consists of the 15 Forum countries plus past and present colonial powers and their overseas dependencies or territories. Most island nations have also become members of regional and international organisations, and several UN agencies are represented in the region. The focus on the Pacific Forum is mainly due to relative similarity and independence as regards policy formulation, planning and management. With this proviso, however, some reference is made, examples drawn and comments expressed regarding the wider Pacific, and much of the book is relevant to developing island countries and land-locked 'island' communities and countries elsewhere.

Pacific island nations are developing countries, and some are included in the UN 'Least Developed Country' category. Pacific islands are fairly unique — they have generally low average per capita income levels, with over half their populations living in small communities in rural areas or outer islands in relatively traditional lifestyles, although there are few of the particular hardships associated with some larger developing countries. One of the problems of discussing Pacific issues are the many myths, ancient and modern, that continue to be propagated in the popular and tourist media. These myths need to be transcended in any meaningful discussion of development in the region.

Themes and Objectives of the Book

Technology and Pacific island development are, separately and together, subjects of considerable breadth and depth. To make the subject matter as clear and approachable as possible, the book has been organised into five parts, with each part focussing on specific topics. As with any system of classification, however, this should not obscure the essential interconnectedness of the various parts and and the issues they address.

Issues of technology and development involve significant consideration of social, cultural, political and economic factors. These factors are mentioned explicitly in some chapters and regarded as implicit in others. The focus in certain chapters on technical or social issues does not infer separation, as in the case of agriculture and women in development, for example. Indeed, combining these two topics, island women have a close historical role with agriculture, and the introduction of new technology has particular effects on women and the gender division of labour, often marginalising and adding to the work of women. Cattle projects aimed at men (even though women have as much experience of keeping livestock), have had a general effect of relocating gardens, mainly worked by women, further from villages.

The overall theme of the book is the central role that technology plays in development, and the need for the management of technology to be appropriate to development in the island context. Various topics address this overall theme. These include discussion of the role of technology in development in such areas as the promotion of small industry and institutional support and strengthening. General areas of interest include technology policy and planning, the choice and assessment of technology, project management, technology transfer, innovation and diffusion, research and development, education and training. Several contributions focus on technology in various economic sectors, including agriculture, marine resources, shipping, marine and land transport, aviation, communications, food technology, health, water supply and sanitation, building and construction, mining, energy and banking.

Many contributors mention other literature on the South Pacific, although there is not a large body of writing on development in the region, and very little on the subject of technology and development. Whilst all independent island states now have development plans dealing mainly with economic development, these are often little more than organised shopping lists prepared at the behest and often with the assistance of aid donors. Some comparison of development theories based on other country and regional contexts has been made, including neo-dependency and modernisation theory. Such a comparison is often of somewhat limited applicability, due to the specific context of island development, as is a comparison with the experience of technology and development in larger developing countries. Several important studies of technology and development in the South Pacific have been made, however.[2]

There are similarities and differences in the various contributions. Differences are mainly of perspective and perception. As may be expected, there are different notions of what constitutes 'development' and how this may be best achieved. Contributors with an economic background tend to link development with infrastructure, economic growth (through import substitution and export promotion), industrialisation and modernisation, achieved through the transfer of Western technology and expertise. Contributors with a background in community development, on the other hand, question notions of development focussed on economic growth, and have wider interests in an improvement of the quality of life, socially and environmentally sustainable development, the need for technology to be appropriate and the broader social effects of technological change, such as shifts in gender and demographic structures.

Technology is closely linked to important needs and issues of development in the South Pacific. The increasing transfer of Western technology occasions increasingly rapid change and dependence on outside technology and expertise and hence the increasing displacement of indigenous technology. As noted above, significant changes relate to gender, the redefinition and organisation of work (or 'economic activity') and need of access to the cash economy, especially for poorer urban and rural people. The focus of many aid projects on men and 'economic' activities often overlooks the traditional role and activities of women. The displacement of many traditional skills by Western technology via imports and aid has created a pressing need for re-skilling and the support of local technology and technological institutions in the region. The preference for tinned fish, for example, is largely due to factors of convenience and status, even though tinned fish is of lower nutritional value and requires monetary exchange (often for fish caught in Pacific waters), and has led to fewer people engaged in fishing and increased food imports.

In addition to re-skilling at the individual level, there is also a need for enhanced information and activity in the management of technology at the project, policy and planning levels. Technology policy and planning at the governmental level should complement rather than contradict village and community development activities at the 'grass-roots', as often happens. Non-government organisations have an important role to play in the promotion of appropriate technology and community development. A related debate concerns economic and technological criteria in the choice of technology, and the need for closer consideration of technical performance, efficiency, resource use, availability and user preference. The question of who makes decisions, how technological decision-making takes place — particularly as regards the role of donors and consultants — and the assessment, appraisal and monitoring of technology from cultural and environmental perspectives are all considered important.

Information and communication are of great importance in the innovation and diffusion of technology to potential users. Technological research, development and innovation is another important but neglected area in small developing countries. There is a need to develop local research and development capability, particularly in the field of appropriate technology. In this way new technology, and associated research, design and development, can be encouraged to build upon rather than displace indigenous technology — incremental rather than radical innovation is generally more successful, and creates less impact. The issues of technology and gender, work, re-skilling, choice and decision-making can also be more thoroughly addressed from this perspective.

The need to develop local research and development capability is linked with the need for institutional development and the support of education and training at national and regional levels. Institutional development and appropriate technology is discussed by various authors, with several references being made to the development, innovation and diffusion of the Wokabaut Somil — locally developed for the on-site production of building timber, but used increasingly for high-value timber (although some specialists question this use of the Somil). Regional cooperation and education and training are two issues on which all contributors agree, although there are differences in opinion regarding the type and level of education and training required.

Organisation and Layout of the Book

In the organisation of the book into five parts, Part One introduces overall issues and considerations relating to technology and development in general and the island context. Part Two considers various specific issues relating to technology in development and the appropriateness of technology in the Pacific. Part Three covers particular technologies and areas of technological application from a mainly technical perspective. Part Four examines the management of technology for development. Part Five discusses the role and issues of technology policy and planning.

Technology is recognised as a powerful agent of change that should be appropriate to social, cultural, environmental, economic and other conditions. General themes include the 'technological revolution' occasioned by the increasing technology transfer to the region through trade and aid, and the benefits and problems of technological change. Ben Higgins examines the role of technology in development from the perspective of the economist. The general constraints of size and isolation are noted, although opportunities for island agriculture in a possible 'green revolution' are discerned. The culture-power of technology in the process of change and the consequent need to balance technology, development and culture is emphasised by Stephen Hill. The relationship between technology, society, development and the environment is discussed by Suliana Siwatibau. The need to protect sensitive island ecosystems and the increasing unsustainability of larger 'corporate technologies' and their potential for serious environmental impact is noted and contrasted with the benign 'peoples technologies' of the Pacific islanders. Stuart Kingan and Tony Utanga look at this trend and the role of science and technology in the Cook Islands over the last fifty years.

In Part Two various specific issues relating to the appropriateness of technology for development in the Pacific are examined. Don Mansell presents general guidelines for appropriateness and notes the 'cuckoo effect' in the displacement of traditional by imported technology. From a background in community development, Ruth Lechte observes that Western technologies are male-oriented and notes how Western aid programmes have diminished the traditional importance of island women as technologists. Lechte also emphasises that 'appropriate technology' must be appropriate for women, which is not always the case. This theme is continued by Elizabeth Cox, who discusses the declining interest and concern for women, appropriate technology and village development in PNG since the 1970s and early 1980s.

The importance of information and communication in the innovation and diffusion of technology are examined using the example of the message and the media in the promotion of cooking stoves. In this context, the capacity of islanders to absorb and apply new marine technology is noted by Phillip Muller and Andrew Wright, who counter the view that the Pacific is a difficult place to test and innovate new technology. Helen Molnar examines the choice, effects and vested interests associated with the considerable technological change in the print, radio and TV media. Technological change in the media promotes both the independence of the 'small' local media, and at the same time reinforces the dominance of and dependence upon the 'big' national and international media. The final chapter discusses the considerable interests vested in education, and the issues, needs and approaches relating to formal, informal and non-formal education and training in the field of technology for development.

Part Three looks more closely at particular technologies. Keith Leonard notes the appropriateness and benefits of combining improved techniques with traditional agricultural methods and systems, and the need for further research and training. Tevita Moengangongo reflects on agricultural mechanisation, the performance of the government tractor pool and use of horses and tractors for ploughing in Tonga, which illustrates a lack of complementarity in technology policy and planning between the governmental and village or 'grass-roots' levels mentioned above. Sue Parkinson and Bill Aalbersberg also stress the importance of combining traditional and modern technologies of food processing and preservation to improve nutrition, reduce disease and food imports (the second highest category of imports by value to the region, after technology).

Research, design, development, demonstration and training in the area of affordable housing using local materials in Kiribati are discussed by Clive Stewart. A similar examination of technological appropriateness in water supply and sanitation follows. Transport and communications epitomise problems of smallness, isolation, high capital and operating costs in the Pacific. In the field of high-tech communications, Jim Wilkinson takes a technical view of the potential for and constraints of regional cooperation in national and international telecommunications. Air transport is discussed from a similar perspective. The relevance of low-cost road construction techniques are also discussed in this context. In the important area of marine transport, Tony Finch notes the problems of technological choice between older, affordable but often unsafe and newer, aid-supplied and overly complex ships. In a similar vein, Don Stewart examines technological choice between large-scale mining, with high returns but considerable environmental and social impacts, and the potential for small-scale operations, with less total return, but less environmental and social impact.

Part Four focusses on technology projects and management. In an interview, Lukis Romaso, discusses the establishment and support of small industries, with particular reference to the Wokabaut Somil — an example of a technology developed in PNG that has been transferred within PNG and the wider South Pacific. David Williams looks retrospectively at the production of 'Liklik Buk', a world-famous self-help and training manual focussing on appropriate technology and village development in PNG. Also from the home of the 'Liklik Buk', Dick Burton reflects on the development of the Appropriate Technology Development Unit (now Institute) of the PNG University of Technology in Lae. Energy, mainly in the form of liquid hydrocarbon fuels, is the largest single category of technological imports, and issues of energy management are examined with reference to the potential for conservation, new and renewable sources of energy. Lisiate 'Akolo discusses the importance of 'soft' finance, advice and support for technology through development banks — major providers of loans for smaller private-sector development projects. Continuing the theme of women and community development, Sue Fleming describes the work of the Women's Development Training Programme of USP in promoting the access to and training of women with such technologies as cooking stoves, ferrocement water tanks and ventilated pit latrines.

Part Five covers technology policy and planning. David Abbott discusses the role of technology in development policy and planning from the perspective of the economic development planner. The need for explicit attention and experience regarding the assessment of technological aspects of aid projects by donors is noted by Rodney Hills. The importance of technology policy and management is outlined by Stephen Hill, and the need for an interest in technological change and support in strengthening technological capability. Particular initiatives in technology policy and planning in Fiji and PNG are examined in this context. The final chapter looks at technological trends in the West and the likely futures in the South Pacific, noting particular areas of future technological need and the limited scope for industrial development. This, coupled with the potential of Western technology for change and the frequent inappropriateness of Western technology, underlines the need in island countries to develop the capability for 'minding the machines' — of effective technology management in terms of technology choice, transfer, policy-making and planning.

Technology, Development and the South Pacific

Tony Marjoram

It is important to ensure a common understanding of what is meant by technology. The term 'technology' is actually quite difficult to define, partly because technology is so pervasive. Because of this pervasiveness, a wide view is needed to comprehend technology. Part of the problem of definition is that 'technology' has different meanings for different people, meanings that change over time, as technology itself changes. Technology is the embodiment of ideas in tools, machines, products, processes or practices used by human beings in their interaction with the 'natural' and 'human' worlds. Technology is partly the application of science — the 'appliance of science' — although science and technology overlap in a continuum of interest and activity.

Technology may be described as traditional or indigenous, low or high, intermediate, alternative, soft, and appropriate technology. These terms essentially refer to the origin, complexity, age, competitiveness and suitability of technology with respect to the context of its use. They should not imply any hierarchy, or the superiority of new technology; whilst new technology may be an improvement on what went before, this is not necessarily the case. What is important is the appropriateness of the technology to the given context.

Hardware, Software and Infrastructure

Technology consists of hardware tools and machines and software knowledge relating to the design, choice, operation, maintenance, repair and overall management of that hardware. Each item of technology can be considered part of a system or 'infrastructure' of hardware and software that connects with other technology, technologists and the wider society, economy and environment. This connection is necessary to supply various inputs — for example, for successful operation and maintenance, and in turn to provide various outputs. The presence of a developed technological infrastructure is partly what defines the 'developed', industrialised countries; the lack of, or limitations in, the development of a technological infrastructure partly define the 'less developed', non-industrialised countries.

Shaped by and Shaping Society

Technology, society and language developed together. Technology is a social product. It involves group or social activity: in cottage or communal industry, and increasingly in the modern factory, requiring specialised production and the division of labour. The larger-scale production and application of technology began in the Industrial Revolution in Europe. Technology was developed or shaped in the Western context, in the image of the West, in response to certain Western needs. The motor car, for example, developed to suit the transport needs of the West, in turn leading to the development of decentralised cities like Los Angeles, and such attendant problems as urban pollution. That situation has not changed much, although technology is increasingly the result of research, design and development by teams of scientists and technologists working for transnational corporations, with global corporate interests.

Changes in technology and major technological innovations also significantly influence the direction or 'trajectory' of future technological change and, in turn, the development and societies of industrialised nations.[1] Technology and Western industrialised nations are closely interrelated; they shape each other. The significance of this for developing countries, and particularly small non-industrial countries such as the Pacific islands, is that they have become takers rather than makers of technology. They are thus shaped by Western technology, with little contribution to the generation of that technology.

The Acquisition and Impact of Technology — the Neutral Fix?

Technology acquisition is the result of a process of research, design and development, often called 'invention', followed by innovation and, if innovation is successful, of technology transfer, acquisition and diffusion. Technology transfer consists of the purchase, exchange or gift of technology, usually from the innovator, agent, wholesaler or retailer to the user. Technological innovation is the introduction of a technology into a new context or market. Technological diffusion or distribution takes place if the technology is accepted and propagated. Most technology transfer is between developed industrialised countries. Technology transfer from developed to less developed, non-industrialised countries is of equal importance, and often problematic.

Because of its social and cultural roots and 'shaping', technology cannot be considered neutral or value-free. Technology embodies and reflects the society in which it was developed. This understanding is important, particularly when considering the transfer of technology from the society in which it originated to a different context with different values. When technology is transferred from one context to another, it is frequently only or mainly the hardware that is transferred, with the software being partly or totally left behind. Also, because of the dominance of technology and the technological outlook, problems involving social, cultural and other aspects are often perceived as purely technological and economic, and therefore amenable to a 'technological fix'. This frequently happens in the South Pacific, and is partly an example of the 'toys for the boys' syndrome — of technologist 'boys' and their technological 'toys'.[2]

Technology has to be chosen carefully and the hardware and software adapted as necessary to suit the different context of use, and/or that context of use has to be changed or adapted to suit the new technology, otherwise problems frequently arise, often leading to negative effects and the premature demise of the technology. Due to realities of small population, isolation, and social and cultural factors, transferred technology is often a poor 'fit' to island conditions, particularly in rural areas. Outboard motors, for example, are generally designed for Western leisure boating; when they are used in the Pacific, operational life expectancy can be reduced dramatically.

The introduction of technology can lead to both positive and negative effects on different groups of people or sections of society. Technology can be both part of the problem of development, and part of the solution. Technology shaped by production conditions and consumption patterns in developed countries is liable to have significant impacts upon less developed countries, particularly small islands. As Stewart points out, 'the continued domination of technology creation by the developed countries has meant that the developing countries are locked into the technological trajectories determined by the developed countries . . . technologies have tended to have characteristics corresponding to conditions in developed countries — being capital and skill intensive, and relatively large scale, producing products with characteristics suited to high income markets — relative to the conditions and needs of developing countries'. Stewart observes an increase in this trend, and the generally increasing inappropriateness of Western technology to developing country contexts and needs: 'For the most part, these tendencies have increased over time, as real incomes have risen in the developed countries, accompanied by rising capital per head and expanding education and skills, with the generation of demands for an ever-changing variety of increasingly sophisticated products. The technology emanating from the advanced countries has thus tended to become inappropriate over time, in relation to the needs of developing countries, especially low-income or slow-growing countries, both with respect to product characteristics and to techniques'.[3]

Technology and Development

Defining development is as difficult as defining technology. 'Development' means different things to different people, and different groups of people have different development priorities. Development is concerned with social goals and ways of prioritising and achieving these goals, and is therefore inherently political. Whilst an economist may use GDP per capita as the dominant indicator of development, it does little to indicate income distribution or other criteria that most people would equate with development: access to and standard of housing, education, health services, water supply, sanitation and opportunities for income generating activities and small business growth. The role of technology is important in all of these areas.

Although some analysts equate development with economic growth, with finance or capital as the main input and output of development, technology is better regarded as the main engine of development, with finance or capital as the fuel for that engine. The link of technology with development began with the slow but revolutionary development of agriculture. Of particular interest for the South Pacific, it now appears that agriculture was first practised in Melanesia around 30,000 years ago, nearly 20,000 years before Mesopotamia, the 'fertile crescent' and 'cradle of civilisation'.

The link between technology and development produced profound change after the Industrial Revolution in 18th century Britain, with the growth of mechanisation and capital available for investment. The role of technology in industrial development increased, as illustrated by military-industrial production during World War II. Preceding the NICs (the Newly Industrialised Countries — Hong Kong, South Korea, Singapore and Taiwan), postwar reconstruction in Germany and Japan was facilitated by the Marshall Plan, the first example of international development aid, primarily involving the large scale transfer of technology and capital.[4]

Following the pattern of development in the NICs, the application of advanced technology and industrial development have been promoted as the model for development in other developing countries, with the particular goals of import substitution and export promotion. However, this model of industry-led development would seem to have limited applicability in the South Pacific, mainly for reasons of population size, isolation and limited technological infrastructure.

Management of Technology

The management of technology relates to all aspects of technology, including research, design and development, installation, adaptation, innovation, diffusion, operation, maintenance, diagnosis and repair; technology choice, transfer, negotiation and decision-making; and the formulation and implementation of technology policy and planning. Technology management applies at the 'micro' project and 'macro' policy and planning levels.

Technology Choice and Decision-Making

Criteria for technology choice include factors such as the availability of capital, supply and cost of labour, the skill level of available or potential employees, the productivity, durability, complexity, ease of maintenance and repair and the possible environmental impact. Technologies may be capital/investment- or labour-intensive. Considerations relating to technology choice are closely connected to size. Although larger projects may have a higher technological component, a greater technological content and sophistication does not necessarily imply greater capital intensity, or increased economy of scale.

An important consideration relating to technology choice is that incrementally improved or adapted technology is usually more reliable, a better 'fit' and more successful than totally new technology, which is more likely to encounter operating and other problems. More basic, labour-intensive technology also generally involves lower overheads and less risk. Status, aspiration and neophilia are powerful but sometimes misplaced stimuli for purchasing new or radical technology.

Technology Policy and Planning

Technology policy and planning is the prerogative of governments and larger corporations. Governments set the framework in which public and private organisations choose and use technology. Technology policy can be explicit or implicit. Explicit policy consists of specific statements addressing technology policy issues. Implicit policy consists of statements or actions that do not refer specifically to technology, but nevertheless have an impact on technology; for example, fiscal policy is an important reflection of implicit technology policy, and fiscal policy should be formulated and implemented as part of an overall approach to technology policy.

The Small Island States of the South Pacific

Adjust Your Mind — Island Realities

Whilst the Pacific islands share some similarities with other developing countries, the overall realities of Pacific islands and island life relate to the generally small size of islands and island communities, and their isolation at national, regional and international levels. Most islands have limited physical and human resources. Many experience natural catastrophes such as tropical cyclones and hurricanes, tsunami, earthquakes, drought and various tropical health problems. Despite overall similarities, because of their isolation, a multitude of unique social systems, languages and cultures have evolved in the Pacific. Most island states, and even small communities in larger countries such as PNG and the Solomon Islands, are quite distinctive. There is only a limited unity in their diversity.

Physical and Demographic Conditions

Available resources reflect regional diversities. The larger Western Pacific islands have mineral and natural resource potentials that many regard as a rich natural resource-bank or gene-pool of flora and fauna of significant potential. The range of flora and fauna decreases moving east from PNG, and smaller islands and atolls are extremely resource-poor, especially in regard to land, with environments in fine ecological balance, and particularly sensitive to change.

Overall data for the South Pacific is presented as Tables 1–6.[5] Islands range from Papua New Guinea (462,243 km² and 3.5 million people), to the 21 km² of Nauru or 1600 people of Tuvalu. Overall population density ranges from 7 people/km² in PNG to 419 in Nauru and nearly 2500 on Ebeye, mainly outer-island Marshall Islanders dependent on the US missile testing station in Kwajalein. With the exceptions of Nauru and Niue, countries of the region typically consist of countless islands spread over vast areas of ocean. Kiribati, for example, has an oceanic Exclusive Economic Zone larger than continental Europe or the ASEAN region. Population growth is high, and there is increasing population drift or internal migration from rural areas and outer islands to urban areas, and considerable external migration from some countries.

Life expectancy in the region ranges from 50 in PNG to 67 in the Cook Islands and Niue, with an average of 52.5. As elsewhere, women usually live longer than men, although in PNG and the Solomon Islands life expectancy is less for women than men (the world average is around 59 years; 76 years in Australia, New Zealand and the US). The median age of 18.5 years illustrates the youthfulness of island populations, reflecting the high population growth rate. Most households, especially in rural areas, consist of extended families.

Social Conditions

Over 80% of islanders live in rural areas, mainly in villages of fewer than 100 people, in relatively traditional lifestyles. Most island countries are typically characterised as rural-urban 'dual economies', in a state of transition towards a more Western or 'modern' society. The overall quality of life in the rural and urban island Pacific is relatively high compared to many developing countries. Water supply and sanitation are often problematic, particularly on the outer islands. There are few problems with food production and supply, although the incidence of nutrition-related problems in urban areas is increasing, as urban drift, poverty and the consumption of imported foods increase, giving rise to increasing 'Western' diseases including cancer, heart disease, asthma, diabetes and ulcers. It is with the increasing populations and rising aspirations that the need for and problems of development arise.

Educational opportunities are limited in many islands. On average 35% of those eligible attend primary and 9% attend secondary school (this compares with world averages of around 91% and 43%). Gender differences are reflected in local language literacy rates, reportedly ranging from an average 32% in PNG (male 39%, female 24%) to nearly 100% (Tonga, Western Samoa).[6]

Health services are also limited, and extended families and communities traditionally act in a social welfare role. Average food intake for the region is relatively low at 2200 calories/day (compared to around 3000 for many developed countries). Crude birth rate is high, averaging 30.6% (world average 27.5%, 16% for Australia, New Zealand and US), reflecting high population growth. Infant mortality is very high, particularly in some countries, averaging 63.2 per thousand (the average in most developed countries is around 10). The number of people per doctor in the South Pacific is also high, on average just over 3000 (around 600 for most developed countries).

Economic Development

As prices for island exports have generally declined, and volumes and prices of imports increased, island governments have attempted to encourage economic growth by promoting exports, reducing budgets (through structural adjustment) and increasing aid. At the microeconomic level, around 70% of island adults are 'economically active' in the 'informal' non-cash economy, with 39% in the 'formal' cash economy. There are many problems in defining and identifying 'economically active' adults outside the cash economy, as many people are engaged in traditional activities in the 'informal' sector. In those countries with high migration, remittances from migrants are an important income to islanders and island economies, and approach half the national budget in some countries.

Macroeconomic information dominates national and regional statistics.[7] Gross Domestic Product ranges from A$440,000 (Niue) to A$4.4b (PNG), and GDP per capita from A$550 (Kiribati) to A$3000 (Cook Islands), with an average A$1330 (GDP per capita in developed countries is around A$13,000). Due to increasing imports, balances of trade around the region are all increasingly negative, except for Nauru, PNG and the Solomon Islands (the main commodity exporters). Imports consist mainly of machinery and transport equipment (average 29%), food (21%), manufactured goods (16%), fuel (11%), miscellaneous manufactured goods (10%) and chemicals (7%). Apart from food, most of these goods are clearly 'technological'. Exports consist mainly of minerals (average 45%; mainly of gold and copper from PNG, phosphate from Nauru and nickel from New Caledonia), coffee, tea and cocoa, fish and fish products, sugar and unsawn timber. Agriculture is the main economic activity, at 39% of GDP, with manufacturing at 8.7% of GDP (typically 3% and 20% in developed countries). The share of agriculture ranges from 11% in Tuvalu, to 34% in PNG and 49% in the Solomon Islands. The share of manufacturing ranges from 2.1% in Kiribati and Tuvalu, to 11% in Fiji and 13% in Western Samoa.

Government revenue ranges from A$3.2m (Niue) to A$1.3b (PNG), and from A$180 (Solomon Islands) to A$2280 (Cook Islands) on a per capita basis. Government revenue derives from direct taxes (average 28.1%), indirect taxes and duties (24.1%), budgetary aid (17.3%; mainly from Australia to PNG) and government operations (12.8%). Government expenditure ranges from A$9.3m (Niue) to A$1.4b (PNG), and from $300 (Kiribati) to A$2251 (Cook Islands) per capita. Government expenditure is mainly on administration (13%), education (15%) and health (10%). This does not include the 'black economy' or significant remittance income of some islands. Total aid (bilateral and multilateral) to the independent island Pacific has increased significantly in recent years, and per capita aid is among the highest in the world, giving rise to some concern about dependence and problems of assimilation, if island life and economies are not to be distorted. Total aid ranges from A$7m (Niue and Tuvalu) to A$500m (PNG), and on per capita terms from from A$34 (Fiji) to A$2900 (Niue). It should be noted that a significant percentage of aid funds is expended on central infrastructure (such as wharves and airports), overheads, consultants' fees and the supplemented salaries of expatriate workers, and is therefore not directly 'seen' by many islanders and that, in the wider Pacific context, 'aid' to the French and American territories far exceeds aid to the independent countries of the region.

Overall Development and Development Constraints

The most important needs and problems regarding development in the South Pacific arise primarily from the small size, isolation and general dispersion of islands and islanders, sensitive social and environmental systems and the fact that most of the island nations have only recently reached independence, emerging out of a secluded and undisturbed colonial past. A mixture of small development projects might be the ideal, but the size and dispersion of islands can make the small projects difficult. Added to this problem is the trend for aid donors, whilst they may be sympathetic to small project development, to be administratively unaccustomed or disinclined to work on such a diminutive scale (this partially accounts for the increasing activity of non-governmental organisations in the South Pacific). The potential for rural development also relates directly to these considerations; if decentralised development does not take place, then rural-urban drift is likely to increase, and with it the problems of dualism and unbalanced urbanisation.

Major constraints to development in the islands include shortages of capital and limited infrastructure, particularly technological infrastructure. This includes both the 'hard' technological infrastructure of transport and communications — of roads, wharves, shipping, air and telecommunications services — and the 'soft' infrastructure of human resources that mobilise and manage technology for national development. An example is the vast but problematic opportunities offered by marine resource use and management, constrained by required knowledge and finance. These constraints have given impetus to calls for increased regional cooperation and the sharing of resources, and the doubts expressed by some economists regarding the feasibility of sustainable development in smaller island countries.

Technology and Development in the South Pacific

Most technology used in the Pacific is relatively basic, with relatively low productivity. Pacific islanders are becoming increasingly dependent on the outside world for technology and finance. Efforts towards industrialisation have been constrained by size, isolation and limited technological infrastructures. The conventional economic model of industrialisation and export-led development is not particularly appropriate in the region.

The 'Technological Revolution' in the South Pacific

The South Pacific was thrust into the modern world during and following the Pacific war, and during the later colonial period, with the early steps towards decolonisation and political independence. It is from this period that the start of a 'technological revolution' in the South Pacific can be dated. The islands have therefore been effectively exposed for a little more than a generation — within living memory — to the processes and products of industrialisation that began centuries ago in Europe. The subsequent process of change is one of increasing transfer of technology in imports and aid, increasing exploitation of forest, fisheries and mineral resources, and a drive towards a degree of industrialisation in many of the islands. The Pacific continues to be affected indirectly by more distant effects of technology in the region and elsewhere — such as drift net fishing and the overwhelming prospect of global warming and sea-level rise. Despite its name, the Pacific continues to be used for nuclear testing at Mururoa, missile testing at Kwajalein and the disposal of toxic waste at Johnston Atoll.

Technology Transfer

Technology transfer to the South Pacific is often problematic, largely due to the limited technological infrastructures of island nations, in particular the shortage of trained personnel involved in technological decision-making, choice and innovation, and also the reliability, performance and impacts of new technology. The main way in which technology innovation occurs in the South Pacific is by technology transfer, rather than by research, design and development. Because there is little R&D or manufacturing in the region, most technology is acquired through purchase or loan, overseas aid or transnational corporation (TNC) transfer (either in joint ventures or as licensees). As most technology acquired in the South Pacific is 'mature' or 'off-the-shelf', or transferred within projects involving TNCs, franchise, copyright or licensing agreements are not generally involved, or are problematic.

Technology transfer to the Pacific islands began with traders, whalers, settlers, missionaries, beachcombers, sailors, settlers and colonists. Most initial technology transfer was in exchange for various commodities; first sandalwood, then copra. Slowly the demand for imported goods increased and the cash economy began to displace traditional and trader exchange. Overseas trading houses (for example, Burns Philp and Morris Hedstrom) entered the South Pacific around the turn of the century, often linking retail commerce with commodity production and purchasing operations. Various 'cargo cults' developed largely in response to the desire for overseas technology and trade goods. The Pacific war was the first exposure of islanders to the full and frightening power of Western technology.

An increasing amount of technology is being transferred to the South Pacific, as imports and aid. 'Technological' imports constitute around 50% of total imports, and well over 50% of aid is technology-related.

Technology imports account for approximately 70%, and aid projects approximately 30%, of total technology transfer to the region. Over the last decade, technology transfer into the region has been increasing at approaching 30% per year. This trend indicates an increasing technological dependence in the region. (Technology transfer to the South Pacific is explored further in the next chapter.)

Technology Transfer, Human Resource Development and the Role of Consultants

Technology transfer is often viewed as the transfer of hardware tools and equipment, while important software and management aspects are often neglected. People are an essential element in technology transfer. People need technology, and technology needs skilled people to make it work. The development of technological infrastructures in the islands requires local technological expertise, although few islanders have access to technical education. Indigenous expertise with Western technology is limited (which is not to deny traditional and indigenous technological skills, but points to the marginalisation of these skills). Overseas expertise and consultants are therefore required. A technological 'Catch-22' situation thereby arises, where outside technical advice and assistance is needed because of a lack of local expertise, with local expertise is needed to appraise this outside technical assistance, but is unavailable because of the dependence on outside technical assistance. Aid donors may face similar constraints, as most donor officials are economists, not technologists.

The Effects and Impacts of Technological Change

Western technologies exert profound social, cultural, political, economic and environmental effects in the South Pacific. On the macro scale, many contemporary Pacific news items relate to technology, including nuclear testing, drift-net fishing, large-scale forestry, the disposal of toxic weapons and wastes and, most recently, gold and copper mining in Papua New Guinea. On the micro scale, more profound are the social, economic, environmental and other impacts of individual technologies such as the motor car, refrigerator, stove and outboard motor. It is important to understand technology change to enable improved planning and management of technology, to maximise the positive effects of technology and minimise negative impacts.

Island countries have become more dependent on Western technology partly due to the high status and opportunities offered by Western technology (despite high capital and operating cost and likely maintenance and repair problems). Development is shaped by the opportunities offered by new technology. As in the West, new technology also creates new needs, wants and markets. But the displacement of traditional technology can overwhelm and undermine limited local technological infrastructures, leading to increasing technological dependency. The technological 'fix' can also compound an ignorance of social, cultural and other aspects of development problems.

Traditional, Indigenous and Introduced Technology

Pacific islanders have invented, developed, adapted and applied technology creatively to maintain their livelihoods in very specific situations. Their marine technology of canoes, navigation and fishing techniques, and their sophisticated agricultural practices, evolved to cope with unique and frequently unfavourable conditions, especially on atolls. Resourceful people with limited resources produced suspension bridges, traditional medicine and a whole range of domestic technologies. Islanders also applied a practical, empirical 'folk science' to understanding their world.

In the overall matrix of technology in the South Pacific, traditional and indigenous technology and new technology are all important. Indigenous technology is well understood by local people and is a basis for development and the introduction of new technology. Most successful technology innovation is incremental rather than radical; building upon rather than displacing existing technology. Western technology, improved materials and efficiency, should enhance and complement rather than displace indigenous technology, otherwise the dependence on overseas technology will increase, to the detriment of islander resourcefulness.[8]

Appropriate Technology

All technology should be appropriate in the context to which it is introduced. The prefix 'appropriate' was initially coined partly because much technology transferred to developing countries can be regarded as inappropriate. For technology to be appropriate it should be economically, socially, politically, environmentally and technologically sustainable; it should fit the local situation for maximum overall benefit and minimum negative impact. Technology may be suitable in one context and not in another, and some technology may not be suitable in any context.

Interest in the appropriateness of technology grew in the 1960s and 1970s. It reflected increasing interest in questions relating to the supposed economies and diseconomies of scale, possible limits to growth (caused by increasing populations and finite resources) and concern with the narrow focus and likely consequences of economic growth, especially for environmental degradation. Much of this interest found expression in concepts such as Schumacher's 'small is beautiful' and Illich's 'convivial tools', which focus on a technology for people rather than industrialised production and consumption.[9]

Technology that has been developed and propagated elsewhere (whether appropriate or not) may not necessarily work throughout the South Pacific, where operating conditions are tough, technological infrastructures and support are generally limited, and physical and social environments are sensitive to change. Technologies may be under-utilised or over-utilised, may lack durability and face problems due to a lack of maintenance, diagnostic and repair skills and few locally available spares.

The Acquisition of Technology

Most technology in the Pacific is acquired through technology transfer rather than indigenous research, design and development, followed by a process of innovation and diffusion. Technology is transferred by government departments, transnational and local companies, regional, bilateral, international and non-government organisations for final acquisition by the user. Due to limited capital and technology management skills in the small and medium scale private sector, there is a continuing need for public sector support of technology innovation and acquisition.

Technology in the Public and Private Sectors

Apart from larger mining and agriculture operations, all business ventures in the region are small by international standards. On the island scale, businesses consist of small to medium local companies, and medium and larger overseas companies. The main criteria affecting technology acquisition in the private and domestic sector are context of use, cost, mode of acquisition and availability. Larger-scale technology transfer, particularly involving overseas companies, introduces more complex factors, such as joint venture operations and licensing agreements. Joint ventures are increasingly common, mainly because of the island desire to gain better local control and a share of profits, as well as the promotion of technology transfer. Questions remain, however, regarding the relative merits of joint venture and licence operations; they depend much on contractual arrangements and implementation.

Smaller companies acquire technology with grants or preferential loans designed for small borrowers from the national development banks now established in most island countries. Smaller joint ventures are increasingly common, combining overseas expertise and technology and local entrepreneurs with access to preferential loans. Despite the attractiveness of such operations, the area is fraught with potential problems, again depending much on contractual arrangements.

Bilateral and Multilateral Aid and Non-Governmental Organisations

Bilateral donors provide most of the funds and expertise for development projects (rather than supporting recurrent budgets). Bilateral and multilateral donors provide expertise and training. Despite the interest in smaller scale projects involving appropriate technology for community and rural development, there is some concern that this interest has steadily declined over the 1980s, and about whether the involvement of non-government organisations (NGOs) in appropriate technology and development indicates a lack of knowledge, interest, resources or commitment among national, regional and international agencies.[10] Most agencies have administrative and technical difficulties working on such a diminutive scale, and often support NGOs in these activities. Although NGOs are effective media for technology transfer at national and regional levels, activities may be duplicated. There is, however, need for increased NGO cooperation within the guidelines and goals of national development.

The Management of Technology

Because of the sensitive nature of the social, cultural and physical environments, limited technological infrastructures and consequent potential for negative impacts of inappropriate technology choice, the management of technology in the Pacific is crucial.

Technology Choice and Decision-Making

The increased quantity, range and sophistication of technology transferred into island countries requires increasing attention to the choice, appropriateness and application of technology. Considerations of size, supply, durability and support are particularly important. Decision-making regarding technology in trade, aid and industrialisation is complex, and effective technology choice requires adequate information and involves technological, economic, social, environmental and other relevant considerations.

The status of and aspiration to new and high technology are powerful factors compelling technology choice, even though support may be unavailable, especially on outer islands. Incrementally improved rather than totally new and high technology is often more reliable and cheaper, although some high technological products, processes and industries facilitate increased smallness, efficiency and lower cost. New technological industries have encountered various problems, including marketing, financial management, recruitment, training, retention of trained personnel and the supply of raw materials. These relate to problems of size, isolation and complexity of the available technology.

Technology Policy and Planning

As Fairbairn observes: 'After the fashion of contemporary development economics, almost all Pacific island countries have formulated official development plans . . . the style, scope and level of sophistication [of which] vary widely from one country to the next, depending on planning objectives, technical capacity and predilection of national planning offices and their expert advisors, availability of data on key economic variables . . . and political biases'. The plans focus on economic growth and the presentation of macroeconomic frameworks and development investment programmes or 'shopping lists' for potential donors, but also include goals of 'social justice, national self-reliance, decentralisation, rural development, resource conservation and strengthening of local cultures and national identities ... (which may be interconnected, yet contradictory)'.[11]

There is little explicit technology policy in the South Pacific, although there is an increasing interest in the role and problems of promoting technology and industry in national development. The importance of appropriate technology is stressed in most development plans, but deciding on the most appropriate technology for particular situations, and how this may be encouraged, generally makes for difficulties of interpretation and implementation. A range of implicit policies, such as fiscal policy, have direct effects on technology acquisition and use in the region, although such policies are not generally formulated and implemented as part of technology policy. Also, following Fairbairn, whilst some policy measures may be interconnected, others appear contradictory. Technology planning activity in the region is mainly confined to project planning.

There is clearly a role for improved technology management, policy-making and planning, particularly among development planners and bankers.[12] Given the recognition of the need for technological self-reliance and problems with the inappropriateness and impacts of technology, the production of guidelines regarding technology policy and planning, and strategies regarding technology assimilation, would be most useful.[13]

TECHNOLOGY TRANSFER

TONY MARJORAM

◆◆◆

Technology transfer is the transmission of technology from producers or innovators to users and consumers. Most technology transfer takes place between developed industrialised countries, some from developed to developing (non-industrial) countries, and a little between developing countries. Technology transfer includes the innovation and diffusion of technology; it brings new technology to the market place, and promotes that technology for adoption by potential users. A technology is an innovation if it is new to the context of its use, even though it may not be new elsewhere.[1]

Technology is the major engine of development and economic growth in all countries. Its transfer is important. Development depends upon the application of knowledge, which is essentially what the transfer of technology is all about. Technology transfer empowers people. They do things for themselves, rather than depend on others.

Technology transfer is complex. It involves a mix of social, cultural, economic, environmental, technological and other factors, which are frequently ignored or neglected. Caution is necessary, as external technology transfer often displaces local technology, which may increase technological (and other) dependence, and even cause de-industrialisation in the modern urban sector. A balance between upgrading traditional technology and the careful choice and transfer of new or improved technology is required.

The technology transferred should be appropriate to the needs and situation of actual and potential users. Technology should be chosen, adopted or developed with an eye to the practicalities of its transfer. Technology transfer can only be judged successful if the technology is innovated, diffused and adopted by users. It should maximise positive and minimise negative impacts.

Innovation and Diffusion

Technology transfer through innovation and diffusion is the 'transmission' of technological hardware and/or software from technology producers to technology users. In the South Pacific, the bulk of technology transfer is from developed countries, with very little between island countries. Developing, less-industrialised countries tend to have become importers of technology — technology takers rather than makers. This characteristic, as observed in the previous chapter, is most pronounced in the small island states of the South Pacific, where imported Western technology has significantly displaced traditional technology, which has limited modern sector productive capacity. Whilst larger developing countries may have some input into adapting or otherwise shaping technology, this is less so in the Pacific.

Technology is transferred directly or, more usually, indirectly from producers to users. Technology producers or innovators include overseas companies and transnational corporations, which produce technology initially for consumption in Western markets. Technology users include the public and private sectors, and the many smaller consumers in the domestic and rural sectors.

The main types of technology transferred to the South Pacific are machinery and equipment, fuels and chemicals (refer to the second part of this chapter for greater detail regarding technology imports and aid). Within the region, technology is transferred to larger extractive 'enclave' mining, fishing and forestry industries (significant in value rather than quantitative terms), to the larger public (government industries and services) and private sectors, and to the domestic and informal spheres (significant in quantitative terms).

Technology innovation and diffusion involve various agencies and activities. Agencies include exporters and importers, wholesalers and retailers of technology, aid donors, their consultants and recipient bodies. Customs authorities, shippers and freight handlers are also passively involved. Activities include technology procurement and supply, marketing, information dissemination and promotion through public, commercial and professional media.

Modes of Technology Transfer

The main mechanisms of technology transfer into island countries are imports and aid. Transnational corporations also transfer technology for their own use in resource-extractive enclave industries, but because of the scale and speciality of this technology transfer, there is almost no potential for transfer outside enclave industries. Within island countries the main mechanisms of technology diffusion are local markets and extension services.

The transfer of technology may take place by purchase (by cash, or with a soft or hard loan), as a gift, commodity exchange, lease or franchise, through information dissemination, and formal or informal training in technology. The mode of transfer very much depends on the type of technology involved, and the producers and users of technology, of whom there are a great variety. Technology may be 'high', 'intermediate' or 'low', transferred from overseas, adapted or developed locally, and intended for professional or domestic use (in which case, it may be less durable).

Technology transfer can be a one-way process, with no feedback from potential users, or two-way, involving feedback. Feedback from users to producers is obviously useful. It should enable the technology to address user needs and facilitate any necessary adaptation of the hardware, operation or support for the technology, although this is only really possible with technology developed or adapted for local use. This is a powerful reason for a local input into technology, and for the enhancement of support through the development of local technological infrastructures. Technology transfer should be more than a straightforward introduction into the market place, with little attention to its local needs and context. Better vertical integration is needed when technology is transferred into new conditions. This is the main reason why many imported technologies and technology projects fail in developing countries.

Technology Transfer Differentials

Technology is shaped in developed industrialised nations for local production and consumption. It in turn shapes the development of industrialised nations, creating new technological paradigms and trajectories that shape the direction of further and future technological change. Because of the domination of Western technology, developing countries are locked into technological paradigms and trajectories determined by the developed countries. As technological products and processes become increasingly complex, the amount of technology that may be appropriate for transfer to developing countries has decreased over time. Developing countries have become more constrained in the choice of technology most suitable for their development needs, and at the same time, more dependent upon Western technology.[2]

Technology transfer to developing countries is different in different sectors: there are gaps and lags. These differentials illustrate the unevenness of technological change (or change in the technology paradigm) between countries. It is most imbalanced between developed and developing countries. There is a 'crisis of structural adjustment' in coming to terms with the new technological as well as the economic paradigms of developed countries. The crisis will increase as the technology transfer differentials between the West and the developing countries of the South Pacific also increase.[3]

Problems of Technology Transfer

The issues and problems of technology transfer are frequently ignored or neglected, primarily because technology transfer is a problematic area, involving a mix of technological, economic, social, cultural, environmental and other factors. Social and cultural constraints are the main obstacles to successful technology transfer.[4] Many examples from the Pacific are mentioned in the following chapters. Public sector innovators of technology (through aid) tend to neglect economic aspects of transfer, and private innovators (especially wholesalers and retailers) tend to neglect technological aspects of transfer. Both neglect wider aspects of diffusion. Technologists often consider technology transfer not their problem. Economists neglect technology transfer because it is exogenous, treated as an aspect of capital, subject only to market forces and the choice of their mythical 'rational man'.

Inappropriateness of Transferred Technology

Technology transfer to developing countries is often inappropriate for their needs and situations. As Stewart notes, imported technology may be inappropriate for production and consumption needs, and lead to increasingly dualistic societies, slower growth and environmental degradation.[5] Examples of inappropriate technology can be found in the South Pacific. Technology may not respond to the needs and situation of actual and potential users, or is difficult to transfer properly because it is complicated or difficult to operate and maintain. Technology may be overused, underused, misused, cause problems in use, face increased breakdowns and decreased life expectancy when compared with the same technology used in its place of origin. This situation may be unconsciously masked and perpetuated by aid donors, who are generally ready to replace old technology with new, thus maintaining or increasing technological dependency.

Impacts of Transferred Technology

Developing countries, particularly small island nations with limited technological infrastructures, are generally unable to assimilate the transfer of foreign technology without economic, social, cultural, environmental and other impacts. This should not be surprising. Western technology is not designed for the needs and conditions often found in developing countries, particularly in rural areas. These problems often arise because technology innovators are removed from technology users (as noted above), and because technology diffusers may have little knowledge of either the technology or its potential users; donor agencies, for example, generally have little technological or industrial expertise.

Technology Transfer Within Developing Countries

Technology transfer between less-developed non-industrial countries is complicated because few developing countries are very similar. They have little to offer each other (compared to the higher status Western technology), and the difficulties of communication and transport between them. Technology transfer between developing countries may also receive little effective support. These factors are especially true in the South Pacific, where there are significant differentials between island countries, and between urban and rural areas and outer islands.

Awareness of Technology Transfer

Technology transfer is important but problematic; it is often ignored or neglected because it is not regarded as a problem, or as someone else's problem. No matter how good the technology in the laboratory or workshop, if little attention is paid to innovation and diffusion to potential users, the technology is effectively useless. In developing countries, particularly small islands with limited technological infrastructures, the 'Catch-22' of technology and development mentioned in the previous chapter arises — local expertise is needed to appraise outside technical advice and assistance, but is unavailable because of the dependence on outside technical assistance. The goal of technology development should be reduced outside dependence.

A related constraint is that of the compartmentalisation of expertise. Technologists mainly focus on the technological aspects of technology transfer (as economists focus on economic aspects), perceiving problems to be technological (or economic). This narrow view of technology and development partially accounts for the technological (and economic) 'fix' to problems.[6] Whilst understandable, these perceptions are unfortunate, especially in small island states, where technologists (and economists) need to be more aware and active regarding technology transfer, innovation and diffusion.

An example is the desiccated coconut factory in Tonga, built with Australian aid. This factory was proposed in a consultant's report noting trends in coconut production which recommended processing into desiccated coconut as a means of value-adding and export promotion. The factory was designed by a consulting company, based on an innovative but untried use of updraft cyclone drier technology used for the production of dried milk. The factory initially cost around A$3m, did not work properly, was the subject of litigation between AIDAB and the consulting company and required around a further A$1m in re-engineering to function properly. There were no Tongan engineers able to comment on the proposal, and no independent engineering, economic or other comment was sought by the committee established to evaluate the proposal.

Greater awareness and training is required regarding technology transfer between developed and developing countries, between developing countries (or 'TCDC' — technical cooperation between developing countries) and within developing countries into the informal and rural spheres, in such areas as agricultural extension work, where much informal technology transfer takes place. As Basu points out, it is in the field of agriculture, rather than industry, that many developing countries lag behind.[7]

Technology Transfer Into and Within the Island Pacific

Trade, Aid and Transnational Transfer

An increasing amount of technology is being transferred into the South Pacific. Of the total technology transfer to the region, around 70% derives as imports and 30% as aid.[8] Around half the total imports to the region consist of technological goods.[9] Over the last decade, technology transfer into the region has been increasing at approaching 30% per year. This trend indicates an increasing technological dependence in the region.

The main mode of technology transfer in the Pacific islands is from overseas and within each island state, with less transfer between island nations in the region. Technology is transferred through imports, bilateral, multilateral and non-governmental aid agencies, overseas companies and transnational corporations. Primary technology transfer takes place into the urban public and private sphere, with secondary transfer and diffusion into the domestic and rural sphere. The public or state sector in most island countries is relatively large, due to limited private sector development, although a recent trend in most island states is to encourage privatisation and private sector growth.

Technology procurement and transfer face constraints of size and time; apart from common goods, little technology is available 'off the shelf'.

Technology ordered from suppliers can take months to arrive, delayed by the fact that a large order from the South Pacific is small by overseas standards. The dumping of outdated models, stock and substandard equipment also takes place. Transfer pricing may occur within transnational corporations (where technology is purchased and transferred within a TNC in a way that minimises costs to the TNC, but may increase costs to island countries). Technology can be tied to what hardware, knowledge or expertise is available from aid donors.

Trade

In the period 1975–86 the percentage of technological imports increased from around 40% to 50% of total imports, at approaching 20% per annum. This increase was due partly to an increase in volume and cost of imported fuels, although the value of imported machinery and equipment also increased. These increases partly reflect the influence of enclave extractive industries, and the effects of the recession and reduced investment in the smaller islands. In 1986, technological imports as percentages of total were as follows: machinery and transport equipment — 29%, fuels — 11%, chemicals – 7%. Other categories are: food — 21%, manufactured goods – 16%, miscellaneous goods — 10%, beverages and tobacco — 2%, crude materials — 1% and oils and fats — 1% (other transactions — 2%). Most technology imports derive from Pacific rim countries, mainly Australia, New Zealand and Japan. Data regarding total imports, technological imports by country and category over the period 1980–86 are presented in Tables 1, 2 and 3.

Aid

A significant part of development aid consists of technology, although it is difficult to analyse technological aid, as donors and recipients publish often imprecise and different data, and the technological component of aid can be difficult to define and disentangle.

In a study for the period 1975–80/82,[10] the data for bilateral aid, constituting around 80% of total aid to the region, was examined from the point of view of technological components of aid, using both donor and recipient data. An overall analysis of aid data for three donors (Australia, the UK and New Zealand) revealed that the increase in total aid to the region over the similar period 1977–80 was around 18% per annum. Australian aid increased from A$18m in 1978 to A$38m in 1983, with the technological component of aid increasing from 85% to 90% of total, mainly due to the increase in project aid. UK aid slowly declined over the same period, although the proportion of technological aid increased from 35% to 40%, mainly due to increasing technical cooperation — the provision of technical expertise — which increased from 77% to 88% of total aid over the period.

Transnational Transfer

Technology transfer within large transnational corporations, in licensed operations or as joint ventures with local companies and TNC partners, is usually confined to larger industries such as natural resource exploitation (mining, fisheries and forestry), telecommunications and civil aviation.

The scope for technology transfer or spin off from larger, specialised enclave industries into local formal or informal spheres is limited.[11] Technology used in both types of operation is not generally applicable to wider transfer and diffusion, and can be regarded as inappropriate for the wider production and consumption needs of island countries as a whole, causing slower rural growth, increased urban-rural dualism and environmental degradation. Whilst licence fees may yield more revenue than joint ventures, technology transfer through licence operations is often minimal, with greater potential for technology transfer in joint venture operations. There is a strong argument for the need of government intervention to influence the choice towards technology that is more appropriate for balanced development, particularly in rural areas.[12]

Technology Transfer — A National Perspective

It is interesting to examine technological aid with respect to a recipient nation. Tonga is used as an example.[13] Over the years 1975—80, aid to Tonga increased at an annual rate of 34.1%, and amounted to 97% of the development budget (aid is aimed at the development rather than recurrent budget, except in the case of Australian aid to PNG). The technological component of development expenditure over the period averaged 56%, fluctuating from 35% to 71% depending on the technological content of major aid projects (the technological component of development expenditure was measured by looking at development expenditures in various 'technological' sectors, for example, agriculture, forestry and fisheries, industry, manufacturing, electricity and water supply, transport and communications, and is therefore subject to the same provisos of definition and precision noted above).

Averaging the period, the technological component of development expenditure increased by 46% per year, from A$1.3m and 38% of total in 1975 to A$14.0m and 71% of total in 1980. This compares with a non-technological increase of 17% over the same period. Expenditure on agriculture, forestry and fisheries, electricity and water supply and building and construction all showed significant increases. The transport and communications sector showed the biggest increase, mainly on roads and wharves (from A$0.6m to A$9.1m).

Over the period 1980–85 development expenditure in Tonga levelled out at around A$18m per year. The technological component of development expenditure over the period averaged 55% (similar to 56% from 1975–80), fluctuating from 41% to 67%. The major expenditure was on marine transport — for the acquisition of a large inter-island vessel in 1980/81, and a programme of foreshore and wharf improvements, starting in 1982. Other technological expenditures fluctuated during the period. The increasing technological aspect of aid illustrates the central role of technology in infrastructural development.

Examples of Technology Transfer
It is also interesting and useful to look at some practical examples of technology transfer in the region. Desktop computers are one of the few examples of 'high' technology that can also be considered appropriate in certain situations (although inappropriate in others). Desktop computers are highly popular with aid donors and recipients, although they encounter some problems of performance in the tropical island Pacific, are often under-utilised and may not be needed — in this sense, computers represent a microcosm of the problems of technology and development in the region. Modern brewing and food processing factories have encountered, and introduced, problems into the islands. An out-of-date canning factory was relocated (successfully) to the region. Reconditioned cars are imported into many Pacific islands, but maintenance costs are high. Road-making costs are also high — in one country, meetings of the Roads Committee cost more than the roads; in others there is increased interest in labour-based construction techniques. Various projects appear to have been established for the primary purpose of getting rid of worn-out or out-dated technology and making an overseas loss for metropolitan tax purposes.

Twenty case studies of projects involving technology transfer around the Pacific were presented at the UNESCO South Pacific Technology and Development Workshop in 1987.[14] These case studies examined larger and smaller scale industries, village and infrastructural development projects. Of the projects, six were judged successful, eight unsuccessful, and eight partially successful, or had encountered some problems (broad criteria of success were applied). Problems encountered were technological (breakdown, poor performance, inappropriate choice of technology or product, limited technology management expertise, poor performance of consultants through inability to understand local needs and conditions, bad advice given by potential competitor and insufficient training); financial or economic (cost over-runs, high capital and operating costs, high depreciation costs, problems caused by loan repayment commitments, limited markets and poor market research); administrative (regulations did not help) and political (unviable project promoted).

Guidelines for Technology Transfer

Various technological, economic, social, environmental and other factors should be considered for the appropriateness of transferred technology. Technological questions relate to size, operation and operator skills: is the technology too big (or small) for intended use; can the technology be operated and maintained adequately; are requisite skills or training available for the operation and maintenance of the technology? Economic questions relate mainly to capital and operating costs: is the return on investment in the technology affordable (in terms of loan repayments or increased productivity or profitability)? Social and environmental questions relate to the positive and negative impacts of technological innovation and diffusion.

Various practical guidelines on the transfer of technology were discussed at the UNESCO Workshop:

1. Provide information and train local personnel in the operation and maintenance of transferred technology.
2. To maximise the chance of successful technology transfer, use or upgrade local existing technology rather than introduce totally new technology.
3. Make sure that overseas consultants have some local knowledge and always try to evaluate 'expert' advice.
4. Always try to attach local counterparts to overseas consultants to help transfer knowledge and experience.
5. Always try to prepare supply and maintenance contracts and agreements regarding the transfer of technology.

Factors Affecting the Transfer of Technology

Various interrelated factors affect the choice of technology transferred to the South Pacific. They relate to cost, size, the context and how the technology is chosen, the mode of procurement, modernity and status of the technology. Techno-economic criteria predominate. Technology is often chosen on the grounds of lowest capital cost. Low cost technology may be a false economy, as the technology may not perform appropriately, with high operating costs. Non-techno-economic factors are also important, especially the status and fashionable desirability (or otherwise) of certain technologies (on the part of islanders or expatriate advisors). Overseas suppliers may also attempt to dump unwanted or uncompetitive technology (although such technology may not necessarily be inappropriate in island conditions).

Size factors affect technology transfer. They mainly relate to the small size of the islands and increasingly large size and scale of much modern technological processes and industrial products. Process technology may be too big for island needs, and small process technology may not be available. Donors generally design, fund and manage larger development projects with limited technical input from local governments, giving rise to the 'Catch-22' problems of technological dependency. Whilst small technological products such as computers readily enter the islands in imports and aid packages, they may not address real needs, and thus may cause further dependence. Generally, there may be little choice of technology for transfer, or, alternatively, a duplication of similar brands, causing problems for limited support services.

No Free Technological Lunches

The increasing transfer of technology through imports and aid is causing increasing technological dependence in the South Pacific and decreasing capacity to assimilate and use aid and technology effectively. Despite the high levels of aid — much of it technological — there is no such thing as a free technological lunch. Increasing technological dependence has serious consequences for development in the region, as the technological infrastructures of island countries remain relatively undeveloped, traditional technologies are displaced and the islands face increasing problems of industrialisation.

Technology consists of hardware and software. But technology imports and aid to the South Pacific are often transferred as unpackaged 'black boxes' of hardware, not as a total package of hardware goods and software knowledge. Technology hardware and software should both be transferred. To achieve this, it is preferable to 'unpackage' the technology; to break down the hardware and software of technology to better operate; to maintain and, where necessary, to adapt and improve new technology; to promote technological self-sufficiency, reduce technological dependency and help develop local technological infrastructures. Such a process can be facilitated by increased training in technical skills and management, and the maintenance of contact with related technological activities in the region and overseas.[15] Because of the size and isolation of Pacific nations, this is difficult. It presents a strong case for the active participation of governments in all aspects of technology transfer and development.

Table 1.2.1: Total Imports for South Pacific Island Countries, 1980–86 (A$000)(1)

Year	1980	1981	1982	1983	1984	1985	1986
Cook Is	20,353	22,101	19,928	26,183	23,639	30,457	39,928
FSM	–	–	–	–	42,044	55,040	64,999
Fiji	493,284	562,403	505,948	541,962	512,614	612,040	649,471
Kiribati	16,851	22,830	22,771	19,606	20,877	21,582	21,452
Marshall Is	–	15,714	12,265	19,234	25,691	40,522	42,906
Nauru (1)	–	14,920	13,075	14,351	14,268	14,266	15,913
Niue	2,916	2,952	2,541	2,357	2,752	2,195	2,491
PNG	888,536	958,619	1,002,224	1,086,488	1,107,309	1,267,788	1,409,483
Solomon Is	64,784	66,636	58,604	69,247	75,530	101,648	94,843
Tonga	30,137	34,999	41,621	42,085	46,152	60,133	60,833
Tuvalu	3,147	2,592	2,890	2,953	3,965	4,125	4,056
Vanuatu	63,804	45,270	58,381	70,691	77,892	85,209	83,960
W Samoa	56,421	60,051	49,683	52,385	58,301	75,212	72,175
Total	1,640,233	1,809,087	1,789,931	1,947,542	2,011,034	2,370,217	2,562,510
Total ex PNG	751,697	850,468	787,707	861,054	903,725	1,102,429	1,153,027

Table 1.2.2: Technological Imports by Country, 1980–86 (A$000)(2)

Year	1980	1981	1982	1983	1984	1985	1986
Cook Is	7,104	8,247	6,796	10,769	8,394	11,487	14,690
FSM	–	–	–	–	–	–	14,574
Fiji	258,062	306,000	270,087	271,270	250,367	296,175	315,297
Kiribati	5,620	12,253	10,634	7,788	10,242	10,676	7,632
Marshall Is	–	–	–	–	–	–	–
Nauru	–	3,441	1,925	2,112	1,429	2,306	2,223
Niue	1,183	1,308	1,046	936	1,372	905	–
PNG	468,542	543,110	554,407	618,936	579,701	697,567	754,705
Solomon Is	39,136	38,573	32,062	39,740	39,778	53,415	50,335
Tonga	11,092	13,136	14,533	15,915	15,522	23,124	22,104
Tuvalu	998	888	1,136	985	1,249	1,559	1,446
Vanuatu	–	17,409	21,602	26,383	30,872	32,380	34,373
W Samoa	24,293	33,182	19,564	23,767	20,197	–	–
Total inc PNG	816,030	977,547	933,792	1,018,601	959,123	1,129,594	1,217,379
% Total Imports	49.8	54.0	52.2	52.3	47.7	47.7	47.5
Total exc PNG	347,488	434,437	379,385	399,665	379,422	432,027	462,674
% Total Imports	46.2	51.1	48.2	46.4	42.0	39.2	40.1

Table 1.2.3: Technological Imports by SITC Category, 1980—86 (A$000)

Year	1980	1981	1982	1983	1984	1985	1986
Mineral Fuels (SITC3)							
total value	295,675	398,501	385,670	402,033	357,042	407,179	295,694
% total imports	18.0	22.0	21.5	20.6	17.8	17.2	11.5
Excluding PNG:							
total value	142,606	193,304	190,879	178,861	162,367	184,291	149,688
% total imports	19.0	22.7	24.2	20.8	18.0	16.7	13.0
Chemicals (SITC5) **Including PNG:**							
total value	91,302	111,875	105,637	144,975	147,540	160,958	207,000
% total imports	5.6	6.2	5.9	7.4	7.3	6.8	8.1
Excluding PNG:							
total value	43,790	53,387	53,212	59,575	64,687	66,096	79,548
% total imports	5.8	6.3	6.8	6.9	7.2	6.0	6.9
Machinery and Transport Equipment (SITC7) **Including PNG:**							
total value	429,053	467,171	442,486	471,593	454,541	561,457	714,685
% total imports	26.1	25.8	24.7	24.2	22.6	23.7	27.9
Excluding PNG:							
total value	161,092	187,746	135,295	161,229	152,368	181,640	233,438
% total imports	21.4	22.1	17.2	18.7	16.9	16.5	20.2
Total Technology Imports (SITC 3+5+7) **Including PNG:**							
total value	816,030	977,547	933,792	1,018,601	959,123	1,129,594	1,217,379
% total imports	49.8	54.0	52.2	52.3	47.7	47.7	47.5
Excluding PNG:							
total value	347,488	434,437	379,385	399,665	379,422	432,027	462,674
% total imports	46.2	51.1	48.2	46.4	42.0	39.2	40.1

TECHNOLOGY AND ECONOMIC DEVELOPMENT

BENJAMIN HIGGINS

As is already clear from the previous chapters, Pacific island nations are unique in many respects, and not least in the factors governing choice of technology and the rate of technological progress. The fact that they are very small means that for all of them, because advanced technology requires a fairly large scale of operation to be used efficiently, they can choose to use such technology only if it is assured of a fairly large export market. Apart from that similarity, the island nations are alike in not conforming to the general 'laws' of economic and social development. They differ in the ways in which they deviate from these laws, and in nearly every other aspect of the development process. Smallness, insularity and remoteness do not pinpoint any particular country's level, rate, and style of economic and social development, any more than the fact that a country is big, continental and metropolitan does. There is as much difference between PNG and Fiji or Tuvalu and Kiribati as between Brazil and Argentina or India and Bangladesh. One must be wary of generalisation.[1]

The occupational structures and product mixes not only vary greatly from one island nation to another, but for many if not most of them these structures and mixes are highly abnormal. Tuvalu, for example, has an occupational structure that resembles those of very advanced countries in some respects: less than 5% of the labour force is in farming, fishing and forestry, and nearly two-thirds in services. From these facts alone it ought to have a high per capita income. In fact it is in the lower portion of the lower-middle-income range among developing countries. Less than 10% of its labour force is in manufacturing, and around one quarter is in construction. Kiribati has almost no manufacturing, very little primary sector activity, and the overwhelming majority of its population in the services sector, but is in the same income range as Tuvalu.

One can find in recent years other unique features, such as government expenditures in excess of gross domestic product, foreign aid in excess of total government expenditure, exports equal to two-thirds of GDP and balance of trade deficits in excess of GDP. Economies with such aberrations are bound to display peculiarities on the technological front as well. For one thing, choice of technology is virtually dictated by the structure of their economies, and the policy issue is less one of 'choice of technology' than of appropriate technical progress.

Technology and Development

How are these peculiar characteristics of the island nations reflected in problems relating to science and technology policy and planning?

Let us recall some simple home truths:

1.   'Technological progress' means getting more output from a given bundle of capital, labour and resources. Defined in this manner, one can almost say that technological progress is development. Moreover, the concept of technological progress is entirely neutral with regard to capital-labour ratios, scale of individual enterprises, distribution of population among large cities, small cities and villages, 'style' of development and quality of life and so on. Answers can be given to questions about such matters as these only in terms of specific projects in specific countries at specific points of time.

2.   The actual technology in use in any country at any point of time, in the sense of the structure of plant, equipment and tools used, and the managerial, scientific, professional and technical skills applied, is determined by two related but different sets of decisions:

     a)   Decisions with regard to the choice of technology in each enterprise or field of economic activity.

     b)   Decisions determining the product-mix in the national economy as a whole.

3.   The concept of high technology (high-tech) has two aspects:

     a)   A large input of scientific knowledge and training relative to the cost of raw materials, plant and equipment, and

     b)   A large output of final product (in value terms) relative to the input of man hours, materials and equipment in physical terms.

4.   High-tech industries and services tend to be 'footloose' (or footloose industries and services tend to be high-tech). That is, such industries are less tied to particular places by considerations of access to raw materials,

markets, sources of energy, and unskilled and semi-skilled labour, than are the more traditional industries (such as textiles, iron and steel, automobiles, footwear and furniture).

5. While high level research goes on in resource-based industries like iron and steel, pulp and paper and textiles, the industries that are in the vanguard of today's technological advance are the footloose and high-tech ones (such as electronics, computers and scientific instruments). The important factors in choice of location for such enterprises are proximity to universities and research centres, consulting services, excellence of communications, transport connections, cultural amenities and presence of other high-tech enterprises. Thus, despite their basic mobility, there is a strong tendency towards agglomeration of such enterprises.

Technology in Pacific Island Nations

The existing technology in Pacific island nations has been determined more by the product-mix than by specific decisions regarding choice of technology in individual industries, enterprises, or fields of activity. Varying amounts of traditional agriculture, forestry and fishing still exist in the countries of the South Pacific. In these activities the range of choice of technology is narrow: technical coefficients are close to being fixed.[2] Traditional methods of catching fish or growing taro, yams or coconuts are long since established.

The question of whether or not to make the quantum leap to large-scale, capital-intensive modern technology in the same fields is an entirely different sort of decision from substituting one technique for another within the range of traditional modes of production. Whether or not to purchase a modern fishing factory-ship to go 100 miles out to sea and stay there for days at a time is a very different decision from the decision to use lines or nets just outside the reef on a particular day. Similarly, the techniques used in the modern sector are standard techniques used in such activities the world over, whether in mining, forestry, plantation agriculture, manufacturing or services. There is no significant technological lag in the islands in such activities as copper or phosphate mining, sugar refining, manufacture of beer, rum, vodka and gin, banking and consulting services.

Technology, Capital and Labour

As anywhere else in the world, there is no shortage of either capital or advanced technology in resource-based industries if the resources are there and can be exploited profitably. Nor are domestic savings and investment ratios markedly low, or unemployment rates markedly high. There is no clear sense in which it can be said that capital is more scarce than labour, particularly skilled labour. Wage rates are not low in comparison with those in other developing countries. The shortage and narrow range of natural resources certainly inhibits foreign investment, and also domestic investment. But labour-intensive techniques will not help where there are no resources, or where there are resources of too low a grade and too costly to exploit, as in the case of the proposed copper mine at Namosi in Fiji. By and large, capital-labour ratios are not an issue. Certainly it would be desirable to lower the capital-to-output ratio, but it would be equally desirable to lower the labour-to-output and resource-to-output ratios. Indeed, lowering ratios of factor inputs to final output is the very essence of technological progress or development.

Constraints of Smallness and Isolation

The factor inhibiting accelerated development in the island nations is neither availability of capital nor availability of advanced or 'appropriate' technology as such. Where advanced technology is used it is generally appropriate, and where traditional techniques are still used they are still generally appropriate. Rather, the small scale of domestic markets means that an export market is required in all fields of production where economies of scale are important. However, establishing an export market for any product which has low value in high bulk is difficult because of the isolation and distance from major markets. Similarly, the shift into high-tech, footloose manufacturing or services is inhibited by the isolation from major centres of research, the presence of only three universities in the region, the almost exclusive concentration of these on routine undergraduate teaching, and the paucity of other research centres in the region. Further constraints include inadequate communications, and the infrequent and time-consuming transport links throughout the region.

Even Suva, the major city of the region, is so cut off from the rest of the world that the managers, scientists, engineers and other professionals, whose willingness to live in a certain centre is the basic factor in decisions to locate high-tech enterprises, are reluctant to settle there. Flights to Auckland or Sydney that should take three hours may take all day. The range of consulting services is narrow. There are limited links to computer networks. To be sure, particular individuals may be so enamoured of the islands as to be willing to overlook all these handicaps. But there are not likely to be many, and it is unlikely that those few would be willing to locate anywhere in the region but Suva.

Another barrier to a shift into high-tech, footloose activities is psychological or attitudinal. It is not only that the range of available local managerial, scientific, professional and technical skills is limited, but also that decision-makers in the island nations have little experience with such enterprises, and little concept of what is required to establish them. In particular, they often do not fully appreciate the importance of the role of universities and other institutions of higher learning in the establishment and expansion of a high-tech sector in their economies. Indeed, the concept of a university as primarily a research centre, with much of its activity completely integrated with operations of both industry and government, and providing leadership for technological progress, as in North America and Europe, is totally foreign to most decision-makers in the region. The university is seen as a place where secondary school graduates will obtain a few more years of schooling — a slightly higher high school. The result is that the financial support needed to expand research and postgraduate studies is not forthcoming. Consequently, the islands continue to be dependent on foreign institutions to produce high level managerial, scientific and professional skills.

Technology in Agriculture

To illustrate some of the above points, it does not appear that raising productivity in either modern or traditional agriculture is primarily a matter of making better choices among various techniques, although there are, to be sure, some available options. For example, it would be possible to mechanise the cutting of cane, rather than cutting it with knives. But such a change in technique would make sense only if labour were scarce in the sugar growing industry, whereas in fact there is considerable unemployment and underemployment. Using heavy machinery to harvest cane would require a change in organisation of the industry and add to unemployment. Since the industrial sector is growing so slowly, the labour displaced would have to seek a livelihood in the traditional sector. As the majority of cane growers are Indo-Fijian, this would be difficult, since, in contrast to ethnic Fijians, they do not have access to customary land. This demonstrates the importance of the determination of the technology that is actually used with respect to the occupational structure, product-mix and the pace and nature of structural change.

There do not seem to be any clearly superior techniques which are known but not used in subsistence agriculture. Of course, in both modern and subsistence agriculture, new techniques which would raise the output received from the same bundle of factor inputs would be highly welcome. Meanwhile, opportunities for improving levels of welfare seem to lie in structural change and the adaptation of technology to the new product-mix, rather than in better choice of technology in existing operations.

Technology Decision-Making

In discussing problems of technology decision-making in small island nations, it is even more important than in larger countries to distinguish among three types of decision:

1. Choosing the optimal technique for production of each particular product and service.
2. Introducing innovations which bring clear-cut technological progress.
3. Adapting technology to changes in the product-mix which bring increases in the gross domestic product.

Choice of Optimal Technology

In choosing optimal technology, it is necessary to take into account social costs and benefits, such as impact on the environment and the culture, as well as economic costs in terms of relative availability of various factors of production involved. Here it can be said, first of all, that in the island nations both the physical environment and the cultures are in a more precarious position than in most developing countries. The islands are already natural disaster-prone, and having so little by way of natural resources they can afford still less than larger countries to waste or destroy them. The cultures are in a transitional state from which the outcome is uncertain, and the societies are so small that external shocks that would be easily absorbed by larger and more diverse cultures can have dramatic effects.[3]

Also, the range of both human and natural resources is so narrow that some techniques, although known in the island nations and having proved superior in other countries, may not be feasible. Finally, not all methods of production are infinitely divisible or efficient on any scale — witness the failure of Mao's backyard foundries and Nehru's handlooms. Thus many known techniques that are 'appropriate' elsewhere become inappropriate in the Pacific. Within these limits, however, it can be said that if all costs and all benefits are taken into account, there is never any reason for preferring a less efficient to a more efficient technique.[4]

Technological Innovation

By the same token, there is never any reason for not introducing a new technique which increases the net benefits obtained from a given bundle of physical and human resources, all things considered. But many innovations are tied to particular kinds of natural or human resource which are not available in the island nations, and which would be too expensive to import. Others require a scale of production efficiency that cannot be attained in the islands. Some innovations may produce environmental or cultural effects and impacts which on balance render them undesirable in the island setting. Also, the risks entailed in innovation are greater in the islands than they are in larger and more diversified economies. The failure of one copper mine can be offset in a country like Canada or the United States by the success of another, or even of another mining venture in nickel or uranium, or in another field altogether. But if the Namosi copper mine project went ahead in Fiji and then failed after a few years, the results could be disastrous.

Technological Adaptation

The third kind of decision, regarding the adaptation of technology, is of particular importance for the island nations. Structural change of one sort or another will be needed if the islands are to absorb their population growth and achieve continuous improvements in their levels of welfare. But structural change, like technological innovation, requires change in the technology already in place. Once again, however, a wide range of products may be excluded from consideration in the islands, due to a lack of physical or human resources, or because the necessary scale of output is unattainable.

High Technology

For high-tech, footloose enterprises, producing either goods or services, the local availability of natural resources and markets is less important, because transport costs are a small fraction both of the costs of factor inputs and of the price of the final product. With higher technology, it is possible to consider filling gaps in the domestic supply of human resources by education and training. It is precisely here, however, where one of the most complex and intractable problems of technology decision-making in the Pacific arises.

Education and Training

In countries with large populations, or, as in the case of Switzerland, Holland, and the Scandinavian countries (which are part of a grouping of countries into what is effectively a single economy), it is possible to train people in virtually every professional, scientific, and technical field. If too many mining engineers are trained at one time, there is always the likelihood that a resource discovery, an innovation or change in product-mix will come along to provide them with employment later. And even if it doesn't, there are related fields where they may be employed and still use much of their training. This is not the case in Pacific island nations. Even a single aeronautical engineer may be more than the South Pacific is capable of absorbing, although the problem tends to arise at much lower levels of training than this. A steel-maker would be equally unemployable, and even the number of power-loom operators that can be absorbed is small. The problem is magnified when a single small island country is concerned, and magnified further still when plans are being made for regions of each country.

Nor is it merely a matter of limiting training to the kinds of jobs that are already available. The problem is to predict what sorts of jobs will be available in five, ten and fifteen years from now, and to begin providing relevant training. Moreover, the island nations are essentially private enterprise economies. Most jobs are provided in the private sector, while most education and training is provided in the public sector. Planning in the two sectors must therefore be integrated — which is no easy task. Large industrialised countries can afford to let students choose their own fields of concentration, or let the students' parents choose for them, even if the career prospects in some fields are limited. The risks of unemployment are shared between the individuals and the state, which provides unemployment insurance. But the islands simply cannot afford to train people in skills they cannot use, while leaving shortages of other skills which will be needed as the society evolves and the product-mix and occupational structure change in response. Nor is there any unemployment benefit or welfare support in the South Pacific. The inescapable conclusion from this analysis is that structural change must be programmed well in advance, by private enterprise and government working together.

Regional Cooperation

It is also clear that the range of high-tech enterprises which any one Pacific nation can successfully launch is very limited, because of the exacting manpower requirements of each. It is equally clear that if any number of island nations are to succeed simultaneously in high-tech enterprises, their planning must be coordinated, and there must be some degree of agreed specialisation. Such coordinated structural change would be far more important for the future prosperity and stability of the South Pacific than anything yet attempted by the Pacific Forum or the South Pacific Commission.

A 'Green Revolution' for Pacific Island Nations?

While the long-term development of the islands lies with such activities as plantation agriculture, scientifically oriented manufacturing, modern fishing, the search for seabed minerals and more sophisticated services — all activities with a major reliance on advanced technology — it will take a long time to achieve these economic structures of advanced industrialised nations. Indeed some of them, particularly the atoll countries like Kiribati and Tuvalu, are unlikely ever fully to achieve such goals, or even to want to achieve them. Such structures would mean something like 20% of the labour force engaged in modern, capital intensive, high technology manufacturing, up to 70% in sophisticated services and perhaps 10% in the primary sector using large-scale and capital-intensive techniques to produce a food surplus. For all the reasons stressed above, few of the island nations are likely to replicate this typical structure of an advanced economy in all of its aspects for a long time to come.

Meanwhile, varying but large proportions of the populations will continue to be engaged in traditional agriculture, forestry and fishing, hopefully in a state of 'subsistence affluence'. The absolute numbers of people so engaged are likely to increase in most of the countries of the South Pacific. Some of them can deal with the increasing numbers by bringing more arable land under cultivation, others cannot. All of them would welcome ways of increasing output per household without radical changes in social organisation, patterns of landholding, geographic distribution of the population, basic methods of cultivation or product-mix in the traditional sector. Particularly regarding rural development, it may be relevant, therefore, to think more on the lines of a small-scale 'green revolution' in the South Pacific, and the improved cultivation of such traditional products as yams, taro, coconuts, kava, bananas, citrus fruits, papaya and mangoes.

Indeed, in traditional farming, fishing and forestry, the barriers to improvement in technology seem to lie less in science and engineering than in institutional and cultural resistance to change. Traditionally there was little trade in foodstuffs, and the land tenure systems that emerged were designed to provide each household with all its needs. The result was 'a scatter of land rights, such that each person or group had access to some swamp (for taro), some flat gardening land, some bush land for foraging, some source of stone for tools and usually some access to the sea; i.e. fragmented rights in different parts of the overall tribal or clan territory'.[5] Such splinter holdings, still essentially within the traditional framework, are not particularly compatible with many kinds of technological innovation. Technological innovation is easier with larger estates, unified management and few or single crops, although technological innovation and diffusion at all levels is of obvious importance in the South Pacific.

Importance of Higher Education

Given the limited natural and human resource endowments, any South Pacific country facing continued population growth, and wishing to provide continually rising standards of living for its people, must sooner or later encourage scientifically oriented industry and more sophisticated services. This is only a matter of time, which will vary from one nation to another. That being so, the expansion and improvement of the three universities of the independent Pacific — the University of PNG, the PNG University of Technology and the University of the South Pacific — is of the utmost importance for future development in the region.

Furthermore, it is not just a matter of providing the scientific, technical and professional skills needed for such enterprises. It is also a matter of contributing to the creation of an intellectual and cultural environment that would be attractive to the scientists, engineers, managers, entrepreneurs and other professionals that are their key ingredients.

All three universities have their problems, mainly associated with insufficient support, both from local or member governments and foreign donors. Instead of establishing new centres of excellence in postgraduate studies and research, which are necessary if the South Pacific is ever to escape the 'cultural imperialism' of Australia, New Zealand, the UK, the USA and France, the three universities spend most time facing more immediate and severe difficulties in maintaining satisfactory standards of undergraduate training. Foreign donors have retrenched too soon in their support. Ultimately, however, expansion and improvement of UPNG, UniTech and USP are the responsibility of the governments of the region. Meeting that responsibility will take place only when the governments and peoples of the South Pacific fully understand the crucial importance of their universities for future development in the region.

1.4

BALANCING TECHNOLOGY, DEVELOPMENT AND CULTURE

STEPHEN HILL

◆◆◆

The Idea of Culture

The culture of a society, or of any social grouping, is the meaning system that allows that group to make sense of their world and to know how to act within it. Culture, is not however, an easy concept to grasp. As anthropologist Ralph Linton has pointed out, because our lives are so enmeshed within our culture, understanding it as a concept we can reflect upon is about as difficult as it would be for a super-intelligent fish living within the depths of the ocean to understand what water is. It is only when the fish, by some accident, is brought to the surface and introduced to air, that it experiences anything different.[1]

Anthropology came to grips with culture by a somewhat analogous process — through confronting and needing to explain totally different kinds of society. What anthropology thus came to realise was that all societies hold together because they have a shared view of what social reality is, and how people should act together to maintain it and survive within it. Culture therefore concerns the meaning system of society that provides a 'design for living'[2] in the 'shared ways of thinking and believing that grow out of group experience and are passed from one generation to the next'.[3]

The 'shared ways' however, are likely to be subject to continuous contest and negotiation as different power groups and different power objects come to have influence in the society.[4] The contest is between meanings that are conveyed in the expectations, norms, taboos, rules,

---

symbols, and even the structures of language that society uses. Produced out of human interaction, these cultural vehicles then set the framework for what goes on in further interaction.[5] Culture is therefore simultaneously produced by humans acting together towards a collective purpose, and reproduces the frameworks for continued collaboration, for giving members of a society a sense of how to behave and what they ought to be doing.

All cultures are therefore in a permanent state of change, sometimes slow and sometimes — as specifically is the case for the South Pacific island nations over the past century — very rapid. Professor Fisk describes why this happens: '"Culture" is best understood as man's total adjustment to his total (physical, climatic, economic, social and political) environment. If any part of that environment is changed, as, for example, by the introduction of external trade or by the imposition of national, as opposed to island, government, then some changes to the culture must be admitted or maladjustment will result. Failure to face this fact in development planning can be disastrous; it is like adding salt to water, but planning on the assumption that the freezing point can be maintained as it was before'.[6]

Consequently, development will change culture. Alien objects and alien social practices will intrude on the cultural ways of the people who experience their introduction. Where the introduced objects and practices are quite literally so alien as not to be able to be incorporated into pre-existing meanings, the society may simply consign them to an entirely separate domain from their own reality, as the Aborigines of the Australian Western Desert did to 'whitefella' material technologies.[7] This separation can be maintained, however, only as long as the objects and practices can be insulated from everyday life and daily practices. Far more commonly, the form of alien cultural practices is transformed and in some way filled with meaning by the group into which the innovation is incorporated.[8] The people therefore become involved in a continuous struggle to reintegrate their lives around the newly evolved and potentially conflicting understandings of what is happening to them.[9] As Clifford Geertz affirms, 'The drive to make sense out of experience, to give it form and order, is evidently as real as the more familiar biological needs'; the organism 'cannot live in a world it is unable to understand'.[10]

The Culture Power of Technology Transfer

Therefore, one of the central players in changing the cultural environment is introduced technology. Technology is not only a tool that people can choose to use according to their own culture and assumptions, it is itself a cultural force[11] — refashioning the social relations people form in producing together (for example, as in the introduction of a factory system of production into a previously rural culture). Technological artefacts are symbols that beam out messages about those who possess them (as a foreign automobile implies 'international' status). And, most importantly, technology concerns technical and organisational knowledge. This knowledge is involved in the artefacts, but is also embodied in people, books and organisations. The knowledge that is associated with technology transfer is therefore transmitted into a developing country through many different channels — not only in the technological objects themselves, but also in training, education, publications, visits by foreign experts and so on.[12] Cultures of small island states such as those of the South Pacific are therefore continuously adjusting to the encroachment of the modern technological outside world, for it arrives on their doorsteps from all sides at once, and in ways that deeply penetrate into the very processes of social interaction and meaning-making by which they are able to re-constitute the meaning of their worlds.

The depth of the effect of modernity on island cultures is reinforced by the fact that the knowledge associated with foreign technology transfer also involves economic and social expectations of the foreign culture from which the technology is derived — for example about size, sophistication, the balance of factor costs of technologies and consumer preferences. In the importation of technologies and their associated cultural values into developing countries, the transfer of all of these elements is incomplete.

In general, the main part of technology that is transferred to developing countries, particularly small ones, is physical artefacts. These carry with them cultural expectations and organisational implications of the advanced nations from which they are derived. The transfer and absorption of technical knowledge is the lesser and often neglected part of technology transfer. This is so because the absorption of technical knowledge requires the presence within the developing nation of a level of technical knowledge that can understand and integrate new technological artefacts into the technological fabric of the nation. Usually, in most developing nations, this level of human technical capability is inadequate.

A number of skewing cultural consequences follow from the general pattern of technology transfer where there is such an imbalance between the absorption of artefacts and associated cultural values, and the absorption of technical knowledge. The overall effect tends to be a growing incoherence between different sectors of the societies of developing countries in terms of cultural expectations and economic opportunities. An associated effect tends to follow — an increasing gap opens up between traditional and modernising sectors of the nation. Specific considerations that arise include:

Modernised consumer tastes

An elite tends to develop with tastes for Western goods and lifestyle. The demands of this modernising elite tend to spread, by demonstration, to other sectors of the society. And the demands require the import of Western consumer products (and often brand names), as well as the technological equipment that supports a Western lifestyle. This is probably one of the main engines of change in developing country societies.

Unequal benefits

The greatest benefits of this pattern of cultural change flow to those who have advantaged access to foreign trade or the imported technologies and technical knowledge that makes these technologies work. Least benefit flows to those who maintain their traditional ways (and traditional technical and economic stocks of knowledge). Awareness of unequal advantage provides a strong force for those members of society who are involved in the traditional culture to 'convert' to following the modernising culture and its assumptions.

Unequal participation

However, the opportunities for the whole society to participate in the modernising sector are severely restricted. More 'efficient' technological practices tend to displace traditional methods of making the goods used in society. For example, nylon fishing nets tend to replace hand-woven rope nets, and powered fishing boats tend to replace canoes. And the technologies of the modern sector tend to place less reliance on the inputs of the traditional sector because traditional inputs are frequently of a level of quality that cannot be handled by more sophisticated technological processes.

Because of the economic and organisational factors associated with technologies related to the modernising sector, relatively fewer people are employed to produce the same goods. This smaller number of people tend to earn higher wages than people in the traditional sector, thus taking a relatively higher proportion of the overall national income. The result tends to be a growing gap between a small, more wealthy, modern sector, and a larger traditional agriculture-based sector. The more modern sector is dynamic, whilst the traditional sector remains relatively static — although the traditional sector is little able to resist the impacts of change, and at the same time is not readily able to absorb the impacts of change.

Costs of imports

The dynamic effect of the modern sector therefore tends to accelerate the growing demand for associated modern technologies and capital and consumer product imports. High costs tend to be associated with the import of such equipment and products. For example, these include the increased costs of fuel, spare parts and foreign technicians to run larger-scale technologies. Often, very few benefits follow in terms of employment creation or enhanced internationally competitive productivity. The overall level of economic wealth is not increased at a rate that can keep pace with the accelerating demand for modern technological artefacts and consumer products.

As a consequence of each of these factors, foreign technology imports tend to foster growing consumer expectations that cannot be met by available economic resources. In addition, there is a fundamental impact on traditional cultural ways that follows from the sheer power, efficiency and 'modern' symbolism of the new technologies and products. Along with the breakdown of traditional values, there is an even stronger drive from the whole population to find a new way of identifying with the modernising economy and its consumer products — as a means of filling the space left by traditional values that no longer help to make sense of the new consumer world.

This drive towards Western-style consumerism is likely to remain the case as long as a nation does not have access, on its own terms, to the technical knowledge component of technology that is transferred. For it is control over this element that could allow the nation to direct the process of change, for example to integrate imported technologies with traditional techniques or traditional cultural and organisational values.

These general observations are potentially very significant for South Pacific island states. Except that national technical capabilities may be less developed than in some other developing nations, and that many of the states may be significantly smaller and more exposed to international influences, the story appears to be the same.

Therefore it is highly desirable to consider both economic and cultural questions together in making decisions that relate to imported technologies. For the two are opposite sides of the one development coin. Development plans should therefore quite explicitly examine cultural linkages and consequences associated with capital investment, trade policies, agricultural and industry promotion, foreign aid and other factors relating to technology transfer.

The Relationship between 'Appropriate Technology' and Culture

As a solution to the need for development that balances economic and cultural change, considerable attention has been paid to the introduction of 'appropriate' technologies that form a bridge between traditional and modern sectors. This attention has mainly focussed on larger developing countries, although there is some interest in appropriate technology in the Pacific island context.

The idea behind discussions of smaller scale appropriate technologies is that, by making more incremental adjustments to existing techniques and products, the level of cultural dislocation is likely to be minimised. In small island states, where the economy is largely based on traditional agriculture rather than on secondary industry, the consideration of appropriate technology is therefore an issue that deserves special attention.

Appropriate technologies allow a nation to capitalise on the most abundant of its present resources (for example, relatively unskilled labour and agricultural produce), rather than on the introduction of modern technologies that may not link well at all. The use of appropriate technology is likely to make a more limited demand on scarce resources, such as technical skills and foreign exchange. Appropriate technology is therefore resource-efficient, and at the same time maintains economic linkages and forestalls the drive towards more Western-style consumerism.

Depending on the technical resources available to national governments, the appropriateness of technology can be enhanced by considering existing practices and the cultural and economic goals that are being sought through:

1. making careful choices among technologies that are available;
2. making significant adaptation of available technologies; and,
3. developing new technologies that are designed specifically for particular purposes.

The experience of designing and using technologies over the last 20 years suggests, however, that some cautions should be heeded. There are often hidden costs as well as benefits.

The Cost of Choosing

There is often a wide range of alternative technologies from which to choose. These variations may include considerable differences in size, capital intensity and varying requirements for energy, types and levels of skill and management expertise. Also, there may be many different suppliers, so that scope exists for bargaining over the terms and conditions of supply, for example, concerning credit, training that is provided and restrictions of management contracts.

However, large costs could be involved in searching for and evaluating alternatives. The costs of obtaining information could be too high for a single project or country to bear. Where some of the available alternatives are relatively new, there may be high risks involved in being an early user.

Scope for Adaptation

The core elements of a technical system are often inflexible, so that there may be limited scope for choice at that level. This is particularly likely to be the case with manufacturing systems that are oriented towards import substitution or the development of export industries. In these cases, the characteristics of the product (which are related to what is supplied by or to overseas markets) tend to restrict the range of choices about production equipment.

However, there are often many options in the peripheral parts of the production system (for example, in materials handling), and in the way that the technological system is organised (integrating both low-scale cottage industries with high-scale manufacturing, or by employing traditional organisation practices). Adaptation can perhaps be most effective in these peripheral areas.

The primary costs, however, lie in the dependence of adaptation, even in peripheral or social components of production, on skill and knowledge resources. Costs also lie in the difficulties that can be experienced in integrating new production practices into traditional organisational ways.

Integration into Traditional Social and Cultural Practices

A study of these difficulties across a number of South Pacific nations highlights what may need to be considered. To quote from a report by Standingford:

> Over the years many attempts have been made, by Governments, churches, colonial administrators and aid agencies, to evolve approaches to development which incorporate and make use of established culture and traditional structures rather than threaten them. The creation of co-operatives is perhaps the most prominent example and, while there have been successes, the general picture is a discouraging one. Many countries have sought to channel development resources through existing organisations at the village and island level — in Western Samoa the *fono*, *taulele'a* and *aualuma*; in Kiribati the Island Councils; in Fiji the *soqosoqo vakamarama*. The current Fiji Development Plan states that: 'The possibility and desirability of reintroducing the *Turaga-ni-koros* and *Bulis* through the Fijian Affairs Board will be examined. Government recognises the contribution that local community leaders can make to development efforts and will encourage them whenever possible'.
>
> In Western Samoa the traditional economic unit is the *aiga*, controlled . . . by the *matai*. Since individuals reap little personal benefit from work performed on *aiga* land, production of marketable (and in particular, exportable) surpluses has fallen behind national expectations. Some success has, however, been achieved by encouraging competition between villages based on export crop production. This method exploits the traditional competitiveness which manifests itself in enthusiastic inter-village cricket and publicly announced church donations.

In traditional society it is common for activities to be undertaken in groups which bring together people of the same age, sex or rank. Thus projects executed by women's groups (such as the Fijian *soqosoqo vakamarama* mentioned above) or young men's groups (such as the Samoan *taulele'a*) work through and may be seen as reinforcing traditional social structure rather than undermining it.

It is hazardous to make generalisations about the success of initiatives in widely different countries, but it has been our observation that attempts to harness the energies and organisational skills of existing village women's groups have been the most promising. In many countries the women in rural areas have well established organisations which traditionally involve themselves in such matters as public health, infant care, tending food gardens and livestock husbandry. The historical reasons for this, in a situation where men have been warriors and fishermen, are not hard to imagine.[13]

Distortion by Local Social and Cultural Practices

Where the introduction of technologies can be integrated with the strength of existing social practices, as in the case of involving women in rural areas mentioned above, there may be a recipe for successful transfer of technology that is accompanied by little disruption of traditional culture.

In many cases where 'appropriate technologies' have failed, what can be seen is that these social, cultural and political characteristics were not adequately taken into account. An observation by Standingford illustrates how the 'technical' success of a project may be in direct opposition to social success regarding the adoption of new technology within traditional communities:

> We would make the general observation that the lack of appropriate technology is rarely an obstacle to outer island development, if appropriateness is judged in purely technical terms. However, failure of development initiatives is often attributable to incompatibility between introduced technology on one hand and the complex and infinitely diverse pattern of custom, values and motivation which characterises human society on the other. It is unlikely that more research will overcome this problem of incompatibility. What is required now, in our view, is a slow process of trial, error and adaptation on a scale which allows mistakes to be made, and with substantive involvement by the people who will be responsible for and benefit from the systems in question.[14]

Standingford also provides two other examples of the affect on technology of social and cultural factors. After noting how, in developed countries, older skilled craftsmen often resist technological change, apart from any other reason because it reduces the significance of their skill or replaces their employment entirely, he comments:

It is understandable, then, that technological innovations of any kind are examined rather carefully by the older men who enjoy political and economic power in most Third World communities. If an innovation appears to carry within it the threat of diminution of their power the old men will sit, impassive and expressionless, until the most committed 'appropriate technology' enthusiast is reduced to tears of frustration and goes away. In many parts of the world resistance of this type has been met when proposed schemes would have given village women or young people access to the money economy through poultry, dairying or market gardening activities.

Another example from Western Samoa is appropriate here. A scheme was introduced to supply village fishermen with small catamarans, powered by outboard motors, to enable them to make day-long fishing trips outside the reef. Training in the care and maintenance of outboard motors was given before delivery of the boat. But community and family obligations in Western Samoa are such that the owner of an outboard motor frequently comes under irresistible pressure to lend it for many purposes, economic and otherwise. Indeed, he may come to his boat prepared for a fishing trip only to find he has lent his motor to a person or persons unknown during the night. Toolkits suffer the same fate and, like books in our own society, seldom find their way back to their original owners.[15]

Developing Culturally Sensitive Technology Planning

The idea of assessing the appropriateness of technology is the central element of any technology policy. But appropriateness can be judged against many different criteria — ranging, for example, from upgrading the productive efficiency of the traditional rural sector to the replacement of traditional technology with modern manufacturing techniques and imported consumer goods.

Given the small size of many Pacific island states, as well as the dominance of the traditional agricultural sectors, there is a particular place for the consideration of smaller scale technologies that allow integration of the traditional with the emerging modern sectors within the economy.

However, in all cases — whether consideration is of more modern or small-scale technologies — an essential dimension to be taken into account is the existing culture and social practices. Modern technologies can have a seriously distorting impact on traditional cultures. But, where competition with imports or on international markets is required, there may be no other alternative. Smaller scale technologies, which at first sight appear to be minimally disruptive, may simply not work because of a lack of integration of new techniques with traditional social structures and ways of doing things.

Culture is therefore an essential feature of 'design space'. Decisions about the appropriateness of alternative technologies that are available, or could be developed, need to be made within and for particular national situations. Decisions need to align economic objectives of government with objectives that concern maintenance or managed change of cultural ways.

Because the introduction of new technologies — at any level of scale, modernity, or complexity — is essentially a social process (with extensive social consequences), it is advisable to pay attention not only to the technology artefacts themselves, but also to the process by which the technologies are developed, chosen, or introduced within what is always a complex social, economic and political system. Success is usually directly associated with attention to this social process. One particularly important feature of many successful programmes has been the involvement of the community in all aspects of the processes of change.

Social participation in technological choice and transfer is potentially the key to a small island society being able to find its own most resilient balance between the past cultural values they wish to retain and modern world forces that are shaping their future.

TECHNOLOGY, DEVELOPMENT AND THE ENVIRONMENT

SULIANA SIWATIBAU

◆◆◆

Technology, as has been defined earlier in this book, is a set of techniques within a structure. The techniques comprise ideas, means and know-how. These are developed, disseminated and utilised within a given social, political, economic and cultural structure. They are designed to exploit the physical environment within which they were developed. Much of the technology imported into the Pacific since European contact was developed within a different social structure, to meet development needs under different conditions.

Two major challenges arise in the utilisation of technology introduced to the Pacific. The first is to ensure the technology is adaptable to Pacific social structures, so that it promotes rather than hinders the development of those societies. The second is that this may also involve some adaptation on the part of Pacific societies, so the technology can be better assimilated. Such adaptation would include, for example, the building of technical colleges to train technicians to operate and maintain the increasing amount of technology introduced with the promotion of industrial development in the region, and the establishment of low-cost housing near industrial development sites to provide easy access for industrial workers.

The second challenge is to ensure that technology will service development without destruction of the environment on which that development depends in the long run. This is the challenge that is often left unmet in the desire for rapid and maximum economic gains. This chapter deals with the interaction of environment and technology as Pacific societies utilise the latter to service their development efforts.

Technology, Society, the Environment and Development

The importance of the link between technology, society, the environment and development is stated in the development plans of most Pacific countries. These goals include both economic and social development, as well as some maintenance of cultural integrity. Economic development is possible without much regard to shorter-term social and environmental consequences, but such a course often implies heavy longer term social and environmental costs that are unsustainable. Social development, on the other hand, cannot be envisaged without simultaneous consideration of the sustainability of the environment in which society exists (or subsists, in rural areas, where most islanders live).

In Pacific societies, culture is still closely intertwined with the environment, so that maintenance of the environment is a necessary condition to maintaining certain aspects of culture. If technology is to service the process of development effectively, it is necessary that a suitable structure exists within society for the active assimilation of technology, and to minimise the adverse effects of technology upon the environment.

The interrelation between society, technology and the environment may be considered as a compound of factors which multiply rather than add together. A decline in the quality or value of any one of these factors can have serious adverse effects on the process of development.

The Pacific Environment before Human Settlement

Before the advent of human societies into the region, the Pacific Ocean and its scattered island land masses were a rich diversity of ecosystems, populated with a great variety of species, many of which were found nowhere else in the world. An ecosystem is a living unit of interdependent plants and animals, existing within a common set of physical environmental conditions. Thus a coral reef is an ecosystem, separate from a mudflat ecosystem, which is again separate from a mangrove or forest ecosystem, although all these ecosystems may be interconnected in a biogeographic area — a collection of ecosystems in a geographic expanse, where the plant and animal species are more closely related to each other than they are to species outside the area.

Through natural processes, these biological societies evolved from one stage to another, changing both in form and composition. New species arrived or appeared, old species moved on or died out. Finally, in each case, a relatively stable association emerged, where a balance was achieved between the different species that live in association with each other and their surrounding environment. This is the end of a long process of biological settlement, and is called a 'climax association' – a final form that no longer changes to a different form through natural processes. This association or balance is maintained in a dynamic and delicate equilibrium. Each member plays an integral and important role in maintaining the climax association as a whole, similar to the way the different organs keep the human body as a whole in a healthy and delicate equilibrium. For example, a sand dune becomes a lightly forested sandy island, a lava flow is finally covered with tropical forest, or a boggy expanse is turned into a mangrove swampland.

Human Settlement

With human settlement, of course, the equilibrium is disturbed. New species and new associations, such as cultivated gardens, are introduced. The introduction of new species accelerates change, including the death or extinction of old species. The physical environment is changed, and the fine balance between the climax association and its environment is disturbed. The natural balance is often not able to survive, and many of its more vulnerable members die. This occurs, for example, when timber trees are removed. The animals that depend on them for food and/or shelter and the small plants that thrive in their shade cannot survive. They disappear, along with the timber trees. New and possibly more aggressive species replace them. Similarly, removal of corals from coral reefs deprives little fish and other small marine organisms of their shelter, and robs larger fish of their food supply. The reefs then gradually become barren and die.

Pre-European Pacific societies caused only limited damage to their environment. Their technology was relatively benign, and many societies had developed quite sound conservation practices enabling them to live in equilibrium with their environment, ensuring their mutual sustainability. The terraced gardens of hill country in Melanesia, the pit agriculture of coral atolls, the systems of taboos practised everywhere that restricted eating turtle meat and turtle eggs to chiefs and forbade wildlife harvesting from certain areas for certain periods are examples of widespread environmental management practices in traditional Pacific societies.

European Impact

The increasing visitation, settlement and colonisation by Europeans, and especially the introduction of their technology, began to change the fragile ecological balance in the Pacific. The introduction of the axe, for example, highly desired as an early trade good, was instrumental in cutting down, almost to local extinction, sandalwood trees that were highly desired by Europeans in their trade with the Far East. The arrival of increasing amounts of Western technology increased the capacity and potential for environmental damage. This is particularly the case where natural resource exploitation is concerned — such as mining, fishing or forestry — or some other feature attractive to Western powers — such as the advantage of regional isolation for nuclear testing, toxic waste or chemical weapons storage and disposal.

To date, despite some glaring exceptions, such as the abandoned island of Banaba and the mined moon-like landscape of Nauru, much of the rich diversity of Pacific ecosystems has remained. A survey of the South Pacific[1] reported an estimated total of 2000 types of ecosystem in 20 distinct biogeographic areas in the region. Many of the ecosystems are tiny and located in restricted areas, with unique conditions, that often also give rise to unique endemic species. The Pacific has one of the highest degrees of endemism in the world. This diversity of ecosystems and high degree of endemism is extremely fragile, as destruction of a given valley or raised limestone island (phosphate mining), or mountain top (gold mining), often means the loss of a whole unique ecosystem, with several endemic species.

For this reason, the International Union for the Conservation of Nature has begun an inventory of ecosystems, plant and animal species found in the Pacific, as part of its worldwide inventory programme. The programme is already finding that the rate of species extinction in the Pacific region is, sadly, one of the highest in the world.[2]

The Need to Protect Species and Ecosystems
It is important to protect species and ecosystems (or collections of species) for the reasons set out below. The main cause for the loss of species and decline of ecosystems is the activities of human beings. The application of technology, particularly larger-scale Western science-based technology, has enabled human beings to be more active in the Pacific islands, and the use (or misuse) of Western technology must therefore be seen as a major factor in the degradation of Pacific island environments. The application of Western science and technology may, however, also offer a means to understand and provide a basis for sound and sustainable development in the South Pacific.

Why save Species?
Pacific readers need not be reminded of the wealth of useful natural products that Pacific societies currently depend upon for medicine, shelter, food, handicrafts, dyes, ornaments, traditional monetary systems and other uses. Very few of these have been cultivated or farmed to any extent. Those few include timber species such as *Agathis vitensis* in Fiji, food species such as the wild yam *Dioscorea nummularia* and fruit trees such as the Pacific lychee *Pometia pinnata*, and the crocodile now commercially farmed in Papua New Guinea. Before any species can be farmed successfully, some basic information about its survival requirements and breeding habits

needs to be established. A commercial industry based on the domestication of any wild species cannot be viable unless it is based on a strong gene pool with a great range of variability, from which selection can take place for the development of desirable characteristics. Therefore, not only do we need to preserve wild species for future use, but enough of each species needs to be preserved for a strong, healthy population.

Outside the Pacific, particularly in developed countries, the usefulness of wild relatives of cultivated species is well known. Crossing a domesticated species with wild relatives of corn, rice or cattle, increases specific useful characters, which include adaptability to new conditions of soil or climate, yield and resistance to diseases. The farming of marine resources (mariculture and aquaculture), as performed elsewhere, has great potential in the Pacific, yet we know so little of the resources we have.

Why save Ecosystems?
Except for simple pioneering plants, such as algae, lichens and mosses, wild plant and animal species do not survive in isolation, but always in finely balanced interdependent communities or ecosystems. An ecosystem is itself like a living organism, where every member (species) plays a vital role, like the organs of a single living body. The loss of a species is therefore like the loss of an organ, rendering the organism sick. The degree of sickness depends on the importance of the species in the life of the ecosystem as a whole. Unfortunately, human activities usually affect the more important rather than the less important members of an ecosystem. As the ecosystem gets 'sick', many of its members begin to die, just as a sickness in a single organism spreads from one organ to others, as the complications of a disease set in. Thus many valuable and potentially valuable species are lost before humanity even has a chance to understand their roles and potential uses for future generations.

Technology in the South Pacific

In the countries of the South Pacific, as in developing countries elsewhere, technology includes small-scale, mainly traditional or indigenous technology, generally found in rural areas; medium-scale or 'intermediate' technology, typically including domestic, transportation and small-industrial technology, found in urban and rural areas; and larger-scale, modern Western technology, mainly associated with larger industrial and natural resource enclave operations. At either end of this technological scale, technology in the Pacific can be seen to consist of two types — 'people's technologies' and 'corporate technologies'.

Both corporate and people's technologies are necessary for the development of modern Pacific societies. People's technology is necessary for the economic and social development of the common people, particularly in rural areas. Corporate technology is necessary for the economic growth of the nation. While the use of people's technologies may have slowly accumulating negative effects, the use of much larger corporate technologies in government and private sector development projects has an enormously greater potential for severe environmental impact, and allows little or no facility or time for redress. It is the choice of specific types of technology within these divisions that will result in either environmental degradation or sustainability.

People's Technologies

These include small-scale, rural technologies, developed either by traditional societies, or appropriated by modern rural communities. These truly belong to the people. They are no- or low-cost, generally well understood and have no system of patents that forbid the free dissemination of their know-how, development and use. The knowledge and skills associated with them are transmitted through the informal training system of the people. Examples include subsistence fishing, house construction, traditional medicine and introduced activities such as the construction of simple wood-burning stoves by village women and village artisans. People's technologies are usually relatively environmentally benign.

Regrettably for the Pacific, there has not been enough formal or governmental interest in people's technologies to ensure their survival. Some examples are mentioned below to illustrate how the use of environmentally benign traditional, improved or new technologies can help to meet modern needs and development goals of Pacific island countries. Cautious reference is also made to some of the dangers of indiscriminate modification and application of traditional technology. These examples are drawn from the fields of fisheries and agriculture.

Fishing Technologies

Apart from a few island societies, such as Kiribati, most Pacific people's fishing technologies were and remain restricted to the reef zone and inshore waters. These continue to fulfil the bulk of subsistence fisheries needs of Pacific societies.

Unfortunately, fisheries yields from these areas are rapidly dwindling — not only because of increasing population pressure, but also through the use of environmentally damaging fishing technologies and environmental degradation from other sources. The devastation caused by dynamite and various types of fish poisons are well recognised by governments throughout the region. Less recognised but equally damaging are modern adaptations of older fishing and marine resource collection methods, and some new demands on reef and near-shore marine resources. These include:

Fish Drives

Unlike the muro-ami fish drives of Japan and the Philippines, where heavy weights are used to pound the reef top, fish drives practised in the Pacific traditionally used floating thick ropes of leaves and a tightening wall of swimmers to drive fish inwards. This was environmentally benign, as it created little damage to the reef surface.[3]

Nowadays, with the availability of modern fishing nets, which may be obtained in any length desired, more efficient modifications of the traditional fish-drive are possible. One of these, practised by women in Fiji, involves herding fish into a tightening circle of net by running them in over the shallow reef surface. This pounding of feet over the reef surface and dragging of net, damages live coral. An excessive use of this type of fish-drive can kill many corals on the reef, leading eventually to depletion of reef-life and eventual death of the reef.

Fish Traps

An efficient and environmentally benign method of catching fish in coastal waters is the building of reed walls and funnels on reefs or mudflats, and the herding of fish into such traps as the tide falls. This method, widely used in the Pacific, selectively traps only large fish, and was very effectively used by skilled traditional fishermen to catch selected species. In Fiji for example, traditional knowledge of fish habits included deciphering their droppings and 'swimprints' on the exposed reef and mudflat at low tide. One could tell which major species of fish were feeding in the area and where they travelled over the flat at high tide. One could then construct a fish trap in the right place and at the right time to catch the desired fish species. Unfortunately this folk science is now almost lost in Fiji, although the traditional knowledge persists in other Pacific societies, including the Solomon Islands, Vanuatu, Papua New Guinea, Tonga and elsewhere, particularly in outer islands and rural areas. The official recognition, preservation and use of such folk-wisdom would aid the understanding and management of fisheries resources and enhance the importance of traditional knowledge throughout the Pacific.

Some modern modifications of the reed-wall trap can be environmentally destructive. The use of chicken-wire instead of reeds is indiscriminate, catching unwanted fish, injuring smaller fish and blocking detritus to interfere with the current over the reef or mudflat. Such interference can affect the growth of more sedentary organisms, such as shellfish, a very important food source for many Pacific societies.

Harvesting the Reef

An important but underemphasised aspect of food production in the rural and traditional island Pacific is the 'fossicking' for and harvesting of various marine resources of the reef at low tide, mainly by women. In terms of quantity, more seafood resources are gathered in this way than by subsistence or artisanal fishing.

Besides their role in food production, the reefs of the Pacific are becoming increasingly used as tourist attractions, the source of shells and fish for the overseas aquaria market and for the provision of sand and corals for building materials.

Catching fish for the overseas commercial aquaria market is a growing industry already well developed in Hawaii. In the rest of the Pacific, with careful management, this could be developed as a small income-generating or business activity. According to Randall, most coral reef fish collected for aquaria appear to be in great natural abundance, and may recover from relatively heavy harvesting under careful management.[4] The problem with aquaria fish-collection lies more with some of the methods of collection currently employed, which can be very destructive of the reef ecosystem. Such harvesting technologies have included the use of chemical poisons and dynamite, which harm all reef organisms indiscriminately. Good fisheries management requires the education of all people involved with marine resources. It will be advantageous to link modern understanding and management with traditional knowledge and conservation methods.

Agricultural Technologies

The majority of Pacific islanders continue to live in rural areas, where they depend largely on techniques of traditional subsistence agriculture for daily survival. Even in rapidly growing urban centres, vacant lots and backyards are used for traditional gardens to support or supplement family food requirements. The demand of cash crops, and of human settlements for better land, has driven some subsistence farmers onto marginal lands, often to steep hill slopes with poor soil and growing conditions. Here the traditional methods of slash and burn continue, but fallow periods diminish, so that soil fertility is progressively destroyed, and soil erosion encouraged.

Despite this, however, it is worth noting that some small scale farmers, pushed onto such marginal lands, have developed modifications of traditional agricultural techniques to minimise environmental damage. These include the control of burning, the use of rubble to build contours and the wise choice of crop mix.

Where environmental conditions are limiting, such as lack of soil and soil moisture, traditional technologies have been used to create appropriate conditions, as exemplified by the pit taro gardens of coral atolls. Modern adaptations have also been developed for the cultivation of smaller scale gardens for vegetables such as beans and carrots. One such adaptation (used by a woman home-gardener in Tuvalu), uses a bed of coconut husks to retain moisture, over which soil and organic compost are piled to build a vegetable garden. Such people's technologies are eminently suited to their own environment, and should be adapted where necessary and promoted for widespread dissemination.

Corporate Technologies

Larger scale corporate technologies are generally developed, owned and controlled by organisations that are outside or alien to local Pacific island communities. These technologies have been developed within different socio-economic, cultural and political systems. They are expensive, complicated and the motives behind them, ideas that give rise to them and means of their development are often highly protected through systems of patents and licences. The know-how for their operation and maintenance has to be acquired through the formal education system. They are mainly used by multinational corporations operating in the region, larger governmental or paragovernmental agencies.

Because the control of such technologies does not reside in the Pacific, it is difficult to modify the technologies for better adaptation to Pacific environments. Financing and other administrative arrangements associated with the application of technology often leave little choice for Pacific decision-makers regarding the type of technology to adopt. Under such conditions, the way to minimise environmental damage lies in good management of technology, and the introduction of environmental management measures to offset the unavoidable impacts of modern technology (especially as the promoters of such technology may neither know nor particularly care about island environments and the impact of technology).

From the environmental point of view, corporate technologies are employed and have impacts in three main areas:

1. *Earth*

    Those that utilise geological resources of the soil and earth. These include mining, excavations for roads and other infrastructure constructions, agriculture, forestry and human settlements.

2. *Water*

    a. Those that utilise hydrological resources of freshwater or seawater. These include hydro-electric power stations and the large-scale use of water in such industrial applications as cleaning, heating, irrigation and food processing (for example, in brewing and fish-processing).

b.   Those that do not use water directly, but have a major impact on them. These include the use of agrochemicals in commercial agriculture, the use of the sea for dumping wastewater and solid matter (including toxic and radioactive waste) and the use of small atolls for nuclear weapons tests.

3.   *Air*

Those that impact on the quality of the air and atmosphere, largely through release of air pollutants. These cover a wide range of activities including home insecticide sprays, vehicular traffic, factory emissions and waste incineration.

Environmental Impacts of Corporate Technologies

Zone of Impact

The impact of a technology on the environment is not limited to the immediate site of application, and occurs both on-site and off-site. It may extend great distances away through the movement of water or air. Thus, erosion inland through forest clearing may result in heavily silted rivers, damaged coral reefs and ruined coastal fisheries. This has happened in many areas of the Pacific. Areas downwind of a fertiliser plant or food processing factory may receive a heavier load of pollutants than other areas that are closer but upwind of the factory.

Mechanism of Impact

The environmental impact of a technology on ecosystems occurs through two interacting mechanisms or pathways — through direct biological impact on biota or biological systems, and through indirect impact on life support systems of the physical environment. The impact through each mechanism or pathway can be analysed both on-site (where the technology is located) and off-site (a distance away, where the impact of the technology can be traced).

Physical Environment

Technological impact on the physical environment includes disturbances of the soil and earth, pollution of waterbodies and atmosphere. In general terms, technological activities that are related to the earth have more widespread effects and impacts than those which involve water or the atmosphere.

Biological Environment

Once the quality of the life support systems is affected, living organisms that depend on them (including human beings) are also affected. Vulnerable members die. Unexpected mass deaths of fish near urban centres and commercial farms have often been reported, their deaths evidence of the deteriorated waterbodies they inhabit. Plants have been found to be highly sensitive to levels of air pollutants. Some pollutants produce specific responses from specific plants. For example, the tobacco plant has been used to monitor and map ozone pollution, and the alfalfa plant used similarly for sulphur dioxide pollution.[5]

Interrelation between Physical and Biological Environments
The impacts of technology in the physical and biological environments are interrelated. Technology may have a primary effect on the biological environment and a secondary effect on the life support systems of the physical environment. This happens after forest logging, where the removal of trees affects the quality of the air and waterways, which then impact on other living organisms.

The interaction of technology with the physical and biological environments may be illustrated thus:

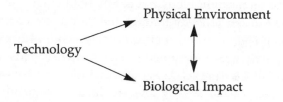

Impacts of Technology on Human Environment
In terms of development, the effects and impacts of technology on the human environment and society are of particular interest. For decision-makers, these effects and impacts need to be quantified in terms of costs and benefits, in order that environmental concerns be given the attention they deserve.

Assessing the Impacts of Technology
Careful analysis should be conducted of the expected impacts of the technology proposed for use for any development project before the total impact of technology can begin to be quantified. This analysis should include the following considerations:

1. *General Technology*
   What is involved in the use of the technology?
   Where can the major impacts of the technology be expected?
2. *Physical Environment*
   What are the on-site and off-site impacts on the physical environment?
   List effects and impacts with particular reference to soil, waterbodies and air. These effects should be quantified as far as possible. For example, to

take one effect of a proposed mine, increased silt loads in rivers as a result of mining should be estimated.

3. *Biological Environment*

What are the on-site and off-site impacts on the biological environment? Identify and list impacts with particular reference to individual species of plants and animals, ecosystems and biogeographic regions as a whole. These impacts should be quantified as far as possible. For example, to continue the above example of a proposed mine, the area of coral reef which would be affected by heavy flooding should be estimated.

4. *Human Environment*

It is important in the assessment of the impacts of technology to make particular reference to the human environment.

The following direct and indirect impacts on the human, biological and physical environments should be identified and quantified in terms of costs and benefits, where possible, so that those impacts that are of economic importance to human societies may then be singled out and some value placed on them by decision-makers:

1. *Direct impacts on the human environment.*

For example, in the case of industrial chemicals, what is the health effect of air pollutants on factory workers and downwind homeowners?

2. *Indirect impacts of altered biological systems on the human environment.* For example, will the clearing of forests reduce mosquito population and hence the incidence of malaria?

3. *The indirect impacts of altered life-support systems of the physical environment on the human environment.*

For an overall assessment of the impacts of technology, the effects on the human, physical and biological environments should be tabulated and quantified where possible. Although this is a difficult task in the case of the 'macro' physical and biological environments, an attempt to value these effects should prove a useful exercise in itself. These values may then be added to computations of project cost/benefit analysis. It is important that those effects that are unable to be quantified have their zones and levels of positive and negative significance literally if not economically indicated.

At the rate at which Pacific governments are promoting development projects that impact upon the environment, and noting the accompanying rate of destruction of these fragile ecosystems, it is a matter of urgency that environmental concerns must be taken into account in the planning of any development projects and initiatives.

However, even with the best internal environmental measures they can take, Pacific island countries and people are unable by themselves to have much effect upon certain overwhelming external threats to their environment. These include those created by technologies serving the interests of highly developed nations outside the region – such as the effects of nuclear weapons testing, toxic waste disposal, destruction of the ozone layer and the particularly terrifying prospect of the 'greenhouse effect' (caused by carbon dioxide build-up), consequent global warming and sea-level rise, which would destroy many low-lying islands and atolls, and the sense of identity of many islanders.

* * * *

While it is heartening to note a greater interest in environmental issues, both in the Pacific and in the world generally, much of this is more rhetoric than reality. Many of the advances made in the Pacific in recent years have been in areas outside individual national jurisdictions, where Pacific nations have been able to unite against a common threat such as driftnet fishing or global warming. Unfortunately, within their national boundaries, governments of the region appear to have found it difficult to act effectively. This is due to a variety of reasons.

Given their high population growth rates (now averaging well over 2% per annum), their limited resources and vulnerability to all factors causing change, Pacific countries must now seriously examine their development priorities. The correct choice of technology to facilitate development priorities is vital, for that choice will influence the total way of life of future Pacific societies, the culture they will evolve and the sustainability of the environments within which future Pacific societies will exist.

Fifty Years of Science and Technology in the Cook Islands

Stuart Kingan and Tony Utanga

Early Days — Technological Resourcefulness and Self-Reliance

In the 1940s, although there were only 6000 people in Rarotonga, science and technology were positively accepted by Cook Islanders, and many had a remarkable degree of technological ingenuity. It is interesting to begin by recounting what happened after an important electric motor burnt out. In New Zealand, a similar breakdown would have meant that the motor would need replacement, as no rewinding company would fix it, claiming that rewinding would be too difficult. Technical people in Rarotonga had a different approach, and the next day had completed a perfect rewinding job, with the motor eventually outlasting the rest of the equipment.

The isolation of Rarotonga prompted a local desire to listen to overseas radio broadcasts. There were many short-wave receivers from the US that were very ingeniously maintained, and at least five had been built by local people. Some were powered by imported dry batteries, some by car batteries. Charging batteries was carried out rather expensively at the government freezer, and many people had small generators. There were at least two small hydro-driven generators, and two wind-driven generators.

The best microsope in the hospital had been borrowed from an engineer, who had made the instrument locally. There was even a locally made film projector. The cinema was the scene of another major technological innovation — silent films screened on a hand-cranked projector and using limelight had been introduced in 1907, and modern photophonic sound films had been screened in Rarotonga before they were introduced into New Zealand in the 1920s.

Cook Islanders knew well what technology was appropriate for island development. (Unfortunately, they were not always able to obtain such technology, and sometimes were given technology that was inappropriate for their needs, as we shall see.) In 1944, local people watched or operated bulldozers brought in to build Rarotonga's first airstrip. They were impressed with the potential usefulness of these machines, and asked the NZ colonial government to supply one. When local colonial officials said that a bulldozer would be of no use, interested islanders were able to obtain a small D4 from another source. That machine was then worked almost continuously for 20 years, maintained by local mechanics.

Land Transportation

The Cook Islands Public Works Department is responsible for roads and water supply. Fifty years ago, roads were practically the same as now, but without sealed surfaces. The main road in Rarotonga had been sealed earlier, but by 1944 very little evidence of this remained. So gravel surfaces continued for a long time. Those with motor vehicles complained, and various surfaces were tried, but no real solution was achieved until sealing began in the early 1960s. Today, most of the roads in Rarotonga and some in Southern Group islands are sealed, but resealing is frequently necessary, and expensive.

In Rarotonga, before World War Two, a change in transport took place from horse-drawn buggies, imported from the US, to motor vehicles, mainly medium-sized trucks. However, during the war, when there was little shipping, exports dropped and there was an economic recession. Most motor vehicles deteriorated and their wheels were used on a new generation of buggies, which once again became the main form of transport for both goods and people.

At that time, three businessman still had trucks operating, and the Public Works Department had a small pickup which served as an ambulance when required. Bicycles predominated for private use — bicycles were the main means by which individuals moved around and went to work, and remained so for many years. Later, mainly because of increasing theft, bicycles had to be registered and given number plates. In Rarotonga there were over 3000 registered bicycles for a population of less than 10,000.

At the end of the war, there were only three private cars on Rarotonga. With the end of the recession, wartime hardship and isolation, imported trucks and a few more cars began to appear. A few motorcycles were also imported — small ones of European origin — but all gave a lot of trouble, and were soon discarded. Then, in the early 1960s, the small Honda motorcyle made its appearance. Unlike previous motorcycles, the Honda did not seem to break down with such regularity, and soon practically every bicycle was replaced by a Honda 50 or similar small and reliable Japanese motorcycle. Young people would no longer ride bicycles. The new Honda culture led to the gradual displacement of most bicycles by small Japanese motorcycles — the rubbish dump began to fill with perfectly good bicycles.

Gradually, two wheels gave way to four, and trucks, pickups and cars began to replace the small motorcycles that had previously displaced most bicycles. Today in Rarotonga, with a population of 9000 people, there are over 4500 registered motor vehicles — trucks, cars and motorcycles, more than one for every two people, and the bicycle, no longer needing to be registered, has made a comeback in these times of increasing awareness of fitness, increasing vehicle costs and pollution.

Outer islands now all have some motor vehicles, but the vehicle culture has grown more slowly on the outer islands than in Rarotonga, as outer island maintenance and repair have always presented problems. On one small island in the 1950s, an enterprising resident returned from a visit to Rarotonga with a bicycle (perhaps from the dump). Although there was less than a mile of road on the island, the bicycle created great interest, and was hired out at high cost to all the young people for single rides through the village. Soon, the enterprising owner was able to import two more bicycles, and they continued to bring in cash. The owner then bought a small two-stroke motor that fitted on the back of a bicycle, powering the back wheel through a friction drive. This was too much for the Island Council, who took him to court for dangerous driving, going through the village at about 15 miles per hour. The Council passed a new law limiting vehicle speed to five miles per hour, but the government in Rarotonga refused to approve the law.

On another island, sudden wealth through pearlshell exports prompted a businessman to import a brand new pickup truck. Maintenance problems, repairs and rust soon beat him, however, and three years later the pickup was buried in a ceremonial funeral. Aitutaki and Penrhyn were ahead of other outer islands in terms of motor vehicles — many surplus jeeps and trucks were left behind by departing US forces after World War Two, and these vehicles lasted for many years.

Shipping

Up to the war, the only way to travel to Rarotonga was by ship. In 1944 the NZ Government Motor Vessel *Maui Pomare* was the only overseas shipping connection to the Cook Islands, making ten trips a year from Auckland (sometimes via Lyttleton). The *Maui Pomare* normally took ten to twelve days to make the trip, carring 34 passengers and quite a lot of cargo. It was a good ship, but hardly adequate.

Before the war, Union Company ships serviced Samoa and Rarotonga from New Zealand. Ships crossing the Pacific fortnightly between California and New Zealand also called in to Rarotonga. These brought a lucrative tourist trade to Rarotonga. Passengers went ashore for the few days while the vessels, anchored off the reef, were being unloaded by lighters. Two large auxiliary schooners were owned by local trading firms. But as copra prices dropped, outer island trade declined. The larger of the two schooners, the *Tagua*, was put up for sale, but there were no buyers, even at a bargain price. Then the war came along and the NZ government rented the vessel from its owners and undertook to maintain it. It was used during the war to service islands from NZ as far east as Pitcairn, as far north as Funafuti and as far south as Campbell Island. During the war an occasional phosphate vessel from Makatea to NZ called in to Rarotonga, but this was mainly to transport Cook Island indentured labourers, who worked the Makatea phosphate mines.

The other ship, the *Tiare Taporo*, was left to serve the Cook Islands. Through a special agreement, the *Tiare Taporo* was contracted to carry freight for the owners of the *Tagua*, although it would not carry freight, or even mail, for other traders. Technology is often as closely associated with politics as economics. This situation was soon broken by local businessman, and later prominent politician, Dick Brown, who purchased an old schooner, the *Tahitienne Auckland*, and started trading in the Cook Islands. Several other ships were acquired, operated and retired in quick succession — the ships had short lives because of the poor condition they were in when cheaply purchased. The ships ran at an overall loss, but trading in the outer islands was lucrative, and soon business grew and became well established. Various ships followed, mostly short-lived, but all operated either by writing off losses against trading profits, by accepting a government subsidy, or both.

Following the war, more trans-Pacific ships from NZ called on their way to and from North America, but carried only freight. In the early 1960s the *Maui Pomare* was replaced by a new NZ government vessel, the *Moana Roa*, which carried more passengers and cargo, was faster and gave an excellent service for many years. As trade increased, the monthly *Moana Roa* service was replaced by two smaller ships giving a fortnightly cargo service to and from NZ. This service has continued, and today small ships unload at the wharf, connecting Rarotonga with NZ, Samoa, Niue, Honolulu and Tahiti.

Until the mid-1960s no ship could enter harbour at Rarotonga. Fuel was brought in by tanker rather than drums (the practice in most other Pacific islands), and unloaded by a pipeline from an offshore anchorage. As harbour improvements continued, smaller ships could soon enter the harbour, including small oil tankers.

Over the years, marine technology has changed little, and although satellite navigation, automatic engine monitoring and automatic steering have all reduced crew numbers, overall costs have soared, and it is doubtful that modern ships can pay their way on small island routes without subsidy. Local shipping, with small cargoes and long distances between islands, has always been a doubtful economic proposition.

By 1990, local inter-island shipping was becoming almost prohibitively expensive, due mainly to the large crews needed on local routes. The alternative, small motor vessels, are also very expensive to run. A new radical technological innovation in inter-island shipping is badly needed.

Aviation

Before the war there were no aircraft based in or regularly visiting the Cook Islands, except for a Walrus amphibious aircraft. This aircraft was initially carried by a NZ warship. The warship was persuaded to part with the Walrus after the plane impressed local people and at least one local businessman. The Walrus remained in the Cook Islands, and eventually sank near Aitutaki.

During the war, airstrips were built in Penrhyn and Aitutaki, where American troops were located, and both islands got used to regular calls by military aircraft — Liberators, Flying Fortresses, Catalinas and others. An airport was built in Rarotonga in late 1944, and the first flight from Auckland to Rarotonga was an RNZAF Hudson. Then, using airforce Dakotas, the RNZAF started a fortnightly passenger service to Rarotonga, travelling via Fiji, Tonga, Samoa and Aitutaki. In 1947, the Dakotas were changed to DC3s, and NZ National Airways took over the service for the next five years.

NZ National Airways started the coral route using flying boats — the only aircraft that could then land in Tahiti. The service called at Fiji, Samoa and Aitutaki en route to Tahiti, but had to bypass Rarotonga due to unfavourable landing conditions. Passengers to Rarotonga had to travel to and from Aitutaki by ship. When an airport was built in Tahiti, the flying boats were replaced by Electras and DC6s, but Rarotonga still had no air service. The RNZAF started air services to Rarotonga using Hastings, Hercules and later DC6s, until Polynesian Airways started flying to Rarotonga with DC3s. After the opening of the new airport in 1973, Air

New Zealand flew in firstly with DC8s, then DC10s, 747s and now 767s. The tourist trade, plus the large numbers of Cook Islanders flying overseas, now supports four Air NZ flights per week, one via Nadi. Other airlines fly two flights to Hawaii, two to Tahiti and one to Sydney, via Pago Pago, Apia, Nadi and Brisbane.

Local inter-island air services were slow to start. Cook Islands Air began a service from Rarotonga to Aitutaki in 1974, and added flights to other Southern Group islands as airstrips became available. Later a private company, Air Rarotonga, was formed, and now has five aircraft servicing all Southern Group islands, and Manihiki and Penrhyn in the Northern Group. Their latest acquisition is an eighteen-seater turbo-prop Bandarante (the type earlier flown by Air Pacific, based in Fiji).

Radio beacons were installed in Rarotonga, Aitutaki and Penrhyn during the war. After the war the Penrhyn beacon was removed. Recently, new beacons have been installed in Penryhn, Manihiki and Atiu. Some local planes are now equipped to use Omega navigation.

Water Supply

The water supply piped to all residences and other buildings in Rarotonga was operating fifty years ago, using open weir intakes high up on the mountain streams. Water was clear during good weather, but very muddy in floods. There were insufficient intakes, however, and the delivery pipes were too small to give sufficient daytime pressure to some areas. Over the years, some intakes have been replaced by effective water galleries, small pipes have been replaced with larger pipes, and more intakes have been added. Some recent experiments with open reservoirs did not meet expectations, and these are now out of use (but can be reopened if needed).

Energy

Fifty years ago, cooking was performed either in traditional earth ovens, or on wood or kerosene stoves. Clothes were mainly ironed by charcoal irons, although there were a few benzine irons. House lighting was by benzine pressure lamps, kerosene wick lamps or simple candles. One or two buildings had 12-volt electric lighting from batteries charged either by wind generators or by small petrol engines.

One photographic business had a large 32-volt generator charging batteries to run equipment, and the local cinema operated its arc lamps from a large DC generator. The government-owned freezer was the sole supplier of meat and butter, and had a large engine-driven compressor. It also had a generator for charging batteries. The radio station had a large 110-volt battery, charged by a large DC generator.

For refrigeration, people either had iceboxes, supplied weekly by large blocks of ice bought from and delivered by the government freezer, or they had Crossley Icyballs imported from the US. These devices consisted of an insulated cabinet and two balls connected by a pipe. One of these balls was heated for about an hour on a kerosene stove each morning, and then the other ball was placed in the refrigerator cabinet. This kept the cabinet below freezing for nearly 24 hours, when the whole process had to be repeated. This process was usually performed by some enterprising youths, who would contract to service about six households. They would light each stove in turn, and then it would be time successively to replace the balls in the units. The actual management of technology is an important but often neglected issue.

The government-owned Electric Power Supply (EPS) company was established in 1945. Starting in Rarotonga only with a capacity of 35 kw, the power supply grid steadily grew and extended, until 1977, when the whole island was covered, and generating capacity had reached nearly 2 megawatts. The generation output has continued to grow, and will soon have a capacity of 8 megawatts. Electrical appliances were very popular, and diffused rapidly, although, in the 1970s, imported gas began to predominate for cooking.

As prices of fuel and electric power rose rapidly after the major oil price rises in the 1970s, the 1980s saw an increasing interest in alternative, renewable sources of energy. In the 1980s, solar water heating was installed in about one third of Rarotonga houses. Also in the 1980s, the technology to build and use simple charcoal and woodburning stoves was introduced. These stoves have become popular on some outer islands, but have not proved popular on Rarotonga.

Solar photovoltaic power was introduced in 1978 to replace small petrol generators in outer island radio stations, and has proved very cost-effective over the years. Photovoltaic power systems were introduced for domestic lighting on outer islands in 1981. Photovoltaic systems have a great potential for use on outer islands, where power generation and distribution is expensive, and could be in more widesread use today for outer island lighting, refrigeration, radio and video. However, aid agencies insisted on installing diesel generators, and the EPS, particularly expatriate staff, campaigned against solar energy.

When solar photovoltaic systems were introduced in 1981, outer island residents thought it just what they had been looking for, in terms of their needs and situation. Two factors held up the promotion of this appropriate technology. Firstly, Australian aid experts said the people needed diesel generators. So Australian aid gave the generators for free, and also paid for the wiring on outer islands. On the other hand, anyone wanting solar power had to pay for the entire costs of equipment and installation, wiring and maintenance. Diesel-generated electricity was therefore subsidised. The supply cost was further subsidised — on some islands, the real cost of power generation was as high as $3 per kwh, yet it was sold to the consumer for the same price as in Rarotonga, at 25 cents per kwh. This situation was obviously good for the customer, but unrealistic regarding the real costs of power production. Today, outer island power supplies cost government a subsidy of over $1,000,000 annually.

Secondly, once reticulated 240-volt systems have been installed, a change from reticulated AC power to individual house systems, each with their own solar-powered 24-volt DC equipment, is not easy. Outer island people have invested considerably in AC equipment — refrigerators, power tools, radios and TVs, irons and electric jugs. Although a change to DC leads to improved energy efficiency with most appliances, it also means meeting considerable new capital costs for the new DC solar systems and new DC appliances. Also, while small solar systems are useful, they usually lose their appeal because of their limited capacity for energy storage and power supply. Solar homes need 10 or more standard solar panels to charge batteries and provide sufficient storage for a range of appliances. The change from AC grid to DC solar can only be accomplished effectively if, as in the 25 completely solar-powered islands in French Polynesia, people are helped to be self-sufficient in solar power by being given substantial loans at low rates of interest and a strong supporting government agency, possibly in cooperation with aid agencies, to assist in purchasing and maintaining appropriate equipment.

Apart from problems with reticulated AC systems on outer islands, technical problems have also arisen, and generator system breakdowns have been frequent. Three-quarters of the aid-supplied generators broke down during the first year. These were then shipped first to Rarotonga, where they couldn't be fixed, and then to NZ for repair. Shipping and handling charges alone approached the value of the machines. Because of poor shipping services, fuel supply as well as increasing cost is always a major problem.

Despite these two factors, and because of the problems with generator systems and the subsidies they require, if solar systems are given the support noted above, it seems that a gradual change back to solar power in the most remote islands is inevitable and imminent.

Communications

As early as 1914, the Island Council in Rarotonga requested that the NZ colonial government establish a radio station in Rarotonga, mainly for contact with NZ. At every Council meeting the delay was questioned, until finally, in 1917, a radio station was set up. This comprised a spark transmitter and what, at that time, was the most modern valve receiver.

The standby receiver was a crystal set, with a galena crystal and catswhisker. Ten years later, more modern equipment was installed, and this continued in use until the late 1940s. More modern equipment came in with the requirements of World War Two, and communications were established with all outer islands. All communications were by morse code telegraphy, and local operators became very proficient.

Cook Island radio operators were more proficient, both operationally and technically, than those imported from New Zealand. In the 1930s, a hurricane completely destroyed an outer islands radio station, but within days it was back on the air. The local operator had carefully cleaned all the components and rebuilt the equipment. After the war there was a great interest in the revival of amateur radio, and many local people become interested. In the early 1940s two people had built their own transmitters, but because of wartime restrictions could not use them. The interest in radio after the war led to many new hams in Rarotonga, and very soon, through the efforts of the Radio Club, there were many more hams per head of population then in any other Pacific Island country (our neighbour, Tahiti, came next).

The central radio station relayed daily morse code news transmissions from NZ and San Francisco to outer islands, and transcripts were placed on public notice boards. This was the only news service in the Cook Islands, and was well received. In the mid 1950s, the daily news bulletins from NZ and San Francisco were incorporated into a duplicated news sheet, and local news, notices, shipping and weather news were added. This was the start of the government-owned *Cook Islands News*, now a privately owned daily newspaper.

Most of the problems faced by outer islands telegraph stations were due to power supply breakdowns. Small petrol generators frequently failed, and even back-up generators had often also failed before the first generator was able to be shipped away for repair. In the late 1970s, solar panels became available. These not only solved the problem of outer island power generation for telegraph, they were also much easier on charging the batteries, whose life expectancy doubled. Telegraph charges to outer islands were also very high. It cost more to send a telegram from Aitutaki to Rarotonga than to send one from Aitutaki through Rarotonga to London — in fact, a 600-word telegram to a relative in an outer island would cost the entire annual salary of a junior public servant.

The late 1950s saw the start of radio broadcasting, with a 30-minute service per week, using a 250-watt transmitter normally used for shipping services. This service grew when the local Amateur Radio Club built a 500-watt transmitter in 1960, followed by a 250-watt transmitter and a one-kilowatt transmitter beamed to the Northern Group. This service soon became Radio Cook Islands, and further transmitters were subsequently added. Radio Cook Islands was operating five broadcast transmitters, all made by local effort out of surplus parts bought, begged or borrowed from overseas. The Cook Islands had a very effective broadcast coverage, better in fact than now. In 1965, NZ made a special grant for the purchase of a 10kw transmitter. This went into service in 1967, and the service was well received in most islands. But the equipment used a lot of power, and with increased power costs, the power cost alone to the government was over $500 a day. This transmitter was duly replaced by a transmitter of lower power and increased efficiency, but the broadcast service coverage of the group declined, and is now relatively poor.

A small manual telephone exchange was established 50 years ago in Rarotonga, at the post office. The exchange operated during office hours between key government offices such as hospital, radio station and Resident Commissioner. The exchange was joined by a shared party line at night. This service grew, and soon the exchange offered a 24-hour service. More lines and operators were added, and in the early 1980s the manual exchange was replaced by an up-to-date electronic exchange and push button phones. Although ground-based radio is capable today of giving excellent telecommunication service to outer islands, local telecommunications, still operated by the post office, are now establishing satellite earth stations in outer islands.

Technically, there had been nothing to stop setting up a radio-telephone service to outer islands years ago. But the government argued that such a service would reduce their telegraph revenue, and it had to wait till the late 1960s, after a radio-telephone service had begun to NZ and other overseas destinations. In 1979, the British firm of Cable and Wireless took over the international service through a satellite earth station in Rarotonga. Satellite communications were not new, however — in 1972 a locally built earth station had joined the PEACESAT network, and is still operating.

In December 1989, television was introduced to Rarotonga, and includes live NZ news. It is paid for by a universal increase in income tax, plus advertising revenue. Video recorders have now become widespread in all parts of the Cook Islands. Despite the introduction of broadcast TV, videotape rental shops are big business in Rarotonga. In December 1990, television commenced in Aitutaki, showing tapes of the previous night's programmes in Rarotonga.

Business and Office Technology
Complicated mechanical accounting machines were used 50 years ago. These have now been replaced by new electronic devices. Typewriters first

became electronic, and were then replaced by computer word processors. Copying machines have become a must, and earlier mechanical teletypes introduced in the 1970s have been replaced by fax machines.

All these new electronic devices are easy to use, but expensive if overseas contact is involved. Unfortunately, however, most have been found to be adversely affected by the tropical climate — with constantly high temperature and humidity. Life expectancy of all modern business machines is low, maintenance expensive, and replacement frequent. Many offices and businesses have therefore opted to install air conditioners in rooms where such equipment is used. The major problem that then arises is that an air conditioner in Rarotonga can cost hundreds if not thousands of dollars per year to operate, and generally itself only lasts a few years.

A related problem is the social impact of such new technology. For example, although computers enable banks to reduce staff numbers and gain better control over transactions, customer queues seem to have lengthened. Now that tellers need to spend a long time getting the computer to clear and record a transaction, banking operations can take much longer than they used to.

It is interesting to note that one mechanical accounting machine that came to the Cook Islands in the last century was still working perfectly 70 years later. Modern electronic computer technology may be a big step forward, but only if it becomes far more reliable — once such equipment can last 70 years or more in a tropical climate without air conditioning, then it will be really good.

Medical Technology

Fifty years ago, hospital facilities in Rarotonga were somewhat behind overseas standards of the day (apart from the locally-made microscope). The hospital X-ray machine was primitive and difficult to use — when an X-ray was needed, two outsiders had to be sent for, one to start the engine which powered the machine, keeping a hand on the throttle and an eye on the voltmeter, the other to operate the X-ray machine and develop the film. The Americans in Penryhn and Aitutaki has much better equipment.

Now the hospital has a very modern X-ray department with the best equipment available. It also has a well equipped laboratory, and many modern devices such as dialysis and ECG machines. But again, these have to be maintained, and despite good training in NZ, hospital technicians have their hands full.

Educational Technology

Fifty years ago, education in Rarotonga had little technology beside chalk and blackboards, pencils and paper. In the late 1940s, two 16mm projectors and a regular supply of educational films were sent to Rarotonga from NZ, and were regularly shown. Filmstrips were also sent, and schools in Rarotonga obtained filmstrip projectors. The Department of Social Development in Rarotonga produced filmstrips of local interest, and because there were no suitable projectors for outer islands use, the Department developed a very efficient projector that operated from a 6 volt battery, using only 20 watts. These projectors were widely used in outer islands, both by the Education and Health Departments.

When tape recorders became available, nearly all schools obtained one. But these were not much used, and largely became toys for teachers. School radio broadcasting to outer islands started in the 1960s, and the service was very successful. But later, when the Education Department was asked to pay for broadcasting time, the service was discontinued. Although video recorders have become widespread in all parts of the Cook Islands, their main use is for entertainment rather than education.

Reflections
Progress? — Aid, Dependence and the Need for Appropriate Technology
What has happened to the technological ingenuity and self-reliance which were characteristic of the Cook Islands in the 1940s? The post-war period was followed by internal self-government in 1965, and the coming of 'development' to the Cook Islands. With development came increasing aid — bilateral aid from specific countries, and multilateral aid from agencies such as the UN. Aid is useful for development if it is appropriate, but in practice it was often inappropriate aid that was forthcoming. Although a request for a bulldozer may now be granted without question, if that bulldozer breaks down, all that is required is to ask an aid agency for another. The need for and the art of perpetual maintenance that existed in 1944 are now largely gone, with the increasing dependence on technological aid.

The Importance of Science and Technology Education
More important than the promotion of appropriate technology is fundamental science and technology education. As education in the Pacific islands has expanded, the development of science and technology education has been poor, particularly at secondary level. The teaching of simple fundamental scientific principles is part of general technical knowledge, and essential to clear technical thinking. Because of limitations in secondary school science, college graduates today often get confused, lacking the simple foundations of science. A look through textbooks in general science shows why many secondary pupils remain so backward in science and technology. Any teaching that ignores fundamentals will achieve only confusion. This illustrates some of the serious limitations in

science and technology teaching, and represents a real problem for island societies in which science and technology are increasingly important.

APPROPRIATE TECHNOLOGY: AN OVERVIEW

DON MANSELL

The Small Island Context for Technology

The Pacific island states differ so much from most other nations that they have almost unique problems in choosing technologies from among the alternatives available. The choice may be provided through the freedom of the market place so that consumers choose, or by controlling the market so that planners choose, or, as in most instances, by a combination of those. A poor choice leads to the introduction of an inappropriate technology. Although it is difficult to provide a general definition of appropriate technology, the essence of appropriateness is suitability to the social, economic, physical and political context of use.

The main sectors in which technological choice is to be made are housing, sanitation and health, agriculture (including horticulture and animal husbandry), food processing, transport, communication, manufacturing and allied servicing, energy, education and administration. Technology must not be viewed solely in terms of artefacts, however. Technology also includes systems, such as methods and arrangements for doing things, preferably with the purpose of enabling people to live more satisfying lives. The conventional, but rather questionable measure of development in this is the average income per person, so it is usually assumed that increased and improved technology will increase income and consequently the standard of living. Other measures of development abound, ranging from other economic indicators to demographic variables such as life expectancy and infant mortality.[1]

The Pacific island states have such limited economies that their capacity to produce new technologies, their capacity to buy them, and even their capacity to use them effectively, are severely restricted, particularly when one examines the long term economic prospects of members of the region. Their sources of income are scarcely within their own control and therefore are insecure. It follows they will have little hope of improving their lot without substantial assistance, which so far most of them have enjoyed. A population of a few thousand, or even a few hundred thousand, is not large enough to create new technologies that will compete in the world-wide technology market; this forces small Pacific island communities to be net importers of technology. Consequently, careful choice is needed if the cost of those imports is not to get out of hand. 'Cost', of course, refers to social cost as well as financial payments.

Technological Change
The technological development of human society has moved from the mere appropriation and use of natural resources through adaptation of resources, to the creation of new products, processes and systems.[2] Pacific islanders are at the second stage, for the most part. What technologies will help them increase their standard of living according to their own measures of it?

It is necessary to ask of each technology option which is available the following broad questions, each of which implies many subsidiary questions:

- What does the technology offer?
- What does the technology demand?
- To what is the technology sensitive?

The third question can be subsumed within the second, but consider examples of answers to each of the three separately for the moment. A new or newly-introduced technology firstly offers increased variety, whether it be a foodstuff, an entertainment, a tool, or a technique. It is variety and its implied excitement that draw people away from traditional lifestyles to new things — often drawing them from rural communities to the relative glitter of urban settlements. Much imported technology in the Pacific islands has this element of fashion in what is offered, ranging from junk food to sunglasses and including more serious intrusions such as baby formulas. One would hope that a technology innovation would offer higher productivity (less drudgery), improved quality and new opportunities. An important consideration in this respect are the potential users of technology, especially implications of technological change for gender — how men and women will be affected by new technology.

The 'down' side is that technologies do not blossom in isolation — they have important linkages with other technologies. For example a television set demands either a video recorder and a distribution system for video tapes, or a satellite and earth station system. Motor vehicles require fuel supply depots, roads and streets, spare parts and mechanics with their specialised tools, and a safe system of traffic control. A factory requires raw materials, capital, disciplined and trained workers, competent management, a suitable infrastructure including energy supplies and communication systems, an assured market, and, in many cases, related industries. The demands of a technology are not merely technical and economic; they are also social and political. They require certain commitments from the labour force, from the public sector and from government.

An imported technology is sensitive to its market and to regulatory authorities. Therefore those who use capital to introduce it can be relied upon to 'massage' the market (usually with advertising) and to ingratiate themselves with the politicians. That pressure on the market and on community leaders can lead to severe distortions in the patterns of demand and in community decision-making.

If the benefits of the technology are deemed to outweigh the demands it makes on the society, economy and ecology within which it operates, it may be judged to be appropriate. The mere fact that it survives financially is not evidence that it is appropriate. Clearly the judgment whether the benefits outweigh the costs is subjective at least in part. Despite the attempts of technologists and economists to quantify all manner of things in a supposedly objective way, life remains full of subjective assessments.

Assessment of Appropriateness

Factors which need to be considered in assessing a technology include the following:

Climate

The Pacific environment is harsh on many artefacts, being mostly hot and humid. The reliability and life expectancy of building materials, electronic devices and much processing equipment is likely to be lower than in the more temperate places of their origin. Function also is influenced if the design of the artefact is not adapted. Many 'modern' buildings in hot humid climates are unnecessarily uncomfortable.

Organisation of production

The success of much modern technology depends on the economy obtainable from large scale operations, both in the production and marketing phases. It is true that there has been an explosion of small entrepreneurs in the technologically advanced countries but they are viable because they exist in a large and varied economy which has suitable niches for them.

Income Levels

The capacity to generate capital for investment depends on income levels, and, in particular, on average savings from income. Alternatively, the capital comes from outside the country, with a consequent loss of proprietorship. External investment is not necessarily harmful but it is worth noting that most of the developed countries, including Japan and USA, are wary of it. If we focus on internal investment we find that the low level of capitalisation tends to favour the introduction of technologies which do not compete with more capital-intensive plants elsewhere. Therefore, the goods or services offered are protected by artificial pricing or the investment is lost. In either case it can scarcely be claimed that the standard of living has been improved.

Skills

Modern technology demands new skills. In most countries which are regarded as economically successful the proportion of workers classified as unskilled has declined. This has had serious implications for the educational and social systems which have been required to place much greater demands on school-children and to support those who have been unable to cope. It is not merely a matter of skill, but also one's attitude towards work, employment and productivity which is challenged by an enterprise competing in a volatile market. Technological change is so rapid that retraining and discipline is more and more important. That can be stressful for workers in the more developed countries and even more so for communities which have been mostly subsistence economies.

The users of technology also must be skilled because of the greater complexity and sophistication of everything from a house to a bicycle or office equipment. Service industries have expanded to relieve the immediate users of the technologies. But are such service industries developed sufficiently in the Pacific island states to make the new technology appropriate? The problem is particularly acute in those sectors of industry and commerce in which there is a world-wide shortage of relevant skills (for example, in computer maintenance).

Demand

Reference has been made already to the interaction between technologies and the patterns of consumer demand. The infant food formula case is only one of several in which either the demand was not there and the investment was lost, or the demand was created with distortions of other priorities (in that instance in the hygienic feeding of infants).

Social Effects

Traditional lifestyles are peculiarly sensitive to changes in how things are done. The change can disturb customary obligations, duties and practices and can shift the balance of political power within the community. That may or may not be harmful — an assessment must be made. Occasionally the introduction of a technology conflicts with deeply-entrenched beliefs, and taboos are broken. Examples can be found in culturally sensitive aspects of human behaviour such as housing and sanitation, where custom may render unacceptable otherwise perfectly sound and suitable technology — such as taboos regarding human waste leading to the cultural unacceptability of the composting toilet, an otherwise promising technology for the economic disposal and conversion of human waste into fertiliser.

The Cuckoo Effect[3]

Introduced technologies have a tendency to remain, often working well below their normal efficiencies, but nevertheless competitively with what they have replaced. The proprietors commonly have access to finance at much more friendly rates than local entrepreneurs and have other supporting systems to help solve problems. They are able to pay better wages and fringe benefits than a very small local firm and frequently appear to have higher status as an employer. Furthermore, their capacity to buy favours from authorities is much greater. A local business may, however, through kinship and other political ties, have a considerable advantage.

Authorities have other reasons to protect imported ventures and the technologies they sell; they may believe that advanced technology is the only means of development and therefore disparage the local product, and they may be aware that the imported technology is linked to other parts of the economy which depend on its survival. In a large economy these factors may be less than persuasive but individual enterprises become very important in the tiny economies of the South Pacific.[4]

Goals of Appropriate Technology

Definitions of appropriate technology must include the idea of net benefit mentioned above, and must acknowledge the importance of sustainability. In the Pacific island states the question of sustainability is very important because their economies are so weak. Removal of aid and migrant remittances would leave the income of many island nations quite incapable of sustaining much above the subsistence economy from which they have been moving. Assuming their income base is stabilised, they must look to technologies which maximise the following characteristics:[5]

1.   Technologically Sustainable
   ● Use local materials and energy.
   ● Build on locally understood technologies.
   ● Use proven techniques, to reduce the incidence of failure.
   ● Provide a product or service of acceptable, but not necessarily extravagant quality, with high reliability, low maintenance and ease of access.
   ● Meet the demands of the local geography (particularly climate and topography; referring to the effect of environment on technology).
2.   Socially Sustainable
   ● Involve local people in its development and introduction (ideally, responding to a real need).
   ● Use existing or easily adaptable skills with minimum retraining.
   ● Offer opportunities for further employment and economic activity.
   ● Provide work satisfaction.
   ● Minimise the need for movement of labour away from traditional communities and other occupations.
   ● Encourage regional and rural development.
   ● Introduce change gradually, so that it does not appear threatening.[6]
   ● Be environmentally benign (introduced technologies can have harmful environmental impacts on the environment; possible environmental impacts are also therefore matters of social concern).
   ● Avoid disturbance to local customs, traditions and beliefs.
   ● Have beneficial or at least no harmful gender implications.
3.   Economically Sustainable
   ● Require low capital investment per workplace.
   ● Require maintenance expenditure which is affordable.
   ● Provide a competitive product or service.
   ● Fit in with local, regional and national development plans where they exist.
   ● Integrate the participants more into the national monetary system in order to reduce the duality of the economy (to aim for greater economic equality and opportunity).
   ● Provide opportunities for benefits to the people as a whole rather than to a privileged group.

Jequier stated conditions for the success of a new product (whether it be a crop, a pump or a latrine).[7] His list is valid in the current situation in the Pacific islands:
   ● market demand;
   ● well-managed production;
   ● adequately-skilled workforce;
   ● sufficient credit to finance the innovation and its risks;

- effective transport and distribution;
- effective reward, since the entrepreneur must make a profit;
- effective information systems.

Examples of Technology in Use

Two examples suffice to illustrate some of the points made above.

Biogas

The first is biogas technology. The technical social and economic feasibility of this technology have been demonstrated in China and India which have large and highly structured societies providing many opportunities for the technology to flourish. The introduction of biogas plants in the Pacific islands was done by expatriates and not in response to a keenly-felt enthusiasm on the part of the recipient communities. Although simple in principle the technology requires careful management to maintain its efficiency, and the proportion of biogas plants in the Pacific islands which continued past the demonstration phase is tiny.

Wokabaut Somil

The wokabaut somil (portable sawmill) has, so far, been a greater success. It has met a real need for more efficient harvesting and use of forest timber. It is made by a local firm which understands the technology and can maintain it. It is used in the places where people live and do their normal work. It is supported by a dissemination and information system created on the campus of the Papua New Guinea University of Technology. Time will tell; the venture is still not very old, but it has fitted the requirements stated above and will probably prove to be a progressive and sustainable (and therefore appropriate) technology provided it is used judiciously and not to the detriment of the forests.

* * *

The criteria by which to judge the appropriateness or otherwise of a technology are complex and frequently subjective. They are such that judgments may be expected to change over time — societies and economies are dynamic, and so the context for technology is subject to change. It is possible to ask questions, the answers to which help assessments of the appropriateness of technology and enable technology choice to be made.

The most important components of assessment are strongly contextual, and include issues of affordability and sustainability. The features common to a large majority of Pacific island states (small and sparse populations, limited resources, poor economies, geographical isolation etc) make it necessary to assess technologies very carefully and critically. The mere survival of a technology is not sufficient evidence to call it appropriate.

IF IT'S NOT APPROPRIATE FOR WOMEN, IT'S NOT APPROPRIATE

RUTH E. LECHTE

Women of the Pacific have always been technologists. They invented and used tools for basic agriculture, food gathering and preservation, for making clothing, mats, containers and baskets used for storing and carrying almost everything, including babies. They made paint and dyes for decorating these and other craft artefacts. They were water collectors and carriers, and were particularly involved with the technology of traditional medicine. Much of this activity still serves its users well, and, although it is doubtless more appropriate to use a modern bucket or handpump in a well rather than traditional methods of water collection, many traditional skills and products still have practical, art and craft value, and it is fortunate that women retain some status through their ability to produce them. But it is not the status that accrued when these were life-preserving skills.

Many women in the Pacific now perform important functions in contemporary life — as doctors, aeroplane pilots, university professors, computer operators and business entrepreneurs — the list is endless. At the same time, the majority of women are still partly or wholly living traditional self-supportive lives in villages or mountain settlements, where traditional technologies remain very much part of the fabric of life.

Workshop — 'Women and New Technologies'
In September 1989 the Energy, Environment and Appropriate Technology Program of the World YWCA, based in Fiji, organised an international workshop — 'Women and New Technologies'. The workshop was held in

the Netherlands, and attended by young women, from around 50 countries.[1] The intention of the workshop was to overcome ignorance of technological issues, and the fear women often have of 'hard science' resulting from skewed educational systems. It was also intended that the knowledge gained in the workshop would help the women participants to influence programmes and projects for women in their own countries, including the Pacific, and improve their political understanding of the implications of decision-making regarding 'development' issues involving technology.

A skilled resource team organised and led the training workshop. The workshop focussed on the significance and impact of various technologies on women. These included new reproductive technologies, office technologies, communications technologies, the philosophy and application of appropriate technology, biotechnologies and nuclear technology.

In early discussions the participants showed a healthy scepticism about the common perceptions of technology as an abstract and male-dominated activity, especially the development and use of most modern technology. The participants also concluded that there is no clear understanding of how technology can make women's lives easier and more productive, and observed that many new technologies actually make their lives more difficult. Although cautious of the uncritical acceptance of new technology, the group recognised that technology was also a positive force for development and change, and that knowledge of technology is vital for women to assess potential positive and negative impacts of technology.

Questions that then arise include: How will women make informed choices about which technologies serve or harm them? How will women make decisions which take account of their limited resources and time? How can women best integrate new technologies into their daily lives and activities?

In the exploration of such questions, many stories were exchanged regarding the computerisation of the workplace. One woman noted the general concern with 'feeling like a slave of the machine, I was only taught to input material . . . and have to work at the machine's speed'. Women from Melanesia expressed concern at the long-term effects of reproductive technologies such as the depo-provera injection. Food irradiation, genetic engineering and 'brainwashing' through modern technologies of communications and the electronic media were among the many issues noted as being of concern to women in the questionnaires participants completed prior to the workshop.

It was interesting to observe the opinions of Pacific island women before and after the workshop. In the early discussions, where participants as a whole tried to identify technologies which had immediate effect on their lives, everything from cars to refrigerators was mentioned. When participants split into regional discussion groups, Pacific women specifically mentioned nuclear testing in the Pacific and family planning technology as matters of particular importance to them. This called to mind the statement by Margaret Mead in the 1940s — that the world was in the midst of a basic revolution symbolised by the 'bomb and the pill'.

Women and Technology in the South Pacific

In the South Pacific there is no question that women's decision-making regarding technology is hampered by chiefs and government bureaucrats, who tend to think and plan big and rather idealistically. Women generally think, work and plan, at least in villages and settlements, on a more personal scale, at a practical household, homestead and neighbourhood level. Their activities generally succeed because women have limited capital, and are ready to devote time, labour, commitment and enthusiasm to their development projects.

Island women retain close connections with various forms of traditional technologies and knowledge. These include the manufacture of goods for the home, food production and collection, traditional medicine and healing practices — for example, the use of naturally occurring materials such as a plant in the Solomons used to enhance mothers' milk because it is high in proteins, vitamins and minerals.

Much of the drudgery of women's daily toil can be lightened by technology, from improved small-scale transportation to food processing. Despite this, there is little conscious attempt in the Pacific region to distinguish between those traditional technologies which are of benefit and should be retained and improved, and those which could be replaced with new technology for the overall benefit of island communities. In practice new technology of questionable value often displaces traditional technology of proven benefit. The use of a pit toilet is clearly preferable on many counts to the traditional practice of excretion in the bush or near water courses. In other cases a traditional village technology which is low cost and utilises locally acquired materials and skills should be retained and upgraded where possible by modification, but without changing the underlying principles of operation — the recognition of traditional food preservation methods and their improved dissemination is an example of this.

Technology, Politics and Gender

Issues relating to technology and development inevitably involve considerations of politics and gender. Who decides what development will happen, and where? Access to safe drinking water and sanitation is a political issue. Does the introduction of a road, or foreshore reclamation, or the destruction of mangroves, mean women have to change their daily habits and lives?

Technological machinery seen in villages includes tractors, cultivators, sawmills and so on. The use of such machinery has a definite gender bias. In Papua New Guinea the present writer watched as the men of an extended family worked the cash crops with tractors. On the other side of the hill women were cultivating yams with digging sticks. Rural electrification schemes are often installed when and where business and trading centres demand it, rather than in response to the needs of rural households.

Also evident in the Pacific is the same gender bias as in developed countries. Project supervision and mechanical tasks are generally performed by men, with clerical and support work performed by women. This is the result of education systems and sex stereotyping inherited or imported from colonial or aid-donor nations.

As elsewhere, men tend to take over new technologies. This is often due to the 'mana' associated with a new technology (more than status in the Western sense, mana involves a 'spiritual' status). When the novelty value of the new technology wears off, men lose interest and women generally take over, at lower wages. Debates taking place at World YWCA Council meetings early this century illustrate this — there is a report of a discussion as to whether women should be permitted to use the new and dangerous typing machine, because of the adverse physical effects this might have on them.[2] Women are now the almost exclusive users of typewriters (and word processors), in some of the most boring occupations.

Technological Innovation

The introduction or innovation of technology does not necessarily lead to an even distribution of benefits — technological innovation tends to reflect existing social inequalities. The bias of planners and administrators, often Western trained, is to promote 'hardware' — as machines or mechanical processes for doing things. This often leads to the neglect of 'software', which is equally important. Access to technological hardware and software for women is of vital importance, but fraught with difficulty — systems for the acquisition, transmission and control of the technology present particular obstacles for women. Part of the problem here is the perception of men's activities outside the home as 'work', and women's identification with the domestic sphere as non-work. In the Pacific this perception is a cruel joke, especially in Melanesia, where women generally work physically harder, longer and unremittingly for the home, community, church or whatever.

The introduction of electricity, and therefore domestic technology such as stoves, refrigerators and the like does not mean that these technologies are readily affordable. Quite the contrary — islanders have difficulty buying and then running such appliances. But because of the 'mana' of new technology, there is a high aspiration for imported appliances. And because urbanisation and urban-rural connection is high in many Pacific island nations, the aspiration for Western technology is also high in rural areas. Some island nations also have close connections with metropolitan centres on the Pacific rim. In Samoa, for example, there is a constant interaction between town and village, and also between Samoa and inner suburban communities in New Zealand.

The introduction of electricity also neglects the energy reality of many islanders. The large bundles of firewood in Apia market, expensive in terms of local earning power, indicate that this form of energy is still cheaper than other energy sources such as electricity. This illustrates the inappropriateness of much new technology that is introduced in the region. Why not focus on the provision of affordable fuelwood for Apia? How do women manage a fuelwood energy source in crowded urban areas? The cash needed for purchasing fuel must reduce family expenditure on other essentials.

In a crowded housing estate in Raiwaqa, a suburb of Suva, the Fiji Centre of the Extension Services of the University of the South Pacific developed a communal kitchen with lines of wood-burning cement stoves. These enabled women to cook while socialising, and discouraged the use of dangerous kerosene stoves in the tiny flats. Various cooking stoves have been developed in the Pacific region, including drum ovens for baking. There is a powerful argument for more effort to be put into the application of improved cooking stoves for specific situations — particularly the saving of fuelwood in urban areas such as Apia.

Improved woodstoves save fuelwood compared to open fires, although the higher cost of fuelwood in urban areas means that woodstoves may not be as 'cheap' to run as kerosene, gas or electric appliances (which have a higher capital cost that may be offset if purchased with 'never-never' credit). Improved woodstoves are locally produced and use local rather than imported fuel, however. To promote their use, improved woodfuel stoves should be priced somewhere between the 'free' capital cost of open fires and the price of kerosene, gas or electric stoves, and social or community forestry plantation should be encouraged to provide fuelwood at more affordable and competitive prices. An ecological overload on biomass fuelwood resources is beginning to be seen in urban and coastal areas of many Pacific towns. Household fuel shortages are a symptom rather than a cause of such deterioration.

The Pacific is no different from other parts of the world regarding planning and development — where technology, economics and general user value judgments have all to be considered at once. In May 1991 the women's programme desk of the UNCED planning committee held a symposium — 'Women & Children First'.[3] Two comments made at the symposium remain in the mind of the present writer. An agricultural course was mentioned which teaches mechanised agriculture and fertiliser manufacture under the heading 'food', with no reference to cooking or food needs of the community. A plea was made to train more women in engineering, for reasons of equity, and because there was a shortfall of trained engineers coming out the system. Reflecting on these comments, it could be said that engineering, as a resource 'exploitative' discipline, may be in need of reform, and that the general view of technology — as a process of design, innovation and construction, could perhaps benefit from a different vision in terms of operation, maintenance and use which women practitioners could provide.

The present writer attended the Solomon Islands Western Province Environment week, held in Gizo in October 1990, and heard deep and almost tragic concern expressed at logging operations there. The solution of the men was to replace the multinational operators, with their destructive and eroding machinery, by the wokabaut somil, a small and mobile machine. This would reduce output and leave control of timber in the hands of communities. It was pointed out that government was really only interested in the foreign exchange earned by logging.

The women saw the crucial issue differently — they wanted equal representation on provincial councils in order to be a part of the decision-making process about any logging. Although they would not have articulated it thus, overtones of the bioregionalism debate, currently strong in the environment movement, could be heard — of the importance of being native to a place; of living within the limits provided by local resources and creating a way of life which can be passed on to future generations. Interestingly, a few strong women were leading a drive for women to register to vote, and to stand for the council elections in the Western Province, held in late 1991.

Credit — Lightening the Load

The ability of women to use technology for personal or village needs, income generation projects, or general upgrading and 'lightening the load' will often depend on the provision of credit, and this is a stumbling block everywhere in the region. In Fiji, women are acknowledged as better 'risks' by the cooperative movement — they have an infinitely better repayment and development record than men's groups. Nevertheless, lending agencies still hesitate to lend to individual women, or women's groups, especially when the project involves women in non-traditional activities. The appearance of newspaper articles with a tone of amazement whenever a woman graduates in motor mechanics or welding from the Fiji Institute of Technology is a case in point. This has happened twice recently — on marriage one tradeswoman decided to freelance in order to work the irregular hours required by her family commitments. Getting a bank loan for tools she needed proved impossible — a grant was managed through a women's funding agency, but should not have been necessary — she was happy to borrow.

Impact of New Technologies

The major concern of women at a seminar in the Sepik region of Papua New Guinea in 1981 was cash cropping — the meeting was held in an area of new rubber smallholder development. The whole concept of smallholder cash cropping was foreign, especially as women had no control over this new land, compared to the control over land they had in the traditional setting from which they had been moved. The effect of the new technologies some years later was catastrophic: breakdown of families, poisoning by herbicides, pollution of water courses, soil erosion and a huge dependence for family survival on the women's food crops, being grown in a totally alien situation by previously river-living people who had almost exclusively been food gatherers.[4]

Encouraged by deregulation and the setting-up of tax-free zones, women have been moving in numbers around Fiji to provide cheap labour for factories, mainly in the garment industry. The technology is sometimes hazardous, the work repetitive, the environment stressful and the pay generally low. Recent political-economic development and economic theory is to blame here, rather than the technology used, but the effects remain, as does the conceptualisation of women as willing to be lowly paid workers. Trade unions are becoming militant and challenging the government's so-called 'economic miracle', but with increasing urbanisation and increasing numbers of women now the heads of their household, the problem will intensify. A recent video on Indo-Fijian women interviewed workers in garment factories, the domestic situation and the sex industry.[5] Garment industry workers were happy with the availability of the jobs, compared with domestic and sex industry workers, in spite of low hourly rates of pay. The union movement does need to review the technology women are using, in industrial and domestic settings, with a particular view to possible improvement of technology in terms of mechanical and physiological use, and in terms of the impact of such technology on women and the wider community.

New Technology and Opportunities for Women

Although this is not the place to discuss sex stereotyping, either in traditional island cultures or in the modern sector, there are many questions relating to technology and gender issues. Apart from the question of equity, the fact that women may lose status when changing roles should be a problem for decision-makers. In general terms, social and technology development policies should expand rather than restrict women's options. Housework is an essential service, and should be shared by the whole household. Contraceptive technology, labour- and energy-saving technologies are important. Girls in schools need to be encouraged to stay in maths and science streams. Apprenticeships must be open to women so that fear of tools and machines is lost, and positions of responsibility and decision-making also become available to them. Barriers to learning programmes for special skills, and to loans and grants for business endeavour, must be removed. While the extended family is still in place and able to care for children and the elderly if women work, the need for child-minding facilities will increase as time goes by. This should not be regarded as a special bonus for women, but a recognition that families have children and that women's skills as adults are needed in the workforce. Where women are single parents (an increasing phenomenon), this is even more important.

Trade unions in the Pacific, as everywhere else, have traditionally been male dominated, but the establishment by the Fiji Trade Union Congress of their Women's Wing has been a boon for women garment factory workers. With the YWCA and the Fiji Women's Rights Movement, the Women's Wing is now pioneering the unionisation of domestic workers. Apart from the fact that the latter are often exploited and can suffer sexual harassment, they have also been excluded from the benefits of membership of the Fiji National Provident Fund. Other issues will also need addressing, because, in occupations such as word-processing and garment factories, there is an increase of male control over female labour.

Identifying, Evaluating and Promoting New Technology for Women

In 1983, Technology for the People, an organisation based in Geneva, organised a large trade fair in Manila. The World YWCA, in cooperation with Approtech Asia, arranged a parallel meeting — the 'Asia and Pacific Women's Small Technologies and Business Forum'.[6] The idea was to have the women participants move around the displays at the trade fair, and then meet in workshops to assess what was being shown in relation to its impact on women, positive or not.

It was obvious from the outset that exhibitors at the trade fair had not conceptualised their products with women in mind. There were 140 exhibits from 15 countries, and women visitors commonly remarked that there were very few stallholders who could answer the questions of an average rural woman.

As they went around the displays at the fair, participants used technology assessment sheets for identifying and evaluating what they saw. Some of the questions were:

1. Will this technology enhance an activity in which women are already engaged?
2. Will the technology involve women in learning new skills?
3. Are the raw materials readily available?
4. Are service and training packages available?
5. Are women permitted to purchase the process or the manufacturing manuals?
6. What will be needed in terms of finance?

Sessions focussing on problems and possible solutions followed, together with discussions on strategies for introducing and using new or improved tools, technologies and processes. Recommendations were addressed to women and women's organisations, technology developers, legislators and governments. Pacific participants agreed on a need to follow up on the components they felt were of most importance to their learning from the forum. These included:

1. The need for banking and credit associations for women.
2. The need for alternative fuels and the planting of fuelwood.
3. The need for women's organisations to learn to provide consultancy and advice on technical matters.
4. The need to upgrade the skills of women field workers so they can provide training in business.

In the final session, the participants were asked to list on wall charts the kinds of technologies they would feature if they were planning a Technology for the People trade fair. The list consisted essentially of guidelines regarding the use of technologies by women, and included:[7]

1. Technologies that are most suitable for women across the South Pacific should:
   — not need electricity,
   — make maximum use of local materials and traditional skills,
   — form the basis for income-generating home industry,
   — be of low cost,
   — be genuinely labour-saving.
2. Technology should be developed within the region, or adopted, adapted and improved where necessary, and effectively promoted.
3. It should be emphasised that technology consists of hardware and software.

4. Technology for use by women should be designed for easy and understandable use and maintenance.

5. Examples of technologies particularly needed by women include those used in the production of furniture, utensils, agricultural implements, pots, tiles and baskets and in health-care equipment. The promotion of inexpensive and small-scale food-processing is particularly important — for expelling oil, grinding grain, extracting juice and food sterilisation.

6. The dissemination of technological skills through effective and user-friendly instruction and learning is particularly important; such instruction should use a maximum of demonstration and actual use of technologies.

Similar views emerged from meetings held to mark the end of the Decade for Women in Nairobi in mid-1985 and attended by almost 20,000 women — a United Nations Conference, parallel forum for non-government organisations and a 'Tech and Tools Fair', organised by the International Women's Tribune Centre, the World YWCA and the Kenya Appropriate Technology Committee.[8] As in the 1983 Manila trade fair mentioned above, assessments were conducted of the technology on show. These assessments were then discussed in small groups, and a 'Tech and Tools' handbook was produced as the result of requests made by many women for an easy-to-read evaluation and descriptive tool. At the three-day workshop on Women & New Technologies at the forum, Pacific participants were vocal about new technologies, particularly reproductive and other technologies connected to birth control, prenatal testing and the birthing process.[9] Throughout the discussions the underlying theme was that the organisation of technology world-wide is dominated by rich countries, and that the poor have limited access and almost no input to the development of technology to suit their needs.

Women's Access to Technology

An overall question emerging from the above relates to how women gain access to, and have a role in choosing, technologies they themselves need. Part of the answer is to identify and promote the use of such technology in the public and private sectors. This can be done, as in the West, through more effective consumer research and information dissemination. Non-government organisations could have a central role in such activity.

Government ministries and departments focussing on women's affairs and national women's organisations in the Pacific could also associate themselves more closely with institutions working in the field of technological research and development. Closer connection could also be made with local industrial firms and workshops to influence their research and production decisions for the benefit of women at the company and wider community levels.

In the area of grass-roots technology transfer, extension workers in the field of women, technology and development need support and skills enhancement regarding training and information dissemination. In addition to extension training with projects involving technology, credit schemes and business management training must also be available. The transfer of successful technology between different locations and countries should also be promoted — if a pilot project is successful, it should be a priority for extension workers to encourage the transfer of technology as quickly as possible for its wider application.

Technology Information and Communication: Message and Media

Tony Marjoram

◆◆◆

Technology information includes a vast range of spoken, written and visual material. It may be technical or non-technical, formal or informal, relatively complex and user-hostile (unless you happen to be an expert) or generally understandable and user-friendly. Technology information communication is an important part of technology transfer, and a major source of ideas and instruction regarding improved or new technology. It is itself part of the software of technology.

The three main functions of technology information are to inform, instruct and advertise. Poor technology information may not be very informative or may provide little instruction, and advertisements regarding technology (as all advertisements) can be somewhat less than truthful.

The communication of technology information is vitally important in the promotion and propagation of improved or new technology. Without it, technology may stay in the workshop or laboratory, or in the book on the shelf — no matter how good the technology, it is useless unless it is effectively communicated and diffused. Although this chapter focusses on the communication of information about technology, it is important to remember that communication is a two-way process, and that the best form of technology, and information about technology, should first be decided by consultation and a two-way exchange of views between technologists and potential users.

Technology Information and Communication

Although the small size and isolation of Pacific islands make for many constraints, there is considerable potential for the development of information and communication of technology for development in the region. This includes simple leaflets and booklets in local languages, and more innovative activities such as the production of video programmes, community radio and theatre. The 'Liklik Buk', published in PNG, is a good example of a village development technology sourcebook (see the chapter in part four by David Williams). Community theatre is new to the South Pacific, but the Wan Smolbag Theatre Group in Vanuatu, starting in the late 1980s, has already produced plays relating to health, the environment, women and cyclone preparedness. Radio production could be more innovative in the use of local stories as a vehicle to discuss and promote development issues and the use of village technology (the popular BBC radio programme 'The Archers' began in the 1940s primarily to propagate agricultural information).

The four main considerations regarding technology information and communication are as follows:

1. Purpose of the information.
2. Content of the message.
3. Target audience.
4. Medium or media of communication.

These considerations are interconnected rather than sequential. Communication very much depends on the target audience, which also depends on the message to be communicated, and the reason for communication. These factors should be considered simultaneously.

Why Communicate?

The goal of communication is generally to encourage people to change their behaviour — to encourage them to do something new or in a different way. It is important to have a clear idea of the goal of communication, as it may then be realised that the goal is unachievable or impractical, or need refining.

Why Change?

The inclination or disinclination to technological change depends on the perception of the benefits and risks involved in the change, the magnitude of the change and a range of other factors. There is a calculated trade-off between the perceived risks and advantages involved in change — greater advantages may be gained with more radical change, although higher risks may increase the chance of problems or failure (the chapter by Keith Leonard in part three points out that subsistence agriculture is risk-minimising rather than profit maximising). On the other hand, people may be less willing to change if the advantages of change are less readily apparent. Generally, it is easier to encourage people to make small or incremental changes rather than radical changes in technology.

Decisions regarding the choice of technology reflect the background, interests, values, priorities of and pressures upon decision-makers, and their perceptions of needs and problems. A particularly important consideration in whether or not people will be inclined or disinclined to use new technology is their perception of whether the technology will enhance or lower their status — technology change is intimately connected with the sociology of technology, and whether or not technology empowers or disempowers potential users. (Imported Western 'status' foods are more highly regarded than local produce, despite higher cost and often lower nutritional value, and the fact that tinned fish may have been caught in the South Pacific.)

Pacific islanders are generally well inclined to technological change, and can sometimes be considered positively 'technophilic' — as indicated by the drastic changes and 'technological revolution' taking place over the last 40 years. Specific examples of the aspirations of islanders to acquire Western technology go back to the early days of European contact, and now include all the conveniences of modern Western technology. As elsewhere in the world, these technologies are bought on the grounds of new applications and opportunities offered by the technology, improved performance (compared to older technologies) and high status.

Expectations of performance of Western technology are generally high, despite readily apparent problems — durability is usually lower and running costs higher than expected, or elsewhere. Outboard motors have a short life, generally because of a neglect of maintenance, and piles of used batteries often surround larger radio-cassettes. A relatively new, broken-down truck was even ceremonially buried in the outer Cook Islands.[1] Attitudes towards Western technology are becoming more realistic, as awareness of the negative impacts of technology and recognition of the need for technology to be appropriate increase. Radio-cassettes, a boon to local music and culture, can be powered by solar-rechargeable batteries. Although outboard motors and cars need support services that are limited, especially in outer islands and rural areas, basic training programmes in motor maintenance help reduce costs of the technology.

Disinclination to technological change is mainly because of perceptions of limited benefits. This may be because there are no real benefits, or that potential benefits have been poorly communicated to potential users. Which may be due to the different perceptions of the problems or needs by technology decision-makers.

Cooking Stoves

An apparent disinclination to technology change is the response to 'improved' wood-burning cooking stoves promoted by various agencies around the island Pacific (a case study of information communication for an improved cooking stove is presented at the end of this chapter). Improved wood-burning cooking stoves have been promoted mainly on grounds of increased fuel efficiency (use of less wood on a household level, and less forest resources on a national level) and reduction in local smoke pollution (fire smoke leads to increased eye and lung disease among cooks). Overall policy regarding stoves is generally formulated by urban-based male energy sector decision-makers, with little direct experience of stove use, who may not regard stoves as problematic or an energy priority (most islanders live in rural areas, and most stove users are women). In 1990, a group of senior Pacific island energy decision-makers advised a regional energy agency to discontinue activities with improved cooking stoves, despite the desire of the agency, and many stove users, to continue.

Most women who use wood for cooking recognise the benefits of improved stoves, particularly the reduction in smoke and the appearance and hence status of such stoves (fuel saving may be marginal — stoves are generally more efficient in the laboratory than in practice). However, many women also aspire to kerosene, or, better, bottle gas or electric stoves, rather than improved wood-burning stoves. The aspiration is for new, higher status stove technology, despite a general recognition of the high operating and capital cost of these stoves (gas and electric stoves are unaffordable for all but wealthier islanders).

It may be that wood-burning stoves, no matter how improved, do not correspond to aspirations of 'West is best'. Due to running cost and status, people who have acquired a sought-after but expensive gas or electric stove often reserve the stove, and even a separate set of pots, for special occasions. It may not be surprising that the promotion of improved wood-burning cooking stoves has encountered some difficulties.

Part of the problem is that improved wood-burning stoves may not be as improved as their promoters contend. New technology also needs to be considered in the context of use. With cooking stoves, this means that stoves should be considered as part of the kitchen and overall kitchen improvements, not alone. The stove is the central piece of kitchen technology, and the installation of a new stove is liable to alter kitchen function and use. For example, the chimney of improved cooking stoves enables the kitchen to be moved closer to or even integrated with the house (most island kitchens are built separate from the house, to avoid smoke contamination of the house).

Overall, the seeming disinclination to technology change in the adoption of improved wood-burning cooking stoves may be more apparent than real. Technology change is a more complicated and slower process than most innovators think. This underlines the need for more attention and care devoted to getting the technology right, and the innovation and diffusion of new technology.

What Message?

Information about technology should be produced in a user-friendly way where possible — technical information can generally be written in a user-friendly manner, even though technical people easily lapse into jargon. Some information, however, is necessarily technical or user-specific, and hence will be limited to a particular audience. If this information is directed at a general audience, it may appear 'user-hostile'. This should be borne in mind when writing or preparing information — if the message has to contain technical information, then it should be focussed at a particular audience. If wider communication is also required, multi-audience material or even two documents can be produced — one for technical information and instruction, complemented by another with reduced technical content for user-friendly information or advertising to a general audience.

It is important to be aware that it is not usually necessary to become overly technical to accurately communicate a technical message. Giving unnecessary scientific information to people can cause confusion, reduced confidence and motivation to act. For example, people building ferro-cement water tanks do not need to know about the theory of thin-wall ferro-cement-reinforced shell structures, budding mechanics do not need to know about applied thermodynamics, and people making ventilated pit latrines do not need to know much about the germ theory of disease, although a little knowledge may be useful. In such situations, the use of explanatory metaphor to convey the meaning is helpful, especially when used with visual illustration. There is considerable scope here for innovation in the use of leaflets and video.

Attention should also be paid to the language of communication. Because English is the second or third language of most Pacific islanders, information should be presented in the local language where possible. If this is not possible, then information should be presented in such a way as to be readily understandable or translatable. Care is also required regarding the cross-cultural transfer of metaphors or colloquialisms. For example, following the comment, 'there is more than one way to skin a cat', several workshop participants informed the author that they understood there was only one 'best practice' technique.

Who? — the Target Audience

Considerations regarding the content of the information to be communicated are closely connected with the target audience. It is important to identify the target audience fairly precisely, so that information about technology can be produced and presented in the most 'user-friendly' fashion. This will maximise the chance that people will take an interest in and use the technology — the goal of the information communication. It should also be noted that technology information communication is frequently indirect, through intermediaries such as training officers (the training of trainers is important).

The most important questions regarding the target audience relate to the technical proficiency, knowledge and attitude to the technology concerned. These considerations are important in view of the technical content and general description of the technology. Inclination or disinclination to change may be due to attitudes toward technology based on inaccurate preconceptions of the technology. It is important to correct inaccurate impressions of technology through the use of accurate user-friendly information.

For example, a slight misconception regarding the potential use of charcoal stoves took place in a discussion between a stove expert and an economic planner (with an interest in energy matters). The economist correctly observed that the production of charcoal itself lost energy, and therefore that it is better to burn wood in efficient stoves, but would not accept the point that it may be more efficient to use charcoal if transportation is involved (charcoal is less than half the weight of wood for the same energy output). The stove expert was unable to present user-friendly information to dispel this impression, and the debate, like the subject, began to generate more heat than light. A project partly involved with technology and development activity with Australian Aboriginal communities found that information directed at decision-makers and politicians was most effective if produced in multi-colour brochures, with a high image-to-text ratio, using few words, in large print, noting project successes and the contribution of decision-makers and politicians.

When producing technology information (as well as technology), it is very helpful to meet and talk to typical members of the target audience. This helps check real needs and usefulness of the technology concerned, and helps answer the question of what message will be the most effective way of communicating information about the technology. It may also be useful to model technology communication in a role-play (where technologists and information communicators take roles from the target audience and play out the process of introducing the technology and exploring the best ways of communicating information to promote the technology). Audience participation also helps determine the most meaningful form of communication in terms of language and modes of explanation — especially the 'translation' of technical information to non-technical people.

How? — Media and Style

The main considerations regarding the best way to communicate information relate to the presentation and style of the material. Presentation includes the form or media in which material is presented, and style is the fashion in which the material is presented in the chosen media.

Considerations regarding the presentation of information are as important as considerations of content and target audience. Interesting information is more easily communicated, understood and accepted than boring information. Different types of information may be presented in different types of media — including spoken (eg live talk, extension worker, radio), written (newspaper, leaflet, computer disc), visual-still (eg slides, posters), spoken/visual-still (eg slide/tape, blackboard, live slide), or spoken/visual-moving (eg film, video, live TV). Because of the importance of training, mass media should be produced in a form and style most useful as source for trainers to use in direct communication.

There is a close relationship between the information to be presented, the target audience and how the information is presented — the type of media and style chosen for presentation. Some material is inherently more visual than others, some may be particularly suited to video — although video is mainly known in the region as a medium of entertainment rather than of communication or education, there is considerable potential for the use of video for community development. Technical information is often regarded as more suited to written or visual-still media, which may explain the frequently boring nature of such material, and is another reason for using more modern media such as video for technical information communication.[2]

It is important to organise information to make it as straightforward as possible to the target audience, especially non-technical people. Technologists, like other professionals (such as medical doctors), are often not good at this. Making information user-friendly relates both to the media, form and style of presentation.

Language

Language communication is in two forms — oral and written. The Pacific islands have strong oral traditions (such as memorising genealogical records several generations back) and should be considered significantly oral rather than written cultures, especially in rural areas and outer islands. The oral tradition persists in the importance of face-to-face communication

— islanders are generally keen to ask questions directly, whereas few would write for information. This is another pointer to the potential for recorded video material, and for the use of satellite facilities (at USP Centres around the region) for live (voice) technology information sharing and discussion.[3]

Written communication is valuable for the transfer of technological information. An increasing amount of written information, usually in English, is appearing in the South Pacific, through the increased information flow into and within the region and increasing activity of regional institutions and agencies. This is obviously good, provided the information is received by those in need of it. There are constraints with written information, however, as the literacy rate is less than 50% in certain parts of the Pacific (lower in English). In printed information, the local language should be used for preference. When English is used, it should be kept relatively basic and unambiguous, and translated into the local language where possible. Technical language or jargon should be restricted to the absolute minimum necessary. All information should maximise visual content.

There are also constraints on the use of modern media, such as video — chiefly in costs and durability. A related constraint is the shortage of locally relevant recorded information. There is much potential for the development of material dealing with appropriate technology for national and regional radio programmes and the increasingly popular and available video TV.

Case Study — 'Making a Smokeless Wood-Burning Stove'

Background — the Technology

Problems relating to the isolation of island states are common to all extension activities, but particularly for technology, primarily because it is difficult and expensive to move tools and equipment. This prompted the decision in 1983 to begin a leaflet series on the 'Transfer of Appropriate Technology' at the Institute of Rural Development of the University of the South Pacific (IRD/USP), intended for distribution around the (then) 11 member states of USP. The leaflet, 'Making a Smokeless Wood-Burning Stove', was produced in 1984.[4]

Following the international literature and experience, two basic stove designs were developed at IRD/USP — a two-pot 'smokeless' wood-burning stove and single-pot wood or charcoal burning 'bucket' stove. Two stoves were chosen to match expressed cooking needs, which required two pots for general cooking, and one pot for water boiling. The two-pot stove was designed to burn wood (or similar material) and was termed 'smokeless', following general usage of the term, in using a chimney to reduce local smoke emission (no wood-burning stoves are perfectly smokeless).

Both stoves were designed and developed to respond to stove needs in the Pacific the author felt were not fulfilled by other 'improved' stoves that had been developed but not widely propagated in the region. The main problems with other stoves were that they were often expensive, complicated to make and difficult to operate. The USP two-pot smokeless stove is of modular design, constructed of sections cast in moulds to maintain correct shape and quality, and was designed to be affordable, relatively straightforward to make by women at village level and easy to operate.

Why Communicate?
The stove leaflet arose out of an interest in wood-burning stoves at IRD/USP, in response to a need recognised and expressed by energy agencies, women's groups and NGOs. The goal of the leaflet was to propagate information about the wood-burning stove: to inform, instruct and advertise. It was anticipated that the information and advertising roles may predominate, as a degree of technical proficiency would be required to translate the leaflets into reality.

What Message?
Under the subheading 'Why Better Stoves?', a cartoon stick-character was used to make the points that the stove uses less fuel (which means less wood-gathering work for women), burns a variety of fuels, reduces smoke in the cooking place, is clean cooking, a substitute for gas or electricity, of relatively low cost, easy to make and repair, and can be carried in pieces. Other subheadings addressed the topics 'What is a Good Stove?', 'What You Need — Tools and Materials', 'What You Do — Building and Assembling the Stove', and 'Using the Stove'.

Target Audience
The main direct audience for the leaflets were women's groups, relevant NGO's, energy agencies, energy policy-makers and relevant regional organisations. The indirect audience were of course women cooks of the South Pacific. Drafts of the leaflet were evaluated by sample members of the above audience.

Media and Style
The intention was to produce information that would reach the widest possible audience. It was decided that this would be best accomplished in the form of a folded panel leaflet, rather than a booklet or other material. The leaflet format was chosen because leaflets are fairly user-friendly,

relatively inexpensive to make and easy to distribute. The leaflet used a 50% balance of text and illustration to promote the appearance, accessibility and understandability. The leaflet was produced using an electronic typewriter, with pen and ink illustrations consisting of simple sketches, 3-D views and the stick-character cartoon, and was printed in black ink on light white card. Light card was chosen mainly for durability, but also because of a salutory story of an extension leaflet, produced on lighter paper, that was considered highly successful until it was discovered that leaflets were being used for rolling cigarettes and other unintended purposes (which is acceptable, provided the leaflet was read before use).

The Stove Leaflet

As with all information designed to communicate and encourage change, information can be judged in itself, although the acid test is the amount of intended change it has actually brought about. The wood-stove leaflets were well received throughout the island Pacific, and could be considered fairly successful in advertising, providing information and promotion — the stove became more widely known in the region, leading to enquiries for more information, stove demonstrations, a stoves workshop in the Solomon Islands, and inclusion in regional and national women's technology and development workshops.

The instructional role of the leaflet, as a working drawing from which stoves are made, is difficult to assess, because of the unknown number of stoves that have been built. A constraint with the leaflet was the prior need to make moulds to maintain the quality of construction, and consequent need for a reasonable amount of technical knowledge and motivation to produce stoves from the leaflet (although moulds, once made, can make many stoves, and can be kept for community use). Sets of moulds were distributed to USP member countries, with over 20 sets each going to the Solomon Islands and Cook Islands. Although further research would be required to determine how many moulds and stoves were made, it can be reported that a picture of the stove even found its way onto a postage stamp in Fiji.

It is now considered that the information was too densely packed on the leaflet. The content of subsequent leaflets was given more space. Because of the extra space required and increased information content of subsequent leaflets, it was also decided to change the format from leaflet to booklet. The use of a word processor facilitated the production of later booklets.

It is considered that the best use of the leaflet is to promote improved stoves, preferably as part of an integrated program to improve kitchens. The leaflet should be followed by media promotion, stove demonstrations and workshops at national and local level, teaching stove construction in the community, or manufacture in small enterprise workshops, and providing technical and financial support as necessary. Technology diffusion is a complicated and time-consuming process, requiring considerable effort that for these main reasons is generally neglected or underemphasised in technology and development activities.

COMMUNICATION TECHNOLOGY: IN WHOSE INTERESTS?

HELEN MOLNAR

When the models for development are all from one source, when external cultural stimulation is from a single cultural tradition, and when the technology and philosophy of communicating a national and cultural consciousness are external, then the possibility of fostering a heritage based upon indigenous models is significantly diminished.[1]

Background
The Pacific has been ignored for many years, but a number of countries (America, England, Japan, Germany, New Zealand and Australia) are now taking an increasing interest in the region's communications because of the Pacific's economic and strategic importance. There has also been very little academic interest in Pacific communications, and it is only since the mid-1980s, with the establishment of UNESCO-sponsored training schemes, that more detailed information about Pacific media activities has begun to emerge.

Pacific countries are now 'looking more closely at their broadcasting services in an effort to gear communication more directly and effectively to the goals of the newly independent states'.[2] The most pressing communication problem in the Pacific is inter-island and intra-island communication. This is complicated by the number of islands, the distances between islands, the small size of the total population and its spread over the island states and the cultural diversity in the Pacific.

Communication is an integral part of any culture, and communications technology is an extension of that culture. Control, or access to communication technology, gives people access to the media which in turn can shape and inform public opinion. There is a view that communications technology is culturally neutral (and this is certainly the way it is marketed). But along with any communications technology comes a host of existing practices, from maintenance requirements to training and programme techniques, which determine how the technology will be used.

In the West, the introduction of radio and television technology preceeded content, and this is the situation in the Pacific. When Pacific countries acquire communications technology there is a demand to use it. But many Pacific countries do not have established media infrastructures and practices. Just over half the Pacific radio services have been established since 1961, only seven of the 22 Pacific countries or territories had television prior to 1980, and while there are a number of small newspapers, there are only six daily newspapers in the entire region.

Lack of local expertise, combined with the cost of local production in television, has meant that Pacific stations are importing Western programmes to make use of the technology. Where TV does exist in the Pacific it is usually sold as an entire package, for example technology and programming, whether this be American, French, Australian or from New Zealand. The Pacific media are developing their own programme forms in radio, but overall, they are disadvantaged because producers are unaware of the diversity of forms available. To date, Pacific countries have only been exposed to limited media, eg. Radio Australia, BBC, Voice of America (VOA), with the result that some media practitioners see these as the only models for production.

The availability of communications technology alone does not guarantee local programming. If communications technology is to be effective, it needs to be part of an adequate infrastructure, rather than just being 'dropped in from the sky'. Local production requires staff resources, training in production techniques, producers who have an awareness of the potential and diversity of media forms, and funding for hardware and software. Expertise in administrative and technical areas is also essential. For instance, there is a chronic shortage of trained broadcast technicians (radio and video) to install, maintain and repair broadcast equipment, and this can result in lengthy delays in these areas.

The argument for local content is a powerful one. Given the potential influence of the media and its extensive reach, it is vital that different cultures be able to listen to and view images of themselves — not just 'alien images'. Ian Johnstone (Radio New Zealand International) made this clear when he said, 'Perhaps the most useful contribution TV can make to a community is the opportunity it offers for increased self-awareness. By holding up a mirror to a society, more effectively than any other medium,

TV vastly increases the flow of information, ideas, entertainment, opinion, and can encourage involvement by all levels of society in the development of a sense of identity. But this is only possible if local people have control of the medium and access to it'[3].

But in the Pacific, where radio, and to a lesser extent print, has been government initiated and funded, and where television is operated by foreign interests, this sense of communication technology as an extension of culture is not widely expressed.

Choice of Communications Technology

One of the major problems facing the Pacific media is the choice of technology. Media development in the Pacific has been very ad hoc. Communication and resource difficulties have made regional planning difficult, and the Pacific's isolation from the rest of the world has meant that information about a range of communications technologies is not available to Pacific countries. This concerns some Pacific broadcasters, because it makes them vulnerable to overseas corporations selling their equipment, and to large overseas media groups who work directly with governments to set up media services.[4] Consequently, the choice to adopt a form of communications technology can be based more on 'political' interests than considerations of national media needs.[5]

Pacific countries to date have tended to favour the 'big' media (national radio, television) rather than the 'small' media (community radio, video, newsletters). But the 'small' media lend themselves more readily to indigenous use, and have the advantage of being able to provide local programme alternatives to the 'big' national media.

Satellite technology is often referred to as having potential in regions like the Pacific because it can cover large distances. However, experiences with satellite technology in other non-Western countries indicate that this technology has done little to increase local, indigenous communication.[6] It has instead been used to extend the interests of Western commercial media, and this is clearly the case in the Pacific.[7] This one-way flow of Western programmes (radio and television) does not encourage active indigenous involvement because it reduces the audience to an object of that communication. It is also not providing a greater diversity of information and entertainment to the Pacific, but is instead delivering a Western media product that is standardised for consumption by Western audiences.

State of the art equipment is not necessary for small Pacific stations nor is it necessary for good production. However, at present, in too many instances the standard of equipment and studios available is directly impacting on the type of programmes that can be produced. Broadcasters are unable to use the equipment easily and this affects the on-air sound of the station and their enthusiasm for their work. Some Pacific broadcasters are literally defeated in their efforts to go out and record material because of the lack of tape recorders and software, or because their equipment is so antiquated that it is impossible to produce a reasonable level of programming. In Tuvalu, in 1989, there was only one operational portable tape recorder which was being used for news, developmental programmes, and to record the choir for Sunday. When station equipment is so limited, the staff usually produce basic forms without recorded inputs. This result is a very conservative form of programming, and is not stimulating to listen to. Moreover, because of the complexity of the funding situation, purchasing another piece of equipment is not a straightforward matter. The bid for this equipment has to be put to the relevant government department and may or may not progress further.

The acquisition of communications technology in the Pacific is further complicated by the fact that a number of countries are dependent on aid organisations or overseas companies for equipment because of the expense. But funding from aid organisations is often tied to a particular choice of technology. Moreover overseas consultants and agencies usually recommend studio designs and equipment that they are familiar with, but these may not be the most suitable choices. There are numerous examples of inappropriate equipment, one of which involves a radio station which received a new studio, transmitter and equipment; 'Everything was installed by the donors, ready for use, complete with service manuals, at first in a foreign language only, later in English as well. But none of the staff had an idea of what possibilities the new equipment offered, or even of how to operate it properly. No local technician had been instructed about its maintenance. And the whole layout of the studio, following traditional Western models, was quite unfit for the needs and established work patterns of this particular small station'.[8]

If aid is to be of real value, the choice of equipment needs to be made in consultation with the station staff, and the projects must be properly resourced and include funds for installation, training of operators and the software necessary for operation. There are many examples of equipment being imposed on stations in the Pacific, without any thought being given to the necessary resources to support its operation. One of the more recent involves a Japanese funded professional multi-channel mixing desk and equipment worth SI$500,000 donated to a Pacific station in 1990. The equipment was not used for two years because no one at the station knew how to operate the mixer. But even when a producer had been trained, there was still no recording as the necessary microphone outputs in the studio had not been installed and the station concerned could not afford these. Some years ago, the station had received an outside broadcast van from an aid donor, but stopped using it because they could not resource it. The amount of equipment in the van was more than the station needed. Aid agencies justify their funding of studios and equipment in this fashion by arguing that Pacific stations will 'grow into' these facilities, and also appear to assume that the bigger and more sophisticated the technology the better. Small Pacific stations, however, while in need of uprgraded studios and equipment, cannot resource large studio complexes and state of the art equipment, nor do they need these for good production.

In other instances, consultants do not appear to have spoken to station staff about the staff's equipment preferences. For example, in 1988, 2AP in Western Samoa received funding for a new production studio from an overseas foundation. The equipment was very sophisticated, and could only be operated by a technician, thus limiting the producers' use of the studio, and increasing the labour necessary to operate the mixing desk. Meanwhile the station presenters worked from two on-air studios using equipment that was so antiquated and cumbersome that reasonable on-air presentation was extremely difficult. In 1989, Radio Tuvalu was waiting for the completion of a second on-air studio with equipment funded by a UNDP/UNESCO grant. This had taken five years from when it was first proposed, to become a reality. The delay was partly due to the fact that the equipment was coming from Europe, but it also reflected the bureaucratic nature of aid funding. However, the broadcast console that was installed (on the advice of a consultant), is not what station presenters wanted. It is difficult to operate, and makes presentation procedures harder. A broadcast console is a relatively inexpensive piece of technology, and there are a number of easy-to-use models readily available. One could have been imported quickly from Australia, and this would have had the advantage of providing a reasonably close supply of spare parts, which is a problem for Pacific countries.

The other problem with aid is that application processing and the eventual receipt of the aid can take years. Radio Tuvalu, as noted above, waited five years for the equipment from the UNESCO/UNDP grant. Moreover, the equipment was not delivered all at once, but came separately over the course of the five years. The Pacific is in a double bind on such matters. It is expensive to deliver equipment to small Pacific countries, and manufacturers often feel that it is not worth their while, particularly when it is a one-off order with no follow-up. Aid agencies deal with a range of different suppliers, and until there is some standardisation of equipment across the Pacific, the potential for the Pacific stations to lobby manufacturers for a better deal is minimal. If Pacific radio stations did attain some level of standardisation, they could band together to demand better service from the major equipment suppliers.

At present, the lack of trained Pacific island technicians/engineers means that Pacific radio stations are reliant on technical information from foreign experts. This factor combined with the Pacific's isolation from major markets has meant that Pacific island stations often lack the information necessary to make informed choices about equipment and studio design. This situation will not change until more Pacific technicians are trained and the information flow improved. PACBROAD has addressed this issue by seeking funds to standardise equipment and it also provides independent advice on radio equipment. PACVIDEO worked in a similar way with television stations and video centres. However, despite this, Western consultants dealing directly with station managements and governments can still impose their designs on the stations. This is because consultation with the broadcasters is not a major feature of Pacific radio.

Equipment is not the only area affected by lack of funds. Software barely exists in the Pacific, with the result that there are few blank tapes, and minimal editing supplies. Producers, however, cannot make programmes without the basic materials of production (tapes, cassettes and editing equipment). Reel-to-reel tapes are expensive, especially for the smaller stations, so tapes supplied free with overseas transcription programs from the BBC, VOA, RA, and Deutsche Welle are used for recording local material. These tapes can be re-recorded over many times and still be in use when they should have been discarded.

One of the most serious aspects of this problem is that Pacific stations are using tapes that should be kept for archival purposes. The NBC, for example, has been using its older tapes to record current programmes. Yet these tapes are the most extensive record of significant cultural, historical and political issues in PNG since 1973. This in turn defeats one of the important features of indigenous radio, its ability to record indigenous culture and history and preserve it for future generations. But radio archives in the Pacific are almost nonexistent.

If communications technology is to be effective, the choice of technology needs to be tied to present and future production requirements. This requires an overall level of planning and coordination that is difficult for smaller Pacific media because they are putting all their resources into daily production. They are also disadvantaged because they often do not have access to the technical expertise needed to make these decisions. The regional training projects in radio, print and video are beginning to have an effect in this area, as they have the resources to coordinate technical planning across the region for the first time.

Pacific Media Outline

The major source of media information in the Pacific, even in the larger countries of Fiji and Papua New Guinea, is radio. Radio was often introduced into the Pacific to service the needs of Europeans working there. The first radio service was set up in PNG in 1933, followed by Fiji in 1938. Other Pacific countries had to wait until the sixties for radio — Niue 1967 and Nauru 1968. Over the years, the expatriates have been phased out, and all the stations are now run by local people.

National radio services operate in Fiji, Kiribati, the Cook Islands, Niue, Vanuatu, Western Samoa, Tuvalu, the Solomons, Tonga, Nauru, and PNG. These services are mostly government funded with degrees of commercial sponsorship. There are three privately-owned commercial stations in the Pacific — in Fiji, the Cook Islands and Western Samoa, and there is the independent Kanak station in New Caledonia. The existing economies in some Pacific countries would be unlikely to sustain commercial, privately-owned media. Commercial stations are dependent on advertising revenue, and need to operate in reasonably large markets where there are competing businesses. But, in a number of the smaller Pacific countries, this would be very difficult.

Radio's popularity is enhanced by programmes in indigenous languages, and by the fact that it is very much an extension of the 'coconut wireless', the network of interpersonal communication that exists in the islands. One of the key advantages of radio is that it is a personal, informal medium, well suited to oral cultures. Its technology is user-friendly, and encourages one-person operation which is ideal for the smaller Pacific stations.

Radio has established itself as the most effective medium in the Pacific because it can cover the distances involved cheaply and effectively, and because radio sets are affordable. They can also be run on batteries, avoiding the need for electricity.

People describe radio 'as a way of life' and a lifeline in the Pacific.[9] A number of the outlying islands and rural provinces in the larger islands do not have telephone systems, and rely heavily on radio for contact with the outside world. This is especially important as the delivery of mail and newspapers is very unreliable outside urban centres, and radio has the advantage of offering the most immediate form of communication.

The lack of a telephone system in parts of the Pacific has meant that radio is used like a telephone. Many Pacific stations have message programmes where relatives and friends can communicate with people in other parts of their countries. Radio is also a vital link for messages from government departments.

The ability to produce local radio material varies greatly between stations, but overall, Pacific radio lacks programming diversity. Moreover, a major criticism of some Pacific radio stations is that they suffer from what is described as 'jukebox syndrome' — mainly playing music (usually from overseas) with little local input. The need to 'fill' broadcast time has resulted in some stations using overseas transcription programmes which have little relevance to their audiences (eg. BBC, Radio Australia, Deutsche Welle, VOA). Similarly, Pacific stations rely heavily on overseas news services like Radio Australia for their overseas news.

In countries where there are pressing development problems and minimal information outlets, the media can be used to disseminate information widely. But owing to a lack of resources and a lack of understanding of media potential in this area, opportunities to incorporate the media into Pacific development campaigns are often overlooked. Well produced developmental programmes could have an important place on Pacific stations. Existing programmes focus on literacy, health, nutrition, agriculture, fishing, mining, women's issues, and managing small businesses. There are also educational programmes made for primary and secondary schools. However, many are not imaginatively produced, and tend to consist of talks only, or long interviews which are unlikely to promote audience interest, let alone change. They are also not very numerous. According to Pamela Thomas, one of the reasons for this is that radio programmes and newspaper articles 'are still produced by health personnel who have no media training and are unaware of the needs of individual media'. Thomas adds that there is little consultation between health professionals and the media, and the media messages are often not pre-tested and evaluated.[10]

The success of developmental programmes also requires a detailed understanding of audience listening habits so that programmes can be properly targeted. But there is very little audience research conducted in the Pacific because this requires training and resources which many Pacific stations do not have. As a result, much Pacific radio programming is based on assumptions about when audiences are listening, and there is very little data on how and why they listen. This presents another problem for Pacific broadcasters as a number of stations are under pressure to reduce government funding by attracting more advertising. But if stations cannot give advertisers a breakdown of their listeners, this will difficult to achieve.

Radio in the Pacific is also constrained by staffing factors which also effect newspaper and television recruitment. Broadcasting is disadvantaged by the fact that it is often viewed as a second-class profession. This results from a combination of factors, the key one being that broadcasting is not being used to its full potential, and therefore it does not have the impact or the image that it could. Another factor is that there is not a readily available pool of media practitioners, particularly in countries with a brief media history. Consequently, radio broadcasters in some Pacific countries also produce the local newspaper, and in other countries they produce programmes for the television station. Recruitment problems are further exacerbated by high staff turnovers. Broadcasting is poorly paid and talented broadcasters often leave for better paying government jobs.

It is surprising, given radio's importance as a source of local information, that Pacific governments do not appear to have given media training a higher priority. Some Pacific governments are very suspicious of the media, and attempt to restrain its influence. This further disadvantages Pacific media development because funding agencies react to government priorities.

PACNEWS

The Pacific Broadcasting and Development project (PACBROAD) funded by the German Foundation, Friedrich Ebert Stiftung (FES), is the major regional radio training project in the Pacific. PACBROAD set up PACNEWS in 1987, the first regional news service to operate in the Pacific. One of its aims is to balance the 'coups and earthquakes' coverage of regional events by international news organisations and agencies, by covering not only so-called 'hard' news, but positive, development news as well. Prior to PACNEWS, countries had to rely on foreign news services for information about other Pacific countries; they received news about the Pacific from a Western viewpoint.

PACNEWS is an excellent example of what can be done with minimal technology. Other regions in the world have used satellite technology for the gathering and transmission of regional news, but this option would be too expensive for Pacific stations, and would have required a much longer set-up time. PACNEWS operates very simply. Each of the 13 contributing stations sends news items to the PACNEWS centre in Honiara via fax, with some of the stronger newsrooms sending around six stories daily. (PACNEWS moved to Honiara in December 1990, and PACBROAD to Vanuatu, after being expelled from Suva by the Fijian Government.) PACBROAD, with the assistance of the German Foundation for Technical Cooperation (GTZ), has equipped all member stations with fax machines, which has reduced costs and increased the reliability of the transmissions. Initially the bulletins were sent via telex but this proved expensive and unreliable.

In 1992–1993, PACBROAD aimed to further upgrade PACNEWS by setting up an electronic mail system. PACBROAD estimated that this would reduce transmission costs by another 15–20%. The ease of operating this system will also increase the overseas subscribers, because a number have indicated that they will subscribe if they can edit copy directly on a computer screen. PACNEWS receives half its funding from PACBROAD, and the other half is made up of subscriptions from media organisations in the Pacific rim, and commercial media services in the Pacific.

The impact of PACNEWS has been significant. It gives the island states the opportunity to hear about their neighbours for the first time, and has introduced a very important Pacific perspective into the news. In addition to this, PACNEWS has stimulated some Pacific stations to develop their own local news services. The use of PACNEWS by overseas services like Radio Australia is also helping to counter the one-way flow of news from the West to the Pacific. PACNEWS would eventually like to produce Pacific news on video, further increasing its influence in the Pacific and the Pacific rim.

Pacific Newspapers
In the Pacific, with the exception of government and church publications, newspapers are privately owned and therefore dependent on advertising. In 1989 private newspapers represented more than two-thirds of the newspaper copies circulating in the Pacific, with 93% of all circulation being produced by non-indigenous publishers.[11] At the same time, newspaper ownership is becoming increasingly concentrated, with two global corporations, Rupert Murdoch's News Limited and the French Hersant group dominating. Their interest in the Pacific emphasises the capital intensive nature of newspaper production, and makes it even less likely that smaller private indigenous newspapers can find the necessary capital as these corporations will have cornered the advertising markets.

Newspapers in the Pacific appear in English, in a combination of English and indigenous languages, and in indigenous languages only. 'In all cases, newspapers serve a very basic educational function as one of the few regular reading materials in the Islands'.[12] For some people newspapers are the only source of printed material apart from the Bible. Consequently they can have quite a long lifespan, and unlike radio can be constantly referred to and passed from household to household.

Print journalism, like radio broadcasting, suffers from the lack of a professional base. Part of the problem is that many Pacific newspapers are of recent origin, and the well established papers like the *Fiji Times* and *Post-Courier* (PNG) have overseas owners, and have drawn heavily on expatriate journalism expertise. Production standards vary greatly between islands and can be quite haphazard. There are only six daily newspapers published in the region (Cook Islands, Western Samoa, American Samoa, PNG, and two in Fiji). But the circulation for weekly papers is higher than dailies, which reflects the market realities in the Pacific and the population spread. Daily newspapers would be completely out of date by the time they reached some areas, whereas weekly papers have more chance of being timely.

In 1989 a UNESCO training project — PACJOURN, was set up, based in PNG. A UNESCO report in 1986 had concluded that print journalism needed a programme like PACBROAD, and that the print media was starting well behind radio.[13] The existing print technology in a number of countries also needed to be updated, and one of PACJOURN's roles has been to provide better equipment.

Print technology historically has not been as user-friendly as radio or video, as the production of daily newspapers is labour intensive. However, with advances in computer technology, there is the potential for one person operation. PACJOURN has recognised this, and supplied hardware, software and training to a number of Pacific countries at no cost to them. Most daily and weekly newspapers now use desktop publishing techniques. This has had a major impact on newspaper production since 1990, as the ease of producing newspapers in this way has increased the number of papers, and has also considerably improved the appearance of the papers. In Western Samoa, the *Samoa Times* was able to change from a weekly paper to a daily (five days) because desktop publishing combined with a laser printer meant that the newspaper could be produced easily, and the lengthy typesetting process was no longer necessary.

Training is still required in this area so that Pacific journalists can use the computer technology to its fullest potential. However, funding for PACJOURN finished in August 1991, and in 1992–1993, UNESCO funded a very much smaller print training project, PACPRESS, for one year only.

Television, Community Video and PACVIDEO

Television is the most expensive medium to operate and it has a low priority in many Pacific countries compared to radio and print. But at the same time, the use of video recorders in the Pacific is increasing, despite the costs. Video hire shops are springing up throughout the Pacific, hiring out overseas television programmes, sporting events and films. In the American Pacific Territories, US television is beamed in via satellite. In the French Pacific, New Caledonia and French Polynesia, the situation is similar, with television and radio services coming straight from Paris to the Pacific. Australia has moved in a similar direction with Alan Bond's EM-TV service to PNG. EM-TV is dominated by imported programme material, and little has been done to develop local production inputs.[14] Of the 22 member countries of the South Pacific Commission (SPC), 17 are able to receive some form of television, mostly via satellite or cassettes delivered by overseas companies. Indigenous production is not extensive.

Pacific television services, through their transmission patterns and programme content, favour urban middle classes, at the expense of rural communities. Television in PNG is a good example of this. The mainly imported programmes are in English, and TV is restricted to urban areas and electricity subscribers. In comparison, PNG has the largest radio network in the Pacific, with a national and regional system consisting of 19 provincial stations broadcasting in a number of languages.

The introduction of television has also highlighted the lack of legislation to protect local interests. The existing legislation appears more concerned with technical standards, rather than questions of local content, advertising content, and the number of indigenous languages to be served.[15] This has made it difficult for Pacific media groups to insist on a local content quota. In 1970, a Broadcasting Review Committee in Fiji suggested that Fiji set up TV without delay, with 'an immediate goal of 30 percent local programming with an emphasis on Fijian news and sports, processed and edited in the islands'.[16] However, when Alan Bond won a contract to supply TV to Fiji in 1988, his company PBL was given a 12-year monopoly and control of at least 80% of the content (this contract has since lapsed due to complications that arose as result of the coups). Similarly, PNG, prior to their acceptance of the PBL proposal, stated a preference for community video as a stepping stone to television. But PNG was not in a position to do this because it did not have trained television personnel, nor the resources to run national television.

A number of people in the Pacific are concerned that television has started without adequate thought being given to other options. There also appears to have been little consideration of the economic and socio-cultural implications of the introduction of television. Pacific broadcasters did come together to discuss issues raised by the introduction of television at the UNESCO sponsored meeting in Suva late in 1989, but it is difficult to hold regular regional meetings because of the costs involved in Pacific travel. Cultural and economic differences also make the possibility of a regional television service unlikely, yet this has clear economic advantages for the small Pacific countries.

It became clear at the Suva meeting that the countries were divided into three groups — the first group felt television should be introduced because it would be of benefit to their economies, the second group felt that only developmental television was appropriate, and the third group dismissed television as too expensive.[17] Media interests at this meeting also strongly asserted that the entire Pacific would eventually have television, and 'that the population of the Pacific Island Nations is regarded by television company owners as one of the last untapped television markets'.[18]

Broadcasters at the Pacific Islands Broadcasting Association meeting held in Vanuatu in August 1990, discussed their concerns about television. Ian Johnstone said that the decision to adopt television is usually made by government. The interests of Pacific countries could therefore be displaced by large business interests from outside the region 'who do deals with Ministers'.[19] And despite any rhetoric about national development needs, these deals have clearly favoured foreign media owners who need to sell equipment and increase audience markets shares for their programmes and advertisements.[20]

Secondly, the question of whether a Pacific country will adopt television is being increasingly bypassed by advances in technology. With direct satellite broadcasting, and point-to-point multipoint capability, individuals can make the decision about whether they will receive television, thus doing away with the need for a national system.

Lack of trained television personnel is a major impediment to local production. In some countries (Niue, the Cook Islands), radio broadcasters have been asked to assist with local video production. But this inevitably weakens the national radio service, particularly in the smaller countries where strong and viable radio stations have yet to be established.[21]

In 1989 a regional television project — PACVIDEO, was set up at the South Pacific Commission (SPC) in Suva, funded by the International Programme for Development Communication (IPDC, of UNESCO) with Australian funds-in-trust. PACVIDEO's long-term objective was to provide basic training for the future development of television in the region. As a first step, the project encouraged increased local production distributed through the existing VCR and video hire networks, as a way of establishing community television. These video programmes were seen as a useful precursor to national television because they gave audiences the opportunity to develop an interest in local programmes. At the same time, Pacific island producers would gain valuable production experience working on smaller projects. PACVIDEO also hoped to set up a regional programme exchange, but this has not eventuated due to lack of resources and personnel.

As well as providing indigenous content, video programmes also play an important role in development work. Techniques can be demonstrated, the images can be frozen, and replayed, leading to a greater understanding of the subject. This is why there is increasing interest in this area from government departments such as health and agriculture, because they see the educational value of video for extension work.

However, one of the greatest threats to local video production is the glossy, sophisticated production techniques used in overseas programmes. These can make the local productions look amateurish, and discourage local producers from developing their own forms. But research has found that audiences generally prefer local productions to overseas ones, because they enjoy seeing images of themselves and their country.[22]

In 1992, PACVIDEO had not been re-funded, and its future was unclear. Without PACVIDEO the main training in the region will come from the SPC, but it cannot resource as many courses as PACVIDEO did. The lack of training is particularly problematic as a number of the newer stations (Niue 1988, the Cook Islands 1990, Fiji 1991, Tonga 1985 and 1991) are committed to indigenous production and need further training to increase the quality and quantity of their productions.

Further Considerations

Radio will remain the most significant medium in the Pacific for some time because of the geographical nature of the islands. However, there is a sense of inevitability about the introduction of television, and if the existing systems are to be taken as examples, this would suggest that there will not be extensive discussion about local requirements.

The global dominance of Western commercial media forms, and the subsequent importation of Western commercial media into the Pacific, appear to have obscured the potential of the media to be used for local production, and for cultural maintenance and regeneration. This greatly disadvantages the development of Pacific media, and raises major questions about impact of overseas material on Pacific cultures.

Continued training in radio, video and print is vital if the Pacific media are to develop and produce local content. This training should not concentrate only on Western forms, but seek to encourage the growth of indigenous media forms. Pacific countries also need to be in a position where they can have much more influence over the control and access to communications technology in their countries. Only when this happens will concern about the dominance of foreign media be lessened.

TECHNOLOGY AND MARINE RESOURCE DEVELOPMENT

PHILLIP MULLER AND ANDREW WRIGHT

◆◆◆

The South Pacific is no different from the rest of the world in terms of the changes that have occurred through the development and transfer of technology during the last century. The rate and extent of technological change in the Pacific have been dramatic, however, despite the common misconception that it is a difficult region in which to innovate new technology. Pacific islanders have exhibited an outstanding capacity to absorb and apply new technologies across a broad spectrum of activities. This is typified in the field of fisheries and marine resource development. Although the South Pacific has not generally been at the forefront of developing new technology, it has been an excellent testing ground for new technology, and islanders have been quick to adopt innovations that have contributed toward fisheries development in the region.

Islanders also developed sophisticated traditional systems of marine science and technology. This included detailed knowledge of fish behaviour and appropriate lures, marine technology and navigation. This knowledge was developed according to available materials and demand. New materials and equipment, new markets and demands, new means of processing and preservation that were unavailable to islanders before European contact have slowly changed the nature and size of fishing activities and operations in the Pacific.

These changes in technology and fisheries exploitation began with the first visits of European explorers to the region some 250 years ago, searching for new lands and commodities. In the field of marine resources, they were mainly interested in whales, beche-de-mer, mollusc and turtleshell, all of which had been historically exploited for subsistence purposes by local coastal communities. The early transfer of technology from the West included steel hooks and multistrand string for fishing lines and nets, and multipurpose steel knives and axes, useful for processing catches. With increased contact, these and other technological developments were applied not only to improve the efficiency of local fishermen to supply subsistence needs, but also to supply the crews of visiting ships, traders and settlers.[1]

Apart from Melanesia, the South Pacific is generally poor in terms of land-based commodities offering sustainable development opportunities, although the whole region harbours a huge diversity of marine resources. In terms of commercial fisheries development, it is mainly the oceanic, as opposed to inshore resources that to date have been successfully targeted for development. Among the reasons for this are the relative abundance of individual oceanic resources offering development potential compared to inshore resources, the world demand for the oceanic resources of the region and the fact that oceanic resources in general do not fall under claims of traditional ownership. The latter point has inhibited commercial exploitation of some inshore commodities. However, it has possibly also resulted in their preservation.

This chapter examines changes that have occurred as a result of technological developments applied to marine resource exploitation in the South Pacific. The various marine resources are profiled in general terms, together with a description of methods applied to their capture, processing and distribution. The impact of technological change applied to the development and management of marine resource exploitation is assessed and some forecasts concerning likely future developments proposed.

The South Pacific

With regard to their geography, cultures, and economies, Pacific island countries are diverse. Relative to the development and management of fishery resources they are united by two common characteristics: small land masses and jurisdictions over large areas of ocean. Coupled with this is the fact that most countries have limited agricultural or other renewable resources, and so place substantial reliance on living marine resource development to offset an increasing trend towards import dominated economies. The importance of marine resources to the region is underlined by the general reference to the development, management and conservation of fishery resources and the marine environment in the national development plans and strategies of all countries and territories of the region.[2]

Pacific island governments stress the need to maintain traditional lifestyles and values to mitigate against the social problems associated with urbanisation and the growth of cash economies, largely brought about as a result of the application of new technologies. Balanced against the need for economic development is a wish to ensure that marine resources continue to contribute sustainably to the cultural and social wellbeing of island communities.

Marine Resources

The fishery resources of the South Pacific can be broadly divided into two classes: coastal, or inshore, and oceanic, or offshore. While there is some overlap, these resource categories support different user-groups and exploitation regimes.

Inshore resources are typically subject to forms of marine tenure, have supported extensive subsistence use, are relatively easily accessible, and offer some economic development potential, but may be fragile and, in some countries, liable to over-exploitation by the present fishing capacity, especially in locations adjacent to urban areas. Inshore resources are the normal basis of small-scale fisheries development activities and the major source of income generation for local fishermen.

Offshore resources are not normally subject to traditional tenure, are of only localised subsistence importance, are relatively less accessible for coastal communities, but are orders of magnitude larger, and beyond the present capacity of South Pacific countries alone to overfish. Because of the industrial nature of fisheries and the international marketing structures that exist for their products, there has been and continues to be extensive foreign involvement in their exploitation.[3]

Despite the costs of accessing distant international markets, demand for marine commodities from the region has resulted in significant increases in exploitation of South Pacific marine resources. This has largely been achieved by application of new technologies by indigenous peoples of the region and foreigners. Rapid changes in this area commenced 50 years ago, when the Japanese began targeting marine shell and tuna resources of the region.[4]

Inshore Fishery Resources

Inshore resources, which include a wide variety of reef and lagoon fish, as well as crustaceans, molluscs, echinoderms and algae, have traditionally been a mainstay of the subsistence diet in all coastal areas of the Pacific, and they continue to make a major contribution to the protein intake of coastal people. Nevertheless, the true importance of subsistence fisheries to the nutrition and health of coastal peoples and the economies of countries of the region remains poorly known. This is despite the fact that increased coastal populations exploiting inshore resources throughout the region have resulted in local resource depletions.

Inshore fisheries development activities, generally interpreted to mean the application of new approaches for improved exploitation, processing and distribution, have typically focussed on the more accessible inshore resources, as a means of generating income-earning opportunities. In most cases, new technologies are applied to such development initiatives. The 1980s saw a growing awareness of the limitations of basing development on inshore resources: as well as being finite and fragile, inshore resources tend to be thinly dispersed and highly species diverse, which makes post-harvest distribution and marketing complex and costly.[5]

Fishing Gear and Vessels

Fishing gear and vessel development has improved the relative catching efficiency of local inshore fishing activities, and expanded the resource base available for exploitation. Many donor agencies, regional and international fisheries organisations have had, and continue to have, active programmes either to improve traditional fishing craft and gears, to develop new craft specifically for South Pacific conditions or to adapt designs from elsewhere.

Gear development, through the successful deployment of synthetic materials for fishing lines and nets and more effective hooks and artificial lures, has contributed significantly to improved catches by local fishermen. This does not mean that traditional technology has been entirely superseded. In many areas, plant material is still used for the manufacture of lures and nets, and the outrigger canoe has been in the region for at least 4000 years.[6]

Throughout the region, fishing in sheltered inshore waters from dugout canoes, with or without outriggers, provides the majority of local finfish catches, although these fishing activities remain largely undocumented, and the catches unquantified. Quantification would be difficult, as transportation of catches between outlying islands and central markets is carried out by diesel or petrol-powered vessels and, to a lesser extent, aircraft.

With respect to nearshore pelagic species, such as tuna and mackerel, almost all present-day fishing activity by indigenous coastal residents utilises introduced technology. Diesel and petrol-powered vessels have increased the area over which fishermen can range in search of fish and, together with the utilisation of new fishing gear, catching efficiency has improved. Storage for the catch aboard these vessels, through the installation of ice boxes and/or refrigeration systems, has extended the period of time between capture and sale of fish, and improved the general quality of the catch presented to buyers.

Although technological developments have been responsible for the increasing effectiveness of local fishermen in the inshore area, there are indications that, at least with respect to finfish, increased populations rather than increased fishing efficiency have been the major cause of local resource depletions where they occur. In rural areas with access to productive agricultural land, such as is the case throughout much of Melanesia, local fishermen fish to supply subsistence needs, and fishing for cash is often only a secondary activity to cultivation of crops.[7] On low islands and atolls, such as exist throughout much of Micronesia and Polynesia, fish are relatively more important as a commercial resource, due to the lack of alternative resources offering commercial development opportunities, although many such islands are distant from large markets.

In association with new technology regarding fishing gear and vessels has been the development of handling and processing technology. This has improved the quality of marine resources presented for sale, and increased the period between capture and consumption. This has increased the ability of fishermen in remote areas to access more distant markets, and in many cases to prepare a product for international distribution.

Although many finfish products are susceptible to poor handling, and without adequate freezing deteriorate rapidly, other non-perishable resources, such as beche-de-mer and marine shell, have been targeted by Western and Asian traders throughout the region for almost two centuries. However, in the last 30 years, and especially during the last five, these commodities have been the target of increased effort by local fishermen. Throughout the region, centrally located buyers consolidate small quantities supplied by local fishermen for grading and shipment to international markets.

Aquaculture and Mariculture

In response to resource depletion, numerous projects to breed and distribute local marine resources and culturing systems have been proposed and experimented with throughout the South Pacific. Aquaculture and mariculture have not developed to the extent expected by some a decade ago, for a variety of reasons, mainly economic and social. However, there remains potential for such activities to contribute to the resource base available for local fisheries development through the introduction of species outside their natural range of distribution, and the enhancement of local populations. In addition, re-establishing populations in areas where they have been depleted through overfishing, or as a result of environmental perturbation, has been identified as an important product of such activities.

The Inshore Future

Present aquaculture trends are characterised by increasing interest in non-traditional species, and in the use of aquaculture to enhance natural fisheries. This is an important area, and one in which significant research effort and funding will need to be concentrated in the 1990s to evaluate the economic potential of coastal aquaculture programmes, and to develop appropriate technology for broad application throughout the Pacific.

The biological and socio-economic constraints to inshore fishery development will continue to fuel the present trend towards widening the inshore fishery resource base by promoting alternative fisheries accessible to small fishermen. The identification and subsequent exploitation of the deepwater (greater than a depth of 80 metres) finfish resource is an excellent example of progress in this area. This resource, generally beyond the range of traditional fishing techniques, and thus not targeted for subsistence purposes in the past, offers good potential for commercial fisheries development if that development is properly managed. In addition, the establishment of fisheries for coastal pelagic species based on fish aggregation devices (FADs) is a promising way in which previously inaccessible resources can be made available to small-scale fishermen. Programmes of FAD deployment will continue in the coming decade, and greater support will be needed to assist Pacific countries maximise the benefits from them.

Offshore Fishery Resources

During 1989 it was estimated that 650,000 tonnes of offshore species (tuna and allied types), valued at US$1–1.2 billion, were harvested in the South Pacific region.[8] The South Pacific countries, determined to ensure that the tuna resource is managed for long-term sustainable exploitation, are currently examining means by which tuna fisheries can be regulated. Given the enormous areas through which the tuna fleets range in search of tuna in the South Pacific, and the lack of national capabilities to monitor the activities of the fleets, the countries pool resources to explore new technologies that may be applied to management of the tuna resource through the collection and analysis of information relevant to fishing activities and the international markets the fishing fleets target.

Joint Ventures

In general, South Pacific countries lack the capital to establish extensive industrial fishing fleets and the associated shore facilities required to service them. The expertise needed to operate and manage such fleets is only now beginning to develop. There is still extensive foreign involvement in such industrial fishing ventures, and this is likely to persist well into the next decade. In addition, the international nature of marketing arrangements for industrial fishery products also makes foreign involvement almost a prerequisite. Joint ventures have been used as a means of ensuring foreign involvement in the past, providing the potential for commercial development and technology transfer. They are likely to remain a viable option for industrial fishery development in the future, although the actual benefits accruing to South Pacific countries through joint-venture arrangements has not always been positive, and such arrangements require careful monitoring to ensure objectives are adequately addressed.[9] At present in the Pacific there is a shortage of local expertise, especially among civil servants who are normally appointed to represent governments in joint venture arrangements, to adequately monitor joint ventures.

The direct involvement of Pacific countries themselves in offshore fishing activities is limited. Progress by coastal states in developing their own tuna resources has been slow, despite a commitment on the part of all states to increase local involvement in the region's surface tuna fisheries. The rapid expansion and growing dominance of the capital-intensive and technically complex technique of purse-seining has further exacerbated the situation. The transfer and adaptation of technology and skills, product development and marketing support will all be required in future collaborative programmes to develop industrial fisheries based and technically serviced within the region. In particular the dynamics of markets, and their product preferences, require continued monitoring and study if South Pacific countries are to effectively compete in them.

Licensed Fishing Operations

Most offshore resources are presently harvested by the vessels of distant-water fishing nations (DWFNs) operating under access arrangements of one sort or another. The value of access fees paid by DWFNs in 1989 was approximately US$30 million, or about 4.3% of the value of the tuna catch on international markets.[10] There is an obvious desire among South Pacific countries to increase their share of returns from offshore fisheries, rather than continue with the resource rental arrangements that predominate at present. The development of locally-based and operated industrial tuna fisheries should thus be a priority area for economic development programmes in the region in the next decade although success in this area will require perseverance on the part of island governments and industry.

At present, the involvement of Pacific islanders in commercial offshore fisheries development is largely confined to less technologically complex fishing operations such as pole-and-line tuna fishing and longlining for tuna and deepwater demersal finfish. Although a number of pole-and-line vessels have been successfully 'localised', the key positions on such vessels largely remain in the control of expatriates. The more capital- intensive and technically advanced methods, such as purse-seining, are likely to be directed by Westerners and Asians for the foreseeable future, although Pacific countries are increasingly insisting that employment opportunities on such vessels be included in access arrangements. The Federated States of Micronesia (FSM), Vanuatu and Kiribati actively pursue this requirement and the FSM, in its 1990 access discussions with Japan, successfully negotiated for shore-based fleet management training for its nationals. This offers enormous potential as a means of transferrring technological and managerial experience to South Pacific island nationals.

The Offshore Future

As the direct involvement of coastal states in industrial tuna fisheries grows, their share of the catch will increase and result in a reduced share allocated to DWFNs. In addition, it may be necessary to allocate catches according to fishing gear type, especially where the use of one gear by a DWFN may have an adverse effect on another used by a coastal state. Resolving problems of catch allocation among states with different levels and types of involvement in local and distant-water fishing activities will become one of the region's most pressing long-term issues.

The Costs and Benefits of Innovation

The application of new technology in both offshore and inshore marine resource exploitation in the South Pacific is, as elsewhere, related to the cost of implementation, and the relative net financial return that may accrue as a result of implementation.[11] With respect to offshore fishery development, the cost of implementing technically advanced commercial fishing operations, requiring a large amount of training, has been met by joint-ventures or foreign-owned companies active at the harvesting and distribution levels. The capital outlay necessary to establish and operate such large scale fishing ventures is generally beyond the financial resources of most private companies in the region. However, governments, through joint-ventures, have promoted such activities and some of these operations, such as pole-and-line tuna fishing, have been successfully established (although many have failed).

Environmental Impacts

Although monetary costs are of paramount importance in assessing the suitability of new technology to marine resource exploitation throughout the South Pacific, many countries are increasingly conscious of possible environmental damage associated with technological innovation. An example of the inappropriate application of new technology to marine resource harvesting in the South Pacific has been the widespread use of explosives salvaged from disgarded World War Two munitions for concussing schools of inshore fish. Many countries now have legislation against this, making the practice illegal. More recently, driftnets have been used by Asian fleets in the South Pacific to target albacore tuna, a practice widely condemned not only in the South Pacific, but also internationally, because of its non-selectivity.

Technology Transfer

In inshore fisheries, technology transfer has mainly been introduced by regional fisheries organisations financed by donor agencies. Experimental programmes including a large training component for local fisheries extension officers and private enterprise involved in the fisheries sector have generally been carried out at little or no national cost. Although some inshore fisheries (for example, trochus, green snail and beche-de-mer) in the region are of local economic importance, these fisheries involve little modern technology. New methods have been introduced for the exploitation of finfish resources, but success in this area is limited by the large diversity of species in a catch which has never been large by international standards, and the remoteness of fishing grounds from suitable markets. Generally a lack of confidence regarding the sustained supply from inshore resources constrains potential market development beyond local artisanal needs.

Control and verification of the activities of foreign fishing vessels (FFVs) operating in the region will be enhanced by effective vessel surveillance and the enforcement of fishery and maritime regulations. However, surveillance is costly and in most cases cannot be carried out effectively at the national level, given the geography of the region and the small size of most national economies. There is therefore a strong case for establishing a harmonised regional programme to develop vessel surveillance, monitoring and reporting practices. The first step towards this has been the establishment of the Forum Fisheries Agency's (FFA's) Regional Register of Foreign Fishing Vessels, which, since its inception in 1983, has effectively induced a pattern of conduct that allows for more ready compliance with national fishing regulations on the part of FFVs.[12] The harmonisation of fisheries legislation in the region by standardising legal provisions that relate to the control of FFVs would also be beneficial and warrants further consideration. The relatively recent introduction of computers to national fisheries departments has played a large part in the successful monitoring and documentation of fisheries activities throughout the region. In the last five years almost all national fisheries departments have installed computers, largely with the assistance of various donor agencies and regional fisheries organisations. Staff have rapidly acquired the knowledge to utilise computers to assist their work across a broad range of activities including administration, analysis of research programme data, monitoring fisheries, information storage and retrieval and documentation. Computers will play an increasingly important role throughout the fisheries sector in the South Pacific in the future.

* * * *

Despite the high degree of social, economic and political diversity among Pacific islands, and the costs of communicating and servicing cooperative activities across the huge distances that lie between them, South Pacific countries have succeeded in achieving an exemplary level of cooperation on fisheries issues. In many situations, greater national benefits can accrue when countries unite in pursuing common development and management goals, rather than acting in isolation. This is particularly the case in the areas of environmental protection and conservation, atmospheric pollution, resource management, technological exchange and information sharing. Because of the need to deal with extra-regional interests on a collective basis, and because of intensifying interest in issues related to the quality of life, South Pacific regional cooperation is set to increase in the 1990s.

The success with which the Pacific island countries have explored and experimented with new technology and applied it to fisheries resource assessment, development, management and conservation is largely due to the collaborative action countries generate through the two regional fisheries organisations, FFA and the South Pacific Commission. The benefits of coordinated approaches to technology transfer to the Pacific have been real in the past. The role of regional organisations in keeping member countries abreast of technological developments will not diminish in the future.

SOCIAL AND POLITICAL CONSTRAINTS ON
APPROPRIATE TECHNOLOGY IN PAPUA NEW GUINEA

ELIZABETH COX

No aspect of development occurs in a political or social vacuum. Developing countries are greatly influenced by the conditionalities of aid and trade, and the constraints imposed by global economic relations, international and national social structures. These influences too often compete with and overwhelm the efforts of organisations with appropriate technology and community development in Third World countries.

This chapter deals with the choice, transfer and application of technology, and the opportunities for people to create and control desired change and improvement within their communities. It is concerned with the kind of problems people and communities face when, in spite of the invasion of videos, fast cars and fast foods, they have decided to stay in their villages. It is concerned with the organisation and development of food production, housing, energy supplies, educational and health services based on what people already have, or can potentially access, control, manage and maintain.

Community development is taken to mean change and improvement in the social and material quality of life, which the people themselves choose and implement. Genuine development of the community can never be a process imposed from outside, an appendage of a larger and very differently directed and motivated process of economic development.

Throughout the chapter, points will be illustrated by personal anecdotes, gained from working with one rural resettled community of

___

3000 people in a planned Integrated Rural Development Project (IRDP) in East Sepik, and close association and involvement with a province-wide network of village-based women's groups who have devised and led their own programmes for development for the past decade.

The resettlement project is made up of a community in which people's lives have been organised, ordered and directed by local authorities and external agencies. In the face of this, many people and small groups have demonstrated a clear determination to decide upon and do things for themselves — to teach, lead, organise and innovate for local development through the formation of peoples' organisations. With the support of some NGOs and individuals, local leaders and activists have been given the opportunity to gain experience in and exposure to new and alternative technologies.

By reference to the general context of Papua New Guinea, and the particular experiences of these community and women's groups, it is hoped to elucidate and illustrate the development trends in PNG which currently limit the possibility of applying technology to community development, rather than to exploitation and destruction for profit.

Technology, Resource Exploitation and Development

Papua New Guinea is a resource-rich country. There are vast tropical rainforests of precious hardwoods. PNG also contains some of the world's richest gold and copper deposits. Not surprisingly, the nation has experienced an invasion over the past five years of mining multinationals and entrepreneurs from Australia, Japan, Malaysia, the Philippines, South Korea, Taiwan and Thailand, who wheel and deal directly with local politicians and landowners in their drive for quick and unfettered profiteering. The local landowners are bought off with promises of schools, hospitals and the other basic services that they have wanted and expected for the past fifteen years. Many people make the claim that the PNG government has failed to deliver the basic goods and services — and that they see no alternative other than betting on the multinationals and other foreign businesses.

Logging, which is occurring at a devastating and uncontrolled rate, and the various multinational mining companies have become the most significant influences on the economy, the environment and the lives of the people. Cash cropping, so vigorously promoted as rural development throughout PNG since the 1950s, is failing.

In spite of the Bougainville crisis and the closure of the nation's biggest and most profitable mine, forced by popular armed uprising by landowners, the PNG government still seems to believe that mining will be its economic salvation. Most people recognise that many local communities, cultures and environments will be sacrificed in the process. Basic needs are being overridden by economic 'development', which limits the diversity of productive activities and the development of people's initiative, enterprise and participation. The single-minded economic pursuit of resource exploitation is catalysing PNG's current 'law and order' problem.

When mining sets the development stage, the symbols of development are massive machines, pollution and profit — with the benefits occurring to a very visible rich elite. When landowners have to be relocated, they may be given matchbox houses and ablution blocks, but they are certainly not inspired to seek or develop appropriate technologies to bring change and improvements to their communities.

Some of the more specific problems associated with the choice and transfer of appropriate technologies for community development are a result of the combined effects of these macro development influences and the relative weakness of a less spectacular and poorly supported appropriate technology movement.

The current mode and operation of development in PNG is not only by-passing people's basic needs, but in many cases is preventing them from ever meeting them for themselves in the future. For example, the fact that food is often hunted, gathered or fished in PNG is often overlooked. Logging and the dumping of mining wastes in rivers and seas has for too long proceeded unchecked.

Agricultural development in PNG has almost exclusively concentrated on export cash crops. Agricultural officers often receive training based on inappropriate overseas practice. They see themselves as agents of organising production, rather than promoting the subsistence production of surplus food products for community consumption and supplementary income. Cash-crop based development projects typically promote and subsidise various agricultural technologies including nurseries, fertiliser, insecticides, pesticides, contouring, budding, pruning and planting-out technologies, as well as training, transport and marketing, many of which are inappropriate in the subsistence sector. Any transfer of useful and appropriate agricultural technologies to food production is accidental rather than intended and regular practice. Through commercial outlets and as part of farmers' loan packages, agricultural chemicals and hybrid commercial seeds are made available. Services for local seed production, supplies and basic hand tools are scarce, and in many cases non-existent.

Economic Gain or Community Development?

One problem is that most externally planned and funded development is concerned with mobilising money and machines for economic gain rather than motivating people for community development. Power is being vested in the structures which support and reinforce new hierarchies of authority and dependence on bureaucracies. This works directly against creating opportunities to develop the potential for local leadership, local community organisations and the optimum input of NGOs into community development. There is an underlying fear that people who are educated and engaged in debate about local development issues might be critical and propose alternatives for local development. This fear becomes exaggerated when the state as external agent of mainstream economic development worries that control or authority might be lost.

Appropriate Technology and Community Development

In Papua New Guinea, 85% of the population live in rural villages. 93% of the land is held under customary ownership. 65% of men and 72% of women are illiterate. The extended family system is still alive and well. There is no official state social security system as such. Most people who live in town still derive a great sense of security from the knowledge that they can resign or retire and 'go back' to 'their place', and live from the land. These conditions require slow and careful change based on simple and small technologies with integrated literacy, awareness and other basic education activities.

In the first decade of independence, from 1975 to 1985, there was much interest in appropriate technology and community development. This era was filled by the rhetoric of self-help and self-reliance, local ownership and equal distribution of the profits of natural resource development. There was a substantial and significant effort in PNG to promote appropriate technology through organisations involved in community development. Agencies like the South Pacific Appropriate Technology Foundation (SPATF), Appropriate Technology Development Institute (ATDI, based at UniTech), Village Equipment Supplies (VES) and Village Industry Research and Training Unit (VIRTU) have, through networks with people's organisations across the country, played an important role. PNG has, in fact, been a leader in the Pacific region with its well known provincial and national appropriate technology research and development organisations and publications. Transfer and dissemination has proved much more difficult, although active networking among researchers, extension workers and village and community organisations during the decade proved valuable and inspirational to thousands of ordinary villagers and local leaders.

Information systems have been set up and popular publications produced, of which the 'LikLik Buk' has been the most significant.[1] The 'LikLik Buk' Information Centre (based at ATDI) has prompted the production and facilitated the distribution of local publications, songs and drama related to the introduction or evolution of appropriate food, agriculture, health, household and other technologies.

Despite the above activities, and for various reasons, many avenues and opportunities for the promotion of appropriate technology have been missed. PNG's appropriate technology organisations and programmes have always been working against the odds. They rely largely on non-government funding sources, and on voluntary staff and services. In 1990 most of these organisations were struggling to survive, and some of their leading advocates had moved to the 'high-tech' mining sector.

No major overseas aid development programme package has seriously incorporated the promotion of resource centres, providing training, resource people or publications regarding appropriate technology. Where these activities have evolved in the context of large planned development projects, it was inevitably despite, rather than because of the objectives, conditions and controls written into the official development project. There are a few cases where the appropriate technology consultant was included as an obligatory appendix — just as a nutrition or women's consultant might be — to a mainly masculine, economistic approach to development. Some examples of technology and community development follow.

Water Supply and Gender Bias

Water is a major problem for many communities. When water is far away or contaminated (often by primary industrial activities, especially mining) it poses particular problems for family health and increased workload for women and children. Too many technologists or government service departments suffer from a gender bias. This blinds them to recognising and supporting self-help community efforts to solve problems of water supply. In one district of PNG water authorities of the local health department refused to allow specially trained women, their supportive community and community organisations to utilise the hand-driven auger and water pumps lying idle in government workshops. They did not believe that women could drill water bores for themselves. This frustrated and delayed the women's self-help efforts for two years, until they began water supply work financed by the production and sale of traditional string bags, with subsidies from some small overseas non-government aid agencies.

In a resettlement scheme, where development was planned and implemented from the top down, the government had bought and delivered galvanised iron tanks to farmers as part of their loan package. However, many were damaged during delivery. There was no workable repair or maintenance system. When farmers sent their tanks back to government stations for repairs they often didn't see them again for another one or two years.

Things were more complicated when a local community-based building project was set up. Part of the aim of this project was to maximise the use of local timber. However, the treated hand-split shingle roofs put copper sulphate into the tanks, where it reacted with the zinc and aluminium to promote rapid rusting. The people who owned and used the tanks watched this happening and complained, but their observations and correct conclusions were rejected by people who had an interest in the rapid, unimpeded and unquestioned promotion of these new building technologies.

In another example, local development activists sent members off for training in the production of domestic, household cement water tanks. They brought back skills, equipment and materials to introduce a technology appropriate to a very pressing basic need. However, the tank mould was delivered by a government truck and misappropriated by an expatriate agricultural officer. He used the tank mould to make small fish ponds for his aquatic weed collection, then brought in Rotary International funds and Australian voluntary labour to build an enormous demonstration 20,000 gallon cement tank for community water supply. He has since left the area. Now the mould for the small tank cannot be found, and no one knows how to construct the larger tank.

Health Care
In the health field PNG, like many other countries, has an historical problem with the frequent use of inappropriate technologies. Local traditional medicines and methods of health care have too often been dismissed and discarded. Not surprisingly, penicillin has become a convenient if magical panacea to all manner of ills presented at clinics, which could actually be easily prevented by community based education and actions. In family planning programmes, depo-provera injections — more easily 'administered' but with serious potential side effects — have been promoted in preference to the less dangerous and more easily comprehended contraceptive technologies such as condoms and diaphragms, that require a little more explanation, education and training but allow for a lot more self-reliance and control.

The failure of DDT spraying and other attempts to address the critical problem of malaria have led to a new strategy of promoting pyrethrum-dipped mosquito nets. This is combined with the wholesale importing of high quality nets by the government Health Department. However, this new programme depends on the Health Department to advertise and distribute this appropriate technology. An additional problem is the reluctance of the Health Department to allow community organisations to take over the dipping process (which must take place every six months). They claim that villagers could not cope with the careful mixing processes required. No such reluctance or doubt has accompanied the distribution and availability of toxic agricultural chemicals which are promoted in the cash crop industry.

This underestimates the potential for people's technical capacity and understanding when they are determined, trusted and in control. For example, rebel landowners, tribal warriors and urban rascals seem to have no problem making home-made guns and explosives.

Misuse of Development Resources

Beyond the problems associated with the introduction and adoption of appropriate technologies there is another serious social and political problem. This is the appropriation of development resources and their exclusive and wasteful use by the very people and organisations who are responsible for implementing development projects.

One example is the water tank noted above. Another is the ubiquitous four-wheel-drive car or bus which is purchased with overseas aid or loan funds to provide transport for rural development activities. In theory, these vehicles are government-owned and for official use between 8am and 4pm. If used efficiently and wisely, even within the constraints of these inflexible bureaucratic hours, they could be a great boost to development projects — supporting people's organisations, resourcing and facilitating community education and aiding the production and marketing of food crops. However, this is rarely the case. Project and government cars often serve more as personal vehicles for the local elite. They facilitate visiting the relatives, promoting family businesses and feathering nests in distant home villages, ready for the public servants' retirement. One hardly hears of a car facilitating people's development or appropriate technology, unless it is owned by a non-government organisation.

The case of government buildings constructed as part of planned rural development packages is much the same. In many parts of PNG costly community facilities such as classrooms may be left idle to deteriorate, rather than someone arrange for them to be occupied, repaired and utilised by NGOs or community organisations.

Diesel generators are often set up in remote government stations established to administer rural development projects. Large volumes of fuel are used to light up the lives of a few privileged government workers. In one case K$15,000 per year was spent on diesel fuel for the exclusive provision of power for two people — an oasis of light and sound in the blackness and bleakness of a rather poor rural community, where only 20% of the families owned small kerosene lamps, and even fewer people could afford fuel for lighting on a regular basis. Requests for power connections to provide community entertainment and to run the local women's group freezer for fresh fruit and ice block production were declined.

Constraints in Promoting Appropriate Technology for Community Development

The above kind of development 'assistance' leaves the people in the dark in more ways than one. It leads to the kind of resentment and despair which discourages efforts with appropriate technologies. It can also inspire acts of destruction and disruption — as statements of dissatisfaction by the people about their limited role in the development process, and in the future of their community and country.

Outside Organisation

These problems are linked to a widespread lack of confidence, interest and trust among local people in government and politics. Development programmes are often externally funded and planned, hierarchically structured and implemented. This approach fails to entrust or empower people with the information, skills, confidence and resources to decide upon and direct their own community development. Rather, they impose new systems and values, and encourage attitudes and behaviour by local authorities and technicians which deny participation and deprive people of the most basic opportunities and options for self-determination. Individuals, community groups and grass-roots organisations which promote appropriate technologies in this context are very likely to be resented and even harassed if they do not share the ownership, management or control of their resources for development.

Back-up and Follow-through

Another limitation on the successful adoption of technology is the lack of back-up and follow-through support for development projects, including those involving appropriate technology. When development projects are planned and implemented they are generally regarded by planners as completed. In practice, this is generally not the perspective of those on the ground. All projects, particularly those involving technology, generally require back-up support and follow-through to maximise the chance of their effectiveness and success.

Preaching and Practice

There is often a great gap and contradiction between what is promoted and what is practised in lifestyle, housing, daily diet, mobility and access by the proponents of appropriate technology. Some senior government officials and politicians have seen fit to sit on the boards and committees of organisations which promote environmentally sound farming, nutrionally sound food processing and other appropriate and ecologically sound technologies. Meanwhile, wearing another hat, they sign agreements to establish chemical fertiliser factories on their beaches, promote highly mechanised rice production or the rampant logging of their own people's forests. When the people start to see that these 'big men' do not do what they say, they drop appropriate technology programmes out of sheer disillusionment, as a statement of despair and protest in response to this hypocrisy.

Training and the Flying Circus

Ineffective training is another limitation to the successful promotion and adoption of appropriate technologies for community development. As Government field extension officers often receive inappropriate training, they too often become technocrats, rather than friendly helpers of the people. In development projects, they are often slotted neatly into management rather than service roles. It is hardly surprising that ideas for appropriate technologies rarely emerge from within government departments or planned rural development projects.

Attempts by appropriate technology networkers and organisations to provide training have met with very limited success. In Bougainville village outreach and hands-on training was reasonably successful, but could not survive the social crisis provoked by the presence of the huge copper mine. The community extension programmes of major appropriate technology agencies, according to their own evaluations, have too often provided training in the form of a 'travelling circus' or 'hit-and-run' rural workshops. This problem is not simply the fault of these agencies or their staff. It is related to the problem of the failure, throughout PNG, to develop appropriate methodologies, timing and venues to provide back-up for community-based education for community development.

Information and Communication

The appropriate technology movement in PNG has suffered from the limited distribution, promotion and use of appropriate technology publications. In spite of the now world-famous 'LikLik Buk' and other appropriate technology publications, there are very serious limitations to this material reaching and being used by rural and largely illiterate community leaders and members of village-based organisations. The scope and potential for translating this important information into drama, songs, or simple literacy materials is enormous.

PNG has quite a good range of documentary videos developed over the past decade, dealing with many of the development issues and problems associated with the role and application of appropriate technologies. Yet they have hardly been used. The potential for using video to promote appropriate technology has hardly been explored. Video machines and cassette recorders reach the most remote villages. People are overdosing on diets of Rambo and other high-tech, high-violence, high-impact video material. There is a pressing need to turn this dismal scenario around.

Technology for Development or Toys and Tokenism?

With externally-planned rural development projects, 'alternative' activities involving appropriate technology have often failed to motivate or mobilise village communities with a vision of a locally-managed, environmentally-safe and sustainable community development.

Given the current serious political and economic constraints, renewed vision, vigour and approaches are required. If technology is to work in favour of community development, we need, alongside the development of tools, machines and publications, the parallel development of social structures and organisations which build and promote people's power and knowledge of new and useful technology. If we are to learn any lessons from the Bougainville crisis and breakdown in law-and-order throughout PNG, then appropriate technology organisations must make links with the various awareness-raising groups promoting people's participation and choice, to encourage programmes and strengthen the capacity of people to reject inappropriate technologies at the planning stage by peaceful means.

In spite of a decade of intensive promotion, networking and training in appropriate technology by various quasi- and non-government organisations, the impact of high-powered, high-technology development has relegated appropriate technology operations and aspirations to 'toys' and tokenism. The current political economy of PNG is shaping a society heading in the opposite direction.

The impact of mining, logging and agribusiness 'development' has devalued traditional lifestyle, housing and diet. It has divided rural communities and discredited the simpler technologies which might evolve spontaneously and be applied to local development. It has dismissed and disempowered the community-based people who could lead, initiate and adapt development strategies at a local level and continue to link the village groups and activities to appropriate technology research and support networks.

Political and economic forces in PNG are overwhelming people and marginalising their participation. PNG's future development must be based on a concern for people at least as much as it is driven by the desire for money. People are being served a diet of Rambo, rice, tinned fish, and beer. They would be better served by literacy and awareness programmes, 'LikLik Buk' and appropriate technology projects promoting local agriculture and fisheries development. If the choice is the former, people would be well advised to prepare for the possibility of a new era of poverty, instability and violence. If the choice is the latter, then government, foreign aid donors and lending agencies should make sure their money is put where their mouth is.

EDUCATION AND TRAINING FOR TECHNOLOGY AND DEVELOPMENT

TONY MARJORAM

The needs for human resource development through education and training in the South Pacific are many and diverse. There is a particular need to develop technology infrastructures in the region through technology education and training, which are themselves a soft technology — imparting the knowledge that is necessary for technological hardware to work properly. Education and training needs include the development of different skills and levels of skills, in different fields, requiring different methods of training.

Technology training needs range from active information exchange to in-depth coursework, from basic trades training to technology policy, planning and management. Skills development needs include the acquisition of additional or secondary skills, where an interdisciplinary mix of skills or multi-skilling is required, and retraining or re-skilling, when new skills are required as older skills become redundant in the wake of new technology and work practices. Technology training is required in the public, private, non-government and community sectors in the formal and informal sectors.

Formal, Informal and Non-formal Education and Training

Education and training can be formal, informal and non-formal. Formal education is the graded, age-structured and usually state-run system of education, running from primary and secondary schools to the college or university. Formal education can be 'academic' — where the main goal is to study and pass theoretical exams in the 'classroom situation', and/or 'vocational' — with a more practical orientation. Formal education is usually full-time, although tertiary education may be part-time. Formal education in the island Pacific started with Christian mission schools.

Informal education is the non-organised lifelong process of information and knowledge acquisition from informal sources, including the acquisition of cultural and traditional knowledge ('folk' science and technology) in hunting, fishing, agriculture and craft production. Much knowledge in the Pacific islands continues to be gained through the informal education system and techniques.

Non-formal education is organised goal-oriented educational activity outside the formal system, generally consisting of short courses or workshops. Non-formal education also refers to those education techniques which are outside the formal system of education and the 'classroom situation'.

There is often little relationship and may even be some antipathy between formal, informal and non-formal education. Education is a powerful form of socialisation. It is unfortunate, for example, that formal Western educational systems have had the effect of displacing traditional informal education systems, knowledge and skills in the Pacific. Non-formal education often 'fills the gaps' of formal education.

Education and Training — For What and For Whom?
Education took place in the Pacific islands before the coming of the colonists and colonial systems of formal education and instruction. With colonialism came Western systems of education based on Western practice and background.[1] As with technology, the transfer of educational systems into different contexts can be problematic and inappropriate.

Education and Development
Conventional development theorists began to equate development with economic growth and the building of institutions in the later 1950s. Education was seen as an investment in the creation of 'human capital', without which rapid economic growth could not take place.[2] Educational strategy focussed on expanding the structure of formal secondary and tertiary education to produce skilled and educated people to act as a professional and middle-class elite to lead the process of economic development.

By the late 1960s shortcomings of this approach were evident — the excessive focus on the modern/urban sector, wage employment and industrialisation had led to the development of urban elites, social inequality, continued rural poverty and rural-urban drift. Interest focussed on the need to redirect development goals towards the reduction of poverty, unemployment and inequality.[3] In education, a critique developed of the formal emphasis on academic subjects, criteria of excellence, excessive individualism and competition, lack of relevance to the majority of school students and negative impacts on other forms of knowledge and knowledge acquisition.

A report for ILO commented that 'Children learn, and are encouraged to learn, not in order to satisfy a carefully stimulated intellectual curiosity, not in order to acquire knowledge which they could use in their occupational lives, not in order to enrich their experience, but in order to fulfil examiners' requirements. The school's function to educate becomes superseded by the demand that it should qualify. One consequence of this is that the knowledge and skills acquired by the majority who fail the tests (which are designed to prepare the minority who gain access to further education) are inappropriate to their needs and those of the nation'.[4] The formal education system in developing countries was described by Coombs as of low 'internal efficiency' and 'external productivity' and a 'world educational crisis'.[5]

Attitudes and expectations instilled into pupils also limited independence and innovativeness — 'schooling has conditioned them to become employees . . . the modern sector is an employee sector . . . its employee teacher, the representative of the modern sector in the village, demonstrates the employee model . . . the would-be employee has learned to take orders not initiatives'.[6] From a rural point of view, the relationship between agricultural productivity and primary schooling 'remains ambiguous, and there is insufficient evidence to justify the claim that primary schooling helps to make people better farmers'.[7]

The demand for and provision of formal eduction, however, increased into the 1970s, despite the increasingly apparent disparity (to many outside observers) between the need for formal education and qualifications and the slower expansion, stagnation or even contraction of employment opportunities.[8] This was considered largely due to the 'hidden curriculum' of education, where education is seen as a way of acquiring credentials necessary for personal advancement in the 'status-conflict' model of education, also observable in the South Pacific, although formal education began relatively late in the region, with the establishment of mission schools.[9]

Alternatives were presented, mainly from the perspective of non-formal education — 'The school must not be replaced by another dominant system: alternatives must be plural . . . should not manipulate individuals but . . . prepare individuals to direct and re-create institutions . . . education should not be separated from work and the rest of life, but integrated with them . . . education should be a self-justified activity designed to help people gain control of themselves, their society and environment'.[10] The relevance to other issues of Third World development is clear. Also clear is the connection of alternatives with traditional pre-institutional, non-alienating forms of education in developing countries and elsewhere. This also applies to education and training for technology and development. There is a particular need to develop the technological infrastructure in developing countries, and a commensurate need for relevant education and training. This is at the formal 'certificate' level, and also for non-formal training regarding village technology or appropriate technology.

Education and Development in the South Pacific

The average regional attendance at primary school in the South Pacific is 34.7% (46.5% excluding PNG), and for secondary school 9.0% (19.5% excluding PNG). The average regional figure for non-attendance at school in the 5-19 age group is 56.3% (19.5% excluding PNG). Particular problems of education are highlighted in the largest country of the region, PNG, where only 30% of eligible children attend primary school, and only 4% attend secondary school.[11] This also reflects reality — in PNG, 85% of school students do not enter formal employment. Drop-out rates increase at the transitional points between primary, secondary and tertiary education. In PNG, for example, only 1.6% of secondary students reach grade 12 — the level generally required for entry to college and university (compared to 40% internationally), with just less than 1.0% entering college or university.[12]

Education in the South Pacific is relatively formal and traditional, with a deficiency in technical subjects, despite widespread concern to promote technical education — as the 9th Fiji Development Plan observed, 'Technical and vocational education were given high priority during the DP8 period. Although attempts made by government strengthened technical/vocational education, educating parents and pupils to appreciate the advantages of practical skills proved difficult'.[13] There is also the problem of putting knowledge or 'book-learning' into practice, particularly following post-secondary technical training. This is similar to the situation in developed countries, one difference being that in developed countries secondary and tertiary graduates generally receive further on-the-job or work-related training.

The majority of Pacific islanders live in rural areas. The rural/informal sector contributes significantly to the national economy and development, providing many raw materials, cottage craft goods and labour. Despite an increase in population and education across the region, there has been little real increase in employment opportunities in the formal sector. This results in rising but unfulfilled aspirations. There is a pressing need to create employment in the formal and informal sectors, to improve formal, and expand informal and non-formal education and training opportunities.

Vocational training policies and programmes have been developed around the Pacific, but generally focus on formal/modern/urban sector training needs and models through apprenticeships and skill-upgrading. With particular reference to rural and non-formal education, it is important to take training to the people, rather than the reverse, and to establish a local base for training, which should be directed at self-employment rather than certification. Bamford observes that 'it must be emphasised again that training for rural living cannot itself solve the problems of urban drift and unemployment, particularly of youth. It does increase a person's potential for employment and when it has sound community support and is an integral part of broader rural development programmes it can, in national terms, make an important contribution to the alleviating of such problems. Furthermore, and of equal importance, it can in personal terms lead to an improvement in the quality of life for rural people who, for years to come, will continue to be the majority in the islands of the Pacific'.[14]

Guidelines for Training

Guidelines for training needs in the South Pacific, focussing mainly on non-formal rural development, have been suggested by Bamford.[15] There is considerable overlap in these guidelines, which are compressed below into a single list (no order of preference):

1. Ensure community interest and support for training.
2. Identify specific training needs.
3. Develop courses with flexibility to meet specific needs.
4. Ensure training has relevant content, facilities and equipment.
5. Link training with productive work activities.
6. Develop economically viable projects during training.
7. Select mature and motivated trainees.
8. Develop effective system of follow-up of trainees.
9. Recruit experienced and committed staff.
10. Collaborate closely with related development agencies.
11. Carry out periodic evaluation.
12. Undertake careful planning of capital and operating finance.
13. Develop locally-based training programmes.

Education and Training for Technology and Development

Education and training in science and technology in the South Pacific faces almost every constraint in terms of institutional support, teacher training, course content and approach. In PNG, for example, science is only taught in the final two years of secondary school, grades 11 and 12. As in other fields, planning for technical education continues to be dominated by labour needs assessments based on economic and structural planning, rather than a more functional assessment of real needs. In PNG 'there is ultimately a conflict between the demands and needs of the country to train a relatively small number of scientists and engineers . . . and the majority of the population who need an awareness of science . . . sufficient to allow them to more fully participate in the development of their traditional communities and to adopt appropriate technology'.[16]

Technical training in the region largely continues to be a reflection of technical training overseas, often on the recommendation of overseas advisors. A constructively critical approach to the use of overseas advice and resources is needed, with the primary goals of increasing local technological self-sufficiency and reducing overseas dependence.

Education and training facilities for technology and development around the region consist mainly of the descendants of technical institutes set up in the colonial days (Fiji Institute of Technology; Solomon Islands College of Higher Education, formerly Honiara Technical Institute; Lycee Technique in Vanuatu and Tarawa Technical Institute in Kiribati).[17] These technical institutes had the prime function of training technicians for colonial needs. Their successors continue to focus mainly on formal trades training, although some changes have taken place to update courses and approaches.

A welcome addition to technology education and training in the region is the PNG University of Technology (UniTech also accepts some regional students, and houses ATDI — the Appropriate Technology Development Institute). Other new or 'alternative' additions include education and training institutions in Fiji (the Centre for Appropriate Technology and Development, CATD), Tonga (the Community College) and Vanuatu (KITOW — the Kristian Institute of Technology, Weasisi), using formal and non-formal approaches. These have had mixed results — despite the significant German aid funding of CATD (reportedly over A$2m, mainly for buildings), the CATD programme of village technician training has had limited success, for reasons including poor participant selection (sons of village chiefs do not traditionally become manual workers) and the distribution of expensive electric tools to villages with no electric power. Apart from these institutions, there are few technical education and training centres in the region.

Other education and training institutions operate at a regional level. These include the University of the South Pacific — with an Institute of Rural Development in Tonga (which closed in 1991), Institute for Research, Training and Extension in Agriculture at the Alafua campus in Western Samoa, Institute of Marine Resources and Department of Technology in Suva and USP Extension Centres around the region. The South Pacific

Commission and Forum Secretariat are also involved in supporting shorter training workshops, as are international organisations — the UNDP, ILO, WHO and FAO. Although there are obvious needs for regional technology education and training, such programmes face problems relating to the high cost of regional travel and difficulty in follow-through and support. Apart from UniTech, there is an acute need for an education and training institution focussing on technology for development in the South Pacific.

Needs

Although much island education has an academic leaning, there is an increase in practical, basic technology subjects and non-formal educational techniques in post-primary schools. Technical subjects are, however, often taught as 'industrial arts', 'a singularly inappropriate title for most Pacific island countries with their basically non-industrial economies'.[18] Industrial arts, like 'domestic science' and 'home economics', hangovers from colonial days, may teach little about industry or the arts. Particular attitudinal changes are required regarding agricultural technology — 'The introduction of new crops, as well as new ways of producing the old, requires new skills as do supportive services and industries. The impact of development makes necessary more than just new technical know-how and skills, it also requires adjustment to new ways of living brought about by contact with the wider world'.[19]

An increase in technical education and training in the rural sector requires a future emphasis on shorter-term non-formal education. This emphasis should focus on disadvantaged areas and groups, 'even for the few who receive training, further technical advice and possibly training will be necessary. While this applies both to men and women, it is particularly the latter who will require special attention as their needs have frequently been overlooked'.[20]

There is a particular need for 'barefoot' engineers at village level. Training needs include both formal and informal education, training syllabi and approaches. The above general guidelines for training are very applicable to technology, complemented by the following considerations: 'Are technology maintenance, repair and spares services available locally? Provide information and train local people in the operation and maintenance of technology. Always try to evaluate "expert" advice. Attach local counterparts to overseas consultants to help transfer knowledge and experience'.[21]

Approaches

Various education and training approaches are required to most effectively address the above needs. Formal education for young people should be more practically focussed toward technical needs. Non-formal approaches should be used in the formal sector, and it is a good sign that this is happening, despite the inbuilt resistance of formal education systems to significant change (as noted above in Fiji DP9 — 'educating parents and pupils to appreciate the advantages of practical skills proved difficult'). The content, approach and status of 'industrial arts' need to be updated. This problem relates to the training of technical teachers in the region.

In the informal sector, for young people not in the formal education system and post-schoolers requiring basic or further training, non-formal education and training is the most relevant approach. Ideas such as 'village polytechnics' have been suggested for the training of barefoot engineers and similar personnel.[22] More seminars and courses should be available for in-service training in the rural/traditional and urban/modern sectors. Workshops for further training or retraining should preferably be held in-country, bringing the workshop to the people. Regional workshops are also useful, however, especially for comparing different national approaches. Overseas training is indicated in some instances, although increasing expertise is available in the island Pacific. In all training the selection of those participants to maximise gain is important. This depends primarily on real interest and connection with the subject of training, and ability to put theory into practice and communicate acquired knowledge.

* * * *

Education and training methods should include formal, informal and non-formal approaches, in longer and shorter, full and part-time courses and workshops, local, regional and overseas. Training must be relevant to real rather than anticipated needs, and avoid 'certificationism'. Education and training must be carefully tailored to suit needs in content, length and mode of delivery. The provision of improved training facilities and opportunities is a significant means through which rural-urban and overseas migration drift and brain-drain may be reduced.

Improved education and training, however, itself is often not enough — post-training follow-through and support is generally needed to make the most of education and training. Many valuable and stimulating training courses and workshops have been organised in the region, only for the participants to return to work or home to find that they cannot put what they have learnt into practice because of limited funds or interest.

TECHNOLOGY IN AGRICULTURE: AN OVERVIEW

R. KEITH LEONARD

Agricultural production in the Pacific is commonly divided into subsistence and commercial systems. Pure subsistence production involves the production, gathering or hunting of a variety of crop and animal products (together with food from the sea in coastal areas) for the nutrition and housing of the family or extended family unit.[1] In addition, subsistence production gives rise to a number of other useful products such as pandanus for basket making, paper mulberry for tapa production and so on. In pure subsistence production no surplus is produced for sale, although some products may be exchanged with other subsistence producers. Subsistence production operates outside the cash economy.

Commercial production, on the other hand, involves the production of a surplus of either traditional or introduced crops for sale. The commercial production can either be sold on the local market or exported. Cash is involved in commercial production. Pure commercial production involves selling all the product. In between subsistence and commercial production are many variations of semi-subsistence or semi-commercial production, where farmers produce both for their own needs and for the market.

Subsistence Production Systems
Subsistence production systems characteristically involve very low levels of inputs other than labour. Few, if any, cash inputs such as fertilisers, herbicides or pesticides are traditionally used. The main input apart from labour is planting material or seeds. While the digging sticks and stone axes

of former times have given way to the bush knives and metal spades of today, often not much else has changed in pure subsistence production systems.

It can be said, therefore, that subsistence production systems involve low levels of technology. Closer examination reveals that subsistence farming technology, while appearing quite simple, is in fact a carefully developed system which has evolved over a very long period of time in response to a particular set of environmental factors (such as climate and soil type).

Subsistence systems commonly involve mixing a number of species, including tree crops, root crops, annuals and perennials, in an apparently haphazard fashion on the same plot of land. After years promoting the virtues of mono-cropping and 'high technology' production systems, agricultural research and extension agencies in the South Pacific are now promoting agro-forestry and multi-cropping. Research is increasingly organised along farming-systems lines. Often these supposedly 'new' systems are remarkably similar to subsistence systems practised by farmers for centuries. This should not be surprising — subsistence systems evolved through an empirical process of observed trial and error in a system of traditional knowledge or folk science not unlike that of modern scientific research.

All crops require nutrients to grow. The roots of perennial species go deep and wide to gather nutrients leached downwards by the heavy tropical rainfall, while the falling branches and leaves result in a nutrient recycling system through the breakdown of organic matter into forms which can be reused by the plant. Annual crops, such as most of the root crops, have a short growing cycle and need a relatively good supply of nutrients in the surface layers of the soil. For this reason many subsistence production systems for short term crops involve the use of slash-and-burn or shifting cultivation, where a plot of bush or jungle is cleared, burnt and used for one or more plantings until the fertility is exhausted and a new plot is developed. The old plot is left to regenerate (revert to bush) during which time its fertility is restored through the actions of the tree species which re-establish themselves. Obviously the degree to which the fertility is restored depends on the length of the fallow time and the species which regenerate.

Traditional and Introduced Technology

In the same way that subsistence systems evolved through a process of trial and error, the choice of technology was also driven by what worked over a long period of time. The process of natural selection and refinement of systems by trial and error produced systems which gave a high chance of success. A subsistence farmer wants to minimise risk rather than maximise yield. Not producing enough means going hungry, while producing a surplus is of no particular value unless this can be stored against future periods of shortage. The attitude to risk explains why many small farmers are not interested in borrowing money to purchase inputs or in concentrating on a single cash crop when commercial agriculture projects, which have been proven to be financially viable, are introduced into the subsistence sector. The technology selected had to be reliable. Of course, before European contact the choice of technology was also driven by the limitations of locally available materials and tradeable resources.

Technology transfer in subsistence production was most commonly from generation to generation and family member to family member. While the rate of technological change was slow, new technologies were introduced from time to time as a result of voyages of discovery and trading. Even where contact did exist, the ability to transfer technology between regions was limited by environmental factors and the inability to modify or control these.

While subsistence production is a careful adaptation to a set of local conditions, problems exist. Subsistence production systems often have a relatively low yield per unit of land area. This is particularly so if the total area of land required for a slash-and-burn system to work properly is taken into account. This may involve an area of eight to twenty times the area actually cultivated in any one year. Rising populations put subsistence production systems under increasing pressure. Subsistence systems can cope to a certain extent with adverse conditions, but still suffer from droughts, cyclones, pests and diseases (often introduced) and other 'natural' disasters. Traditionally, there was limited technology to call on to deal with these problems.

As indicated, subsistence production generally requires a high labour input. In many areas of the Pacific there is now a deficiency of rural labour. In some cases this is an absolute shortage of labour, in other cases the shortage is due to the unwillingness of people to work in agriculture because of its low status and/or low returns. This places subsistence production systems under pressure, and is a principal reason why alternative technologies such as the use of mechanical cultivation and herbicides have now been incorporated into subsistence production systems.

Commercial Production Systems

Commercial production is the production of surplus crops for sale. The dynamic of commercial production is the need for cash. Most farmers in the Pacific now need money for a number of purposes, ranging from school fees to purchase of clothing and other consumer items. Countries need to generate foreign exchange to pay for imported items. As a result, governments promote the production of export crops, and rural people in the Pacific increasingly produce for the market, either for export or the domestic market. Commercial production of traditional food crops can be extended to the export of significant amounts, as illustrated by taro exports from Western Samoa to New Zealand.

Generally the first step made by smallholders towards commercial farming is the production of a surplus of food crops, which is sold in a local market. A small surplus can be produced using traditional technology. However, to produce a larger surplus (and so to generate more income), either a greater area must be cultivated or new technology utilised to increase output per unit area of land. While increasing the area is theoretically an option, in practice land is often not in plentiful supply. Also, traditional systems rely heavily on labour, and the ability to increase output by increasing the area cultivated runs into the problem of labour shortage. The use of new technology such as tractor cultivation and the use of pesticides is often the only viable option.

In addition to the production of a wide variety of traditional food crops, farmers in the Pacific also produce many other crops for sale on the domestic market, including stimulants such as betel nut, kava (also exported), as well as products for handicraft making. In the main, traditional technology is used in the production of these crops.

The first, and for some Pacific nations still the main crop commercialised for export production was coconut — with products including copra, coconut oil and desiccated coconut. The Pacific colonisers established large plantations for the production of copra. Production by smallholders was also encouraged. Today, copra production is no longer a particularly viable alternative, although it accounts for a considerable amount of the foreign exchange earnings of some countries. The technology adopted and still used is simple, consisting of planting, weed control (sometimes), fertilisation of young palms (sometimes), harvesting and drying. Few if any cash inputs are required, capital equipment is limited to a bush knife. Harvesting time is non-critical. The principal development of technology in coconut production has involved the introduction of hybrid varieties, biological control of pests, and production of intercrops such as cocoa and bananas.

Introduced Crops

While commercial farming can and does involve traditional crops, the great bulk of commercial agricultural production now involves non-traditional or introduced crops. In the Pacific these include sugar (Fiji), cocoa, coffee, rubber (Papua New Guinea), oil palm (Papua New Guinea), bananas (now almost non-existent as an export crop in the Pacific), together with a wide variety of minor crops including vegetables, vanilla, spices, tea, pepper and various fruits.

Cash crops have been introduced into smallholder systems and into the largeholder and estate sector. In Western Samoa an effort was made to revitalise the export banana industry based on a single large plantation. In Tonga, on the other hand, a significant effort was made to revitalise its banana industry through smallholder production. Coffee production in Papua New Guinea is largely in the hands of smallholder producers, while crops which require further processing (such as oil palm) often use a nucleus estate smallholder model of production. Whether introduced into the smallholder or estate sector, commercial production almost always involves monocropping (the main exception being the interplanting of coconut with a variety of crops).

Introduced cash crops have generally come with a complete package of technology, usually of the high-input/high-output model.[2] This production system aims at maximising output per unit area of land by the use of fertilisers, herbicides and a range of other agro-chemicals to control pests and diseases. Smallholders taking up cash crop production have often done so on the basis of low-input/low-output, thus many agricultural development projects have failed to achieve their target production levels.

The reasons why small farmers react in this way is due to a complex of factors involving attitude to risk, production for immediate needs and not for future wants and lack of adaptation of the introduced technology to local conditions. A multi-disciplinary study (sociological, technical and economic) may well reveal that smallholders make the right decision, from their points of view.

Technology of Commercial Production
As already indicated, the technology of commercial agricultural crop production was generally introduced to the Pacific along with the crop itself. For almost all these crops, the Pacific is an insignificant or very small producer in world terms. For this reason, Pacific nations cannot afford basic developmental research. Generally the most that is possible is aimed at adapting and testing technology developed elsewhere.

The technology of commercial production has been introduced into the Pacific by many different groups of people including colonialists, commercial entrepreneurs, development workers, technical consultants, expatriate lecturers, Pacific islanders studying overseas, agro-product salespeople and through a wide variety of written material. Within a country, the principal means chosen by most Pacific nations to diffuse agricultural technology through the rural sector is by an extension service, usually government-funded, but now increasingly involving commodity corporations and private management consultants.

The poor performance of government-funded extension services is widely blamed for the failure of smallholders to adopt new and supposedly better technology. While it is undoubtedly true that most extension services are underfunded and consist of large numbers of staff with deficient pre-service training and lacking in support, supervision and in-service training, the premise that small farmers' failure to adopt new technology is due largely to an ineffective extension service remains to be proven. It is the opinion of this author that other factors are equally if not more important. Some of the problems of commercial production in the Pacific are well illustrated by the failure of efforts to revive the once thriving export banana industries of Fiji, Tonga, Western Samoa and the Cook Islands.

The Banana Industry in Tonga

Records indicate that bananas were first exported from Tonga in 1953. Between that year and 1964 exports averaged 4600 tonnes per annum. In the five years between 1965 to 1969 production and exports increased dramatically, with exports averaging 14,000 tonnes per year. Peak production was achieved in 1967, with total exports of 20,700 tonnes (equivalent to over a million cartons). In 1970 production collapsed back to former levels. For the next 16 years production averaged only 2600 tonnes per year.

The experience of the Tongan export banana industry mirrored that of all other Pacific island producers. Up until the late sixties all New Zealand requirements were sourced from Fiji, Tonga, Western Samoa and the Cook Islands. New Zealand consumers only knew Pacific island bananas, a flavoursome, but mixed-ripe and often disfigured product, roughly handled and squashed into wooden boxes.

In the late 1960s, Pacific island banana production started to collapse. The collapse can be attributed to a number of factors but most important, at least initially, was the arrival of new diseases, particularly Black Leaf Streak (*Mycosphaerella fijiensis*). As a result, it became impossible to grow export standard bananas without a regular (every 10 to 14 days) and expensive spraying programme. Other diseases and pests also arrived or manifested themselves more strongly as the area in production increased. These included bunchy-top virus, nematodes and root borers. Other factors also had an effect, including inadequate industry organisation, the lack of a disciplined commercial approach to banana production by the growers, infrequent and unreliable shipping, the vagaries of the climate (droughts and cyclones particularly) and, in the 1970s at least, the lack of support from the importer.

With the collapse of Pacific island banana industries, imports of bananas from Ecuador and the Philippines exposed the New Zealand consumer to a totally different type of banana, produced largely by multinational corporations, a banana more bland in taste but larger and with almost no skin imperfections and no mixed-ripe. This rapidly became the standard to which any producer had to aspire.

Bananas had been formerly grown using simple technology with little requirement for agrochemicals. Large areas were planted and weeded by hand and the resultant crop harvested and packed into wooden boxes for shipment. Subsequently, the industry not only had to cope with a variety of pests and diseases which required expensive and timely control measures, but also it had to compete with a visually much more pleasing product from Ecuador and the Philippines. This too required that the industry pay much more attention to quality control to eliminate scab-moth damaged fruit, sap staining, bruising and mixed-ripe. The wooden box (produced locally) had to give way to the cardboard carton (imported) and a whole range of new technology was introduced.

A number of reviews and studies during the 1970s recommended the steps necessary to revitalise the Tongan export banana industry. Two schemes, with largely local funding, were implemented during these years, with little result in terms of improved export production.[3] In 1979 a study of the banana export industry in Tonga was published. This outlined a programme to develop a viable export industry. The Tonga Banana Export Revitalisation Scheme, with funding of NZ$5,000,000 over five years, was launched in 1982/83. The project provided technical assistance (in post-harvest handling, project management and production), capital equipment (trucks, project and extension vehicles, sprayers), subsidies on selected areas of disease control costs and price support. Both the price support and the disease control subsidies were phased out over the five year period.

Although the project showed many encouraging signs of success during its operation, and introduced many valuable ideas to aid commercial agricultural production, it failed in the fundamental objective of re-establishing a viable export banana industry in Tonga. Once again there are various reasons for this failure but these are the most important:

1. Towards the end of the project the New Zealand Government ended the arrangement whereby Tongan bananas had guaranteed access to the New Zealand market.
2. The Tongan Government failed to take key decisions regarding industry structure and operation.

3.   The project was based only in southern Tonga (Tongatapu and 'Eua) where it suffered the effects of several cyclones and droughts, as well as extended periods of low temperature.

The question that also remains unanswered is whether the technology adopted was appropriate. From the crop budgets and monitoring carried out, it was clear that banana production was financially attractive for growers, and certainly there was never a shortage of willing producers. Lower cost and lower risk production models could have been explored. For example, the economics of phased production (to minimise the risks from the cyclone season) to serve the New Zealand market for a more limited period of the year could have been assessed. If the main reasons given above for the project failing to achieve its objectives are correct, then it would appear that external factors were largely to blame rather than the technology used.

The Way Forward
It is increasingly recognised that the technology adopted for agricultural production must be appropriate — but appropriate for whom? The farmer has certain objectives, such as income maximisation, reduction of risk and assurance of food supply. A country may wish to improve the level of nutrition of its people, reduce the import bill of fossil fuels and agricultural chemicals and reduce pollution and health hazards from agricultural production. Future generations have a right to receive resources not depleted by unsustainable practices of previous generations. The objectives of each group can and do involve conflicts in technology selection, and most certainly this is the case between groups.

Determining the appropriate mix of technology for agriculture will require compromise. The process will be on-going, as new problems arise and technology changes. The important need for Pacific island nations is to put in place the systems and institutional framework which will allow conscious choices to be made about what technology is best or most appropriate for use in particular social, economic, environmental and related contexts. The following points may provide some guidance.

Control on the Use of Pesticides
All countries should have legislation which allows for the control of importation, distribution and application of agricultural chemicals. The responsibility for overseeing the practical working of the pesticide legislation should rest with a national pesticide agency. A committee made up of relevant government officials (agriculture, health, planning), industry representatives and environmental or consumer group representatives is more appropriate for small countries. For larger countries, an agency with a small full-time staff may be needed.

For small countries it is probably not possible to require registration of agricultural chemicals because it will not be worth the company's time to incur the cost of registration for the small market involved. The countries of the region may wish, however, to develop some common registration standards which would see certain products registered for regional use. As well as being involved in regulation, agencies or committees should have responsibility for promoting awareness of safe use of agricultural chemicals and the recognition and treatment of pesticide poisoning.

Control on the Entry of New Pests and Diseases

The countries of the Pacific are islands and as such have a natural barrier against the arrival of new pests and diseases. In order to avoid the need of having to make difficult choices on the introduction of new technology with possible harmful and costly secondary effects, it is well worth while spending some money avoiding the problem by having an effective agricultural quarantine system and service.

Evaluation of Alternative Models of Agricultural Production

The planning or economics units in the Departments of Agriculture have a role to play in defining alternative production models for the crops grown in the country in order to ensure the production models chosen are economically and financially appropriate. A range of options should be analysed including high input/high output, low input/low output and intermediate stages.

Research into Appropriate Agricultural Technology

The Pacific region needs appropriate technology and the research and development of that technology. While technology can be transferred from outside the region, it is important that this be validated as appropriate for regional conditions and demonstrated to encourage its adoption. It is vital, therefore, that resources and direction be provided to regional institutions such as the Institute for Research, Extension and Training in Agriculture (IRETA) and Institute for Rural Development (IRD) of the University of the South Pacific (USP), and the South Pacific Commission, so that they can carry out this task.

It must be recognised that resources are limited. A strong case can be made, however, for greater funding for research in appropriate technology as a means of reducing the great waste of scarce investment capital which is directed towards inappropriate technology, many examples of which can be found in the Pacific.

Training in Appropriate Agricultural Technology

Similarly, training in the concepts and specifics of appropriate technology is required at all levels, not only as 'stand-alone' training but also incorporated into mainstream agriculture, economics, health and other related courses.

Debate on Appropriate Technology

Finally, it must be recognised that what is appropriate for one country, village or person is not necessarily appropriate for another. Also, what may be appropriate for society may also be prejudicial for some individuals within that society. A national consensus must evolve regarding the development direction countries wish to follow. This requires an informed population and an active debate on issues relating to appropriate technology and development.

AGRICULTURAL MECHANISATION:
TRACTORS AND TECHNOLOGY CHOICE IN TONGA

TEVITA H. MOENGANGONGO

◆◆◆

Prior to European contact, agriculture in the Pacific was essentially subsistence production for household consumption. Agriculture consisted of a set of sub-systems of activities and production which included the gathering of land and marine resources, hunting, the cultivation of root crops, tree crops and raising of livestock.[1] Technologies were simple, focussing more on land preparation and planting techniques than food processing and preservation. Nevertheless, early explorers reported some complex and well-planned systems of traditional agriculture. Captain Cook depicted Tongan agriculture as well laid-out plantations linked by an intricate pattern of roads.[2] Brookfield has described the early culture of taro, which frequently required terracing for irrigation.[3] Mulching was also commonly practised.

The major change in agricultural technology in the Pacific relates primarily to land preparation techniques. The choice of technology varies from country to country, depending on local agricultural and other conditions. In most, agricultural technologies have been fully imported, while in others local adaptations and some manufacturing have taken place. This chapter will introduce a case study of agricultural mechanisation to examine a strategy adopted to meet the particular demands of smallholder farmers for mechanised land preparation. The case study is of the hiring of tractors (with driver/operators) to smallholder farmers through the establishment of the machinery pool within the Ministry of Agriculture, Fisheries and Forestry (MAFF) in Tonga.

Whilst the possible use of tractors applies mainly to those countries with soil, landholding and other conditions suited to their use, and the alternative use of draught animals applies specifically to those countries with horses or buffalo (Tonga, Western Samoa and Fiji), the study illustrates general issues of technology choice and transfer across the Pacific.

Land Preparation

Traditional slash-and-burn land preparation in Tonga relied firstly on stone axes for land clearance and burning. This method does not disturb the soil, and loses a lot of organic matter through burning. The use of stone axes for slashing has given way at the household and small farmer level to steel bush-knives and axes. Steel spades and digging forks have also replaced planting sticks. At the larger commercial level, hand tools have given way to mechanised chainsaws and tractors equipped with slashers and ploughs. The bush-knife (cane-knife, or machete; with a blade about 80cm long, sharpened on one edge and wooden handle) is used for clearing small shrubs. Axes, either one-handed (hatchet, tomahawk or chopper) or larger two-handed versions, are used for clearing larger trees.

Small holder planting methods employ traditional and modified-traditional hand tools. The planting of taro (*Colocasia esculenta*) for example, still uses sticks, although these have generally been modified with the attachment of a metal tip. This saves time normally wasted in having to stop occasionally to sharpen the end of the stick. The sharp oval-shaped spade (100–150mm wide, thought to be derived from the blubber knives of the old whaling days), with a long, straight heavy shaft (often of galvanised water pipe) is used for planting and digging yam. The steel digging fork is a multi-purpose tool, used for planting many of the root crops.

Mechanisation

Tractor-Based Land Preparation

More recently, tractor-based mechanised land preparation has become popular among the larger, commercialised farming community. In most island countries, the transition to larger, mechanised agriculture did not go through the stage of using draught animal power (with the exception of Fiji, where Indo-Fijian farmers introduced bullocks for ploughing and related land preparation practices). The main advantage of using tractors for land preparation is that tractors can cultivate a large area in a short time. However, tractors have the disadvantages of high capital input and high operating cost — which 90% of Tongan farmers cannot afford.

Animal Power — an Alternative to Tractors?

Because of the rapidly escalating price of fuel in the late 1970s, MAFF decided to establish an Appropriate Technology Section (ATS) with the primary purpose of developing a low-cost method of land preparation, using draught animals, particularly horses, first introduced by missionaries, and still relatively common in rural Tonga. The use of draught animals for land preparation has various advantages, including low capital input and maintenance costs. Apart from availability, Tongan farmers also have experience in handling horses, and horse-drawn land preparation techniques cause little soil compaction, compared to tractors.

The Machinery Pool in Tonga

In the early 1970s MAFF established a machinery pool, consisting of a few tractors (equipment and driver) for hire by smallholder farmers. At the time, there was a desire to increase both the area of land under cultivation and productivity — primarily through increased mechanisation. The main reason for establishing the pool was the prohibitively high capital cost of farm mechanisation for smallholder farmers. By 1976, 25–30% of the total demand for mechanised land preparation was met by the pool.[4] To meet the demand, government acquired 20 tractors, 5 sets of disc ploughs (3-disc; 1.0m diameter discs), and 5 sets of tandem disc harrows. This equipment was supplied through New Zealand and Australian aid (New Zealand was the main donor to the machinery pool programme).

At the time of establishment, all the tractors and equipment were located at a central depot, from where they were driven by MAFF driver/operators to the work sites every morning, and returned at the end of the day. Some tractors, complete with equipment, travelled from 20 to 30 kilometres on sealed and dirt roads before reaching their destination. On an average day, a tractor performed 3.5 hours of useful work, and spent 4 to 5 hours travelling — around 40% of total time was spent on tillage operations. The driver/operators were paid between A$5 and A$6 a day.

In 1976, farmers hired the tractors and equipment, with driver/operator, at the rate of A$5 an hour. By 1980, the rate was increased to $8 per hour, due to rapidly increasing operating costs. However, this rate was still heavily subsidised by the Tongan Government. To operate the machinery pool at a break-even point, the rate should have been doubled — to A$15 an hour.[5]

Performance of the Pool

During the period 1986–89, the machinery pool, with 16 tractors and full stock of farm equipment, performed at close to full commercial operation on Tongatapu, while the service continued to be subsidised on the outer islands. The 1989 rate for hiring the tractor and equipment was $18 per hour, which was still below a fully commercial rate. While the hire charge meets the operating and maintenance cost (spare parts, labour and fuel), it does not cover the administration costs, and more importantly, the replacement cost of the equipment.

The selection of tractors and equipment was not based on technological or economic information, but trial and error. The mouldboard plough does not suit Tongan conditions, as the ploughshare is easily caught in tree stumps or roots. The disc plough is better suited, and can chop up grass and other plant materials, and furthermore can roll over tree stumps and roots.

Whether to buy a tractor or not is a major decision facing smallholder farmers in many countries in the Pacific. The cost of a tractor (MF 365), a disc plough (3 disc) and tandem disc harrow is around A$43,000. The price of a tractor starts from around A$27,000 (MR 135) for a tractor of 87 kilowatts. In terms of brand, Massey Ferguson tractors were found to be the most durable in the Tongan conditions,[6] although various other brands have yet to be properly evaluated.

Choice of Technology

The demand for the use of tractors and machinery for land preparation is increasing, despite the fact that the hiring rate is being increased to commercial rates, and to meet increasing costs.

Tractor Selection

When the machinery pool was originally set up in the early 1970s, the tractors used were Massey Ferguson 135 and Ford 3000, both with engine power of around 55kw. At the time, the need for tillage was not so great, and tractors were used more for transport. The demand for tillage has since increased rapidly, and with it the need for bigger tractors. Most of the tractors now used continue to be Massey Ferguson (165, 265 and and 365) and Ford (4600 and 6600), with engine power ranging from 85—100 kilowatts.

Equipment Selection

Both mouldboard and disc ploughs, mounted on three-point linkages, were initially introduced. Currently, disc ploughs are more common, with disc harrows used for secondary tillage. The commonly used disc ploughs are tractor-mounted units with 3 discs, each of around 1.0m diameter. For the disc harrows, the tandem type is most common, with four gangs of 560 mm diameter scalloped discs.

The slasher found to be most effective in Tongan conditions is a rotary type around 1.5m wide, using a flail chain. A flail-chain type works better on small shrubs and tall grass than the plain-blade type, which is prone to breakage when cutting thick tall grasses or hitting tree stumps.

Reflections on the Pool

It was initially intended to privatise the machinery pool during the period of Tonga's Fourth Five-Year Development Plan, 1980–85. It was soon realised, however, that this was not possible — private operators, charging $18 per hour, could not compete with the subsidised rates of MAFF, as evidenced by the number of private-hire businesses that had failed. As the government still wished to extend the areas under agriculture and improve production through mechanisation, it was decided that the MAFF machinery pool would continue, but should progress towards commercial operation during the period of the Fifth Five-Year Development Plan, 1985–90.

It was expected that the machinery pool would be running on a fully commercial basis by 1990, with no subsidy from government. The hourly hiring rate was calculated to need increasing to $25, for the pool to become commercial. It is projected that the rate at the end of the Sixth Five-Year Development Plan period (1995) will be $32 an hour.

Based on a study in 1980,[7] the percentage of the time spent performing effective work on tillage operations at that date had been increased to 75% (from 40% in 1976). Table 1 presents information regarding the operational hours and economics of the machinery pool from 1986–89. At this time, more than 2800 hectares was cultivated every year using hired tractors and equipment from the pool, and the average area cultivated per person was 0.6 hectares. Another study in 1985 revealed that 40% of the households in Tongatapu depended on the pool for land preparation.[8] It is apparent from Table 1 that the operations of the pool are levelling at a peak of around 10,000 hours annually. Referring to Table 2, it is also apparent that the private ownership of tractors is increasing, indicating an increasing demand for mechanised land preparation. (Tables 3.2.1 and 3.2.2 appear at the end of this chapter).

Discussion

Animal Power

The use of horse-power did not gain much support from the farming community, mainly for the following reasons:

1. Horses do not have enough power to do the initial breaking of the ground, and lack manoeuvrability (initial ploughing is often of very rough ground, with 1.5m tall Guinea grass — *Panicum maximum*).
2. Extra work is required to look after the animal.

3.   Farmers were reluctant to go back to animal-drawn equipment, which they felt was a backward step.

Problems with the Machinery Pool Tractors

In setting-up the machinery pool, various major problems were initially encountered, which included:

1.   A lack of back-up services such as a fully equipped workshop and qualified or experienced mechanics, and constraints in the availability of spare parts.

2.   The supply of inappropriate equipment from aid donors — for example, a 5-disc reversible plough, which required bigger and more powerful tractors of at least 120 kw, that were not available in Tonga (the discs were later converted to barbecue plates); some of the equipment needed modification to suit local conditions, but no experienced staff were available to make necessary changes — for example, modifying the tail wheel of disc ploughs, and adjusting the weights on disc harrows.

3.   Relatively unskilled drivers — a lack of operator skill resulted in equipment that was often incorrectly set up or adjusted, this led to high incidences of breakages of tractor arms and also increased tractor power requirements; also, as the initial breaking is done when the soil is wet, low operator skill results in greater compaction and crusting.

4.   Driver/operator abuse of the system — largely due to the low pay of A$5–A$6 a day, driver/operators were found to attempt to complete their officially allocated work in as little time as possible, to enable them to undertake 'unofficial' work, for which they were paid on the side. To do this, they would speed from work site to work site, and turn corners with the plough still in the ground. Both practices, because of metal fatigue from vibration and increased stress, resulted in high breakage to the equipment.

5.   Many of the above problems arose because of a lack of experienced personnel to manage the machinery pool.

Problem Resolution and Prospects for the Machinery Pool

Realising the problems, New Zealand, the main donor to the machinery pool, reconsidered the programme. This led to the setting-up of a workshop depot, store and the supply of spare parts (rather than the replacement of tractors). An agricultural engineer, a mechanical supervisor and a mechanic were also provided to facilitate the maintenance and modification of equipment, and a short-term instructor to train the drivers in handling the tractors and equipment. Tongan trainee mechanics were also sent for specialised training to the Ford and Massey Ferguson factories in Australia and New Zealand.

In the meantime, MAFF also undertook some reorganisation of the operation of the machinery pool to alleviate the problems. Three decentralised bases were set up in rural-outer Tongatapu to reduce travelling time of tractors operating in those areas. A bonus system of pay was also introduced, where the driver was to receive 35% of the gross hire fee, after the deduction of fuel and maintenance costs. This was mainly to encourage driver/operators to be more responsible for their tractor and equipment and to discourage 'unofficial' work — the driver/operator would subsequently receive less bonus if they incurred higher than average fuel and repair costs, or if the tractor spent a higher than average down-time in the workshop undergoing repairs for driver/operator-induced faults.

The last ten years, from 1980—90, have seen the biggest increase in demand for use of mechanised equipment for land preparation, and in the number of individuals who own tractors. The increase in demand is due to several factors:

1. The decreasing supply and increasing cost of farm labour (largely due to the attitude of local people regarding the low status of agricultural work).
2. Increase in the number of part-time farmers (who can only spend weekends on their smallholding).
3. A shift away from solely subsistence to a semi-commercial agriculture.
4. The greater availability of loans from the Tongan Development Bank.

* * * *

On an individual basis, farm mechanisation in Tonga cannot be justified. Each landholding is around 3 hectares, and the average area cultivated per person per annum is less than 1 hectare, with an average equivalent input of approximately 4 hours of hand tillage per week. At these levels of smallness, and with the capital cost of a tractor plus equipment at around A$13,000 per hectare, the individual ownership of a tractor is completely uneconomic, and the tractor and equipment would be grossly under-utilised. The machinery pool therefore offers an alternative which allows smallholder farmers to participate in commercial-subsistence agriculture.

The MAFF machinery pool is one of only two hired machinery pools in the South Pacific (the other at the Ministry of Agriculture on Rarotonga in the Cook Islands). Although the operation is not charging full commercial rates, there is potential for it to be self-supporting. The operation has highlighted many of the problems that need to be confronted in establishing such a scheme. Several areas that require to be examined prior to setting up such an operation are:

1. A feasibility study to evaluate the economics of the operation.
2. The suitability of the introduced technology for local conditions, and the acceptance of this technology by small holder farmers.
3. The availability of local resources, especially of required labour and skills inputs.

While the operation has yet to become fully commercial, it is progressing well in this direction, and has accomplished much in 15 years. In view of the success of the project in assisting smallholder farmers with their land preparation, there are many lessons to be learnt and the operation can be used as a model of technology transfer for adoption by other small island states of the South Pacific.

Table 3.2.1: Operation of the Machinery Pool (a)

Year	Total Effective Working Hours	Revenue Collected	Operational Cost	Surplus (b)
1986	8,769	146,929	125,109	21,820
1987	10,544	189,972	109,155	80,817
1988	10,530	188,359	115,709	72,650
1989(c)	7,776	155,300	131,456	23,844

a.   Figures are for Tongatapu only; all A$.

b.   Operational cost does not include element for replacement cost or depreciation of equipment.

c.   Figures for 9 months (January–September).

Table 3.2.2: Private Sector Tractor Ownership (a)

Year	Number of Tractors
1980	35
1985	60
1986	75
1987	80
1988	80
1989	95

a.   Figures from the Annual Reports of the Ministry of Police and Prisons.

TECHNOLOGY, FOOD AND FOOD PROCESSING

SUSAN PARKINSON AND BILL AALBERSBERG

An old man in a Fijian village, when irked by a meeting discussing development, said, 'What kind of development are you talking about? The only development I know is that the cooking pots must not be empty'.[1] This statement represents a widely held view of the role of economic development as related to food production and technology throughout the South Pacific countries. In reality, food technology has been widely used even in subsistence agricultural societies, and its use is increasing as these societies change to market economies. This chapter will look at both kinds of food technology in the South Pacific.

The traditional Pacific diet consists predominantly of root vegetables (such as taro and sweet potato), starchy fruits (such as cooking banana and breadfruit), coconuts, fresh fish and green leaves. Various bush nuts and fruits supplement this diet. During the past 50 years, urban migration has often cut families off from traditional lands and made them reliant on the cash economy. European contact brought along with it changing patterns of food production, distribution and consumption. In general, this has caused people to move away from traditional agricultural and food preservation methods and the consumption of locally grown foods.

As a consequence, there has been an increased reliance on imported foods. Modern diets contain more cereals, canned meat, fish, sugar, salt and fat. The nutritional differences between traditional and Westernised eating patterns, include increased energy from fats, sugar, refined starches and alcohol, accompanied by a decreased intake of fibre, vitamins and minerals. The rapid change in food consumption patterns in most Pacific island countries is considered to be an important contributing factor to the increased incidence of noncommunicable diseases such as diabetes, high blood pressure and heart disease now occurring throughout the region.[2]

Traditional Methods of Food Preservation Technology

In traditional Pacific Island diets the carbohydrate root crops and fruits provided the staple foods, and most food technology has been associated with the preservation of these crops. In times of drought, hurricanes or wars, stores of preserved carbohydrate foods prevented starvation. These foods also enabled sailors to make long voyages and villagers to accumulate surpluses to meet economic and cultural obligations.

Preservation techniques were particularly well developed in the low rainfall atolls and on leeward sides of high islands. Thus in Kiribati and other Micronesian countries, techniques exist for preserving most kinds of sea foods and nearly all the crops and wild foods grown on the atolls. In the more productive islands the only foods preserved to any extent were the staple carbohydrate roots, fruits, nuts and fish. In general preservation strategies involved lowering water content through drying, smoking or baking; salting; acidification by fermentation; sterilisation and the exclusion of air through close packaging.

Food Preservation in the Field

The deterioration of mature root crops is delayed in the field for various lengths of time without affecting quality. In Tonga, farmers aim to have some mature crops underground throughout the year. These are harvested as required. Sweet potato and some yams can be harvested from the same plant twice, whilst mature giant and common taro (*Xanthosoma* and *Alocasia*) are left in the soil for up to six months.[3]

Post Harvest Preservation

Yam (*Discorea*) and taro (*Alocasia*) corms are kept for six months in dry, well ventilated storage houses. Yams are placed upright whilst *Alocasia* and *Xanthosoma* are stored horizontally on racks, great care being taken not to damage the roots. Sweet potatoes are sprinkled with ashes and kept in the same way for up to four weeks. Cassava and wild yams (*Discorea nummularia*) will stay fresh for six months if placed in heaps and covered with grass or banana leaves and soil, under conditions which keep the roots alive. The life of breadfruit is extended for several days through storage under water which slows down the respiration of the fruits.[4]

Drying

This is an important preservation method in all countries. Both raw and cooked foods are dried in the sun or on racks suspended over low burning fires. Foods sliced or grated are laid on plaited bamboo or corrugated iron. The dried material is pounded to make a coarse flour, and later reconstituted and boiled to replace fresh staples or made into porridges or doughs. In spite of long processing, these food products retain useful amounts of the B vitamins whilst carotene is still present in pandanus foods.[5]

In the Federated States of Micronesia and in Kiribati, cooked breadfruit is pounded and spread thinly on mats and dried to the desired consistency. The sheets of dried paste are then rolled tightly and wrapped in pandanus leaves. Formerly this food provided an important reserve. Today it is mainly used for ceremonial gifts. Also, in these countries pandanus fruits are cooked, and the soft ends grated to make a pulp which is spread out on pandanus leaf mats and dried in the sun or on hot stones to a date-like consistency. The mixture is then made into large rolls which are wrapped in pandanus leaves. This product also provides a reserve food and is used for ceremonial gifts. It has a pleasant date-like flavour. The cooked pulp is also enriched with coconut palm syrup and then dried on small leaf mats. The firm pulp is toasted on hot stones until crisp and pounded to a powder. Formerly this food was the mainstay of long sea voyages; today it is included in drinks and puddings. It is stored in pandanus leaf tubes or closed containers.

Cooking

Cooking itself is a method of food preservation. Besides roasting food on hot stones or embers, two methods specific to the Pacific islands are cooking in earth ovens and in segments of bamboo. In making an earth oven, stones are heated over burning logs in a shallow pit. Prepared roots and breadfruit are cooked on the stones. Other foods like meat, fish and vegetables are carefully wrapped in softened banana leaves and placed in the appropriate part of the oven. When all is ready, the oven is covered with layers of banana and other leaves and finally sealed with sacks and earth. Food cooked in the oven is subjected to high temperatures. The steam pressure which builds up inside the wrapped foods has a sterilising effect. Parcels of food cooked this way will last for 4–5 days if unopened. Root crops last longer if previously dipped in salt water.

Bamboo cooking is popular in the inland areas of Fiji and the Solomon Islands. Food is placed inside a section of fresh bamboo. The end is sealed with plugs of banana leaves and an additional leaf is tied over the opening. The bamboo is then rotated over hot coals till the outside is brown. Bamboo containers are stored above the cooking fires. This is considered to be a good way of preserving meat and fish. Fat seals the inside of the container and a vacuum probably occurs on cooling.

Two interesting methods of food preservation also provided sweetening before the advent of sugar. One is the baking of *Cordyline terminalis* root. After cooking for several days in an earth oven the roots become caramel coloured with a sweet taste. In Kiribati, sap obtained from the spathe of the coconut flower is evaporated to form a thick syrup. Traditionally this took place in coconut cups, but today large enamel basins of sap are heated over open fires. The syrup, 'kamaimai', is used to sweeten food and drinks. It is stored in bottles, which are an important item of exchange. 'Kamaimai' has a similar sweetness to maple syrup.[6]

Fermentation

A technology unique to the Pacific is the process of fermentation in pits to store large quantities of breadfruit, taro, banana or cassava. These fermented pastes, buried in leaf-lined pits, could be stored for a few months or many years. It is likely that this procedure was introduced into the region by the Lapita people as long ago as 3000 years ago.

The method is practised throughout the Pacific region with some variation. In most places banana leaves with the central rib removed are made soft and pliable in the sun. The pits are first lined with dry banana leaves and then the folded, softened banana leaves are used as an inside lining. Pits are usually dug in a shaded area with good drainage. The size depends on the amount of food to be preserved. The banana leaves are overlapped and extended over the top of the pit to later fold over the food. Two or three layers of banana leaves are considered essential to properly seal the pit. The washed, peeled carbohydrate food is placed in the pit, the banana leaves folded over tightly and dried leaves placed on top and weighed down with stones.

The food, which was usually well fermented after three to four weeks, became soft. Due to the acidic conditions that had developed it could be safely left in the pit or removed as needed. Usually food that was removed was replaced by fresh supplies, thus providing a sort of batch fermentation. As the leaves that were used to line the pits decayed, the material was removed, fresh leaves substituted and the food replaced. Food removed from the pit was washed, partially sun-dried and pounded before cooking. Longer sun drying and pounding produced a flour-like meal that could be kept for years.[7] Different islands use variations of the fermentation process. Breadfruit may be pierced with a stick, baked or soaked in fresh or salt water before burying in the pit. These procedures seem to start the fermentation process. Sometimes the partially fermented breadfruit is pounded before burying.

Another method is to soak prepared roots in water till completely fermented. The product is similar to that derived from pit fermentation. Material fermented in water may also be stored in the fermentation pits.

Preserved Foods

Starch Making
Europeans arriving in Fiji and the Polynesian islands in the nineteenth century considered starch making to be one of the few activities of the Pacific islanders which had economic potential. The arrowroot plant was widely cultivated for this purpose. Roots were peeled, grated and then soaked in water and strained through coconut fibre. The liquid was left to settle and the supernatant fluid poured off. The remaining starch was sun dried and stored in baskets. Today, cassava is used to make starch in Fiji and Tonga; Niue and some atoll countries still use arrowroot.

Flours and Meals
Dried raw, cooked and fermented root crops and breadfruit are used to make these products. The dried prepared food is pounded to form a powder or a coarse meal-like product. Both types are used to thicken dishes and to make infant and invalid foods. The flour is also mixed with coconut cream and then wrapped in leaves and cooked to make various 'puddings'.

Fish and Shellfish
Fish and shellfish are dried in all areas. Fish is gutted, split and laid flat on a mat, rack or roofing iron. Shellfish are threaded onto coconut mid-ribs and dried in the same way. The smoking of fish and shellfish is also widespread.

Fruit and Green Leaves
These foods are dried in the low rainfall atolls of Southern Kiribati. Fruits like pawpaw and pumpkin are sliced, but the berry-like fruits of 'te bero' (*Ficus tinctoria*) and the leaves of 'te boi' (*Portulaca*) are dried whole.

Nuts
Various bush nuts of the *Canarium*, *Terminalia* and *Barringtonia* species provide important sources of fat and protein in the Solomon Islands and Vanuatu. Nuts are shelled, dried over a fire or in the sun and then stored in sealed containers, bamboo tubes or woven baskets, which are stacked on racks above cooking fires.

Current Use of Original and Adapted Traditional Technologies

The use of many of the food preservation techniques described above is declining for a number of reasons. Improved transportation and communication infrastructure and the ready availability of foreign aid after natural disasters have eliminated the threat of starvation in the Pacific islands and obviated the need for storage of large amounts of preserved foods. Refrigeration exists in many modern urban households (although not in so many rural households) and is used to preserve a wide variety of foods. Introduced foods such as rice and flour have a longer storage life than most traditional crops. Many of the traditional preservation methods are quite labour- and material-intensive, and are therefore less likely to be used by urban islanders or farmers involved in cash cropping. Short-term methods are still practised to preserve carbohydrate staples and fish until these can be consumed, or sold in the markets or abroad.

In some cases, the availability of new materials has led to modification of old methods or the development of new ideas. For example, sheets of polythene plastic may be used to replace the banana leaf lining in fermentation pits, thus reducing the time and labour involved in the process by 80%. Some new ways of preserving root crops, which incorporate similar principles to those used in traditional methods, have proved successful. Freshly harvested taro corms (the edible underground part of the taro), with 4–6 cm stalk attached, are placed in plastic bags. When the top is tied, retained humidity keeps the corm alive for up to 6 weeks.

Cassava roots, cleaned within a few hours of harvesting, are put in plastic bags and treated with a thiobenzadole-based fungicide. This process, which cures the roots, and prevents deterioration, proved successful in Colombia for extending shelf life to 2–3 weeks and could be of value in the Pacific Islands.[8] Research in Fiji showed that freshly harvested cassava could be kept in good condition for up to eight weeks when packed in damp sawdust. Good results depended on choice of variety. Mean deterioration at 8 weeks, in 6 varieties, varied between 43.3–94.8%.[9]

The easy availability of commercially produced salt makes salting of fish a simpler preservation method than in former times. New ways of making more efficient smokers for fish preservation have also been widely disseminated throughout the islands. Smoked and salted fish is now more available in Fiji's urban centres.

Traditional processes such as the earth oven are still widely practised as they are central to island culture and probably the most economical ways to prepare food for large numbers of people.

Fermentation processes are still in practice in some islands, as the unusual taste of the product is relished. Examples are 'poi' production in Hawaii, 'bila' in Fiji and 'bwiru' of the Marshall Islands. However, traditional practices are fast disappearing in many countries.

Food Technology Currently in Use and Potential Future Developments

The situation in the Pacific is quite diverse, as the larger countries such as Fiji, Hawaii and Papua New Guinea have food processing plants that provide products for export, hotels and local markets, especially for import substitution. In the smaller islands little modern food processing is done. In this section we will look at both village-based food technologies and commercial processing.

In the Village

Many of the food preparations in the village involve the scraping or grating of starchy crops or coconuts. Metal tools have replaced sharp shells for these purposes, but there has been little mechanisation. Possible reasons for this include a lack of knowledge regarding hand-powered alternatives, the availability of sufficient time, a desire to maintain traditional practices or the fact that food processing, usually women's work, has not been regarded as a problem, and has therefore not attracted much technological interest. Low cost technologies have been developed in Asia and Africa to perform these processes more quickly, easily and conveniently. It would be possible to use such machines to provide packaged grated roots and coconut for urban working women who desire these traditional preparations, but lack the time to prepare them.

Flour forms a major part of the diet of many Pacific islands, even on remote islands. Inter-island ships are always loaded down with bags of flour. Procedures have been developed to prepare most flour products using cassava or breadfruit flour instead of wheat flour. These flours can be prepared by either finely slicing the crop or fermentating it followed by sun drying. Inexpensive mills (either manually or electrically powered) could be used to prepare the flour. Knowledge of these simple machineries and their potential use is negligible in the Pacific.

The substitution of tropical root crop and breadfruit flours for part of the wheat content of bread, has been well researched.[10] In 1986, a major flour milling company in Fiji indicated an interest in using cassava to replace 10–15% of the wheat content of flour. The development of the project depended on an adequate supply of cassava, at a price competitive with wheat, and a low cost method of preserving large quantities of roots prior to drying. Research in Fiji had shown that raw peeled cassava retained flour-making qualities for up to 4 weeks when held under anaerobic conditions. It was suggested that cassava be put into large sealed pits or tanks. During early fermentation the cellular structure of the roots would break down, releasing moisture. The soft mass could be removed from containers, drained and dried. Drying time is greatly reduced by the fermentation process. Flour produced from a 4-week fermentation was added at a 10% level to wheat flour for testing by a local bakery. The resulting bread was found to be well risen, to have a good crumb consistency, and to make good toast.[11]

The study illustrates how a low cost traditional preservation method could be used to solve a modern food storage problem. Unfortunately the flour millers did not proceed with the project. Cassava grown without mechanisation is not cost-competitive with highly subsidised wheat flour. However, information derived from the research was disseminated through extension teaching to domestic and small commercial bakers.

Other experiments have shown that good bread could be made when raw grated cassava or cooked grated breadfruit is used to replace 10–20% of wheat flour in bread making. Loaves were found to remain fresh for longer than the usual all-wheat bread. In 1985–86 bakeries in Fiji and Tonga made the cassava bread for a time. It is likely that the process would have continued if bakeries could have obtained supplies of ready grated cassava. Indian people often replace part of the wheat content of roti (flat bread) recipes with sorghum, maize and cassava flours. The Food and Agriculture Organisation in Rome has developed a method for a 100% cassava loaf.

Commercial Food Products

As mentioned earlier, there is extensive use of food technology to process local produce, mainly to substitute for imports, but also for export. This activity, however, is generally limited to the larger islands of the Pacific. There is also a significant amount of food processing and production based on imported materials. This is often unfortunate, given the available local produce, which is generally nutritionally superior to imported foodstuffs and additives.

American Samoa and Fiji, for example, have large fish canning factories. Milk is processed in Fiji, where a high temperature, short-time treatment plant has recently been installed. Root and tree staples are almost entirely sold fresh around the region, both locally and as export crops. The production of these crops is small-scale and labour-intensive. There is scope for the processing of snack food chips/crisps from crops such as cassava, breadfruit, taro and bananas, but this has not yet been performed on a large scale. Some import-substituting production of chips and various sauces using local produce did, however, take place in Tonga in the mid-1980s; although the products were tasty, attractively packaged and in reasonable demand (despite the status and popularity of imported snack-foods), production ceased, apparently mainly due to problems of production.

A number of fruits and vegetables are processed in Fiji, mostly by canning. These include tomatoes, coconuts (to make coconut cream), 'duruka' (*Sacharium edule*), taro leaves and pineapples. Some juicing of local fruits is done by two companies. A large citrus plantation in Fiji, which had juice concentrate as one of its products, has not proved viable, and a small-scale passionfruit factory in Tonga has encountered similar problems. With growing international interest in exotic fruit products and the price premium they can command, the production of dried fruits and fruit-based products such as purees and flavours could provide export products as well as nutritious local snack foods. A list of food products manufactured in Fiji is given in Appendix 3.3.1 at the end of this chapter.

In Fiji, a successful fruit crystallising and syruping industry has been established. Ginger and pawpaw preserved by this process are sold locally and overseas. One company is developing jams and jellies made from tropical fruits. There is a local and overseas demand for these products. Honey is produced in Fiji and packed for the local market in bottles and jars, and there is an interest elsewhere in the region. With further development, Fiji could become self-sufficient in fruit juices, tomato products, crystallised and syruped ginger, pawpaw and pineapple, honey and jams.

Frozen foods are well accepted in all countries. The availability of freezing and cold storage in many places has replaced other methods of preservation and permitted the export of several crops. Peeled cassava and taro retain flavour and texture when frozen and sealed in plastic bags. These foods are exported and sold in some supermarkets in Fiji and other countries of the region.

Animal Feeds
The provision of concentrated animal feeds to support livestock is an important consideration for all countries — livestock numbers and costs of imported feeds are increasing, and there is potential for the local production of feeds, or at least some components of animal feeds. Apart from a limited production of coconut, fish and maize meal in Fiji, there is little production of animal feeds on a significant scale around the region. There has been some interest in animal feed production, and several feed projects have been proposed and even begun, although many problems have been encountered, and success has proved elusive on a project basis

(despite the overall fact that local products, labour and industry were used, and foreign capital saved).

Research at the University of Hawaii showed that a nutritious silage could be produced from taro tops by a simple fermentation method.[12] Silaging doubled the dry matter content of taro leaves. Nutritious value and dry matter content were improved by the addition of other foods such as bananas, cane tops, cane trash and fodder grass. The silage was accepted by pigs and yielded good growth results. A small domestic trial in Fiji proved that other taro-family leaves (such as *Cyrtosperma* and *Xanthosoma*), fermented in large plastic bags, provided an acceptable pig food.

The feasibility of making a cassava concentrate was investigated in Fiji.[13] A hand operated peeling and washing machine was made from low-cost, easily available materials. Cleaned cassava was then chipped in a machine powered by a 2 stroke 3.5 hp motor. Chips were dried on a specially designed rack made from bamboo or wire netting. It was estimated that a successful soybean-cassava mix could be produced at $141 per tonne, compared with $176 for a feed based on maize.

* * * *

In the past, Pacific islanders had a rich heritage of knowledge concerning the preservation of many kinds of foods. Survival depended on the storage of surplus crops for times of scarcity. Changing food use brought about by Westernisation and the ready provision of food supplies by beneficent neighbouring countries, following droughts and hurricanes, has caused people to neglect traditional methods of food preservation. The introduction of less labour intensive techniques would make it possible for more people to enjoy local food preparation. The substitution of indigenous tropical foods for imports would require a change in agricultural policies, from export orientation to large scale food production aimed at self-sufficiency.

Appendix 3.3.1: Foods Processed in Fiji in 1990

Alcohol products: beer; spirits — whisky, gin, vodka, brandy, rum
Beef, canned
Biscuits, sweet, crackers
Bread, white, wholemeal, other bakery products
Cakes, pastry
Chicken, frozen
Chocolates, sweets
Coffee
Cordial, fruit and cola

Dairy products, ultra heated milk, homogenised milk, cheese, yoghurt, butter
Eggs (pickled quail)
Fish products, frozen fish, chilled fresh, prawns (frozen, smoked, salted, dried), canned tuna and mackerel
Fruits, fresh, canned, pineapple, guava, mango, passionfruit
Fruit preserves, chutneys, sauces, jam
Honey
Ice cream, toppings and flavour
Kava
Oils, coconut, soy bean, corn
Rice, rice biscuits
Snack foods, spiced Indian extruded starch types, chips
Sugar, molasses
Vegetables, fresh, canned 'duruka', 'palusami' (taro leaves), tomatoes

___

AFFORDABLE HOUSING AND DEVELOPMENT TRAINING IN KIRIBATI

CLIVE STEWART

This chapter will present a brief description of appropriate technology development work in the fields of affordable housing and development training carried out at the Rural Training and Development Centre (RTDC) of the Tarawa Technical Institute, in the Republic of Kiribati.

Kiribati gained independence from the United Kingdom in 1979. Since then, rural development and self-sufficiency have been high on the list of government priorities. As part of the efforts of the Ministry of Education to promote rural development to help improve basic skill levels in village communities, the RTDC was established in 1983. The RTDC has become a focal point for both training and technology research, appropriate to the needs of rural communities in Kiribati.

The RTDC was funded with an initial grant of A$63,000 (from the British Overseas Development Administration). Since that time, the centre has operated on a self-financing basis and has expanded with the creation of four extension workshops on remote outer islands.

Background

Kiribati consists of three groups of small islands scattered over a vast area of the Central Pacific Ocean. The population is over 60,000, with approximately two-thirds living on outer islands, away from the capital island of Tarawa. The rural population live a subsistence lifestyle based on fishing and agriculture. Household income derives from limited public and private sector employment (mainly on Tarawa), remittances from merchant shipping (there is a Marine Training School on Tarawa) and, on outer islands, limited cash income from cutting copra.

It is important to note that Kiribati is a nation made up of small, flat and low-lying coral atolls, with very limited natural resources. The islands possess many features that are unique to the atoll environment and what may be described as an appropriate technology here may well prove to be inappropriate for other areas, in the South Pacific and elsewhere, with a greater variety and abundance of natural resources. Similarly, technology that may be appropriate elsewhere, may be inappropriate in the atoll environment.

During initial training programmes held at the RTDC, feedback from trainees indicated a growing demand for alternative building materials. This demand stemmed from four factors:

1. Traditional materials require regular maintenance. This is time-consuming for home owners and expensive for Island Councils paying for the continual up-keep of buildings.
2. Local construction materials are becoming scarce as demands placed by an increasing population outpace the rate at which stocks of traditional materials can regenerate.
3. The increasing cost of imported building materials puts them beyond the financial reach of most rural communities.
4. General development and progress in Kiribati has stimulated a demand for improved housing and building standards.

The RTDC has tried to respond to these problems by developing a range of low cost products which provide viable alternatives to imported building materials.

Development work concentrated on the following areas:

1. Alternative roofing materials.
2. Utilisation and sawmilling of coconut timber.
3. Low cost building systems using above technology.
4. Demonstration and training in the above areas.

Alternative Roofing Materials

The most common roofing materials in Kiribati are corrugated aluminium and traditional thatch (using plaited palm fronds). Alternatives to both materials are sought — corrugated aluminium sheeting is susceptible to corrosion in salty and humid conditions, and the use of traditional roofing materials is constrained by increasing population and limited stock regeneration. Several alternative materials were considered. These included coconut wood shingles (coconut wood split into tiles), the treatment of thatch with preservatives to extend durability, and cement-based roof sheeting. As coconut shingles would also require preservative treatment, both coconut thatch and shingles could not be considered viable, due to the need to use the roof as an area for rain water catchment, which would not be possible if toxic preservative chemicals were used. Work therefore concentrated on producing a cement-based roofing product.

Eight cement roofing systems were evaluated, ranging from larger corrugated coconut-fibre-reinforced sheets to smaller flat tiles. A variety of production methods were tried — including hand screeding (drawing a flat edge over a mould to give a flat surface), tile presses (using the same principle as cement block moulds) and various techniques using vibrating tables to consolidate cement mortar tiles.

Various problems were encountered during development work. These included the porosity of finished products and the apparent need for reasonable quality control during production. Porosity problems were due to the type of sand available in Kiribati — atoll sand is made up of coral and shell fragment, which is relatively porous compared to silica sand. This problem was compounded by production techniques that called for a fluid plastic cement-sand mortar, using large quantities of water. This factor prohibited the use of existing fibre-reinforced corrugated sheet and curved tile systems,[1] as the increased water content of the mix required to obtain curved profiles induced porosity in the finished product.

The porosity problem was eventually overcome by developing two types of non-corrugated tile — the Diamond Tile and the VersaTile. These tiles require a less fluid plastic mortar that could be produced using a stiffer dry mix (the use of less water means a stronger, less porous mortar). Initial problems of inconsistent tile shape and poor quality control were overcome by simplifying the production process to use a vibration-assisted casting technique. These two types of cement mortar tile were selected from the trial for production at the RTDC workshops. Both tile systems have been used to produce good quality roofs on a variety of buildings, ranging from school classrooms to small houses. The VersaTile system was designed for hip roof structures, which have several advantages over gable roofs.[2] These include an overall reduction in the total amount of materials required to cover a given floor area (roof trusses are not normally required) and less maintenance on the finished building.

Finished tile roofs are attractive. They are also cool to work or live under, compared to aluminium or tin sheeting. They are suitable for rainwater catchment and do not leak, even in conditions of heavy driving rain. They can also be repaired or replaced. Cement tiles therefore provide a durable cost effective alternative to thatch and imported corrugated aluminium sheet. Their use in rural areas is increasing as training and demonstration projects prove the suitability of cement tiles to the Kiribati environment.

Specifications for the two types of tiles are given below:
(See note 3 for explanation of terms, and cost comparison with Australia)

	Diamond Tile	VersaTile
Size	350mm x 350mm	400mm x 400mm
Headlap	75mm	95mm
Coverage rate	12 tiles/sq.m	29 tiles/sq.m
Weight	30kg/sq.m	230kg/sq.m
Batten spacing	190mm	250mm
Batten size	40mm x 20mm	40mm x 30mm
Rafter spacing	1m	1m
Roof pitch	30 deg	30 deg
Fixing method	Integral wire tie	2 integral ties
No. tiles/40kg bag cement	44	33
Material cost/sq.m	$3.42	$3.42
Commercial cost/sq.m	$6.72	$6.72

It is interesting to note that the commercial cost of the tiles compares favourably with the cost of aluminium roofing — over $17/sq.m in Kiribati (A$10 in Australia), and that the commercial rate to buy coconut thatch in Kiribati is approximately $2/sq.m.

Production of Tiles

All production equipment is made at the RTDC workshop. The tile machines simply consist of a flat plate and hinged frame mounted on springs. The plate is vibrated by rotating an off-set weight held in a fixed bearing assembly. The weight is rotated at high speed by an electric motor. A 12 volt system using two 40-watt solar panels and battery, power machines used in rural areas, where 240 volts is not available.

The production process involves placing an aluminium sheet covered by a thin plastic sheet between the hinged frame and plate. The frame is securely clamped to the plate with two levers. A stiff cement mortar is placed on the plastic sheet and vibrated. When the frame is full vibration is stopped. A second frame is then placed on top of the mortar and filled to create support ribs. The wire fixing ties are added at this stage. Both frames are then removed and the tile supported by the aluminium sheet placed in a curing rack. After 24 hours the tile is separated from the aluminium and plastic sheets and placed underwater in a curing tank for 14 days.

One man operating the machine can make upwards of 40 tiles per day producing 4.5m² of roofing. Productivity can be increased by using a double frame machine but this requires a 240 volt power supply. The basic 12 volt machine can be produced for under $1,000. This figure does not include the battery and solar panel system which in Kiribati costs around $1,800. The machines are reliable and require very little maintenance.

Utilisation and Sawmilling of Coconut Timber

The high cost of imported timber has been a major problem in developing an affordable building technology for Kiribati. With costs for imported construction grade timber between A$530 to A$1,000 per cubic metre, a cheaper locally produced alternative was needed (general purpose construction grade F5 timber in Australia costs around A$330/cu.m). A major factor accounting for this price was the high cost of transporting timber into and within Kiribati.

To address this situation, it was decided to investigate the use of senile coconut timber using appropriate sawmilling technology. As coconut palms become senile, the production of coconuts declines. At this stage, the older palms should ideally be removed to make way for new trees. Older palms still continue to produce a few nuts, whereas new trees take a few years before nuts are produced. What usually happens in practice is that older palms are left to produce, unless a use (and value) for older trees can be found. Selective coconut sawmilling is therefore doubly useful and a positive beneficial impact on the environment by encouraging the use of old palms for timber, and helping make way for new plantation. Old senile coconut trees also produce the best grade timber, and this ensures that productive trees are not used.

A coconut timber sawmilling project had operated in Kiribati in the early 1980s. Problems encountered in using that sawmill included the need for and difficulty experienced in dressing coconut timber (coconut is the largest member of the grass family, and blunts conventional cutting edges quickly, which necessitates the use of very hard blade material and, preferably, blade lubrication and cooling with water). A fatal accident with the previous project gave a stark reminder of the dangers associated with sawmilling, and the importance of equipment and operational safety. Following the previous project, a large amount of senile palms had begun to accumulate.

The RTDC decide to reinvestigate the possibility of coconut sawmilling. In deciding what sort of mill would be best suited to Kiribati conditions, consideration was given to the difficulties encountered by the previous project, to address the problems of finishing coconut timber and the overriding factor of equipment and operator safety. As noted, another problem was the high cost of internal freight between islands. Shipping timber immediately pushed up the price, resulting in only minimal cost savings over imported wood. The obvious way to overcome this problem was to use a small portable mill that could cut timber of acceptable finish in situ, where it was going to be used, so that the only effective cost of the timber was the cost of transporting the equipment (assuming the free supply of labour, or the charge of a fee to mill old tress into timber).

The Sawmill

In considering the choice of sawmill technology, RTDC decided that a sawmill with acceptable cutting accuracy would obviate the need for post-mill machining. A band-saw was considered to provide sufficient cutting accuracy and operator safety, and a horizontal band-saw was duly purchased, from a UK company, Trekkasaw, who also offered to provide technical assistance in overcoming problems associated with coconut sawmilling.[4] The sawmill underwent several modifications at the RTDC workshop. These included increasing blade tension, altering the blade guide system and adding a pressurised blade lubrication system.

The saw operates on a portable frame consisting of two 5m long aluminium rails or beams, between which the saw head can roll. The two beams are attached to four adjustable legs. The log to be cut is held on clamps resting on the ground between the two beams. The saw head may be raised or lowered to obtain the required cutting thickness. Once the thickness is set, the saw is pulled through the log by two operators (one on each side of the head) both controlling safety switches which start and stop the blade. The blade is driven by a hydraulic motor powered by either a diesel engine or tractor. Although ordinary blades can be used, hard stellite-tipped blades provide a better cutting edge for coconut timber.

Sawmill Performance and Costs

Cutting with the saw is safe, fast and accurate, producing an excellent surface finish. Cutting accuracy can be demonstrated by the saw's ability to cut very thin coconut timber laminates of just 1mm thickness. The saw is also very portable, and in the first 18 months of operation worked on four different islands in Kiribati, producing timber on site for building projects and village communities.

Using the sawmill, timber costs work out to a commercial rate of $260 per cubic metre — one quarter to half the cost of imported timber (A$530–1000), and less than the cost of construction grade timber in Australia ($330/cu.m). This figure includes labour, freight for the equipment, purchase cost of coconut trees, fuel and running costs and depreciation on equipment. For village communities the RTDC offers a cutting service, with people providing logs and free labour. Timber produced under this scheme costs $93.00 per cubic metre. The timber is well suited to building work, particularly roof structures and internal joinery. As a precaution against insect attack, the timber may be simply painted with creosote.

Low-Cost Building Systems, Demonstration and Training

The low-cost building materials produced at the RTDC have characteristics that require consideration when developing an overall building system. For example, coconut timber, although strong and durable for internal applications, is prone to rot when placed in contact with the ground or exposed to continual damp conditions. Coconut timber must either not be used in such situations, or treated with an adequate preservative. Consideration must also be given to the skills and skill level of builders most likely to use the materials. With most rural builders lacking formal construction training, simplicity of use is an important factor. With coconut timber it is also important to note that cutting tools need to be kept especially sharp and that the use of nails requires careful attention to avoid splitting of the timber.

The building system developed at RTDC is suitable for small single storey buildings up to 12m long by 4m wide. Concrete blocks produced in simple steel block moulds are used to make columns at 2m spacings. These hollow blocks in effect create a permanent form for reinforcing steel and poured concrete used to complete the column. This is used instead of pre-cast or poured columns using temporary timber formwork, as the technique guarantees a good cover over reinforcing steel, which is prone to corrosion problems in Kiribati (especially in the absence of complete quality control).

The columns support a 100mm x 100mm coconut timber wall plate (a strip of timber running along the top of the side walls). The plate is held down by securing bolts which tie in with steel rods extending down to the footings. This ensures the integrity of the building, tying the roof through the walls to the foundations — an essential feature in making buildings storm and hurricane resistant. The block columns and wall plate provide a strong support for the roof structure. It should be noted that larger spans have been built, but need to employ a formal ring beam system (a reinforced concrete beam running along the top of the side walls).

Composite columns of treated coconut logs mounted on top of a block base have been used in an attempt to reduce costs. The vertical log is supported by blocks at a height of 500mm above ground level to reduce the chance of damp-induced rot. The log is also protected by an ant proof-barrier to discourage insect attack.

The two roof tile systems (Diamond Tile and VersaTile) use a maximum rafter spacing of 1m. The gable roof uses formal trusses (triangulated frameworks to support the ridge and rafters) and the hip roof uses a rafter and ridge technique which provides increased head room and an attractive internal appearance (there is no truss). The latter system benefits by using timbers that are cut on just one side and edge. This reduces milling and means more use is made of stronger coconut timber (the outer section of the coconut tree is much harder than the inner core).

The roof and support structure form the most important elements in a building, and a variety of materials can be used to complete the building. For residential purposes, traditional raised floors made of coconut leaf mid-ribs can be used. They are cheap, cool and comfortable. More expensive cement floors may be used for other buildings, such as classrooms and workshops.

The area between columns can be filled with doors or shutters or simply left open to provide a variety of layout options. A precast concrete panel faced with coral stones has also been developed at RTDC, and can be used to provide an attractive low wall between the columns. Various materials have been used to fill the space above this panel and below the wall plate, including coconut timber shutters, glass louvres and locally produced woven coconut leaf products. For school classrooms, a large single translucent glass fibre shutter has been developed to overcome the need for light, ventilation and weatherproofing.

Demonstration and Training
The construction of outer island extension workshops provided a good opportunity to demonstrate the potential of and train local people in the use of low cost materials in rural areas. Four workshops, known as Outer Island Skills Training Centres, were constructed using the above materials and building system, and equipped with basic tools.

The workshops were initially staffed by overseas volunteers. These volunteers were assisted by local counterparts, who underwent training at the Tarawa Technical Institute. The I-Kiribati counterparts have now assumed responsibility for running the workshops. They work with village-based management committees who assist by identifying community training needs and development projects. Additional support is provided by staff visits and project assistance from the RTDC.

Local builders were encouraged to attend training programmes and participate in construction of the workshop buildings. This was followed up by a demonstration low cost housing project, which employed the builders to carry out the work. As a result of this demonstration and training approach, village groups asked the RTDC for assistance in organising local housing cooperatives.

* * * *

Whilst research into improved building technology continues at the RTDC following the development of low cost, appropriate technology alternative roofing materials, coconut timber sawmill and building system, this interest was phased down. A greater emphasis was subsequently placed on the demonstration, promotion and training in appropriate building technology. The Outer Island Skills Centres have created a good base from which training programmes can be conducted. Skilled supervisors have carried out construction of small aid-funded building projects. These projects provide an excellent vehicle for practical training, and have greatly assisted in the transfer of new building technology to the rural population of Kiribati.

TELECOMMUNICATIONS:
POTENTIAL AND PROBLEMS FOR NEW TECHNOLOGY

JIM WILKINSON

This chapter describes the background to and early progress of the South Pacific Telecommunications Development Programme (SPTDP), which was established by the island nation members of the South Pacific Forum. The justification for this programme and the methods adopted for its management are outlined. The programme's aim was to establish a pattern or model of collaboration between the telecommunications groups within the Forum countries which would assist the planned development of new and improved telecommunications services in the small island countries of the South Pacific.

Background to Telecommunications Planning

The South Pacific Forum Meeting held in Canberra in August 1983 approved a proposal for the establishment of the SPTDP, which was tabled for endorsement after extensive consultation between the (then) fourteen island country members of the Forum. The SPTDP reflected the recognition by member countries of the importance of regional cooperative endeavour in telecommunications and broadcasting (international telecommunications and broadcasting are linked through a similar and generally shared use of transmission technology, most commonly using satellites). It was proposed that the countries work together within the programme to ensure that the benefits of modern telecommunications technology would be available to all in a coordinated and cost efficient manner.

The first report establishing the case for appropriate telecommunications development in the island countries of the Forum was produced under the convenorship of the South Pacific Bureau for Economic Cooperation (SPEC — now the South Pacific Forum Secretariat, or Forum Secretariat) during 1981/82. The report, entitled the 'Rural Telecommunications Study of the South Pacific', presented the results of studies undertaken by telecommunications experts from Australia and New Zealand, with contributions from the International Telecommunications Union (ITU) Project Team based in Suva.[1] The report was funded from grants from the governments of Australia and New Zealand and the ITU.

The South Pacific Telecommunications Development Programme

Following the Forum's approval of the SPTDP, and the appointment of a small team of specialists at SPEC in Fiji early in 1984, a Management Group was established, consisting of two representatives from each of the Forum island countries, Australia and New Zealand. The Management Group met at three to four monthly intervals during the early years of the programme. The SPEC team advised the Management Group and undertook tasks set by the Group, which were carried out at SPEC and through visits to member countries.

Working closely with member countries, the SPEC team also updated the earlier 'Rural Telecommunications Study of the South Pacific' into a plan of action, which was duly published as the 'South Pacific Telecommunications Development Programme — Planning Report'.[2] This report was published in April 1986 — two years after the establishment of the SPTDP team and Management Committee.

The main aims of the SPTDP, as approved by the 1983 Forum meeting, included the extension and improvement of the then existing telecommunications infrastructures and the provision of network-connected telephones to communities not yet enjoying such services. One quantification of these aims was the expressed intention to double the 1983 average telephone density of the region from three telephones per hundred population to six. It was recognised that the rate at which this aim could be achieved would be set by the availability of the necessary capital and operating funds.

Early meetings of the SPTDP Management Group accepted that, despite the emphasis given to rural connections in the original studies, attention could not be restricted to improving the rural networks alone, and that growth in rural connections would lead to the need to extend and improve urban networks. Several of the smaller countries also found difficulty in separating the rural from the urban elements of their service networks.

Features of the SPTDP Programme for Telecommunications

Studies of the topographical features of Forum member countries involved in the SPTDP programme established clear priorities, based largely on cost factors, for transmissions systems at two levels — the smaller national level, and larger national, regional and international level. Because of the need for transmission methods to bridge generally long water-paths between communities to be served and the nearest points on existing telephone networks, radio transmission rather than hard-wire systems were clearly the preferred option.

The preference at the smaller national level was for land-based radio transmission systems to interconnect communities (trunk systems), and also, in many cases, for connections to individual subscribers. Many of these radio systems could be of the conventional terrestrial radio systems, operating in the VHF, UHF, and lower SHF frequency bands, where short path-lengths and flat (atoll type) terrain exists.

At the larger national, regional and international level, the archipelagic or mountainous nature of many island countries, such as Kiribati and Fiji, characterised by long sea-paths or heavily obstructed land-paths (in the case of the mountainous countries) suggested an alternative approach. It was apparent from the earliest SPTDP studies and Management Group meetings that the clear preference and most appropriate engineering solution to the problem of trunk connections over many waterpaths was for satellite transmission systems, connected to ground-based radio distribution networks. It was found that relatively few consumer connections would require the establishment of satellite earth terminals at subscribers' premises — in most cases a single small community earth station would suffice, with 'wire' or radio connections through a small telephone exchange to individual subscribers.

Early in the progress of the planning studies it was accepted within the Management Group of the SPTDP that all telephone exchanges should be of the modern, electronic 'stored processor control' (SPC) type. This was based on grounds of availability, reliability, and cost/benefit of SPC systems compared with older but technically feasible electro-mechanical exchanges. Representatives of the smaller, technologically less developed island countries acknowledged that the advantages of much lower fault incidence, lower routine maintenance, reduced spares holdings and much smaller size more than compensated for any increased difficulties of training technical staff on the new advanced technology of electronic exchanges, when compared with the earlier electro-mechanical exchanges.

The Satellite Option

By far the greatest percentage of the time spent on technical planning by the SPTDP staff and the Management Group in the early years of the programme related to considerations regarding satellite transmission issues. These specifically included the availability and configuration of South Pacific satellite networks (at present and in the future) and choice of operating frequency bands.

By mid-1987, after around three years of joint study, member countries had reached the following conclusions and decisions.

Choosing a Satellite

Since no one country, or even a consortium of all Forum member countries could afford to purchase, launch, and operate a new satellite, there was no choice but to seek to hire transponder capacity on an existing satellite. The choice was essentially between Intelsat's Pacific Ocean Satellite Network and a newly launched Aussat Satellite Network, of which one satellite had been belatedly modified by Australia to provide a South Pacific 'footprint'. Because of this modification, the Aussat satellite was of less than desirable radiated power — this was a disadvantage to potential users, however, as earth stations would require larger antennas and higher power consumption. The Intelsat system used 'C' band operating frequencies (6 GHz uplink, 4 GHz downlink), while Aussat used 'KU' band (14GHz uplink, 12GHz downlink).

Because of the higher rain attenuation suffered by transmissions in the KU band, the well-established records of prolonged periods of high intensity rainfall in the South Pacific region and lower downlink radiated power level within the South Pacific footprint of the Aussat system, the decision taken was to express a preference for the Intelsat option using 'C' band frequencies. This choice also enabled the further advantage (particularly to the smallest of the countries) of also using their existing Intelsat international earth station in conjunction with smaller outer island earth stations for domestic satellite services.

Sharing a Satellite

Having decided that the Intelsat system operating at 'C' band frequencies would be the best option for 'within country' (domestic) satellite connections in the Forum countries, there remained the issue of how the countries should share the common satellite. Studies revealed that very worthwhile savings would accrue to all countries if 'Demand-Assigned Multiple-Access' (DAMA) satellite circuit allocation methods were adopted, rather than the permanent assignment of a number of satellite circuits to each country sharing the satellite. With the 'permanent' assigning of circuits, there would be times when one country was not using all its circuits, while another country could experience an over-demand, fully using all assigned circuits, thereby obliging other users to wait until a circuit became available. By hiring sufficient DAMA circuits to meet the expected peak instantaneous traffic demand of all user countries, savings in satellite circuit hire costs of at least 15% could be expected.

Using a Satellite

It was also recommended and agreed that satellite circuit-switching equipment should provide 'full mesh' switching, whereby a connection could be effected from one earth station to another working through the same satellite directly — that is, for two-way traffic on a 'single hop' basis, especially within the same country. This facility would minimise 'double hop' satellite connections (familiar to radio users in the South Pacific), where excessive return delay can prove troublesome to telephone users as well as to interactive computer networks.

Another policy position reached on satellite usage was that the use of the single, shared satellite for 'in-country' services should logically lead to the use of the same network for 'between-country' services (although this arrangement would require agreement within the Intelsat consortium). With regard to the establishment of regional radio and television services to Forum countries, it was also agreed that there were similar and equally logical reasons for using a single shared satellite network, such as that envisaged by SPTDP and the Management Group.

Funding of SPTDP

An unusual feature of the SPTDP concept was the delegation to the SPTDP and Management Group of the responsibility to obtain funds for the programme. The first assessment of the capital required (to finance the first three years of the SPTDP program) was estimated at US$100m.

Grant aid funds available to the Forum member countries involved fell well short of this level. Attempts were then made to secure loan funding from the World Bank to bridge the gap between the available funds and the level needed to begin the proposed regional telecommunications programme.

Serious difficulties were encountered from the outset with these inquiries. Many of the island countries did not yet have access to World Bank loans, whilst others had a preference to use loan funds for activities other than telecommunications. The Bank itself was not fully convinced that the income which would be earned from the telecommunications services (at tariffs which were affordable to the potential users in the small countries) would be sufficient to pay the (low) interest on loans, and ultimately enable capital repayments to be made.

Similar problems arose in the pursuit of aid funds. The Forum countries from the outset had said that they could not divert available aid resources to fund the new SPTDP programme and, despite some promises from countries outside the region (who had aspirations to supply the equipment needed to complete the work), no significant aid funds were obtained during the early years of the SPTDP initiative. By comparison with the good progress achieved with the technological planning work, the progress made in procuring funds to implement the programme was disappointingly slow.

Observations

The SPTDP can be seen as an example of successful collaboration between countries, at various levels, regarding the choice, decision-making and planning of improved telecommunications technology and services in the South Pacific. The concept of the SPTDP Management Group, with representatives of all countries contributing ideas and advice, not only towards the solution of their own problems but also those of their neighbours, represents a commendable achievement in regional cooperation. The highlights of the technical plans were the adoption of electronic, stored processor controlled telephone exchanges to handle the switching requirements in even the smallest communities, and the recommended use of a quota of shared circuits on a satellite of the Intelsat Pacific Ocean network to handle the majority of the new trunk circuit requirements within countries and, eventually, circuits between Forum countries.

Failure to secure adequate funding to allow the responsive implementation of the agreed plans must be identified as an issue of concern to participants in the activities of SPTDP, and similar regional ventures. A project involving a lack of technical planning would not be expected to stand up to the rigorous scrutiny of funding agencies and gain funding. It is unfortunate, therefore, that a regionally agreed telecommunications programme should also fail to gain funds within the time-scale sought by the countries involved. Delays in proceeding quickly with the single shared-satellite concept, and alternative national and regional telecommunications planning, subsequently led to the departure from the consortium of several larger countries, to the disadvantage of smaller island nations.

PIPES AND PITS: WATER SUPPLY AND SANITATION

TONY MARJORAM

♦♦♦

The supply of clean drinking water and the disposal of human waste through safe systems of sanitation are two very important and interconnected basic human needs and key indicators of development. Both are essential for good health. The technology for water supply and sanitation — public health engineering, is therefore one of the most important basic aspects of technology for development. Water supply and sanitation are particularly important and interconnected in smaller tropical island nations, where the main traditional source of water — groundwater — has a high potential for pollution with human waste (and also, increasingly, other forms of pollution, such as the runoff of agricultural chemicals and industrial waste).

Water supply on small island states is problematic, and comparable to that of large land-locked desert countries — the Pacific Ocean is almost a saltwater 'desert', where, to recall Coleridge's ancient mariner, there is 'water, water everywhere, nor any drop to drink'. Whilst human waste disposal was once straightforward — with bush disposal or 'beach-flush', sanitation is also becoming a problem, due to the pressures of increasing island populations.

This chapter will examine the overall issues of water supply and sanitation, making particular reference to rural areas, where most islanders live. Three specific technologies will be used as case studies of the appropriateness of water supply and sanitation technologies suitable for village construction, operation and maintenance — ferro-cement water tanks, a ventilated pit latrine and hand-operated water pump.

Water Supply and Sanitation: Issues and Constraints

Health conditions in Pacific islands are generally benign, compared to other developing country situations, with the absence of several tropical diseases from the region. However, various water-borne and related diseases and health problems do exist. An outbreak of cholera in Kiribati in 1977 led to the banning of lagoon-flush toilets and the construction of an ocean-fall sewage disposal system. There have also been outbreaks of typhoid in the region. Incidences of gastroenteritis, diarrhoea and dysentery are all increasing, particularly in rural areas, as is dengue fever and resistant malaria in those countries affected (PNG, the Solomon Islands and Vanuatu).[1]

In 1985, at the middle of the WHO Decade for Water Supply and Sanitation (1980–1990), 69.5% of Pacific islanders were without an adequate supply of water and 53.7% were without adequate sanitation facilities.[2] The problems were worse in rural areas, where 79.8% were without adequate water, and 63.3% without adequate sanitation. In urban areas, 6.1% were without adequate water and 12.5% without adequate sanitation. The largest and smallest countries face particular problems — 75% of Papua New Guineans are without adequate water and 57% without adequate sanitation, with 85% of rural people without adequate water and 65% without adequate sanitation. The overall target for the region by 1990 was to improve access to rural water supply and sanitation to 54.2% and 54.5% of rural people (the PNG target was 50% of rural people). To make matters worse, the problems are not static — increasing population growth and urban drift mean that it is difficult just to maintain service, let alone improve it.

Constraints

The main physical constraints for water supply and sanitation in the South Pacific derive from the geography of the region — the islands of the region are generally very small, with limited and often non-existent surface water resources. Only the larger volcanic islands have rivers, streams, lakes and relatively consistent rainfall. Small coralline islands and atolls have low and inconsistent rainfall, frequent droughts, very limited supplies of groundwater, consisting as a freshwater lens, and are too porous to hold any surface water, such as rivers (although some springs do exist as the surface overflow of the freshwater lens). The freshwater lens floats above denser saltwater intrusion in the porous coralline bedrock of these islands and atolls (very small islets generally have no lens, or a lens that is polluted with saltwater intrusion).[3] Many islands and atolls are very low-lying, and the freshwater lens is close to the ground level. Because of the low elevation, atolls and small islands are also prone to flood damage, particularly, for example, during the storm surge associated with hurricanes.

Physical constraints overlap with each other and social constraints — particularly the shortage of professional and other staff, limited funds, problems of operation and maintenance, the low status of water supply and sanitation and the need for the introduction or improvement of water resource policy and legislation in all countries of the region. There is a related need for the integrated management of water resources — Public Works Departments are mainly responsible for water supply in urban areas, other government departments are responsible for rural areas of greatest need. Many of these constraints reflect the overall need for improved human resource development and the use of appropriate technological hardware and software.

From the point of view of sanitation, the relative porosity of the bedrock of small islands and atolls and the closeness of the freshwater lens to ground level lead to groundwater pollution with human waste. There is also greater water movement in the freshwater lens within the coralline bedrock, compared to groundwater in other geological formations, and therefore a higher potential for contamination of the freshwater lens by liquid wastes. Because of the problem of groundwater pollution, there is either a consequent need to find non-polluting methods for disposing of human wastes, or the acceptance of groundwater pollution and the use of alternative non-groundwater sources of water, such as rainwater catchment. The main social problems for sanitation include the need for public education to improve sanitation practices in rural areas.

Water Supply

As populations and the demand for fresh water increase, alternative supplies have to be found, populations moved or water brought to them. Because of drought and the saline contamination of well-water, British colonial authorities relocated island populations of over 1000 people from outer islands in Kiribati (then the Gilbert Islands) to the Solomon Islands in the 1950s and 1960s. (Although, with an islander interest in migration, it appears that the drought may not have been as serious or the wells as saline contaminated as the authorities were led to believe.) Drinking water is shipped as back-haul cargo to Nauru on phosphate boats, although this is a special case.

Other demands for water also arise, particularly in agriculture and industry. Fresh water and good soil are both limited resources in most island countries, and the potential demand for water for irrigation is enormous, and way beyond the sustainable scope of the water resources of most islands. It is therefore fortunate that larger-scale irrigation has not been promoted in the region. Industrial demands for water occur in such water-intensive processes as brewing and food processing, industries increasing in the region. It is apparent from some such operations that fears regarding groundwater pollution are well founded.

In situations of limited water resources, islanders are increasingly using direct roof rainwater catchment and storage in cisterns or water tanks.[4] Tanks should be designed to hold sufficient water for average household consumption over average periods of drought. The use of rainwater is also occasioned by the damage to the groundwater lens through pollution and overpumping — which destabilises the lens, causing mixing with deeper, denser saltwater. There is also a preference for softer rainwater — because of the lime content and possible saltwater contamination, groundwater is harder and more difficult to lather than rainwater. There is little use of water filtration techniques (such as slow sand filter) at village or household levels in the South Pacific. The option of accepting the pollution of groundwater with human waste and the use of alternative water supplies, such as rainwater catchment, is not regarded as a particularly viable or attractive option by the present author. This is mainly because the groundwater resource is too valuable to be wasted in such a way, and because the consumption of polluted groundwater could not be altogether avoided, particularly at times of drought, with the consequent increase in the problems of water-borne disease.

Rural Areas

Water supply in many villages and rural areas, and therefore to the majority of Pacific islanders, is the responsibility of individual households, and often the particular responsibility of women. Water supply is generally from a well or river, which may be close, or at a considerable distance from the house. Increasing numbers of island households are using roofwater catchment, necessitating the replacement of traditional thatch with corrugated galvanised steel or aluminium sheets — thatch is not suitable for roofwater catchment, due to the discolouration and contamination of the collected water. A similar concern relates to the possible contamination of roofwater with bird droppings. Whilst this concern is understandable, it presents no real problem to health, provided the roof and gutters are kept clean, the tank properly constructed, with water take-off pipe raised above and pointing away from the tank floor. If the concern persists, water filtration could reduce these problems.

Rainwater is stored in tanks of various sizes and materials — including oil drums (which are not particularly suitable for water storage due to problems of corrosion in hot, humid and salty climates), galvanised steel tanks (which may last less than five years due to corrosion) and various types of fibreglass and ferro-cement tanks. Fibreglass tanks are relatively expensive to produce, use imported materials and are not easily repaired. Ferro-cement tanks are less expensive, should not corrode, use some local materials and are easily repaired — ferro-cement tanks are considered the most appropriate tank technology for island construction and use. Cement tanks have even used local bamboo and coir fibre for reinforcement, although problems of reinforcement degradation and leaking have been encountered. Various tanks, particularly ferro-cement tanks, are considered in the case study at the end of this chapter.

Urban Areas
Water supply in most urban areas and an increasing number of larger villages is through reticulated systems into individual households. The supply may derive from lakes or reservoirs, small river dams or groundwater wells, powered by diesel or windmill pumps. Maintenance of reticulated systems is often a problem, and some urban systems have leaks reported at up to 50% of total supply — from the system itself and individual houses (dripping taps, due to the hardness of the water and a lack of maintenance, are not uncommon). Some of the 'leakage' may also be due to unofficial connections to the system.

Alternative and Appropriate Technology
Water supply technologies that have potential but have not been widely promoted in the South Pacific include hand pumps, solar-electric pumps and wind pumps for larger-scale supply systems. Experience with powered pumps is mixed — they have a danger of overpumping the fragile freshwater lens, (whereas hand pumps are self-regulating, and supply only the demand). Wind pumps, like diesel pumps, have suffered from a lack of maintenance and from hurricane damage. There are as yet few solar pumps in the region.

Slightly more novel water supply technologies include desalination and distillation of brackish or salt water. Desalination, generally using reverse osmosis, is a vital technology in water-poor oil-rich Middle Eastern states and some island states such as Malta. Reverse osmosis plants are, however, technically complex and energy-intensive, and can only be afforded where energy is cheap or plentiful, or where an industry such as tourism can pay for the fresh water needed. Distillation, through evaporation and condensation, is also energy-intensive and expensive, unless a plentiful energy source such as the sun is used. Solar stills, unless they are very large, have limited output, and are only really useful in emergency situations. Household distillation is also illegal in some island countries, due to the prohibition of home-made alcohol. Large non-porous surfaces, such as aircraft runways, are also used for water collection.

Many of the systems noted above have high capital and operating costs, and even though they may be claimed to be 'maintenance-free', still require some maintenance and repair, which may be more difficult than maintaining non-maintenance-free technology. All are susceptible to hurricane damage. Because of these comments, it is apparent that roof water catchment and household water tanks take a lot of beating.

Sanitation

The traditional means of human waste disposal in the South Pacific was through either bush-disposal, 'beach-flush' or a 'swim' in the lagoon or sea (in the Pacific islands, to 'swim' is not necessarily synonymous with personal marine mobility). These methods of sanitation work acceptably well, although lack convenience, especially in bad weather or at night. When populations increase, however, problems of human waste disposal and associated diseases arise. With increasing aspirations to modernity, factors of status also arise — in this case the aspiration to a Western-style water-flush toilet. Cost is the main limiting factor in using a flush toilet and septic tank system.

Various improved methods of human waste disposal have been introduced to the island Pacific over the years to cope with the problems of increasing population, and the desire to up-date traditional methods of human waste disposal. These include several types of pit latrine and, more recently, pour-flush toilets, discharging into pits and septic tanks, lagoons and the open sea. There are various problems associated with these waste disposal technologies — dry pit latrines may cause pollution of groundwater if the pit intrudes into the groundwater layer, although pour-flush latrines discharging into pits have a greater potential to pollute groundwater, and also require flushing water, which may be in short supply (sea water may be used, but the pollution potential increases further). Discharging untreated sewage into the sea, and particularly lagoons, where there may be insufficient flushing action, is a major cause of pollution (as at Bondi Beach, although tourists may not expect to swim in sewage on an island idyll).

The disposal of household waste water when improvements in water supply are made is often neglected. It is not uncommon to see puddles of water underneath taps on water tanks and standpipes. This surface water is a messy inconvenience and increases health risks by attracting animals and providing a breeding ground for mosquitos (and hence malaria and dengue fever). The disposal of household waste water is adequately facilitated by the use of simple and inexpensive soak-pits. These should be constructed at disposal points near sinks, below tank taps, standpipes and around wells.

Rural Areas

Sanitation in rural areas conforms to the general picture presented above. Although some of the more extreme pressures of population growth are absent in rural areas, so are many resources associated with sanitation and water supply. Rural sanitation technology is therefore at the more traditional and basic end of the methods described above.

Urban Areas

There are no extensive sewerage systems in the South Pacific. This is mainly due to the costs and some difficulties of installing such systems — larger islands are often mountainous, with solid rock close to the surface, whereas atolls and smaller islands are flat. Sewerage systems in both require pumping systems (which are also necessary in small coralline islands to maintain negative pressure to attempt to avoid leaks into the freshwater lens). Most urban sewage (and other liquid wastes) is either discharged untreated through lagoon or ocean outfall, or into latrine pits or septic tanks. Problems of human waste disposal are increasing as urban areas increase in size, and as more households install pour-flush toilets. Among the first major indicators of such problems was the cholera outbreak in Kiribati in 1977, caused largely by pollution of the lagoon and groundwater lens by the discharge of human waste into the lagoon. There have been occurrences of typhoid in the region since that time, not to mention other water-borne diseases such as diarrhoea in young children.

Alternative and Appropriate Technology

Because of the problems of groundwater pollution, particularly of the freshwater lens in atolls and small islands, it is of utmost importance to keep human waste out of groundwater, or at least well away from groundwater wells and pump sites (preferably over 50 metres). It would also seem sensible to use water-flush toilets only in conjunction with properly watertight septic tanks, and where there is an adequate supply of flushing water. If these conditions cannot be met, the use of water-flush toilets is best avoided, both to reduce the potential for groundwater pollution and to minimise water use.

Water-flush toilets and septic tank systems are expensive and unaffordable by many islanders, particularly in rural areas (unless there is some element of subsidy). There are also problems of maintenance and operating costs with such systems. Water-flush systems may also be inoperable at times of drought. Alternative methods of human waste disposal that have been proposed and demonstrated in the island Pacific include ventilated improved pit latrines (VIPs), water-seal toilets, dry composting toilets and biogas units (using both human and animal waste to produce methane and a detoxified sludge, very suitable for use as a fertiliser).

VIP toilets are probably the most appropriate all-round system of human waste disposal in most situations in the Pacific — improved designs using raised plastic seats are not unattractive, and reduce odour and fly problems. Such designs can also be raised off the ground in areas with low land and high watertable to minimise problems of groundwater pollution and potential damage by flooding. Water-seal toilets have been introduced into some countries by the WHO. These toilets have proved acceptable, although there are possible problems of increased groundwater pollution, the unavailability of flushing water and the breakage of the plastic moulded water-seal due to the over-enthusiastic clearance of blockages.

Dry composting toilets might appear to have promise, but they have not attracted much local interest, mainly because of cultural aversion and taboo associated with the handling of human waste and particularly the use of such waste as a fertiliser for human food. Biogas systems were constructed in many island countries in the 1970s, although none appear to have enjoyed any success, with one plant finally disappearing in an explosion. Biogas systems appear to be more useful in the detoxification of human and animal waste rather than as gas producers, as similar constraints apply to the use of methane so derived as apply to the use of composted human waste.

Case Studies — Appropriate Rural Water Supply and Sanitation Technology

The three case studies below look at ferro-cement water tanks, a ventilated improved pit toilet (VIP toilet) and village water pump, developed at the Institute of Rural Development of the University of the South Pacific. These technologies were designed mainly for rural areas, to be of low cost and low environmental impact, of simple durable design to be readily understood, and easily constructed, maintained and repaired at village level.

1. Ferro-cement Water Tanks

Various types of ferro-cement water tanks have been introduced to the region, including 'conventional' cylindrical tanks,[5] made with and without formwork, and two tanks of modular construction. Ferro-cement tanks can be made on-site or off-site, in which case they are either transported whole to site, or assembled from modules cast off-site in moulds. The rationale for the modular type of construction is that the components of the tank can be made where equipment and skills may be centralised, thereby allowing more complex techniques to be used and a higher standard of quality maintained. The modules, of less volume and easier to transport, are assembled in the field by trained personnel.

Modular tanks include a 'cubic' tank promoted for a period by the WHO, (sometimes known as the 'Cook Islands tank', although many Cook Islanders are unhappy at this) of 5000 litre capacity, assembled from flat square sides reinforced with steel pins. The tank panels are manufactured at a central location and transported to site, where the edges are wired together and plastered. Another modular tank successfully promoted in PNG (particularly on Bougainville) consists of two deep bowl-shaped sections which are cast at a central location (or on-site) which are then wired and sealed together around their rims. Some of the supposed advantages of modular construction may be illusory, however, when overall practicalities and economics are considered. Problems encountered with cubic tanks include the need for relatively high manufacturing quality control and difficulty in making watertight joins between panels — accounting for leaks in many cubic tanks (costly extra gusseting solved this problem in Tonga).

The 'conventional' type of vertical cylindrical ferro-cement tank has been successfully built for many years in various sizes all around the Pacific, and is durable and economic.[6] The circular floor of the tank is made first, reinforced with woven wire or mesh, and plastered with mortar. Formwork, generally consisting of galvanised metal sheet secured around a wooden or tubular metal framework, is erected on the base, and woven wire or mesh reinforcement wrapped around the formwork and wired to the base. This is then plastered, the formwork removed, and replastered to form the walls of the tank. Formwork for the roof is installed, the roof reinforcement wired on and plastered to complete the tank. The only problems experienced with such tanks in the South Pacific are due to poor quality control and ill-advised cost-cutting — such as the use of a weak mortar (low cement content), leading to unsound tanks.

A Ferro-cement Tank Built Without Formwork

Ferro-cement tanks constructed with formwork predispose tank construction towards series production and an organised small business or project orientation. This is a limiting factor in small islands, where problems in transporting the necessary formwork, materials and skilled personnel can result in considerable delays or the unviability of tank construction programmes. The 'formless' tank, of conventional design and construction, but made without formwork, was developed to overcome these problems.[7]

Based on consideration of typical household sizes and drought conditions across the South Pacific, a tank volume of 6000 litres was chosen, with approximate dimensions of 2m diameter and 2m wall height. The need for formwork was circumvented by the use of three innovations:

1. Sheets of weldmesh reinforcement are rolled into a cylinder to form the sides of the tank, around which chicken wire is wrapped.

2. A piece of flat but easily bendable galvanised sheet steel, with handles affixed to one side, is used as movable formwork and held inside the tank, whilst the reinforcement is plastered from outside.

3. The roof is made without formwork by forming weldmesh into a shallow cone, onto which chicken wire is affixed and an inspection hole cut. A mound of sand or soil the shape of this cone is made and covered with polythene sheet, the roof placed on it and then plastered. The roof is then wired and plastered to the walls of the tank.

The 'formless' ferro-cement tank compares to the 'conventional', 'cubic', 'formless' and galvanised steel tanks as follows:

Tank	Vol	Total cost	Cost/unit vol
	(l)	($)	($/l)
'conventional' tank	6800	147	0.021
'cubic' tank	5000	117	0.024
'formless' tank	6300	160	0.026
galvanised steel tank	4500	300	0.067

2. VIP Toilet

It has been noted above that ventilated improved pit latrines can be considered the most appropriate toilet technology for widespread promotion in the island Pacific, especially in rural areas. VIP toilets do not need flushing water, which is often in short supply and can promote increased pollution of the groundwater. They are also more affordable than other types of toilet, and can be made in attractive materials.

VIP toilets consist of a shelter or cubicle on top of a ferro-cement slab above an excavated pit, usually around 2 metres deep and 1 metre square. The pit is ventilated by a pipe of at least 100mm diameter protruding into the pit through the slab and rising at least 2 metres to the top of the shelter, with a fly gauze fitted around the top of the vent pipe to prevent the entry and exit of flies. The vent pipe should be painted black and face the sun (North) to promote ventilation of the pit through the chimney effect — the principle of the VIP toilet. The VIP toilet may be used in the squat style, with a moveable hole-cover, or a pedestal and conventional closeable plastic seat may be fitted. These measures should keep the shelter relatively free from odours and flies.

On low land with a high water table — conditions typical of atolls and small islands, VIP toilets may be raised off the ground, built on compartments that enable a shallower pit to be dug — reducing problems of water table pollution and flooding. VIP-type toilets may also be built over septic tanks. The VIP latrine developed at the University of the South Pacific incorporated such features.[8]

3. Village Water Pump

Hand pumps are very little used in the South Pacific, although they have been demonstrated in several countries and have considerable potential. Water collectors, normally women, may travel considerable distances, and yet water may be a few feet under the ground. Pumps, over a sealed well or borehole, also reduce the chance of water pollution and issues of safety associated with wells.

Hand pumps suitable for village application should be relatively low cost, simple and robust, preferably made from readily available steel and plastic pipe fittings. The pump developed at the University of the South Pacific addressed such design criteria.[9] In addition to wells, there is also a need for a technique for manual well construction or hand-operated boring equipment capable of cutting through coral.

Choice of Technology in Water Supply and Sanitation

The choice of water supply and sanitation technology for use in the islands depends on a combination of economic, technical, social/cultural and environmental criteria, operating at both the personal and project levels (although rational criteria sometimes seem absent). Economic factors usually dominate — systems need to be affordable. Costs, however, should not be allowed to suppress considerations of technical quality — ferro-cement water tanks, for example, have been constructed using insufficient reinforcement and weak cement mixes (too much sand). Such savings generally prove to be false economies when tanks start to crack and leak. The social factor of perceived status may override environmental considerations — as with the preference for pour-flush toilets, when such systems are expensive, water-intensive and groundwater polluting.

Technical considerations sometimes override social/cultural factors — such as the unsuccessful promotion of composting toilets or biogas systems in the face of social/cultural adversity and taboo. The social preference and perceived advantages of new and sometimes locally unproven technology may dominate — as in the case of the cubic water tank, chosen because of seeming expert preference for something new, when tried-and-true conventional ferro-cement tanks would have been a better choice. Projects designed by overseas experts may employ standard technology used elsewhere, but be unsuitable for island environments and conditions (especially as regards capital and operating cost and complexity, maintenance and repair). It is important to involve local people in the choice, installation and management of projects involving technology.

Provision of Improved Water Supply and Sanitation

Initiatives aimed at the improvement of water supply and sanitation in the South Pacific are generally organised as public projects by government departments, particularly Public Works Departments, sometimes in conjunction with the WHO and bilateral aid donors,[10] or community or village development projects, organised by PWDs, bilateral and multilateral agencies (such as the WHO) and non-governmental organisations (often in conjunction with local organisations such as women's clubs). The activities of PWDs generally focus on community systems, such as reticulated water supply, rather than individual installations, such as roofwater catchment and tanks. This orientation can make for inflexibilities of approach and technology choice.

Other constraints and problems relating to technology include hardware that is often unavailable, in short supply or broken down. There may only be one boring rig in a country of many small and isolated islands, for example. Software problems include limited technical knowledge and operator training. Because of these factors, it is not uncommon, for example, for operators to drill overly deep bores into and beyond the freshwater lens, causing saltwater intrusion and damage to the lens. Government and community water supply and sanitation projects often lack defined responsibility regarding management and maintenance of projects. This again underlines the need for the involvement of the local community, and particularly women, in the discussion, design, construction and maintenance of water supply and sanitation projects.

INTER-ISLAND SHIPPING AND MARINE TRANSPORT

TONY FINCH

◆◆◆

The Role of Inter-Island Shipping

The general pattern of domestic trade in the South Pacific island countries has shown comparatively little change over the past few decades. This mainly comprises the carriage of general cargoes (principally foodstuffs and fuel) from urban centres to outlying areas and islands, with return cargoes of agricultural produce — such as copra, fruits and fish for the urban and export markets. The carriage of deck passengers between the islands is an equally important role in many countries. Marine transport thus plays a vital role in the economy and development of Pacific island countries through the distribution of goods and services and collection of export cargoes, as well as providing the main, and in some cases (such as Tuvalu) the only means of communication between widely scattered groups of national populations.

There has been little change in the pattern of ownership of vessels. In smaller countries such as Tuvalu, Kiribati, Marshall Islands and the Federated States of Micronesia, vessel ownership is still largely in government hands, whilst in larger Papua New Guinea and Fiji, domestic shipping is generally in the hands of private operators, with the role of government vessels mainly restricted to the provision of essential services, such as health and education, to the outlying islands.

The actual sizes of the respective national fleets vary considerably, ranging from Tuvalu's single government vessel, the four 'field trip ships' and landing-craft of the Marshall Islands (also government-owned), to some 50 vessels on the Fijian register and upwards of 150 in the case of Papua New Guinea.[1] The large majority of vessels are very small, in many cases below 20 metres in length or 50 gross tons, and many are old and of varied materials and methods of construction.

Changes in Shipping Technology

Developments in the technology of inter-island shipping have been beset with difficulties, both of a technical and non-technical nature. In the first place, the so-called 'container revolution' of the 1960s and 1970s, which was designed to suit the needs of industrialised countries with high labour costs, has proved ill-suited to the needs of small island countries, with their pools of comparatively low-cost labour and limited infrastructure, such as wharves suitable for container handling and internal road systems. The dramatic reduction in the number of Pacific ports visited by international-trade vessels over the past two decades has also had a marked effect on inter-island transport, as noted by Paul Gini in 1984: 'A further effect of containerisation resulting from a reduced number of direct port calls is the greater pressure on domestic shipping services. More transhipment or feeder services must be provided. Either costly facilities must be provided to handle containers at the destination port, or goods must be unpacked at the transhipment port and shipped as break-bulk cargo, thus nullifying the major door-to-door benefit of containerisation'.[2]

Problems and Constraints

Other basic problems are caused by comparatively small populations, widely scattered throughout many islands, the unbalanced nature of their foreign trade (with an import-to-export ratio of 5 or 6 to 1 and higher in many cases) and the very small quantities of cargo to be handled at numerous loading and discharge points, either at small wharves, or often by means of boat carriage (using lighters) in reef areas. An example of some of these factors is illustrated in the case of the populations of the 26 islands and atolls of the Marshall Islands, spread over a sea area of more than 750,000 square miles. The cargoes and passengers carried between the main centre of Majuro and the outlying islands by the five Marshall Islands government ships in 1987 included a total of 47 voyages, ranging from 12 to 24 days duration, each requiring an average of some 20 port calls (or, more accurately, 'landing stops') to carry out transfers of cargoes and passengers.[3] This pattern is not untypical of many other archipelagic island countries in the South Pacific and elsewhere.

Another problem, of at least equal importance, is the comparative disinterest in domestic shipping which appears to be shown by some island governments and aid donors. This contrasts with their preoccupation with more glamorous projects, such as external shipping ventures and flag-of-convenience shipping registers and, particularly, with their enthusiasm for national airlines and all matters connected with air transport. This attitude has led in turn to a lack of clear-cut policies for the development of inter-island shipping, and a general failure to achieve sufficient coordination between national shipping and civil aviation policies.

Whilst recognising the constraints imposed by the containerisation of cargoes in overseas trade, the imbalance of that trade and widely dispersed nature of the Pacific island countries, there appears to have been a lack of planning for development of domestic shipping services in the South Pacific. This is accompanied by a consequent lack of interest in the problem of suitable technology in some instances.

The following sections of this chapter contain, in broad outline, a summary of the principal factors concerned with the design of inter-island trade vessels and their associated equipment (including cargo-handling gear), the problems of repair, maintenance and the operation of domestic shipping services, including the training of shipboard personnel. An attempt is then made to evaluate the success or otherwise of the current technologies employed, and the possible steps that could be taken to introduce a form of technology that is more attuned to local conditions and capable of assisting the real development of domestic shipping services in South Pacific island countries.

Some Aspects of Ship Design and Operation

There is no single 'regional design' of vessel which can be considered suitable for all areas of the South Pacific. This is due to the varied operating conditions found in the region.

Certain influential factors can, however, be listed, the most important of these being the problems of repair and maintenance within the region. Apart from Fiji and Papua New Guinea, which have reasonably adequate facilities for their domestic fleets, there are generally only slipways of very limited capacity throughout the islands. There are also very major problems regarding the availability of spare parts for both engines and auxiliaries, including deck and navigational equipment. The availability and cost of slipping or drydocking and the availability of spare parts should therefore be primary factors in vessel design and choice of machinery and equipment.

Operating Costs

The second major factor is operational economy. This primarily relates to fuel consumption — a matter which weighs heavily in the budgets of practically all island governments and shipowners, and is a crucial consideration in the choice of propulsion machinery and auxiliary systems.

Three principal causes of excessive fuel consumption lie in the over-powering of vessels, the use of unnecessarily high speeds and additional power requirements imposed by the provision of auxiliary systems such as air-conditioning, electric cooking and other appliances in many modern ships.

Obviously, a compromise between the demands of maintenance and fuel efficiency has to be reached. In very general terms, the ideal propulsion system would appear to consist of a medium speed engine and simple robust gearbox, coupled to a well-matched fixed-bladed propeller. The need to keep auxiliary systems to a minimum should also be borne in mind, with greater use of manual rather than electrical appliances, and perhaps the need for air-conditioning could be questioned in many cases where natural ventilation could be utilised. Overall, there is a need to reduce the complexity of ships' equipment and operational systems, and to attune their design to the available skills of seagoing personnel in inter-island vessels and the standards of training provided by marine schools in the region.

However, in contrast to the problems of design that have priority in the more industrialised countries, South Pacific island states have two mitigating factors in their favour. In the first place, labour costs are generally low, certainly by comparison with Pacific rim countries such as Australia and New Zealand, and much higher manning levels with simpler standards of accommodation can be maintained. This is in fact a very necessary consideration in many island countries, where ships' crews frequently carry out stevedoring functions in addition to their normal shipboard duties. Secondly, in order to achieve necessary economies in fuel costs, a reduction in operating speed can usually be accepted. In the majority of cases, periods at sea between ports or load/discharge points are limited to a maximum of two days, and delays are almost all caused by factors such as awaiting tides or daylight reef passages and slow cargo-handling methods, all of which make a normal running speed of up to 10 knots quite adequate. (It should be noted that an increase of speed from 10 to 12 knots can result in an increase in fuel consumption in excess of 40%.)

As far as cargo services are concerned, there are numerous variations in types of cargo and tonnages to be carried. Here again, however, certain general principles apply: firstly, the need for large uncluttered deck areas for the carriage of fuel drums and other hazardous cargoes requiring above-deck stowage, and secondly, the ever-increasing need for reefer space, both for inward and outward cargoes. The carriage of deck passengers is also an important point to be considered, with the need for clear deck space with adequate protection from weather, by means of awnings and sidescreens, plus adequate toilet and washing facilities and supply of fresh water available on deck. Deck passengers also obviously need to be separate from hazardous and other deck cargoes.

Cargo Handling

Cargo-handling equipment also needs attention in inter-island trade vessels, with simplicity of design, operation and maintenance being all-important factors. In the majority of cases, derricks and manual handling systems have advantages over cranes and more sophisticated types of mechanical equipment, and wooden hatchboards and tarpaulins will present fewer operational and maintenance problems than automatic steel hatch covers. Also, in many areas, particularly in the reef areas of the northern islands, workboats must still be used for ship-to-shore cargo transfer, where topography or very small cargo tonnages make the building of small wharves impractical or uneconomic. Whilst this system is extremely slow and frequently subject to weather conditions, it is difficult to visualise any replacement in the foreseeable future.

Safety

Last, but certainly not least, is the consideration of safety. Two points are particularly worthy of note in relation to small South Pacific vessels, in common with similar types of vessel operating in other parts of the world. First is the problem of stability, which poses ever-increasing difficulties with modern small vessels, with the tendency to build higher superstructures, locating all accommodation above deck, and carrying more and larger containers on deck. As far as new ships are concerned, the problem needs to be tackled in the design stage, whereas with older vessels, continuous watch has to be maintained on the disposition of cargo and fresh water and oil tanks. In some cases, carriage of permanent ballast may be necessary.

There is also a great need for the provision of simple stability instructions to be placed on board vessels, instead of the complicated data currently provided with new vessels, which is insufficiently clear for many ships' officers in the South Pacific. The matter of safety equipment, which again requires simplicity of operation and maintenance, is another key consideration. Special attention also needs to be given to the problems of lifesaving equipment and emergency disembarkation arrangements for deck passengers in small vessels. Conventional appliances such as inflatable liferafts or davit-launched lifeboats may not be the best answer in the case of very small vessels operating in areas where servicing facilities are not available. Simply-constructed foam or wooden rafts and buoyant apparatus, in conjunction with side nets and overside ladders, may be a better solution to the problems of vessel safety in the South Pacific.

Ship Design

The preceding paragraphs all refer to a conventional model of vessel designed for the typical forms of cargo and passenger carriage throughout the islands. However, since World War Two, landing craft have come into general use throughout the region, in particular in areas where beach landings are available, and for the carriage of bulldozers and heavy mobile equipment for construction projects. In roles of this nature, these craft provide a valuable back-up service for conventional vessels. In general, however, they have not proved capable of providing regular services. This is largely due to their inability to maintain speed in adverse weather conditions and their unsuitability for carriage of deck passengers in any but very short-range ferry operations.

A further development of the landing craft has been the roll on/roll off vessel such as the *Olovaha* and *Queen Salamasina* in service in Tonga and Western Samoa. These vessels are suitable for both regular cargo and passenger operations, but are relatively sophisticated in design and require a higher level of technology in operation, and special purpose-built ramp facilities for the loading and discharge of cargo.

At the 'alternative' end of the technology scale, the introduction of wind-powered vessels receives periodic attention from potential aid donors, mainly as a means of reviving traditional methods of transport and traditional skills of Pacific islanders. Studies on this subject have been carried out in Fiji, Solomon Islands and Tonga in recent years, and there seems ample evidence to suggest that the use of sail as an auxiliary form of power in engined vessels would definitely result in overall economy of operation and reduction in fuel consumptions. However, with the possible exception of certain very limited areas, it seems unlikely that anything approaching a regular schedule of cargo and passenger services could be maintained by vessels operating solely under sail.

Operation of Shipping Services

As far as the operation of domestic shipping services is concerned, inter-island marine transport can be regarded in the same way as any other public transport system, in which regular schedules need to be maintained and passenger fares and freight rates need to be kept within reasonable bounds by means of government controls. Thus, it would appear that the more uneconomic services, such as those involving small cargo tonnages to sparsely-populated outlying islands, will continue to incur costs which will have to be borne by governments, either by direct provision of services through their own ships, or indirectly by means of subsidies to private ship operators.

Attempts have been made in some countries to introduce a form of route-licensing, in order to force private operators to undertake the more unprofitable services, instead of 'creaming-off' profits from the trades in inner areas and among larger centres of population. These have not generally proved successful, however, mainly due to the complex nature of the licensing systems which have been introduced and the inability of transport administrations to undertake their supervision. A clear example of the enforcement difficulties encountered by a government in this situation has been described by Anne Dunbar-Nobes in the case of Vanuatu.[4] This appears to have been an experience common to other island states.

The other major problem of shipping operation is that of maritime training. There are numerous small training establishments throughout the Pacific, notably in Papua New Guinea, Fiji and Solomon Islands, with additional schools in Kiribati, Tuvalu and Western Samoa. The latter three schools exist mainly for the purpose of training island seamen for service in foreign-owned ships (frequently flag-of-convenience vessels under West German ownership). A maritime school has recently been opened in Tonga, which appears to have been designed with a similar purpose in mind. Attempts have been made by the Forum Secretariat over recent years to coordinate the training programmes of the three first-named schools, and introduce common standards of crew qualifications under the South Pacific Maritime Code. These efforts have met with only limited success.

The Appropriateness of Current Technology

Under the present conditions in which inter-island shipping operates in the South Pacific, there is in practice little real choice of technology in the field of ship design and construction. As far as private companies are concerned, the great majority operate on a very low margin of profit, and many of the small enterprises can be accurately described as shoestring operations. Under these circumstances, new purpose-built vessels are comparatively rare without some form of government assistance, and even recent acquisitions have often been elderly and unsuitable vessels.

Although higher standards have been attained in some areas, such as Papua New Guinea and Fiji, where improved systems of government inspection have been brought into force, many old and sometimes unsafe vessels have continued in service. A notable example of this occurred in Tonga in the 1970s, where fishing vessels from American Samoa, which had been condemned by the US authorities on safety grounds, were imported and used in the inter-island passenger trade.[5] Although the situation has improved during recent years, it is still possible in some areas of the Pacific to find small vessels employed for passenger carriage over long distances which are clearly unsafe in their low standards of maintenance and operation, and lack of safety equipment.

New Technology

In the case of government-owned vessels, the problem shifts to the higher end of the technology scale, with the acquisition of new ships depending heavily on the ideas and designs (in all senses of the word) of donor countries. The South Pacific contains numerous examples of unsuitable technology which stem mainly from this cause. For example, Australian aid vessels include the *Noel Buxton*, a lighthouse tender supplied to Papua New Guinea in the 1970s, which proved to have severe stability problems in service as well as maintenance difficulties; the *Queen Salamasina* (mentioned above), a roll-on/roll-off vessel supplied to Western Samoa in the same era, which was found to be unsuitable in design for her intended domestic ferry service; and the more recent coastal patrol boats, which many observers believe will be too sophisticated and costly for operation by island countries.

Similar examples occur in the case of the Micro Class 'Field Trip Ships' in the Marshall Islands and the Federated States of Micronesia, built in Japanese yards to an American design, which required the installation of permanent ballast to overcome inherent stability problems, and which are now being re-engined in an attempt to reduce the heavy operating costs caused by their extremely high fuel consumption. The latest example of problems engendered by technology acquisition under the aid process is the new *Nivanga II*, recently supplied to Tuvalu under the British aid programme for inter-island service. This vessel was hailed as bringing 'improved comfort, cleanliness and service' to the inter-island trade, and having a 'spotless and efficient engine-room . . . complete with computer console in an air-conditioned control room'.[6] One may well question the need for the installation of such sophisticated machinery. A similar trend also appears in much of the deck equipment, which includes modern, totally-enclosed davit-launched lifeboats. Overall, the new vessel is considerably larger than her predecessor, *Nivanga I*, and the problem of 50% increase in operating costs which now faces the Tuvalu government is largely due to increased fuel consumption. The comparative reduction in crew numbers engendered by use of more sophisticated equipment is an even more perplexing feature in a small country, with numerous unemployed seamen who have graduated from the national maritime training school, but have been unable to find work.

Maritime Training

From the aspect of maritime training, a similar picture emerges. The efforts of the Forum Secretariat to achieve common standards, through the general adoption of the South Pacific Maritime Code and integration of the maritime school training programmes, have met with considerable difficulties. One of the most notable difficulties has been the failure of aid agencies, both national and international, to coordinate their efforts toward the goals of the regional Maritime Code. Thus the Fijian Marine School, originally intended as the key regional centre for higher grades of training for the inter-island trade in the region, has now received large allocations of Japanese aid, and is diverting much of its resources to training crews of fishing vessels. Similarly, the Tongan marine school has been lavishly equipped under the West German aid programme, but appears to be largely concerned with supplying Tongan crews to vessels of German-owned companies. A similar but even more curious use of aid funds now seems to have occurred in the Marshall Islands, where UN assistance has apparently been given for crew training for vessels under that country's flag-of-convenience register (established in Honolulu), while the crews of the domestic inter-island 'Field Trip Ships' remained largely untrained and unqualified.

Appropriate Technology?
It is difficult to find examples of the application of suitable technology in inter-island shipping in recent times, and only two cases spring immediately to mind. As far as ship design is concerned, the moderate-cost vessels introduced into operation on the north coast of Papua New Guinea (Lae-Madang-Wewak) by the Lutheran Mission during the 1970s were examples of a design that was carefully thought out to meet the particular local-level problems imposed by the trade in that area. The vessels were of some 30–40 metres in length, with simple and easily maintained cargo gear and equipment and well-designed facilities for deck passengers.[7]

The second example is that of the training school in Vanuatu, which was established by the government in Port Vila during the early years of independence to provide suitable training courses for the crews of inter-island vessels. The school possessed a very modest stock of equipment, and received only minute quantities of foreign aid, but offset these disadvantages by means of a very enthusiastic and largely national staff, with carefully designed training programmes to suit local resources and needs.

It is apparent and important to note that these examples had three factors in common: they were small in scale, they depended largely on local initiatives, and, apart from background advice, they received little input from foreign aid donors in the design of their programmes.

Planning and the Development of Inter-Island Shipping

The problems of inter-island shipping can certainly not be solved by means of the large-scale acquisition of new vessels or the introduction of novel forms of technology. The most immediate requirement is to make more effective use of existing resources. For this purpose, the primary need is for island governments to give more priority to domestic marine transport and recognise that long term planning is needed in this area to develop a shipping technology suitable for local conditions. This planning should take into account such matters as the need, in many instances, for improved berthing arrangements for domestic trade vessels, and for improved maintenance and repair facilities.

Consideration also needs to be given to the relative roles of private operators and government in domestic shipping, whilst preserving the primary aims of providing regular services to outlying areas and holding passenger fares and freight rates to a reasonable level. A simple and workable domestic trade licensing system is needed for this purpose. More thought also needs to be given to the coordination of domestic air and sea transport, to ensure that costly resources are not wasted in duplication of services. Accompanying the need for improved planning at government level, there is also the necessity to achieve more coordination among aid donors in order to direct their resources towards the main problem areas affecting inter-island shipping.

In the technical field, careful thought also needs to be given to necessary improvements in the design of vessels to meet local service conditions, with particular attention paid to the following:

1. The problems of maintenance and repair, particularly consideration of the availability of shipyard facilities and supply of spare parts within the region.
2. The need for simplicity of operation and ease of maintenance in the design of shipboard machinery and equipment, and for design to take account of the skills of inter-island ships' crews and standards of training in the region.
3. The need for inter-island ship design to take account of the requirement for the carriage of large numbers of deck passengers.
4. The general need to reduce fuel consumption as the principal factor in operating costs of inter-island vessels.
5. The need to improve safety standards, with particular reference to the stability problems of small vessels and the safety of deck passengers.

In order to overcome these problems, the South Pacific region has one very considerable asset — the supply of available labour benefiting from the existence of strong traditions of maritime knowledge and expertise, combined with training in modern techniques.

One of the most immediate and effective steps towards the development of domestic shipping would be to coordinate the activities of the maritime schools in the region and expand their training programmes in order to improve the standard of crews in inter-island ships.

Land Transport: On Wheel and Foot

Tony Marjoram

◆◆◆

The ease and economy of transporting people and goods is a vitally important aspect of infrastructural development. Land transport provides links between rural and urban populations and commercial centres, improved access to schools, health care facilities and markets, connections with sea and air transport services, facilitating and promoting general social, economic and agricultural development.

Land transport in the South Pacific is complicated however, because most islanders live in small communities isolated by land and sea. The development of transportation is constrained by cost (where low usage means that socio-economic benefits may not justify large capital costs on strictly economic grounds) and other factors such as the environmental impact of road construction. A case in point is the causeway linking the administrative centre and islet of Betio with Bairiki and South Tarawa in Kiribati. This replaced the previous ferry service, but at a cost that was only possible through external aid, and with uncertain impacts on water circulation and flushing in Tarawa lagoon. Other secondary effects included the increased removal of biomass fuel from South Tarawa by Betio residents with improved access, and possible environmental degradation.

Compared to the other components of infrastructure in the South Pacific (airports, sewerage and water systems, telecommunications, energy generation and supply), road construction and maintenance is the single largest area of government expenditure. To give an idea of the total expenditure on land transport, the capital and operating costs of transport vehicles (trucks, buses, cars, motorbikes) should be added to this, because fuel and vehicles represent leading import categories. From the perspective of time and labour costs, people commuting and carrying goods on foot and by bicycle should also be considered, but are often overlooked in transport planning.

Perceptions and Functions of Transport Systems

Transport systems in the Pacific, as in many other countries, fall into two categories — the 'formal' sector of major roads planned, designed and engineered for motor vehicle transport (also used by many pedestrians), and the 'informal' sector of rural or local minor paths and tracks, often unplanned, used by pedestrians and lower cost vehicles, which are often ignored in transport planning and official statistics. As elsewhere, government transport planners and advisors have 'not been explicitly concerned with people and their transport needs', preferring to focus on formal engineered roads, concerned mainly with 'economic rather than socio-economic development . . . whose perception of rural transport is exemplified by lorries laden with crops for sale and vehicles taking busy officials about their business. For the rural inhabitants, on the other hand, the local transport system is the means to simplify the attainment of basic needs such as food, clothing, shelter, education and health'.[1]

Studies in various countries have revealed that rural people are more mobile than had been assumed (by planners), and that an equal if not greater amount of travel was devoted to relatively local socio-cultural and household tasks (such as farming, water and firewood collection) and leisure activities, rather than to more distant tasks (such as taking produce to market), which are the focus of conventional rural transport planning and agricultural development. In the Pacific context, however, Barwell notes that in Samoa (and the comments are relevant in other islands), 'studies provide specific evidence of inadequate transport as a constraint on agricultural production and marketing and indicate how this problem becomes greater with the need to increase farm outputs',[2] which is a general development goal of all island nations. It is therefore important to distinguish in rural areas between local (farm and non-farm) and distant (farm-market and non-farm) transport.

Roads

The technology associated with roads includes design, construction, maintenance, repair, traffic control (for example traffic lights and signs) and road lighting.

The World Bank classifies roads into three types:

Class 1 — major trunk/arterial roads (between cities or large towns)

Class 2 — minor trunk/arterial roads, secondary and feeder roads (between and within cities and towns/villages)

Class 3 — local, access or farm roads (between and within villages and farms).

Class 1 roads include 'primary distributors' — main or arterial roads. Class 2 roads include 'district distributors' — secondary or minor arterial roads. Class 3 roads include 'local distributors' — feeder, access and local and 'bush' roads. Class 1, 2 and some Class 3 roads are usually metalled (bitumen surfaced), whilst access, local and bush roads are generally unmetalled (and often primarily fair-weather roads). This classification does not include smaller informal paths and tracks primarily used by pedestrians.

The main roads in most island countries can be considered as Class 2 minor trunk roads on this classification, with other roads in the Class 3 category, and many informal tracks and paths. Despite an interest in improving smaller rural roads, most aid funding continues to be spent on main trunk roads (indeed, this is the policy of some donors, leaving the construction and maintenance of minor roads to local governments). Although there are undoubted benefits of improved transportation, this also has the effect of creating and perpetuating the dependence on road motor transport, together with the increasing need (and aspiration) for imported vehicles and fuel, consequently increasing import bills.[3] In the South Pacific (as elsewhere) it is useful to note that roads are also used as play areas, for casual sport (for example, for cricket, soccer and rugby), meeting places and as a surface for the solar drying of agricultural produce such as copra.

Road Design, Construction, Safety and Maintenance

Roads should be designed and constructed to cope with the current and anticipated future needs and safety of road users, and at the same time be acceptable and safe for local people and environment. These considerations are rarely totally compatible. Road design and construction includes such considerations as the type of road user, traffic movement and speed; road lanes, junctions; road geometry; road 'furniture'; access (for different types of road user), vehicle parking and bus stops. Safety issues include vehicle hazards close to the roadway, poor or absent footpaths and pedestrian crossings; the separation and protection of different types of road users to minimise conflict and danger; driver training, testing, discipline, and road law enforcement and the education of pedestrians and cyclists in safe road usage.[4]

Many of these considerations derive and relate to the (primarily Western) function and design of roads for (relatively) high speed motor transport, even though many roads began as paths and tracks, passing through residential areas. This is particularly the case in most island countries, and illustrates the need for improved and integrated land-use planning, giving greater priority to people rather than infrastructural development. Road construction also relies on the (primarily Western) use of specialised mechanised equipment, such as dozers, graders, rollers and bitumen-sprayers — to the extent that to many people (including many donor agencies and public works departments) road making is synonymous with expensive Western-style roads made with expensive Western equipment.

There are, however, alternative low-cost, labour-intensive construction techniques, which are particularly suitable for the construction of minor roads.[5] Such techniques have been recently introduced (or, more accurately, reintroduced, as this is how roads were made before the advent of mechanisation) into Vanuatu and the Solomon Islands by the International Labour Organisation (ILO). Low-cost construction techniques are labour-based rather than equipment-based, using local labour and low-cost equipment, such as small hand-drawn carts and rollers, rather than mechanised equipment, which is costly and often difficult to move into and maintain in isolated areas. Such low-cost techniques are particularly appropriate for outer islands and rural areas. In several instances village roads that would not otherwise have been built, due to economic constraints, have been constructed by villagers who want a road and are prepared to contribute an element of 'sweat equity'.

The correct maintenance of roads (road surface conditions, signs and other road 'furniture') is important, as poorly maintained roads are a cause of delay, accidents and damage to vehicles. There is a direct link between road conditions and vehicle operating costs. Roads should be designed to be readily maintained, and maintained on a frequent and timely basis, as the prompt repair of damage slows deterioration and helps avoid more extensive and expensive maintenance and reconstruction. As low-cost, labour-based roads are generally repairable by similar techniques to that with which they were constructed, and by similarly trained people, this is another advantage in their favour. Road maintenance includes monitoring and surveying for road condition and damage, relaying this information to road repair crews, and the training of road monitoring and repair crews.[6] The efficient organisation of road maintenance is also of obvious importance.

Modes of Transport

In the South Pacific, as in many developing countries, it is important not to forget that the primary mode of transport of many people and carriage of goods is by foot, particularly in rural areas. Most travel in the Pacific islands consists of trips of less than 5km, generally carrying less than 25kg and made on foot. Many households do not own vehicles, and there are few hand or bicycle carts. Longer trips tend to be made by bus, canoe or pickup, where larger loads, rarely exceeding 80kg, may be carried.

Vehicles

Technological issues associated with vehicles include vehicle choice, procurement, maintenance and repair. Industries associated with vehicle transport include garages to supply new and used cars and trucks, fuel, spares and provide maintenance and repair facilities, tyre repair and reconditioning (retreading), battery manufacture and bicycle repair. Safety issues include vehicle design, maintenance, operation (such as loading and overloading) and considerations relating to roadworthiness, vehicle licencing and inspection. Particular constraints and needs relating to vehicle transport include the financial resources (or credit schemes) to purchase and operate vehicles, vehicle choice, the supply of spare parts (particularly to rural areas) and the training of mechanics.

A UNIDO report published in 1978 summarised the main issues relating to vehicles in developing countries:

1. 'Access to vehicles of conventional design is severely restricted by the low incomes of the masses in developing countries (where) the local manufacture of these vehicles is enormously expensive. Fragmentation of the market, which is common in countries undertaking assembly and endemic in countries entirely dependent on imports, increases the cost of maintaining the vehicle population.

2. 'The main transport needs that are being met by conventional vehicles are those of long-distance movement of freight and of personal transport for the more affluent members of the urban community. There are major deficiencies in rural transport and in movement of urban passengers and short-distance movement of small loads of goods'.

A third point covering vehicle manufacture observed that interest in 'the design and manufacture of low-cost vehicles of smaller capacity and reduced performance have come from two main sources ... the manufacture of cheap three-wheeled vehicles [often following] the successful local manufacture of conventional cars, and recent initiatives of a number of international companies have led to the local assembly of four-wheeled vehicles that are basically small trucks of very simple design'.[7] Since these comments were made, it is apparent that the local assembly of small vehicles of simple design has not taken off as these companies may have hoped, largely because of the costs of producing limited numbers of vehicles, compared with cheaper imported mass-produced cars and trucks, particularly imports of used and reconditioned vehicles.

The importance of low-cost means of transport and walking should not be overlooked, however. Whilst smaller powered vehicles as described may have had limited success, the primary mode of transportation for people and goods in many developing countries are small engine- and human-powered three- and four-wheeled vehicles such as rickshaws and various types of motorcycle sidecars and 'jeepneys'. Walking remains the main mode of transport in many areas.

Pacific Perspectives

Typical problems faced by Pacific island nations in the transport sector relate to frequently undulating terrain and relatively isolated villages, where limited industrial development restricts the choice of transport alternatives. In the South Pacific, most journeys are made on foot, by bicycle, car, bus, truck or tractor. Public transport is limited and mainly provided by private operators (such as minibus private motor vehicles — PMVs — in PNG). Services tend to be focussed on urban rather than rural areas, where they are somewhat restricted. Apart from more general information, there is little detailed data regarding transport within Pacific islands, particularly in rural areas. Apart from a narrow-gauge railway for sugarcane collection in Fiji, there are no railways in the region (although the possibility of a conducting a feasibility study for constructing a rail system for public transport in urban Suva was mentioned in Fiji's Ninth Development Plan,[8] and there is a 'Railway Road' in Tonga, but no railway).

Because of cost and specific application, most heavy specialised vehicles in the South Pacific are owned by governments, often provided under aid. Many lorries, trucks and tractors are also government-owned, generally located in vehicle pools in public works departments, available for government use and public hire. Light commercial vehicles are mainly owned by small businesses, and private pickups and cars are owned by individuals, extended families, taxi operators and community groups.

In PNG, as elsewhere in the region, 'motor car ownership is almost entirely limited to the more affluent residents of the major centres, many of whom are foreigners'. The same study also commented on the excessively wide range of car and truck types available in PNG, and associated problems, where 'a policy of uncontrolled importation has led to an extraordinary variety of makes and sizes of vehicles' . . . 'sales have ranged over 117 makes and 436 make, size and body-type combinations. This fragmentation has compounded the problems of vehicle repair and has inhibited the growth of the repair industry. Spare parts are in inadequate supply and expensive; there is a shortage of trained mechanics, drivers and spare parts staff; service facilities are costly and inadequately maintained'.[9]

In Fiji the infrastructure and utilities sector accounts for around 45% of government expenditure. For the period of Fiji's Ninth Development Plan, 1986–90 (DP9), out of a estimated capital expenditure of F$231m, 38% was budgeted for transport development (with 29% for water and sewerage, 24% for postal and telecommunications services and 9% for energy). From the points of view of technology and employment, it is interesting to note in DP9 that 'more emphasis will be given to labour intensive options, wherever feasible, when making decisions on technology choice for infrastructure and utilities projects, so as to ensure maximum employment generation in this sector'.[10] Overall transport priorities in Fiji are the provision of an efficient and integrated network of transport services, both to promote development in rural areas and improve busy urban roads and to investigate and encourage the use of more cost- and energy-efficient means of transport. Other issues of interest in Fiji include:

- The unification of three statutory authorities responsible for traffic, licensing and transport.
- Support for the public transport bus industry in the face of problems from unregulated taxis and light goods vehicles.
- Concern over the increase in size and overloading of vehicles, causing increasing damage to roads and bridges.[11]

As elsewhere in the region, over half the population of Western Samoa lives in villages or rural areas, mainly on the coast, where economic activity is focussed on agriculture. Barwell observes that the main transport problems for Samoa relate to small village size, distances between villages and household plantations, limited road system and lack of regional market outlets. The two main transportation needs for most Samoans are between villages and the central market in Apia (to the market with crops, returning with household goods), and between villages and the household 'bush' plantation (to the plantation with tools and equipment, from the plantation with tools, equipment and produce). Village-plantation transportation problems increase as plantations tend to move further away from villages. Barwell reported that, in 1977, a typical small-farming household producing copra and cocoa would transport 50 tonnes of harvested crops from plantation to household per annum.[12] The main mode of transport between village and market is the bus, ute or small pickup truck (the most common vehicle in Samoa and elsewhere in the Pacific). The main mode of transport between village and plantation is on foot (carrying loads with a shoulder-pole) or horseback (first introduced by missionaries, as in Tonga), although a few pickups or rental tractor-trailers are also used for this purpose.

These two transportation needs lie at the ends of the range of possible options — walking or horseback is slow and of zero or very low capital investment (although the horse requires a significant area of grass for food), and whilst a pickup or tractor/trailer is faster, considerably higher capital investment is required. The use of motor vehicles is therefore restricted by their capital and running cost — reported at one pickup per 80–150 people in 1980. Barwell also investigated the potential for modes of transport that were intermediate between traditional and mechanised conveyance, with specific reference to horse-drawn carts, able to carry loads of up to 400kg plus driver. Potential was noted for intermediate transport technology 'which would both contribute to removing transport constraints and to reducing the need to import the alternative — tractors and trailers. While the investigation indicated that there was considerable interest in their use, the acceptability and demand for horse-drawn carts among rural families can only be proven by a programme to introduce this form of transport. Thus the study does not prove that horse carts are the most appropriate choice, but it does demonstrate that there is a choice available for exploration'.[13]

Most of the vehicles in Kiribati are on South Tarawa (the main population centre). Kiribati probably has the largest per capita population of bicycles and small motorcycles in the South Pacific — in 1984, vehicle registrations on South Tarawa comprised 61% small motorcycles (a percentage which has since increased to around 75%), with 36% cars and trucks and 3% buses. To promote the use of bicycles on outer islands and small, fuel-efficient motorcycles, the sale of Chinese aid bicycles is subsidised and motorcycles are limited to less than 50cc.

Organisation of Transport
Only the larger island countries have ministries and departments devoted specifically to transport. The PNG Department of Transport is divided into Maritime and Land Transport Divisions, mainly concerned with finance, development, training, policy and planning, monitoring and evaluation. The Technical Services Division of the Ministry of Works has a Roads and Bridges Branch, mainly responsible for design, with the Construction Branch of the Operations Division mainly responsible for construction and maintenance. The Ministry of Communications, Works and Transport in Fiji has a Road Transport Department incorporating a Transport Control Board and Central Traffic Authority responsible for licensing, law enforcement, taxi, rental and hire car control, driving examiners and schools, vehicle inspection and Road Safety Council. The Fiji Public Works Department is responsible for surveying, design engineering and the maintenance of roads. In smaller and medium size island countries,

government departments generally have joint responsibility for the whole field of transport and communications, with public works responsible for technological aspects and police responsible for licensing and traffic control.

Appropriate Vehicle Technology

Whilst not directly relevant to the South Pacific, the third point made in the UNIDO report noted above illustrates the need for and problems of selecting vehicles suitable for small islands. Although there are particular constraints of market size and difficulties of manufacturing all but the most basic vehicles in the region, it is clear that smaller vehicles (especially two- and three-wheeled vehicles) could take advantage of the small size of many islands and island communities. As the UNIDO report concludes, 'these vehicles have a major part to play in economic development. Moreover, the simpler production techniques involved mean that manufacture can be more readily undertaken at lower volumes of production in countries at an early stage of industrial development. This feature can reduce the foreign-exchange cost of providing an adequate transport system and contribute directly to the enhancement of productive abilities and technical skills ... To secure these developments, the flow of information on vehicle types and productive techniques should be promoted as a matter of urgency. Governments of developing countries should pay attention to the possible role of low-cost vehicles in their economies and frame development policies accordingly'.[14]

In this context, it is interesting to note that a vehicle designed particularly for developing countries — the 'Africar', a pickup made using standard car components in a rugged chassis using flat body parts made from plywood — was demonstrated with a view to construction and sale in Fiji and the South Pacific. Despite the environmental suitability of the car, it was apparent that, as mentioned above, consumer preference was for cheaper new or reconditioned imported cars.

Other low-cost, energy-efficient vehicles include bicycles, bicycle and hand trailer. On the subject of bicycle transport in Western Samoa, Barwell comments that 'it is noteworthy that the bicycle is quite rare in the rural areas, and is certainly not the important means of rural transport that it is in many African and Asian countries. Typical travel distances are quite high, and the humid, high-rainfall climate and undulating terrain in many rural areas are not conducive to cycling'.[15]

Whilst these comments apply to longer journeys and hilly terrain, bicycles are used for shorter distance journeys over flatter terrain in Samoa and most other Pacific islands, and there is considerable potential for the expansion of bicycle use and associated modes of transportation, such as bicycle trailers. Bicycle technology fits well into the wide niche that exists between the extremes of human and mechanised means of transport. Work by the present author (in Tonga) revealed considerable interest in the use of bicycle and hand trailers when such vehicles were demonstrated, and that this is a potential choice of alternative transport technology.

A small platform trailer and coupling was designed and developed for use with a standard, unmodified bicycle. Attention was also directed at the specific problem of the transportation and sale of fresh fish to nearby households and villages from the main fish landing wharf and market. The distances involved were too great for walking and uneconomic for the use of motor vehicle delivery, and the use of bicycle trailers accorded with overall development goals of removing impediments to the sale of nutritious local foodstuffs (in the face of increasing consumption of tinned fish) for the majority of people who do not possess transport or refrigerators, and the promotion of local industry. Interest focussed on the use of the trailer to carry a locally made fibreglass esky (ice-box) for the transportation and sale of fresh fish stored in ice.

The bicycle trailer and ice-box created considerable interest, although only a demonstration model was produced. The acceptability, reliability and demand for bicycle trailers (as for any other new technology), would require further proving by an expanded programme of demonstration to innovate the technology into suitable contexts of use and favourable topographic conditions. Government support would be important for such an undertaking, preferably including the use of bicycles and bicycle trailers in relevant departments to gain maximum 'demonstration effect' and counter some public perception of bicycles as a low-status form of transport. In this context, it is useful to note that bicycles are used by Australia Post as local delivery vehicles, and that bicycle trailers are not uncommon in Europe.

Transport Planning and Policy
Transport policy should seek to improve the capabilities of roads (including paths and tracks) and vehicles to match need with affordability for the majority of island populations — with a particular emphasis on rural areas. As noted above, there is a need for more detailed information regarding transport activities and requirements within Pacific islands, particularly in rural areas. More information is required on the mode, purpose and frequency, distance and typical loads carried, safety and accident data regarding all transport activities and needs. It should also be noted that there is scope for research, design, development and production and the adaptation and modification of low-cost, energy-efficient vehicles in the South Pacific, particularly of hand and bicycle trailers, animal drawn

vehicles and low-powered (5–10hp) motorised vehicles for farm and non-farm application.

At a national level, to address some of the problems attaching to the multiplicity of imported vehicles, it was reported in PNG in 1978 that 'Official motor vehicle policies are being reviewed. It is planned to reduce the range of vehicles imported, perhaps by establishing a government monopoly of imports. Manufacturers of selected vehicles will be required to assist with the training of mechanics, and measures will be taken to assist the setting up of service facilities in remote areas. Attention is being paid to the possibility of reducing the demand for cars by providing a more satisfactory alternative public transport system'.[16]

Although laudable in intent, the implementation of such a policy was fraught with a whole range of problems. The PNG government went some way towards possible rationalisation of imports of four-wheel drives, saloon cars, trucks, buses and outboard motors, with a view to limiting imports to one or two models in each category. The review was dropped, largely due to the negative response of the German government. Although not exporting any vehicles to PNG at the time, but concerned that such a policy could affect possible future exports, the German government indicated that if PNG pursued such a policy, then Germany would have to review the importation of PNG coffee. On related issues, vehicle manufacturers, importers and aid donors have gone some way in terms of mechanic training. Little has been done to improve public transport systems in the region, and indeed services have often worsened as government support has declined with the trend toward privatisation.

Particular problems of transportation in the South Pacific relate to technology choice and decision-making, as often revealed in associated problems of operation and maintenance. Road construction generally continues to be capital- and equipment- rather than labour-intensive, and both roads and road-making plant tend to suffer problems of limited maintenance. Road furniture — such as road signs, traffic lights, crossings and road lights — also has poor reliability. Specific examples include the construction of roads that serve political rather than economic ends, misplaced priorities in such areas as road lighting and the expenditure of more funds on meetings of the roads committee than on roads in one country, the misuse of government vehicles and unsuitable 'tied' transport technology from aid donors.

The operations of government vehicle pools face many problems, including the high indebtedness of government departments, criticism of excessive hire charges, misuse of vehicles for private purposes, damage to vehicles (often due to careless driving), poor maintenance, insufficient tools, equipment and spares. These and other factors have led many countries to consider the reduction or disestablishment and privatisation of vehicle pools, at least as regards less specialised vehicles. Radar speed detectors have also been used by more than one regional police force to raise police revenue as much as to maintain road safety. Many of the above problems are largely a function of the choice and transfer of technology that is partly inappropriate, with insufficient support services.

* * * *

Most travel within Pacific islands is within the village or local community for socio-cultural and small-farmer activities, over relatively small distances, with relatively small loads, usually on foot on (or at the side of) minor roads, paths and tracks. Longer trips are less frequent, and generally by bus or pickup. The problems faced by people with such transport needs are not generally well addressed by conventional transport planning, with a focus on engineered roads and motor vehicles, where much of the transport budget of most island nations is expended.

Greater emphasis on these needs and of lower cost means of transport are required, linking these requirements within the wider conventional national transport systems. Particular reference should be made to the promotion of low-cost, labour-based road construction techniques and low-cost, energy efficient vehicles, as mentioned in Fiji's Ninth Development Plan, such as bicycle and hand trailers. Greater attention is also required regarding transport technology management. Governments, aid donors, development banks and NGOs could be active in these areas, especially as regards technology transfer, innovation and credit support to small farmers, small business, industry and community groups.

A shift towards socio-economic rather than purely economic factors of appraisal is also required and whilst, as Barwell observes, 'the economic rationale for low-cost transport investments remains to be proven, the indications . . . are that a more rational approach to rural transport planning is not only socially desirable but economically viable'. There should be a particular emphasis on the quantification and reduction of 'the drudgery associated with the movement element of subsistence tasks'.[17] This, along with subsistence activities that account for the working time of many rural islanders (particularly women), is acknowledged to have been generally neglected by transport planners.

AVIATION

TONY MARJORAM

◆◆◆

Aviation has been crucial in Pacific island development. Improved air services have increased interest in regional cooperation, the advent of mass tourism and the development of island industry and trade with the outside world.

Aviation has helped minimise the problems of small size and isolation at regional and national levels. Nearly all visitors to the region arrive by aeroplane — a situation that has changed dramatically since the 1950s and 1960s, with the improvement of regional air services. Many Highlanders in Papua New Guinea may have seen and flown in small planes before even seeing motor vehicles. Airport terminals are often busier than local markets as travellers, friends, relatives, business and aid people mingle, particularly in those island nations with high migrant connections.

Like other technology, aviation is a double-edged sword. Aeroplanes have brought positive and negative changes to the region. There are disadvantages as well as advantages associated with increased tourism, migration, economic and industrial development. Both advantages and disadvantages derive from a closer connection with other islands and the outside world — for small resource-poor countries, closer proximity also leads to increased external dependence.

This chapter looks at aviation as a technology vital for Pacific island development. Aviation, similar in many ways and closely related to telecommunications, is the very epitome of many of the problems the Pacific islands face in dealing with sophisticated and expensive Western technology — in terms of technology choice, decision-making, finance and acquisition, management, operation and maintenance.

Background

The year 1928 is significant for Pacific aviation, with the first crossing of the Pacific by Charles Kingsford-Smith and Charles Ulm in a Fokker Tri-Motor, the 'Southern Cross', in a seven-day trip from Oakland, California to Brisbane, via Hawaii and Fiji. The grand old days of civil aviation began with the flying boats, a 15-year cul-de-sac of technology development (a legacy of which was the Laucala Bay flying boat station, which later became the campus of the University of the South Pacific). Floats gave way to wheels, with the Super Constellations, DC-4s and DC-6s, piston engines gave way to turbo-props, narrow and wide-bodied jets — DC-8s, DC-10s, Boeing 707s, 727s, 737s, 747s and 767s.

Like the sailing ships that discovered the Pacific, aircraft were also used in exploration, mainly for exploiting valuable natural resources, particularly gold. One of the busiest routes for civil aviation in the world in the 1930s was between Australia and Papua New Guinea, with the airlift of gold mining equipment into the Wau/Bulolo goldfield.[1]

The Pacific war of 1942–45 introduced aircraft into the region in a big way, when many islanders were first exposed to the wonders and ravages of Western technology for the first time. Many island airstrips date from this period. Aviation continued to be of importance in the region — in 1962 there were nearly as many aircraft movements and as much freight handled in PNG as in Sydney or Melbourne, illustrating the importance of civil aviation in a country without major trunk roads.

Aviation and Development in the South Pacific

Aviation has played a major role in overcoming the constraints of smallness and isolation, by sea and land, of communities and countries in the South Pacific. These constraints present obvious problems for aviation in the region — of huge distances over water and mountainous country, using small and medium-size aircraft for relatively few passengers and little freight — from the aviation point of view small is definitely not beautiful in the South Pacific. Particular problems for aviation in the islands are limited capital and technological infrastructure.

Operating conditions in the island Pacific are also hard — 'the typical Pacific islands airline is under-capitalised, has difficulty in recruiting and keeping pilots and engineers, and works in an environment, including salt spray and high humidity, that puts considerable stress on air frames, engines and electronic equipment'.[2]

There is some debate as to the precise economic benefits of national airlines to Pacific island nations.[3] There is, however, little question regarding the overall benefits of aviation in national development in the region — 'connection is all important'.[4] Apart from profit and foreign exchange earnings (or loss), Kissling points out several benefits of aviation:

1. Strengthening of internal national cohesion by reducing the isolation factor.
2. Assistance in the necessary surveillance of national resources such as fisheries inside the 200 mile EEZ.
3. Assistance with regional development through spreading the benefits of tourism and by providing air cargo services for local enterprises for which speed is essential — aviation can help the economic diversification process.
4. Hastening the spread of new ideas and techniques.
5. Increasing access to medical and educational services.
6. Permitting reductions in inventory and storage costs.[5]

Most of these benefits are technology-related. Kissling also observes that skills acquired in connection with aviation have several useful spin-offs in the transfer of technical and management skills.

Aviation and Tourism

Aviation and tourism in the region are closely linked — aviation technology is vital for economic development through tourism. This is illustrated by the decision in 1989 of the newly elected government of the Solomon Islands to establish a Ministry of Tourism and Aviation — a 'significant milestone' for a regional government in acknowledging the joint economic importance of these two sectors.[6] Aviation also opens a window and door to the outside world for islander travel and migration. Most Pacific islands are significantly dependent on aviation for tourist incomes, even though islands only receive a smaller part of what tourists pay for their holidays, as many island hotels (and airlines) are partly or fully owned by outside interests.

Negative Impacts of Aviation

There are numerous adverse impacts of aviation. These include the disadvantages of tourism and migration — tourism has a significant potential to distort sensitive local societies, cultures and economies, and migration leads to a net loss of skilled people. Light aircraft have adversely affected coastal shipping and further depressed outer-island economic activity, contributing to rural-urban drift and out-migration.

An Overview and Analysis of Contemporary Aviation in the South Pacific

There are two distinct types of aviation operators and operation in the South Pacific — international operators (main system) and local/regional operators, who act as feeder services (sub-system) for international operators.

The main airline operators at the international level in the Pacific are Qantas, Ansett, Air New Zealand and UTA (in the French territories). Local/regional island airlines and aviation operators include over 25 companies, who between them fly (own or lease) 164 aircraft of 40 types ranging from a single 747 down to 46 Islanders, and 44 helicopters of 6 types.[7]

Networks of Power

The international and local/regional systems mesh together, and it has been observed that this arrangement was deliberately set up and maintained in this fashion by international airline operators in their own interest. It is in this context — of the business environment of organisations and the 'political economy' of aviation technology as 'networks of power' that aviation technology in the Pacific has been most penetratively analysed.[8]

As noted elsewhere in this volume, Western technology shapes Pacific island societies. Aviation technology is no exception to this, and is indeed an epitome of colonial and post-colonial development. Transport systems and structures in the island colonies grew in response to colonial needs and the particular exigencies of the Pacific war. The context of more recent development of island aviation is in close connection with tourism and the international airlines who to a large extent control Pacific air traffic and tourism.

To understand Pacific aviation it is important to examine international enterprises (in this case the major airline operators), their access to resources and their relationship with the Pacific rim and islands. It is an analysis of corporate power, control of resources and changing technology, with the added ingredients of international relations and foreign aid. The pattern of analysis follows the approach of dependency theory.[9] This approach is of particular use in looking at aviation in the South Pacific, and is in contrast to earlier analyses, which either focussed on macro-level studies of regional traffic flows, or micro-level studies of individual projects, based on neo-classical economics and profit maximisation. These studies neglected much of the behaviour and rationale of business organisations.

Compared to island countries, the major airlines in Australia and New Zealand have unequal access to resources of technology (hardware and software) and finance, and dominate the South Pacific. The dominant international airlines and the dominated regional and island airlines exist in assymetric 'power networks'. Despite access to soft loans and other forms of aviation support, the main resource advantages or bargaining chips of the islands are landing rights and as tourist destinations. The major airlines have the resource advantages of technology, finance and information in the form of hardware and software systems, and the choice between alternative island destinations. The major airlines are able to negotiate from these positions of power. Island airlines are unequal partners in the development of island aviation. Island nations have unequal access to the resources of the major airline operators, who protect these resources and use them to manipulate and protect their environment. This understanding helps explain the continued dependence of Pacific islands on outside aviation technology. With national sovereignty comes corporate dependence, resulting in 'the creation, perpetuation and intensification of (interacting) "segmented" or "dualistic" economic structures' in island nations.[10]

An interesting example of power-network thinking is revealed in comments on a study undertaken for SPEC/UNDP in 1985, where the prime recommendation was of an integrated network of airline services, which would allow airline costs to be reduced by 10% and revenue improved. A senior commentator on regional aviation observed that 'the report overlooked a considerable number of factors that made the introduction of the prime recommendation of integrating Pacific air services impossible . . . the main factor totally disregarded was that the main players at the time were operators of large aeroplane fleets placed at the rim of the island nations basin: they all have fleets of their own and the resources to fund any type of aircraft appropriate for the region. Ansett, Qantas and Air New Zealand all showed a high level of disinterest in the proposal. Ansett, in particular, considered the plan to be both unworkable and unnecessary'. Regarding cost reduction and increased revenues, the commentator observed that this was a 'remarkable and unsubstantiable claim'.[11]

An implication of these networks of airline power in the Pacific is that the provision of air services between Pacific islands is not a priority of international operators, who would prefer to fly direct to individual islands unless otherwise encouraged or obliged, avoiding increased costs and possible complications of bargaining with islands regarding 'freedoms of the air'.[12] Flying rights are an important consideration for foreign policy and economic development, particularly for small island nations, who have little else to trade when dealing with international airline operators.

Aviation and Development — The Cook Islands

Linking aviation technology with tourism, airline power and aid, the saga of the Cook Islands airport is of interest.[13] From 1960, with the end of the flying boat service from New Zealand, the Cook Islands was faced with a particular problem — the airstrip on Rarotonga was too small to take jet aircraft. To cope with the problem an agreement was reached between the Cook Islands and New Zealand to upgrade the airstrip to accomodate jets up to DC-10 type. The airstrip was completed in 1974, at an eventual cost of $11m. In return for this aid, Air New Zealand was given sole landing rights, giving 'New Zealand useful bargaining chips for its air traffic rights negotiations with Fiji and the United States, in essence the aid buying enhanced commercial viability for the national carrier, Air New Zealand'. New Zealand would also benefit from a degree of control over tourism (the Rarotongan Hotel was built to the same capacity as a DC-10, with 66% NZ public company shareholding). New Zealand also hoped that the need for longer term aid to the Cook Islands would decline as the improved airport would help the country commercially. Technological and other factors intervened, however, with the DC-10s being replaced by 747s, which were able to overfly the Cook Islands, and could not land on the Rarotonga airstrip until further modifications were made. Cook Islands tourism never took off the way it was hoped. Later restrictions also affected air freight to NZ, and several small industries that had developed to make use of the DC-10 connection failed. The Cook Islands then had to exert considerable political pressure for Air New Zealand to provide reasonable services.

Aviation Technology

Aviation can present a 'technology trap' for Pacific islands. Because Western technology is developed for Western needs, more sophisticated and larger aircraft of longer range are able to overfly the Pacific, without using the Pacific islands as 'way-ports' or stop-overs. At the same time, island airlines are less able to afford the latest in smaller aircraft technology. These trends are not in island interests, and islands suffer from the 'limitations of imposed technologies' — being technology takers rather than technology makers.[14] These problems relate to the dominance of Western airlines and operators. To lure more jets down from the skies, Pacific islands need airports built to cater for these aircraft, and related tourist facilities.

There are many problems relating to the choice and operation of aircraft in the Pacific islands. In addition to operating constraints noted above, aircraft are frequently flown to the limit of endurance range, but with low service hours, limited service capability (usually only line maintenance at most airfields), considerable distance to major service centres and the need to hold considerable inventories of spares to overcome service delays (Friendly Island Airways in Tonga had to build a $US200,000 inventory of spare parts to cope with this problem). These problems are such that 'the Pacific needs aircraft that do not really exist'.[15]

Two examples of successful small workhorse aircraft in the Pacific are the 19-seat Canadian De Havilland Twin Otter and smaller British Britten Norman Islander — 'their simple, rugged construction, fixed landing gear, and high-wing format are built for plunking down on rough grass or gravel airstrips in hot climates typical of Pacific island aviation. These two planes should keep their place until the end of this century since the cost of buying, running and maintaining the 'high technology' aircraft offered now by aircraft manufacturers can rarely make economic sense in the circumstances the region's smaller airlines operate in'.[16]

The management of aviation technology in all areas (aircraft, airport, booking, ticketing and reservations, training and air-freight) includes important and interconnected considerations regarding technology policy, planning, choice, decision-making, operation, maintenance and training, regarding both technology software (systems) and hardware. These factors oblige islands to use aircraft inefficiently and unproductively.[17] Because of the cost of smaller planes, islands often buy used aircraft that are uncompetitive, near the end of their service life, requiring more maintenance. If island nations lease aircraft ('dry lease' with crew or 'wet lease' without crew), they do so on terms dictated by lessors — usually international carriers. A problem of buying or hiring is that either island states generally have to use one aircraft in two different roles, or buy two (or more) aircraft at higher cost and maintenance requirement.

Problems regarding airstrips in the island Pacific mainly concern the need for sufficient length and surface strength to cope with aircraft that may use the runway. Tropical temperatures reduce lift and necessitate longer runways. Terminal technical facilities include navigational aids, communications, refuelling, maintenance and safety services. Passenger facilities are required to cope with the number of passengers borne by aircraft using the airport, often at relatively infrequent intervals (there may be less than one flight per day).

Booking, ticketing, reservations, baggage, customs, immigration and quarantine facilities all need to be of a reasonable standard of performance and reliability. A problem for many island countries in respect of booking, ticketing and reservations is that they are dependent on international telecommunications and external computer reservation systems — for example, Air Niugini, Air Pacific and Polynesian Airlines all subscribe to the Qantas QANTAM computer reservation system. Baggage handling problems have long been recognised — 'We are no longer leaving baggage behind. We have had only three complaints this year' (1989).[18]

Training to international standard is important to cope with the many problems and constraints of Pacific aviation, but with low throughputs training is expensive and constitutes yet another problem.

Dennis Buchanan (regional aviation entrepreneur and owner of Talair) has commented that plans for a regional aeronautical college were 'pie in the sky'.[19] Both Air Niugini and Air Nauru use an Australian Airlines flight simulator.

Air Freight

Improved air freight services are essential for small business and industrial development in the islands because of the improved access and speed of delivery of equipment and spare parts. Air freight to the island Pacific is affected by the increasing overflight of the islands with long range wide-bodied jets and use of 'unit load devices' (a sort of aircraft containerisation), as few Pacific airports have ULD handling facilities. International carriers are also keener to accept freight that requires minimal handling over longer distances. For perishable freight (as for human beings), the timing of flight departure, transit and arrival is also important (anyone who has flown in the South Pacific will know that flight times are more to do with the convenience of dominant airlines rather than passengers).

Data produced by Kissling shows what the following categories of goods accounted for in terms of percentages of imported air freight (by weight):[20]

Machinery, Vehicles and Electrical Equipment — 28.9%

Scientific, Professional Precision Instruments and Supplies — 14.3%

Chemical and Related Products — 8.1%

Textiles, Fibres and Manufactures — 7.4%

These are essentially 'technological' goods, and add up to 58.7% of this air freight sample (of the rest, 'Paper, Reed, Rubber and Wood Manufactures' and 'Miscellaneous Goods' represent 13.9% and 14.4% of the remaining 41.3% of 'non-technological' cargo).

Problems of Pacific Aviation

Typical problems faced by Pacific airline operators include inappropriate technology, difficult operating conditions, problems with maintenance and spare parts. Fatal crashes involving DH Heron aircraft in Fiji were considered by the NZ Department of Civil Aviation to have occurred largely because of the age of the aircraft, their unsuitability to local conditions and under-experienced pilots. Island airlines purchase and lease unsuitable aircraft because of difficulties regarding the choice of appropriate technology (technical specifications of aircraft can be difficult to interpret, especially to the uninitiated).

Island governments and airlines are subject to external and internal pressures and influences. Air Pacific purchased BAC 1-11 largely because of the post-colonial British connection, although the aircraft were expensive to operate with low revenue hours. Air Tungaru and Friendly Island

Airways both purchased Casa (NC 212-200) aircraft. Air Tungaru reported problems obtaining spare parts, high operating costs and the unsuitability of the aircraft to local needs, and decided to sell before FIA bought their Casa. FIA subsequently encountered similar problems and also decided to sell. Both aircraft were grounded and remained unsold for some time. The FIA Casa was also allegedly purchased under political influence, as it had a rear drop-door and cargo bay big enough to accommodate a Mercedes Benz. The PNG Minister of Civil Aviation, Mr Okuk, purchased Canadian De Havilland Dash 7 aircraft in 1981 (later found to be unsuitable), with little apparent reference to service needs and aircraft specifications. Whilst aid donors provide navigation and ground control equipment to help island airways and aviation, this may also be seen as serving to assist airlines from donor countries.

Difficult operating conditions due to salty and corrosive atoll environments caused problems for the Dornier 228 of Air Micronesia. Turbines have been found to more reliable than piston engines, but more expensive to purchase and maintain. Problems were encountered in Tonga of inadequate fuel supplies on an outer island, necessitating flying the route with a return fuel load. A Beechcraft Queenair in the Solomon Islands regularly belly-landed due to undercarriage problems, and the rate of engine removal necessary for maintenance on this aircraft type was found to be more than doubled in Micronesia, compared to mainland USA.[21]

* * * *

Kissling noted in 1984 that 'Dominance through the supply of technology may replace dominance through ownership and the deployment of personnel'.[22] Since then, a trend toward technology domination and dependence is evident, with the greater need of island access to international airline technology such as QANTAM and other computer reservation systems.

To reduce the domination of overseas airline interests and operators, inequality and segmentation of island aviation, island nations need to gain more control over their operating environment. To achieve this, greater South Pacific regional and national input and control over resources of technology and finance are essential. Despite international airline concern regarding an integrated network of airline services, island governments should be cautious of operators of large aeroplane fleets placed at the rim of the island nations basin and their judgment regarding the type of aircraft appropriate for the region. Here is revealed the political economy of technology choice and an increasing dependence on outside resources.

Mining: El Dorado or Fool's Gold?

Don Stewart

◆◆◆

In a world where the industrialised nations are increasingly hungry for a larger share of available natural resources, the resources owned by developing countries seem to many of those nations to be their one chance to trade competitively on the world scene. Because of this, South Pacific countries, for the most part, have welcomed opportunities to allow the exploitation of their natural resources, whether they be non-renewable resources like minerals or 'renewable resources' like timber or fish. This chapter will concentrate on the issue of mineral exploitation.[1] The boundary of several mobile tectonic plates occurs around the Pacific Ocean. This is the so-called 'Rim of Fire' which is characterised by volcanoes and epithermal gold deposits. The Pacific 'Rim of Fire' passes through Papua New Guinea, the Solomon Islands, Vanuatu and Fiji, and all these countries are currently the scene of considerable mineral exploration. For Papua New Guinea, mining is a major source of export income. In the Solomon Islands and Vanuatu, mining is developing and could become an important export earner in the future.

Mining is also important in New Caledonia and Nauru, for different minerals. New Caledonia contains 30% of the world's laterite nickel, and mining provides 95% of all exports for that country. Nauru's economy is completely dominated by mining, exporting of 1.5 million tonnes per year of high grade phosphate rock, giving Nauru one of the world's highest GNP per capita figures. The phosphate is, however, running out and the economic policy of the country is directed towards

---

using phosphate royalties to obtain a sufficient portfolio of investments to provide funds for the small island community when this happens.

This is an economist's view of mining in the Pacific. If we are interested in development in any meaningful sense we must look beyond the export dollar figures. The export dollars may be large and the sums of money flowing to the government from taxes and royalties may also be a substantial portion of government income, but most developing countries entered into agreements for exploitation of their mineral resources with the expectation that the substantial investment involved would be a stimulus to economic development in the country and bring broader development benefits. In fact this has rarely been the case. The export dollars may be large but so are the dollars flowing out as loan repayments, dividends and other forms of repatriation. The mines have few links to the rest of the economy and have operated as enclaves. Generally the only significant benefit flowing from mineral resource exploitation has been the share of mine revenue going to government.[2] The size of this has depended on the negotiating skills of the government. Whether or not this has been a satisfactory amount is always a debatable issue.

The question then is: 'In what ways has mining impacted on the lives of the people of the South Pacific?'. In answering this question we must look at the issues in the broadest sense; in terms of economic, social, political and environmental issues. We must also ask ourselves 'Has the technology chosen made a difference to these impacts?'.

Mining in the South Pacific: Past and Present

Apart from mining of traditional items such as obsidian (for stone axes) and pigments, there has been no long term history of mining in the South Pacific. Metalliferous mining came with the white man and as usual the gold prospector was in the vanguard. If he was successful he was followed by many more, in the way of gold rushes the world over. When the easily won gold gave out the individual miner was followed by the mining company in the second phase of mining development, and often the gold led to other metals. The third phase of mining in the South Pacific, as elsewhere, has been the phase of systematic mineral exploration, large multinational mining companies and very big mines.

The local people have not been merely onlookers in all this. The gold digger who arrived at Edie Creek in New Guinea in the 1920s from North Queensland or the Yukon found that his role was different. Instead of enduring backbreaking labour in his search for gold he was now a supervisor and an entrepreneur. He could have had recruited for him a team of 24 natives (16 carriers, 8 labourers) who would operate his claim and carry supplies on the five-day journey from Salamaua on the coast to

Wau. For this the natives received the princely sum of 10 shillings a month (A$1).[3] This has been the pattern in the foreign-owned mining industry to the present day: the local people may drive the dump trucks or work in the assay laboratory but not many are found at the most senior levels. This, however, is not to decry the very substantial efforts which have been made in training of citizens by mining companies; for example, in the years since the mine opened Bougainville Copper Limited (BCL) trained 1070 apprentices (25% of the country's total in those areas) and provided university education for many Papua New Guineans. It simply reflects the fact that multinational corporations such as BCL are fully international and in the managerial and technical areas they buy their expertise on the world market. Few Pacific islanders are selling expertise at this level.

The limited participation of local people in mining in their own countries is not quite the whole story. In recent years there has been the parallel development of an indigenous mining industry in Papua New Guinea with local small-scale gold miners and in the years 1988 to 1990 a totally indigenous full-scale gold rush began at Mount Kare in the PNG Highlands. It would be tempting to see this as phase one of a similar pattern of development to that of the overseas-owned mines, but with a time lag of some 50 years. Time will tell whether this is the case.

Papua New Guinea
The first gold mining in Papua New Guinea occurred on Misima Island in 1888 but it was not until gold was found in the vicinity of the present town of Wau in the Morobe Province that mining began in earnest. The first gold discoveries were in 1922 and by 1926 a gold rush had begun. In September that year there were 30 white miners and 790 labourers and by the next February the number of local people employed in the area had grown to over 3000. The foreigners who owned the leases and supervised the mining were the main benefactors. In 1926/27 £190,000 (A$380,000) was paid for gold exported from the field while the wages bill amounted to £7,800 (A$15,600), that is about 4%.

By 1930 the easily won gold was being worked out and the next phase of mining was starting. This took two forms, underground and open pit mining of the lode deposits, which are the deposits of quartz rock containing veins of gold (the alluvial deposits are produced from these when they are worn away) and dredging of the lower grade but extensive alluvials of the lower Bulolo Valley. Transporting dredges to the goldfields was a formidable task and was accomplished by the pioneering use of aircraft for freight transport. The first dredge commenced operation in 1932 and by the start of World War Two there were eight dredges operating. The dredges were decommissioned during the war but by 1948 all eight were again operating. The general decline in the gold industry, while the price of gold was held at $US36/oz, reduced profitability and the last dredge ceased operation in 1964. In all, these dredges produced 65.72 tonnes of gold and 29.56 tonnes of silver.

Two companies commenced mining lode gold in the early 1930s and one — New Guinea Goldfields — operated continuously, except for the war, until 1989. By 1977 it had produced 13.57 tonnes of gold. In 1982 it was taken over by the Australian mining group Renison Goldfields Consolidated who proceeded to build a new mill and double capacity. In 1990, however, the mine closed due to insufficient reserves, 57 years after commencing operation.

Bougainville

In 1972 there started an entirely new phase of mining in Papua New Guinea. The low grade copper/gold porphyry mine which commenced operation at Panguna on Bougainville Island was the world's largest copper mine at start-up, and throughput has been continually upgraded during the mine's operation. The mine, operated by Bougainville Copper Limited, a subsidiary of the Australian mining giant CRA, which in turn is part of the major British mining house RTZ, has through its operation provided between 15 and 25% of the income of the Papua New Guinea government each year as its share of the profits from the sale of the 150,000 to 200,000 tonnes of copper and 15 to 20 tonnes of gold produced by the mine during its years of operation.

The mine was closed in May 1989 due to the action of militants in sabotaging mine installations and attacking mine workers and is now (January 1993) under the control of the rebels (as is the rest of the island of Bougainville). With much of the mine infrastructure destroyed, the company believes that it would take funds of the order of A$400 million to bring the mine back into operation. The demands of the militants were initially for A$10 billion in compensation, closure of the mine and, most importantly, secession of Bougainville from Papua New Guinea.

In retrospect it is possible to see at least three mistakes which occurred in the original arrangements for the mine. The first was fairly quickly rectified but the other two have a direct bearing on the current troubles. Firstly, the terms initially agreed by the then Australian administration of Papua New Guinea with the company were far too generous to the company. This was largely rectified by the 1974 agreement which made the company liable for royalties, normal company tax and a novel 'Additional Profits Tax', which has since been used in other mining agreements in Papua New Guinea and copied elsewhere in the world. The 'Additional Profits Tax' means that in years of high profits due to high mineral prices, 70% of the additional profits would accrue to the government.

Another decision which can be seen in retrospect to be unfortunate was the Australian administration's agreement that the mine could proceed without a tailings dam. This has meant that some 36 million tonnes of fine solids have entered the Kawerong/Jaba river system and the Empress Augusta Bay each year of the mine's operation, causing massive changes to the topography and ecology of these areas and consequent distress to the local people. Ironically the company was well advanced in planning a tailings pipeline which would have improved the situation somewhat when rebellion forced the abandonment of the project.

Another area of difficulty has been that of compensation to the local landholders. Compensation totalling K750,000 (over A$1m) had been paid by the time the mine opened and has continued at the rate of around K60,000 (A$85,000) per annum. At the time this probably appeared generous but now looks totally inadequate. The company reports that over the life of the mine, from 1972 to 1989 the national government got 61.5% of all the cash generated, the province received about 5%, the landowners 1% and the non-government shareholders the balance of around 34%.[4] Of even greater importance than the sums involved was the way in which the compensation issues were handled. The concept under British law that minerals under the ground are owned by the Crown is currently under constitutional challenge in Papua New Guinea, but is probably the reason why the Australian External Territories Minister Charles Barnes felt he could deal with the issue of compensation in the late 1960s by flying to the area and saying to the local people 'You get nothing' and flying away again.[4] Not all attempts to handle compensation were as crass as that, but the conflict between the precepts of 'British' law and traditional attitudes to land, which do not allow for the 'sale' or permanent alienation of land, and particularly the matrilineal system operating on Bougainville, meant the issue of compensation has been a continuing running sore. The rebellion seems to have been initiated by local people who have not participated in the compensation payouts. The company admits that during the year or so leading up to the rebellion they lost contact with the mood of the local people.[5]

Another problem with the Bougainville mine is that the Bougainvilleans were reluctant partners in the new independent state of Papua New Guinea. The Australians and the new Papua New Guinea government saw the mine as essential to the economic viability of the new country, and so were not going to agree to secessionist demands, although the agreed compromise gave considerable powers to the provincial government. These powers subsequently had to be extended to 18 other provincial governments, which has certainly complicated the government of Papua New Guinea.

Ok Tedi

When a substantial gold/copper deposit was discovered by geologists of the US company Kennecott in the Star Mountains near the Irian Jaya border, the Papua New Guinea government was determined not to repeat the mistakes made with Bougainville. Its tough bargaining stance was a factor in Kennecott's withdrawal from the venture, but eventually a consortium led by the Australian company BHP made an agreement with the Papua New Guinea government and the mine opened in 1982. While mining the gold cap of the orebody the mine was the largest gold mine outside South Africa. It is now a major copper/gold producer, exporting 14.3 tonnes of gold and 170,000 tonnes of copper, contained in copper concentrate, in 1990. The question of a tailings dam has been a continual battle between the company and the government. The government has now agreed that the cost of $US1.3 billion for containment of tailings and mine waste would cause the mine to close and accepted the discharge of 70 million tonnes a year of sediment into the Fly River system and the Gulf of Papua, and the expected fish mortality of up to 80% in the Upper Fly due to increased copper levels. Ok Tedi currently provides one third of Papua New Guinea's foreign exchange earnings. (Before the closure of Bougainville it was 20% with Bougainville supplying 40%.) There have been periodic agitations by local landowners for a larger share of revenue and they at one time caused the closure of the mine for a period.

By the end of 1991 a further two new significant gold mines had opened in Papua New Guinea. These mines at Porgera and Misima Islands are smaller than Bougainville and Ok Tedi, but still sizeable gold producers. A third potential mine at Lihir Island could also become a major gold producer and quite a number of other gold prospects are under active evaluation. These developments should mean that Papua New Guinea will be one of the world's major gold producing countries in the 1990s, providing there is no repetition of the problems which forced the closure of the Bougainville mine.

Small-scale Mining

The above is the story of foreign-owned mining in Papua New Guinea, but for a number of years Papua New Guineans have been mining on their own account. This was first officially recognised in the Mines Department Annual Report of 1949 which said 'During the year a party of natives commenced mining on their own accord on the Wanion River . . . This is the first time in the history of the goldfield that natives have produced gold on their own account'. This activity has continued to grow, and currently some 5000 citizens are involved in small-scale gold mining, producing in total perhaps 2.5 tonnes of gold annually. Over the years most production has come from the Wau/Bulolo area of Morobe Province, the scene of the original gold rush in the 1920s. The typical small-scale operation consists of 6–8 people, usually from the same group, though not necessarily from the area in which they are working, operating a small alluvial claim by manual methods, passing 2–3m^2 per day through two or three simple sluice boxes. Some operators would possibly have a portable water pump as the only mechanical device. In the last few years some of these miners have been buying gold recovery equipment to replace their home-made wooden sluice boxes and in one or two cases have mechanised their operations.

Another new development on the indigenous gold mining scene in Papua New Guinea has been a substantial gold rush at Mount Kare on the border of the Southern Highlands and Enga provinces. This is an area where an overseas mining company (CRA) holds a prospecting licence, but where in the years 1988 to 1990 up to 10,000 local miners at the peak of the rush recovered some 15 tonnes of gold. Separation techniques used were extremely crude, as only manual methods (shovels and panning dishes) are allowed by Papua New Guinea law on an existing lease, but the gold was easily won because much of it consisted of sizeable nuggets. In September 1990 this mining ceased because of an agreement between CRA and the landowners to mine the rest of the gold in the deposit, estimated to be worth $300 million. Under the terms of the agreement the landowners would receive a half share of the gold.

Fiji

Gold mining at the Vatukoula field commenced in 1932 and up to 1987 the mine has produced 125 tonnes of gold and 43 tonnes of silver. The mine, which produced 2.3 tonnes of gold in 1990, is currently operated by Emperor Gold Mines of Fiji and the Australian company, Western Mining Corporation. Further development is occurring at Nasomo, adjacent to the existing mine, and that mine produced 1.7 tonnes of gold in 1990. The goldfield at Mt Kasi, which produced nearly 2 tonnes of gold in the years 1932 to 1946, is currently being investigated for redevelopment, and other gold deposits at Mistry, south-west of Nadi, Wanivesi and Vuda on north-west Viti Levu are all under investigation. The porphyry copper deposits at Namosi, near Suva, which were the subject of extensive feasibility studies, are now no longer under licence because of the failure of the joint venture partners (CRA, Anglo American and Preussag) to come to agreement with the Fijian government.

Although gold mining has been a substantial export earner for Fiji over the years, it has never employed more than 3000 workers or contributed more than 10% to GDP, and so can be said to have only marginally impacted on the lives of Fijian citizens.

New Caledonia

New Caledonia contains 25–30% of world nickel reserves and is the world's third largest producer of nickel after Canada and the USSR. The rich silicate ore is smelted to produce either ferronickel or nickel matte for export. Although nickel constituted 95% of New Caledonia's exports in 1986, its contribution to GDP was only 8%. The major producer in New Caledonia is the French company Societe Metallurgique Le Nickel (SLN) but there are also some smaller independent companies who send their ore to SLN for smelting. New Caledonia is also a substantial producer of high grade refractory chromite from the Tiebaghi Mine in the north of the island owned by Cromical SA, a subsidiary of the Canadian company INCO.

The nickel mines obviously have been a key target for Kanak separatists and the mines were closed because of their actions in 1984. There has been little disruption to the mines during more recent troubles, and in a further twist to the story, in April 1990 Melanesian separatists bought an 85% stake in Societe Miniere du Sud Pacifique (SMSP), which operates one of the mines.

Nauru

The 21 sq. km. coral island contains high grade phosphate rock deposits. The island became a independent nation in 1968 and in 1970 the Nauru Phosphate Commission assumed control of the phosphate mining from the British Phosphate Commissioners (representing Australia, New Zealand and the UK). The royalties from the export of about 1.5 million tonnes per annum of phosphate rock give Nauru one of the world's highest GNPs per capita, as the island has only 8500 inhabitants. The phosphate will, however, be finished in the mid 1990s. In 1989 a commission determined that Australia, New Zealand and the UK should pay compensation to the people of Nauru for the destruction of their island. The cost of rehabilitation was placed at $US184 million.

Solomon Islands

Although named for the legendary mines of King Solomon, the country had never been a significant gold producer until the Mavu mine opened 30km south-east of the capital Honiara in 1986. Almost immediately operation was suspended because of the effects of a tropical cyclone but the mine resumed operations in 1987. Mining only involves 1% of the population of the Solomons but there are more prospects being investigated.

Vanuatu

To date Vanuatu has no producing mines but seven or more gold prospects are under active investigation.

Effects and Impacts of Mining

The mineral activities described above have impacted on the lives of people of the South Pacific in different ways. In the broadest sense, most developments have provided some income to the governments of the various countries for use in the nation's development. They have also provided an element of stimulus to the national economy. To some few people the mines have provided employment, and hence cash income at a level much higher than the national average. To only a very few they have provided the opportunity for participation, not just as wage earners, but as owners, decision-makers and entrepreneurs.

On the debit side, mines have caused the destruction of traditional ways of life, and, indeed, the land itself on which that way of life was based. The lack of adequate provision for handling mine wastes has sometimes caused that destruction to extend far beyond the mine boundaries. Cash compensation for this has been either generous, totally inadequate or inappropriate, depending on one's point of view. Many more people have been caught up in the turmoil which has been brought about by the issue of compensation or the threat to the income generation of a mine. The Bougainville crisis has brought home to the mining companies operating in Papua New Guinea and to the government of that country, the fact that they must pay much more attention to the landholders. In the case of the mine at Porgera, the 10% government equity in the mine is to be made available to the provincial government and to the landholders with the provision of special support grants, increased royalty payments and infrastructure improvements. This agreement has been used as a model for other Papua New Guinea mines, such as Ok Tedi and Misima. Whether such measures are enough only time will tell, although problems at Mt Kare where the landowners have a 49% share, suggest that they will not. What is at stake is not just the funds flowing from the mines but the stability of the society and indeed the nation's existence. The potential destructive force of large-scale mining is very great!

Mining Technology

All mining does not have these sorts of effects. In looking at the impact on the lives of people, and groups of people, the technology used must be considered. There are three interlinked factors which are relevant. These are the level of technology, the scale of operation and the ownership of the mine (local or foreign).

Although there are some middle-scale mining ventures, there tends to be a fairly clear distinction between technically sophisticated, large-scale foreign-owned mining operations, typified by phosphate mining in Nauru, the operations of SLN in New Caledonia or Bougainville Copper or Ok Tedi in Papua New Guinea, and at the other extreme the small-scale, simple technology mines operated by some 5000 indigenous Papua New Guinean gold miners. Large operations require sophisticated technology and large amounts of capital, and so require know-how and funds from overseas, whereas small operations can be conducted with simple technology, with both the funding and the technology within the reach of local people.

Large-scale Mining

The most extreme case of the impact of large scale mining on living patterns within the region is the case of Nauru. Mining has caused the destruction of traditional ways of life and, indeed, the degradation of the island itself. It has brought wealth but has not replaced the traditional lifestyle with any alternative productive activity. Few would consider the present situation in Nauru, combining some of the worst features of both affluence and underdevelopment, to be a positive achievement. As stated, this is an extreme case. It may be repeated in microcosm in situations where compensation has been paid to a few landowners, but in most situations the financial benefits from large-scale mining have been spread across much larger populations than Nauru, with a generally positive effect. What has happened more frequently is that the small number of citizens employed by the mines have become a financial elite, with much higher than average incomes and often tending to adopt the lifestyles of their expatriate workmates. The economic benefits from mining do not tend to extend far beyond the mine itself, and so an undesirable polarisation in social and economic conditions is brought about.

Small-scale Mining

At the other extreme, the impacts of small-scale gold mining in Papua New Guinea are very different. This is a wholly local activity, the capital required is minimal and the technology generally passed on from one group member to another. Because there are no loans to service or contracts to honour it can be stopped or started as desired and so can be combined with traditional patterns of life, or other economic activities such as cash cropping. It provides money in rural communities and that money is generally spent within that community. Our study of this activity over some ten years has shown that it is beginning to develop as miners with more initiative and/or richer deposits introduce more sophisticated technology and move towards mechanised mining operations. A local mining industry which develops in this way will remain integrated within the technological, financial and economic structures of the country and thus provide maximum benefit and minimum distortion. This sort of mining is still not without its problems. It often means an inefficient use of the nation's mineral resources and is a very difficult industry for the government to control, so unsafe procedures, labour exploitation and environmental damage can and do occur.

To Mine?
Decisions about mining always involve weighing costs and benefits. The economic benefits can be real or illusory depending on how the development is handled. The environmental damage is always real but can be minimised by good practice. Also although environmental damage from mining is very visible the long term effects on the ecology of a region can be less that those from other forms of development such as agricultural monoculture. The social impacts are also real, changing traditional patterns of life, but this may be inevitable anyway. The political stresses will always be a challenge and involve balancing the negative effects on a small group of people against the benefits to a larger one. The Bougainville crisis and other troubles relating to mining in Papua New Guinea have brought this aspect very much to the fore.

Traditional attitudes to land are well stated in this quote from three Bougainvillean students: 'Land is our life, land is our physical life — food and sustenance. Land is our social life, it is marriage: it is status; it is security; it is politics; in fact, it is our only world. When you take our land, you cut out the very heart of our existence'.[6]

Open-pit mining deals brutally with the land. In the future miners will need to choose those technologies which treat the surface of the land more sensitively. This will be true not only of those places where traditional attitudes to land prevail but also in developed countries where there is a growing appreciation of the importance of the biosphere.

It should also be remembered that the option of not mining remains real, as only in rare cases does ore left in the ground lose its value. With wise policies there is scope for the peoples of the South Pacific to benefit much more from the use of their natural resources, including minerals, than they have in the past.

TECHNOLOGY MANAGEMENT AND
THE DEVELOPMENT OF SMALL INDUSTRIES

LUKIS ROMASO

This chapter is based on an interview with Lukis Romaso,[1] a senior consultant with Kum Gie Consult — established by the Morobe provincial government in 1987. Kum Gie Consult specialises in providing general technology, engineering and project management consultancy services for local business people involved in industrial development. Kum Gie Consult is connected with Development Engineering Services, also set up by the Morobe provincial government.

Q. What are the main aims of Kum Gie Consult and Development Engineering Services?

A. The main aim of Development Engineering Services is to develop core industries and create or spin off a number of co-industries, feeding off the core industry. We use this approach because Papua New Guineans need more experience with business management. If too much pressure is placed on people to formulate or coordinate a number of activities just in one company, that often places too much strain on business management. The idea is to disaggregate or break up industries into smaller, more manageable units, and to provide support with technical, accountancy and general business management advice for 'nursery' businesses. But these smaller units have to be viable, and you may have to combine a number of activities to make them viable. This is our approach. To do this we set up Kum Gie Consult as a registered consultancy company.

What do you see as the future for such organisations as Development Engineering Services and Kum Gie Consult?

We are encouraging the provincial government to move out of Development Engineering Services — to sell their majority shareholding and privatise it into the hands of Papua New Guineans who want to buy into it. That would be good for the business. I see the role of the provincial government as facilitators — they should develop projects and then move out of them. I think they agree with this.

Foundry

Please give some examples of the activities of Kum Gie Consult and Development Engineering Services.

The main core industry we have established and have running is a metal foundry. As co-industries we have helped people to establish small engineering businesses to do some of the secondary processing of foundry castings. For example, the foundry and co-industries produce coffee pulpers and a woodstove. One co-industry contractor buys rough castings for coffee pulpers from the foundry. The castings are then ground and machined, and the pulpers assembled for sale to smallholders and village coffee producers.

Where does the foundry get its raw materials? Does it use recycled materials?

The foundry uses a lot of iron castings and steel waste thrown out by various local industries. The other raw materials are bought from Australia.

What about aluminium, is that also being recycled?

Aluminium is being recycled — the foundry has a section for non-ferrous metals — aluminium, copper and brass. They have an aluminium furnace there which makes aluminium products, so the aluminium scrap they recycle is actually turned into products such as hubs, pots and boilers for boiling laundry. They are also exporting recycled scrap copper.

What problems, if any, does the foundry face?

I think the biggest problem they probably face at the moment is product development. With product development you need to look at what kind of products can be produced in the foundry, with import replacement or import substitution in mind. To do that you need to develop a pattern shop in the foundry, an area that is very undeveloped at the moment. Pattern-makers are very expensive people because they are really the core of the foundry. They develop every single product, so that the performance of the foundry is really tied to the pattern-maker and the marketing people. Pattern-making is unfortunately an area in which there are no skills in

Papua New Guinea. Pattern-making skills therefore have to be developed or imported, and that is something they are looking at now.

How are Development Engineering Services and the foundry funded, how self-supporting are they, and do they have any problems with funding?

Development Engineering Services and the foundry are presently self-funded. To develop a pattern shop, for example, the foundry would need to apply for a bank loan. A development bank or an industrial bank would be the right people to fund such a programme. The foundry business itself hasn't really got money to capitalise secondary processing such as machine shops to undertake secondary processing into final products, so what we prefer to do is spin off secondary activities to other local companies who have the capacity to invest in co-industries such as a small machine shop or combination of machine shop and welding shop.

Microhydro

I understand that the foundry has made impeller blades for microhydro systems?

Yes, other products include cups for small-scale pelton-wheel turbines.[2]

Is microhydro starting to be a big producer of electricity in Papua New Guinea?

Around 80% of electricity at the moment in the country is produced by hydro. There are large turbines in Port Moresby, Lae and the Highlands region. Previously electricity was generated using diesel fuel, but over the last 20 years power generation has changed completely to hydro systems. Microhydro is being used increasingly in villages. It was a very positive government move, otherwise we would be really suffering from the effects of higher oil prices.

What sort of proportion of the impeller blades that are needed are supplied by the foundry?

A very small proportion. The foundry is only producing impeller blades for micro-hydro systems. These are used in small villages, health posts or schools, where local designs are needed and appropriate. Larger hydropower generation systems are all imported.

I believe there are some problems with these small systems especially in terms of electronic load control.

This is the biggest problem. The loads are not constant because the main time people use electricity is lights at night. This makes power generation hard to control. There are no readily available small electronic load controllers systems to suit the needs of village microhydro systems.

Are these small village systems generally 12 volts?

Yes — 12 volt systems are safer for village application because the danger to housing made of bush materials and to villagers is reduced. The problem is that it is difficult to scale down controllers to suit small 12 volt systems. I think the way to do it would be for each house to have 12 volt batteries charged from the main system.

That would be expensive to set up though, wouldn't it?

It would be expensive because each house would need a battery or batteries.

The Wokabaut Somil, Logging and Forestry Management

Are there other examples of the activities of Kum Gie Consult and Development Engineering Services?

Another example is in the forestry sector. We had an idea to use mobile saws and larger sawmills to create spin-off industries by organising a central coordinating agency to supply timber and other goods to people making furniture and kit housing.

Where did the idea and the design of the wokabaut somil come from?

We really copied the idea and technology of the wokabaut somil from imported mobile sawmills, but we made a lot of modifications to make it suitable for local fabrication, production and use. The only thing that is imported is the Briggs and Stratton four-stroke engine.

What was your involvement with the wokabaut somil project?[3]

My involvement was to facilitate the initial design of the somil, before it went into production.

This is when you were at the Appropriate Technology Development Institute.

Yes. But once the somil started taking off it was best to allow it to be commercialised. The wokabaut somil is now totally commercialised, with exports throughout the South Pacific and even to Northern Territory, with one or two of them in Australia for Aboriginal housing projects.

Is that one of the first examples of technology transfer within the South Pacific Islands?

Yes it is.

What about the sawn timber that is produced from the wokabaut somils, is this being produced in large enough quantities for export?

At the moment the approach is to encourage people to produce for local consumption rather than export. Otherwise people have to go up to hundreds of miles to buy timber from town and take it back to the village. This seems absurd but that's what happened in the past, and still happens in some areas. We would discourage the export of sawn timber until the industry is better organised — this is really the key to the whole thing. Up to now, timber exports have not been well organised, or production for sale in Lae or Port Moresby. I think the next step would be to have a much bigger integrated programme to convince people to stop logging operations, upgrade the sawmilling systems a bit and let the wokabaut somil complement a slightly larger version of timber milling, then you can start talking about export of timber.

Could such an expanded operation be run and controlled by local villagers?

Totally. A slightly larger sawmill could produce something around 6 to 10 cubic metres a day, rather than 3 to 4 cubic metres that is the maximum you can get out of a wokabaut somil.

In the short-term this may not be much of a threat to the forests, but is there a longer-term danger that if wokabaut somils are accepted too enthusiastically in many villages, could there be a problem with excessive extraction of native hardwoods?

One of the conditions on buying the wokabaut somil is that buyers receive training in sustainable forestry programmes, selective logging and cutting techniques, in addition to the operation and maintenance of the somil, before the somils are sent out.

I suppose it is important that the national government tries to protect the forestry industry and make sure it is not exploited by overseas interests.

The other way to look at wokabaut somils and local forestry is that a local programme must offer a really good incentive, because the alternative is that overseas interests are coming in, and they could buy forestry rights and log the place out in 10 years or less if they could get away with it. That is the biggest threat at the moment. The challenge is to come up with an incentive for a forestry management system and technology that is sustainable and locally managed.

Low-Cost Housing

When you were with ATDI you worked on low-cost housing, and were associated with producing the 'LikLik Buk', on small scale appropriate technology and village development. Please tell me about your work with low-cost housing and the 'LikLik Buk'.

The 'LikLik Buk' was part of the ATDI information and education programme.[4] Our approach to housing was basically to look at the type of housing system that people want and the possibilities of using more natural resources for housing construction, rather than imported materials such as steel, which makes housing expensive. Traditional house construction is basically a post and beam system, where the loading is always downwards. This system of round pole construction had begun to disappear over recent years. We were able to update the traditional system using new designs and improved local materials. I am glad to say that pole construction seems to have taken off again, even for recreational facilities — the pole system has been used in the construction of a hotel in Lae, for example.

Does pole construction use local hardwood timber?

Yes, local hardwood is used, but you have to introduce some kind of modern technology to make it more durable — you have to treat that part of the pole that goes into the ground with a bituminous material or tar, and concrete it into the ground.

What about roofing material?

Roofing material needs and availability vary a lot in areas of Papua New Guinea. Traditionally, people used sago leaves or grass thatch, and this can be used on pole constuction houses. In island areas, however, it is much more appropriate to use galvanised roofing to act as rainwater catchment for drinking water. On the underside you can still use sago leaves or grass to insulate from heat.

Small-scale Mining

What other areas of activity could an organisation such as Kum Gie, Development Engineering Services or ATDI become more involved in? What is the potential for small-scale village mining?

Small-scale gold mining is a promising new area of involvement for technical support agencies. I think that the government needs to recognise the potential for small-scale mining as an alternative or complementary to large mining operations. The availability of suitable technology is a constraint — technology for small scale-mining needs to be developed and propagated. Suitable technologies could be initially imported and arrangements made to manufacture the technology here. The people from Wau-Bulolo have been small alluvial mining for the last 20 years, and still pan for gold using similar sluice boxes to those used 50 years ago. Sluice boxes can be improved and fabricated very simply. We need to approach people for assistance, but do not have the capacity or funding to do so at the moment. The innovation of such technology among small-scale miners needs support, and miners need training in using improved small mining equipment.[5]

Are there any problems with small scale-gold mining regarding pollution, particularly the release of mercury into the environment? If so, does the industry need to be very tightly controlled?

There is a particular problem with mercury pollution — villagers have been using mercury as a refining agent for over 25 years and many tonnes of mercury have been released into rivers. This adds to the many hundreds of tonnes of acids and other chemicals that larger mining companies have more recently released into the rivers, compounding the whole problem. There is no education at all on how mercury can be used in a safer way. Most villagers have seen their friends use mercury, and they copy them, not knowing that they are poisoning the rivers and themselves.

Is there any new or improved technology existing or being developed for small-scale village mining which is safer for the operators and environment?

There are various improved technologies suitable for small-scale gold mining, and a handbook of small-scale gold mining for Papua New Guinea was published in 1988.[6] The book makes recommendations of technologies that can be used at different scales of mining.

Has there been much interest in this booklet in terms of trying to promote that sort of industry?

I think that the interest is there, the only problem is making people aware of such information. It is unfortunate that books end up on bookshelves, and that people are unaware of many technologies – we can write so many books and we can make so many recommendations, but results only really happen when people actually go out there to promote technology.

I suppose this is where the agricultural development bank or some other organisation could come in?

The Agricultural Bank will fund projects and activities if there is some weight behind it, but really the Department of Minerals and Energy are the people who should really look at the situation and assist small-scale miners. Even if they don't do the work themselves, they could fund technical and field consultants to do it.

Banking, Overseas Aid and the Development of Small Industry

What other comments would you like to make about the development of small industry in Papua New Guinea?

The commercial banks and the government of Papua New Guinea should be encouraged to do more to help finance the development of small industry. One problem concerns bank loans — commercial banks in PNG want their money back in 5 years. This is unrealistic, because it usually takes at least 2–3 years for a small business to reach a break-even point. Small business often does not have the capacity to repay a lot of money in such a short time. Ten years would be a better repayment period if the banks are going to make a worthwhile contribution to the development of small industry. Another problem of the Agricultural Bank is that it has funded projects that were not particularly agricultural projects, often for political rather than economic reasons.

I suppose this also connects with some of the problems of overseas aid, especially from Australia, where there have been allegations that aid money has not been used for proper development activities. Do you think that it would be more appropriate if some of the aid money was tied to specific projects; do you think that would be a good idea?

It would be a good idea, and I would like to see Australian aid tied more to specific areas and projects. Australian aid has been used for empire-building — to fund departments that are self-perpetuating. I do not know how much this has changed. I think Australian aid should follow the Japanese example by tying into specific areas of research or projects with very tight terms of reference. Then I think Australian aid and taxpayers will start to get better results. At the moment they are not getting good results.

Another problem for the development of small industry development in PNG is that the high value of the kina has made it cheaper for people to import rather than develop technology and production in the country. We have become a nation of consumers rather than producers. We import 12 million litres of fruit juice a year when fruit grows wild and we could produce our own juices if only we had the interest and technology.

More importantly, small industry in this country has not really been encouraged. This is mainly because our policy makers are either ignorant or are not interested in developing small industries — they often do not realise the long term problems of this country continuing to be dependent on overseas sources for many services and consumer goods, when small industry development could help a lot with import substitution. A related part of this problem is that PNG is being used as a dumping area for Asian products which are not necessarily superior in quality. We need to support small industry based on agriculture and small-scale mining in addition to relying on relatively limited and specific spin-off industry generated by large-scale mining, which has been the main industrial interest of government in the past.

Small Industries Development and the Future

What do you think will happen to the development of small industry in PNG in the future?

At the moment we are also working on the development of a new industrial centre in Lae, a K9 million project funded by the Asian Development Bank. I am coordinating that project on behalf of the Department of Trade and Industry until they put their team on the ground here next year. This will be the first industrial centre or project that the Department of Trade and Industry has planned in the country. In the long run I think this is really the way to go.

That also sounds very interesting. Can tell me a bit more about the industrial centre — how was it started, was it an initiative of the PNG government?

It is a government initiative, and the main idea is to solve the problem of finding land in PNG for industrial development. Because of the complicated land tenure systems in the country, with the majority of the land being in the hands of customary land owners, it is difficult to get land for industrial development. So the government has secured land and is going to build nursery blocks for small industries, they will also provide fully serviced blocks and develop large complexes for lease to Papua New Guineans or expatriates who have the capacity to develop industries. It is a good idea because it gives people the options and encouragement to go into productive industries.

If people want to set up small industries, where are they going to get the funding? Will that be available from the PNG National Bank?

They are working on an idea to set up an Industrial Bank. The Ministry of Trade and Industry has come out publicly on that, and the aim is to develop the Industrial Centre in conjunction with the setting up of the Industrial Bank.

And how would the Industrial Bank be funded, would that be partly funded by aid money?

There would be some government money in it, but they would have to borrow most of the funds in soft loans from overseas to set the Bank up.

What about overseas aid grants rather than soft loans?

I am glad that the Minister for Trade and Industry is not in favour of using aid to set up the Bank. If you borrow money on soft terms and use that to set up an industrial bank, then that provides an incentive for the Bank to make sure that people repay their loans. One of the biggest problems with the Agricultural Bank is that it made loans to people who didn't need the money and who often used it for projects that were not viable. Many loans went down the drain.

It makes sense for local small businessmen to be under a little bit of pressure to repay loans to make sure that they manage their businesses carefully, but at the same time, if the Industrial Bank was managed properly from the top and it was set up with aid money, then appropriate projects would still be funded, and it wouldn't need to repay any loan, however soft.

If the government can get aid to develop the Bank, then that's fine, but I think soft loans are preferable.

How would the management of the Industrial Bank work?

The Industrial Bank should be managed by people with business backgrounds rather than bureaucrats or public servants, and be completely commercialised. But it should be run as a development banking activity, using staff with banking experience.

You mentioned that the Industry Centre would be funded by the PNG government, the Asian Development Bank and other possible overseas sources. Are any other financial institutions likely to be involved?

Other agencies who could assist would include aid donors, who could provide training programmes for the Centre. Courses that would need to be conducted include management and trades training, at all levels. The Bank or government might not have the resources or funds for training. This is one area where aid donors such as AIDAB might be able to help.

LIKLIK BUK REVISITED: TECHNOLOGY, INFORMATION AND VILLAGE DEVELOPMENT

B. DAVID WILLIAMS

The mid-1970s, with the coming of self-government and then independence, were a special, almost 'magical' time in Papua New Guinea. Especially vivid in the mind's eye are the images of local groups around the nation discussing what it means to be a new nation. The new constitution was a remarkable document, embodying respect for traditional culture and values and participatory democracy.

Foreign nationals were extremely privileged to work there. In a number of ways we were the winners, and as I now look back, I think that we were working within what now seems like a safe and comfortable cocoon, labouring under a degree of self-deception, even denial.

What were our assumptions then, or were we aware of them, as we merrily tinkered with our often lightweight ideas? Speaking personally, I was not really in touch with the political and economic forces that were busy shaping PNG and the South Pacific. I wonder if I was assuming an essential harmony within the nation which did not really exist. There was certainly small sense of the impending anger, frustration and confusion that were to become so explosive in the years to come.

This chapter is basically a constructive critique of our efforts in producing 'LikLik Buk', a rural development handbook catalogue, to openly discuss various issues that remain as relevant and useful today as in the 1970s. I would like to share some reflections on our earlier experiences with 'LikLik Buk', to raise some questions about efforts in rural community development in the 1970s and 1980s in the main hope that these thoughts will contribute to current dialogue.

The goal of reflecting upon and informing technology policy and decision-making in the South Pacific is urgently important. It reflects a key lesson of the last decade: that economic and political structures play a dominant part in determining the wellbeing of people and the promotion (or not) of development. When a government perceives a priority need for foreign exchange, for example, export-led development and the widespread introduction of cash cropping, or massive natural resource exploitation, or even the pursuit of a tourism emphasis, it can cause a tremendous impact on community livelihood systems and on a nation's social and political institutions.

LikLik Buk

The 'LikLik Buk' was an interesting and, by and large, successful model for information regarding technology and village development. Since it is still in use world-wide among those promoting people's technology and village development, and has now gone through several editions and updates, it seems worthwhile briefly to recount its history.

The 'LikLik Buk' was conceived as a handbook or catalogue designed to give 'community level leaders and trainers in Papua New Guinea better access to rural development information sources, with the goal of village self-help action' and small business development.[1] As stated further in the synopsis, it contains 'Short, rich articles on crops, animals, processes, designs, health, animating rural development; lists of books, pamphlets and organisations; plus comments and editorials from a broad range of contributors'. The information contained in 'LikLik Buk' was described as 'basic, technically sound, and helps the reader to define an interest and find further information'.

In April 1975, when about one hundred church-related grass-roots level rural workers met in Lae, PNG, to share their experience and talk about new directions in rural community development, the need for an effective vehicle for sharing sound technical information became sharply apparent. Peter Hale, a creative Ministry of Agriculture and Fisheries officer based in the Sepik, and I, then Agricultural Secretary for the Melanesian Council of Churches, agreed to prepare the first edition. This was based on a participatory model of development information, using articles from a broad range of contributors — whose only compensation was a free copy of the book! So the first edition of 'LikLik Buk' was born. It was initially hoped to update 'LikLik Buk' annually, but this proved somewhat optimistic.

The first edition of 5000 copies in 1976 contained 136 pages of information regarding 'simple technologies that had actually been implemented in PNG'.[2] This edition was sold out in less than two months, and a heavy backwash of correspondence brought many excellent articles, some corrections, and new information. A 1977 edition was immediately begun, with more than double the content of the first edition, and proved to be the standard and foundation piece for following editions. The LikLik Buk Information Centre, jointly established between the Melanesian Council of Churches and the Appropriate Technology Development Institute of the PNG University of Technology, was established to deal with the large number of information requests.

It is believed that more than 40,000 copies of the 1977 edition were eventually distributed, through several printings, including one print-run in the USA organised by the Volunteers in Technical Assistance. This is unheard of for a publication from countries with populations the size of PNG, and represents the largest printing of any item in PNG, except for some editions of the Bible. The use of 'LikLik Buk' by development workers, principally young volunteers from Western nations, is noticeable throughout the Third World. Perhaps it was the particularity of the book, its distinctive PNG personality and humour, and its 'Whole Earth Catalogue' style which made it so universally appealing. It is interesting to note that a communication was received by the Melanesian Council of Churches in late 1977 from President Julius Nyerere of Tanzania, requesting permission to translate portions of 'LikLik Buk' into Swahili. Permission was granted, of course, although I never heard whether or how this request was implemented.

A strength of the 1977 edition was that not only did it come at a time of lively debate about issues related to development, but it was supported by a system of seminars and workshops, which assisted people with the promotion and utilisation of ideas contained within 'LikLik Buk'. Such an atmosphere is obviously conducive to the propagation and reception of new ideas regarding technology and village development. The heady atmosphere of the heyday of the 1970s seems to have declined through the 1980s and into the 1990s, despite the continued and increasing need of technology for village development.

The Melanesian Pidgin edition of 'LikLik Buk', 'Save Na Mekim', published in 1982, was even more popular than had been envisioned. Few copies remained of the 12,000 copies produced in two print runs in 1986. The monumental effort to produce 'Save Na Mekim' was led by Dr Ulrich Bergmann, a missionary of the Evangelical Lutheran Church of PNG. 'Save Na Mekim' is far and away the most carefully crafted and clearly presented of the editions thus far, and that certainly seems appropriate. It appears that work on a new edition of 'Save Na Mekim' may soon be underway. Dr Bergmann sadly observes that Pidgin does not seem to be treated by the government of PNG as something of major value to be promoted through a quality publication such as this.

A major revision of the English edition appeared in 1986. Since a rather large stock is still on hand, strong consideration has not been given to a further update.The LikLik Buk Information Centre continues to exist at the Appropriate Technology Development Institute of UniTech in Lae.

Much knowledge and understanding has developed in the 15 years since 'LikLik Buk' was introduced. It is difficult, really, to know how much 'LikLik Buk' may have contributed to technology and village development, although it surely helped to accelerate the shift in governmental emphasis towards village agriculture. 'LikLik Buk' was a powerful instrument of practical advocacy for the development and support of village technology and livelihood. In this it is also useful to observe that the success of 'LikLik Buk' strongly reflected the needs of Western devotees of gadgets, as well as the needs of village people.

Some Reflections

Some reflections regarding 'LikLik Buk' as I read through the work now are as follows.

Wider Context of Analysis

With hindsight, it seems we might have benefited from a broader, sophisticated and participatory analysis of the wider social, political and economic systems of which we were a part. While there was a laudable emphasis on self-reliance and independent development, this was performed almost exclusively in relation to micro-level village development, without carefully considering or addressing the broader issues.

We did not place Papua New Guinea in its larger context, especially regarding economic and technological power relationships. In that sense, we often viewed the whole nation as a 'pocket project'. We did not draw our picture large enough. Whilst we were becoming more aware of the sensitive and difficult questions regarding the politics of post-colonial and regional relationships, were we sufficiently aware of the power and impact of commercial and transnational relationships in the fields of information, finance and technology transfer on the nation?

We were narrowly focussed with our project perspective. We tended to start with a pet idea, and then developed programmes out of that narrow project perspective. We were incredibly 'prescriptive' for people knowing so little about the larger picture.

Technology, Culture and Power

We are now more critically aware of the intimate connection between technology and culture, and between technology and power than we were in the 1970s, although it is interesting to repeat the 'sticker' inside the cover of the 1987 and subsequent editions of 'LikLik Buk': 'Caution S7 — Supply of this technology except on consideration of social and cultural factors is inappropriate'. It is now more widely recognised that policy-making concerning the diffusion of technology that does not take into account the relationship to culture and the sharing of power is somewhat naive. The traditional Melanesian view of how 'secrets,' and 'naming' represent power is extremely appropriate in this context — we should have been naming the 'powers' to reveal more of the secrets of technology and development.

In addition to projects, we were also so focussed on 'techniques' that we did not give sufficient emphasis to the promotion of the kind of people's organisations which become the deliverers of appropriate technology. I am talking here about the encouragement and support of groups willing to struggle for social justice, which at the basic level means food, land, jobs and housing — the basic human needs. These groups are distinguished by a heightened social awareness among members, and by a participatory process of decision-making, both of which make such organisations strong and cohesive.

Working with such groups is far more difficult than sharing techniques, and not nearly as much fun — perhaps that is why we did not do much of it. We could always fall back on the excuse that engineers, particularly expatriates, are simply not supposed to dabble in such things. But there were a few who did, and I think particularly of certain Roman Catholic priests in this regard (including PNG nationals and expatriates). They made an outstanding contribution to the new nation by raising the level of critical awareness, helping to organise people's groups, and encouraging the development of creative leadership.

All Technology is Technology

It would seem important to carefully guard against the compartmentalisation of technology into 'village' technology and modern technology. In the 1970s, we appear to have unwittingly accepted the false dichotomy between 'people's' technology and modern commercial technology. Mainstream, modern or commercial technology, as we have learned all too well, has enormous impact on the lives of people. The Toyota four-wheel drive pickup, a new brewery and the VCR, for example, were bringing sweeping changes, while we were fixated on biogas digesters, pedal threshers and hydraulic ram pumps.

It is wrong to divide technology into village/local/traditional and Western/urban/modern — all technology is part of a continuum, differentiated by cost, complexity, origin and, in view of these factors – appropriateness. Surely any one slice of technology, if it is to have integrity, must be seen in relation to the larger system of which it is a part.

To illustrate this point — I once flew to a remote area in a small Cessna to participate in a workshop on elementary blacksmithing. The workshop started with nothing but locally-made charcoal and scrap metals, and proceeded to create an expanding array of basic tools. This was interesting and helpful in its own way, but in that workshop we should have been talking about a lot more than charcoal and chisels! The division between village/local/traditional and urban/modern technology represented by the workshop and aircraft was striking.

Awareness of 'Development'

We should have been more critical of certain styles of development. I think that we did not sufficiently struggle to define progress from a perspective of ethics or values, in a politically relevant way, pressing questions about what really constitutes progress and development.

It is very difficult to stand in the way of the onslaught of homogenised, Western consumer culture, but policy decisions can certainly help to address the rapidity of the change, and sometimes deflect some of the more negative aspects. Policy is certainly needed to help the casualties — the negative impacts of development.

We know a lot more now than we did then about the dangers of export-led growth, debt and other problems of development, but we should have known a lot more. There were some helpful voices pointing to the dangers of rampant development, and indeed there were some fine young expatriate advisers throughout the government planning system. But I now feel that I, personally, should have been crying out 'warning' more than I did.

Role of Women

I also wish we had been more clear and direct in addressing issues related to the roles and status of women. Like other technology and development workers and publications, we did include sewing and recipes, and we gave women a nod with a brief essay or two, but we should have said more. A widely quoted UN study has reported that women make up 50% of the world's population, constitute one third of the world's workforce, put in nearly two-thirds of the world's total working hours, and yet receive only one-tenth of the world's income and own less than one hundredth of the world's real estate. The situation faced by women is particularly severe –

PNG is one of the few countries where a high workload results in a life expectancy lower than that of men.

We should have been far more critical of the impact of modern technology on women. Fortunately, some handbooks by and for women have helped to correct that deficiency. Our present awareness tells us that as sign and substance of this concern, we might have used more inclusive language, something still not done conscientiously in the newer English language editions of 'LikLik Buk'.

Sustainable Development

Today one would put far more emphasis on 'sustainability'. Although we were deeply concerned about soil and water conservation then, we were more often concerned that villagers use more chemicals more effectively, than we were concerned about the possible environmental impacts of their use. The erosion of flora and fauna was already rampant, but the dangers were not sufficiently appreciated. Similarly, on the economic front, foreign investment was considered very good, and foreign debt was not yet a great concern. Sustainability was seen primarily at the 'micro' project level.

A scanning of recent papers on development reveals a wealth of terms such as ecological agriculture, ecologically sustainable agriculture, regenerative agriculture, agroecology, resource-efficient farming, integrated farming systems, biodynamic agriculture, biological agriculture and alternative agriculture. These terms reflect the belated recognition of the importance of sustainable development.

* * * *

As we face the policy challenges of the 1990s, what is the new vision of the future? As the Cold War winds down, and as established systems crumble in Eastern Europe and political change comes to Central America, there might be a temptation to assume, very erroneously, that certain Western development models have now been validated. This is wrong.

Our widening world will almost surely see festering political problems, continued inflation, rising structural unemployment, 'de-skilling' of workers, stagnant growth and continued degradation of the environment.

Decision-makers in the South Pacific have a unique opportunity. Few regions of the world have such a potential for seeking alternatives to mainstream Western models and formulae for development, which have an increasingly questionable track record.

Here is the possibility for promoting policies to encourage creative, local approaches of sustaining development to enhance the quality of life of ordinary people in the region. The role and recognition of technology is central to the success of such policies.

THE DEVELOPMENT OF APPROPRIATE TECHNOLOGY IN PAPUA NEW GUINEA

DICK BURTON

Appropriate technology has a long history in Papua New Guinea, a history which pre-dates the appropriate technology movement. During the 1930s missionaries at Kwato on the Papuan coast taught local villagers how to construct clinker-built boats to avoid the excessive use of timber associated with traditional dug out designs. This skill has been handed down ever since. Village men were trained as aid post orderlies in the 1950s to provide a basic preventive medicine service in rural areas. These men were in effect barefoot doctors (before their more famous Chinese counterparts had been heard of outside their own land). Kiaps (patrol officers) and didimen (agricultural extension officers) used, and taught others to use, a whole range of devices and techniques which would today be described as appropriate technologies. Most of the early roads in the Highlands were hand built by local people under the direction of patrol officers. At the time these technologies merely seemed to be the most sensible to use. It is as well to remember these facts when evaluating the more conscious efforts to promote the use of appropriate technologies in more recent times.

Appropriate Technology at Independence
By the mid-1970s, a number of government and non-government organisations had become interested in appropriate technology, and were referring to their activities as 'appropriate technology' or 'intermediate technology' (following the international usage). Among the efforts of the churches were the Bagi Agricultural Centre in the East Sepik Province, the Yangpela Didiman movement and the 'LikLik Buk'. Government was

involved through Vocational Training Centres, the Department of Primary Industries, Department of Forests, Local Government Section of the Department of Works and Department of Business Development. Also active were the two Universities — the University of PNG (UPNG) and University of Technology (UniTech).

These activities were largely uncoordinated and relied on the interest and enthusiasm of individuals. A series of workshops was therefore organised to bring interested people together to exchange ideas and information. As a result of these workshops it was decided that a permanent organisation was required to provide a focus for appropriate technology in the country. Initially this role was carried out by the Office of Village Development (a project of the Prime Minister's Department).

Appropriate Technology Organisations

The South Pacific Appropriate Technology Foundation (SPATF) was established in 1977 to act as the focus of appropriate technology activity in Papua New Guinea. SPATF was established with three main components: a headquarters in Port Moresby, the Appropriate Technology Development Institute (ATDI) based at UniTech — a research, development and information project in Lae (ATDI was a joint venture with the University of Technology and the Melanesian Council of Churches) and a commercial wing — Village Equipment Supplies (VES), also based in Lae. Since the establishment of SPATF, other organisations have also been set up by provincial governments — such as the Village Industries Research and Training Unit (VIRTU) in the North Solomons Province (Bougainville) and the Kum Gie Development Corporation in Morobe.[1]

None of this more formal appropriate technology activity was intended to displace or control on-going activities by other organisations. Rather, it was intended that it would support such activities by providing information, advice and access to funding (an additional important role for SPATF was to lobby for appropriate technology-orientated policies at national government level).

The Appropriate Technology Development Institute

As noted above, ATDI was established in 1977 as a joint venture between SPATF, the Melanesian Council of Churches (MCC) and UniTech. The author served as a member of the governing board of ATDI from its inception, and as its Director for three years (1984–1987). For this reason, the problems and potentials of appropriate technology in Papua New Guinea will be discussed in relation to ATDI.

In common with most joint ventures, ATDI was viewed as having different objectives for each of the three co-sponsors. For SPATF, ATDI represented an opportunity to tap into the resources of UniTech and to establish a presence in Lae (the centre of communications for the country). For the MCC, ATDI provided a permanent base from which the LikLik Buk Information Centre could continue its work of publishing and distributing 'LikLik Buk', newsletters and booklets, and act as a hub for a network of development workers.[2] And for UniTech, ATDI was a means of linking itself to a movement which sought to apply technology to the basic needs of the population — something which was seen as desirable from the point of view both of teaching and of research. Inevitably, it was not always possible to satisfy all these objectives at once.

ATDI itself comprised an office, workshop and information centre based on the UniTech campus near Lae. These facilities were constructed partly from aid funds and partly from funds provided by the sponsors. Staff were either paid by the sponsors or, in the case of some 'LikLik Buk' staff, from income generated from sales. In all, an average of around fifteen staff were employed (staff numbers have since declined). Project funds came mainly from aid agencies, with a lesser amount from the sponsors. UniTech provided land, power, water, telephones, a vehicle, maintenance and accounting services. A governing board, comprising representatives of the three sponsors plus several provincial governments, oversaw the operations of the Institute.

Broadly, ATDI was intended to act as the research, development and information centre for SPATF, as a focus of appropriate technology development for UniTech, as a resource centre for appropriate technology in Papua New Guinea in general and as a focus for development workers. It was hoped that the resources of UniTech would thus be available to support appropriate technology, without ATDI itself becoming an 'academic' exercise. SPATF's extension team, latterly funded by the Foundation for the Peoples of the South Pacific (FSP), was based at ATDI in order to promote the use of the technologies developed and to provide feedback from users, and to ascertain the other needs of communities contacted. Operationally, ATDI was based on project areas (information, water supply, food technology, small business, energy etc.) with, in most cases, a Papua New Guinean in charge of all projects in that area. Joint projects could of course call on the skills of any staff necessary (including those from UniTech academic departments).

Degree of Success of ATDI

After nearly fifteen years of existence, ATDI can point to some successes in the area of publications — the 'LikLik Buk' has been published in its third edition, and a large range of publications have been produced and distributed. In the extension area, many workshops and demonstrations have been presented all over Papua New Guinea, covering a wide variety of technologies. Numerous projects involving technological research and development have been undertaken, addressing important technological needs of the community. All this represents a great deal of effort and activity. This activity has mainly been carried out by Papua New Guineans, and so a great deal of skills development has taken place. However, the record regarding the dissemination of technologies is less impressive.

One aim of the LikLik Buk Information Centre — to set up an active network of appropriate technology project workers — may have been premature. This is partly due to the fact that many appropriate technology projects are still headed by expatriates, who come and go and thus do not provide continuity, and partly because Papua New Guineans who are involved in such projects are often inclined to communicate orally, rather than commit their ideas and experiences to paper.

Repeated requests by community groups and provinces for workshops covering the same skills year after year suggest that, in many cases, the leaders and facilitators who attended such workshops were not able to hand on their acquired skills. The hoped-for multiplier effect of skills transfer did not appear to eventuate. Having said this, however, it could also be that community groups were using the workshops for routine training. In this case, the workshops may be viewed in a more successful light, although not serving the training-of-trainers function they were strictly designed for.

There was also a tendency for ATDI's research and development projects to become ends in themselves, the focus being on research and development activities, carrying on for long periods, rather than the equally necessary emphasis on technology transfer to the community. Where projects were completed (from the point of view of developing the technology) they frequently did not lead to successful innovation into and acceptance within target communities.

From an organisational perspective, ATDI suffered from having several masters. It lacked representation within the decision-making system of the University (thus missing out in the allocation of funds) because it was not viewed as a 'proper' department. ATDI was also pressured to become a straightforward extension and implementation organisation by SPATF (at the expense of its research and development activities). The MCC was less actively involved.

Despite these problems, ATDI has achieved much, not the least being the number of its staff who have gone on to work with other appropriate technology projects, both within Papua New Guinea and overseas, and the number of UniTech graduates who have made a commitment to appropriate technology work as a result of their involvement in ATDI projects as students. These are valuable resources.

Practicalities of Appropriate Technology Development in Papua New Guinea

Papua New Guinea is both a good and a bad environment in which to promote appropriate technology. In many areas of the country, people's access to 'conventional' technology is limited, and people have an open mind as to the technologies they use. In other areas of the country, where people have considerable exposure to introduced technologies and high expectations as to the financial returns of any proposed activity, things are less simple. Nevertheless, the small size, remoteness and diversity of environments in which communities exist in Papua New Guinea will always leave room for unique technological solutions to the problems faced by them.

Extension will always be a problem, however. For an organisation such as ATDI, it is nearly impossible to have the kind of on-going close contact necessary to implement successful projects, with other than a few communities near the home base. This kind of intimate involvement with projects is vital if nationally based appropriate technology programmes like ATDI and SPATF are to keep their feet on the ground and come up with effective solutions to real problems. One continuing problem is that, being a nationally based programme, there will always be pressure on ATDI to be involved in projects in all areas of the country. With limited resources this inevitably means that, unless a locally based organisation can act as an agent, such projects are not properly serviced and are often not successful. Furthermore, inability to follow these projects up results in little being learned as to the effectiveness of the technologies being trialled, what improvements could be made to them and the whole area of project implementation.

It is essential therefore that organisations such as SPATF and ATDI clearly define their roles, and seek to identify and work through locally based government and non-government organisations which can benefit from their assistance, and which are able to devote the close support required to field projects. Locally-based organisations can also more readily integrate the technologies on offer into comprehensive development programmes for the communities within which they work (nationally-based programmes do not necessarily have the detailed knowledge of remote communities to look at their projects in a wider context).

Naturally, there is no guarantee that suitable locally based programmes will exist, and it is therefore part of the role of nationally based appropriate technology organisations to encourage the growth of such programmes. There is little likelihood that nationally based organisations can successfully implement projects on a nationwide basis at grass-roots level. It is essential therefore that they foster the development of programmes at local level which can enable the technologies which they promote to be extended to the communities which they are intended to benefit.

A good example of the kind of locally based organisation which cooperated very effectively with ATDI was the Village Industries Research and Training Unit (VIRTU) in the North Solomons Province. VIRTU was established by the Provincial Department of Commerce to promote small business activity in the villages of the province. In the relatively small province, it was possible for VIRTU to extend its activities into much of the North Solomons and effectively service the projects which it assisted. ATDI was able to provide technical assistance to VIRTU, and VIRTU was able to field test a number of ATDI technologies (thus supplying invaluable feedback), some of which it took up and promoted. In addition, VIRTU was an invaluable source of suggestions for problems upon which ATDI could devote its resources of research and dvelopment. The relationship was thus highly productive to both organisations, and to the communities which they sought to serve.

The above comments may not apply to nationally based appropriate technology organisations in very small countries, where it may be quite feasible for a centrally-based programme to deliver services to all parts of the country.

Case Studies

When evaluating appropriate technology projects, it is often more instructive to look at those which were not a success (or which produced unexpected results), rather than dwell exclusively on the successes. The three projects considered here have therefore been chosen because they present some interesting aspects of appropriate technology work.

1. Institutional Stoves

ATDI was asked to cooperate in trialling a stove developed by the UN Pacific Energy Development Programme, based in Suva. This stove had been developed to provide cooking and hot water for schools, and had supposedly proved very acceptable for this purpose in Fiji. Constructed from cement blocks and refractory materials, the design was intended as a slow combustion stove which would be kept burning more or less continuously. A team of stove builders was available to construct the stoves at schools in Fiji who requested them.

Several problems arose when this design was tested in Papua New Guinea. Firstly, the concept of a slow combustion stove was alien — the users in Papua New Guinea were accustomed to stoves which could be lit and used almost immediately. The relatively slow response of the Fiji stove was not popular. Secondly, the size of Papua New Guinea meant that a number of teams would have been required to build stoves in all the areas where they might be needed, and these teams would have to be maintained in the field for several days while each stove was constructed. On balance, it was felt that a pre-fabricated stove, with relatively low thermal mass, would be more suited to conditions in Papua New Guinea. Low thermal mass would provide the rapid warm-up required for intermittent use and pre-fabrication would allow for relatively quick and simple assembly by local Department of Works and Supply staff in the provinces.

These comments are not intended to be critical of the design of the Fiji stove, which may have been more suited to the situation for which it had been designed.[3] Rather, they indicate that a successful design cannot necessarily be transferred, even within a specific region such as the Pacific.

2. Drum Oven

These were promoted by the extension team at ATDI mainly for women's groups. Quite a number were built in most provinces. They were intended to provide women with a source of income from baking bread and scones. Their small size and low fuel efficiency, however, made them uneconomic. In addition, in many areas the raw materials for baking were either very expensive or often unobtainable. Although various groups were trained to build the ovens, few, if any, actually built any additional ovens, so the technology did not spread.

In about 1986 the idea of larger drum ovens caught on spontaneously in Simbu Province in the Highlands. These village-designed and built ovens utilised corrugated iron culvert sections and were dug into steep banks in clay soil close to the Highlands Highway. With their larger capacity these ovens were economically viable and their owners were able to supply large amount of bread and scones to trade stores, schools and missions in the area, thus creating a village industry. This was a good example of appropriate technology in action where people had seen a technology, adapted it to their own needs and made a success of it. The only problem was that the original drum oven technology, which had been promoted for women's groups, had been coopted and set up as a business owned and operated exclusively by men!

3. Wokabaut Somil

The development of this sawmill was initiated by a mission group and then taken up by SPATF. Some early work was done at ATDI, but the engineers involved felt that work could progress more rapidly if the project was set up on its own. This was done and a very effective design was developed.

Having a good design does not, however, guarantee success — promotion of the idea is also required. Here Village Equipment Suppliers (the subsidiary of SPATF which marketed the somil) wisely provided a package which included training in the price of each mill. The training covered not only the operation and maintenance of the mill, but also aspects of management of forest resources, business practices and marketing of the timber produced. Follow-up workshops and a users' newsletter were also provided. Various provincial government departments became involved (such as VIRTU) as well as the national Department of Forests.

With this thorough back-up and after-sales service, the success rate of the wokabaut somil has been high, when many far less complex technologies have failed badly in the field. Good design, good planning and having a technology which genuinely serves a need for the target group have been critical to this success, as has the feedback obtained by keeping closely in touch with the users.

* * * *

Nationally-based appropriate technology organisations can fulfil a useful role in countries such as Papua New Guinea, provided that they concentrate on supporting locally-based initiatives, rather than trying to run their own projects all over the country.

It is the people who use technologies who ultimately decide for what purpose and how technology will be used. Quite often technology is used in a manner in which it was not designed or developed, and in ways which the introducing organisation did not intend and would not necessarily wish.

Within a region such as the South Pacific, technology transfer is problematic — technologies will not always transfer successfully. The same applies to a country of the size and diversity of Papua New Guinea — internal technology transfer is often beset with problems.

ENERGY SUPPLY AND MANAGEMENT

TONY MARJORAM

♦♦♦

Development is highly dependent on the effective application and use of energy. This is particularly important in the small and isolated island countries of the South Pacific, where the costs of imported energy are high. There is, consequently, a need for the efficient use of imported energy, together with the maximum practicable and effective use of indigenous, primarily renewable energy resources — such as solar energy, burnable biomass and hydropower.

Technology converts energy from one form into another — for example from fuel energy into light or heat. Converting energy from one form into another and distributing this energy entails inevitable costs and losses, however, so it is usually more efficient to use energy directly, in an efficient appliance, rather than indirectly.

The level of energy use is also an important indicator of household, community and national development — energy helps vitalise human activities. Access to energy is necessary to provide for relatively basic needs such as cooking and water pumping, and to encourage development through enhancing the average quality of life and the promotion of small business, industry and transport. There is also a certain status attached to the use of 'cleaner' energy and, at the luxury end of the market, for the use of energy-intensive technologies — such as large cars, power boats, diverse electrical appliances and air conditioners.

Constraints and Issues

The availability of indigenous energy resources varies considerably over the South Pacific. Patterns of energy use also vary, reflecting this diversity and the supply and access to imported energy fuels. An increasing amount of imported non-renewable fuel, mainly liquid hydrocarbons, is being used in the region. Excepting PNG (with a fledgling oil industry of significant potential), and despite a lot of wishful thinking, there have been no other discoveries or much promise of commercially viable oil deposits in the South Pacific. The prospects for the substitution of imported fuels are constrained by limited resources of new and renewable sources of energy — the region is becoming increasingly dependent on the outside supply of energy fuels.

As in other matters, the main energy constraints facing Pacific island nations relate to smallness and isolation. Markets are small, energy cost is high compared to income, and per capita energy consumption is low, although demand is increasing. Over 80% of commercial energy used in the Pacific derives from liquid hydrocarbon fuels — divided almost equally between electric power generation and transportation.[1] The factor of size leads to particular diseconomies of scale regarding imported energy, particularly of small-scale supply through frequently isolated ports and storage facilities. Transportation adds 5–10% to the cost of imported fuel at primary distribution points (eg Fiji and PNG) and 27–40% at secondary distribution points.[2] The problems of cost and supply are amplified in smaller villages in rural areas and outer islands, where most islanders live.

Similar, but more significant than telecommunications, fisheries and civil aviation, the energy sector is the major area in which island nations interact with large transnational corporations, and therefore a focus of interest in terms of the political economy of technology and development in the region. Unfortunately, however, as elsewhere in the world, the operations of transnational oil companies are not easy to analyse.[3] Small countries have limited bargaining power in negotiations with oil companies regarding the pricing and supply of fuels, and limited human and other resources they can devote to energy matters. Only in recent years, with the development and support of regional energy agencies such as the Pacific Energy Development Programme and Forum Secretariat Energy Division, have island nations gained better price and supply agreements with oil companies. In Kiribati, the use of open tender purchasing saved around 15% of the costs of imported fuels, and many thousands of dollars in foreign exchange.

Because of constraints of cost and supply, and the increasing dependency on imported fuels, two related areas of importance arise — the promotion of more efficient use and conservation of imported energy, and the development and promotion of indigenous renewable energy resources and associated technologies, particularly for rural areas and outer islands. In addition, there is an overall need for increased awareness, data collection, information circulation and, above all, training and human resource development at all levels regarding the efficient use, conservation and management of energy.

Energy and Technology

Because of past needs for performance and efficiency in the use of limited resources, Pacific islanders have a history of efficient and self-sufficient use of energy and energy technologies — for example in the construction and operation of traditional sailing craft and the more recent application and use of 'improved' fuel-efficient cooking stoves in those countries where biomass fuels are in increasingly short supply. The importation of energy fuels has also tended to displace the use of local energy sources — energy, like technology, is often assumed to be imported, and local resources of energy are forgotten or overlooked. Pacific islanders have become less efficient in their total use of energy as they have become increasingly energy dependent.

This trend is primarily due to technological change — introduced technology designed to use imported fuels has in many cases displaced traditional technology using local fuels in the main areas of energy use — transportation, lighting and cooking. Whilst many introduced energy technologies undoubtedly enhance the quality of life (for example — electric lighting), appliances are frequently inefficient, and may also be dangerous, especially older appliances such as ageing kerosene stoves. New technology is almost inevitably accorded higher status than traditional equivalents, despite increased capital and operating costs and problems of limited durability. There is little significant or widespread interest in the region concerning the development or importation of energy technology designed for the more effective use of local energy resources. With the possible exceptions of hydropower in some countries and solar water heaters in wealthier urban areas, there has been a lack of success of projects involving new and renewable energy technologies, partly because of overestimated need and partly because of underestimated technological software, skills and training required to operate such technology.

Energy consumption in the industrialised West has shown signs of decreasing in recent years. This is largely due to the fact that much new energy technology (both improved hardware and the software operation and organisation of energy use) is designed with energy efficiency in mind. New non-energy technology may also save energy — for example, the use of improved telecommunications may minimise the need for personal contact and transportation costs. The question of energy efficiency should be included in the assessment of all-round suitability of technology for transfer and use in the Pacific.

Sources, Supply and Consumption of Energy

Energy used in the Pacific derives from indigenous renewable and imported non-renewable energy resources. Indigenous renewable energy resources include solar, burnable biomass, human/animal, hydro and wind energy (the latter all derive from or are dependent on solar energy). Imported energy consists mainly of liquid hydrocarbon fuels — diesel for generating electricity for domestic, public and industrial use and fuel for trucks, petrol for cars and outboard motors and kerosene for cooking and lighting. Diesel power used for electricity generation has now been complemented by hydropower in Fiji, Western Samoa, PNG and the Solomon Islands.

Although some surveying of domestic energy use has been undertaken in some countries of the region, there is little information on more general patterns of energy use, particularly in rural areas and regarding the needs of transport and agriculture.[4] Most energy is used in urban areas, all of which now have reticulated electricity supplies, although by no means all urban households are connected — the majority of households in the Pacific islands do not have electricity. Most islanders live in rural areas or outer islands, where only larger villages are electrified — in Fiji 35% of rural households have electricity, and in Papua New Guinea, the Solomon Islands and Vanuatu rural electrification is generally well below 10%.

The 'bright lights' of the towns partly account for urban drift around the region, and the need perceived by outsiders for improved electricity supply and use in rural areas. This perceived need is often negated by rural islanders, who frequently place their need for electricity behind those of improved health, education, water supply and sanitation. This underlines the importance of an overall or integrated approach to rural development in the region, rather than a 'technological fix' of electrification for development. Indeed, it has been observed that 'rural electrification follows rural development rather than creates it' in the South Pacific.[5]

Rural electrification schemes have encountered many problems, mostly of initial cost and subsequent maintenance. The safety of 240v systems is another problem. Solar photovoltaic systems are better suited for decentralised individual household application, although such systems also encounter problems relating to cost and maintenance.

Per capita energy consumption in the South Pacific is low, varying from 50–100 MJ/day. Between 60 and 70% of energy used derives from indigenous sources, mainly biomass and hydroelectric power (in those countries with hydro potential). Most of the biomass is used in domestic cooking. Energy imports consist mainly of liquid hydrocarbon fuels — around 50% diesel fuel, the rest including aviation fuel, auto petrol and kerosene. Around 80% of imported fuel use is split roughly between power generation and transportation, with the rest being used in agriculture, industry, mining and for household purposes (mainly kerosene for lighting and cooking).

Total per capita energy use per year in the South Pacific varies from around 0.306 toe (tonnes of oil equivalent = 13.7 GJ) in Kiribati to 0.805 toe (36.1 GJ) in Fiji, with an approximate average of around 0.5 toe (22.4 GJ). This compares to a world average of 1.25 toe (56.0 GJ), and 5.977 toe (267.8 GJ) in Hawaii — regarded as a model of development by many islanders, with a per capita consumption 12 times that of the island average, and deriving almost entirely from imported fuels. The per capita annual consumption of indigenous energy varies from 0.138 toe (6.2 GJ) in the Cook Islands to 0.441 toe (19.8 GJ) in Fiji, and that of imported energy from 0.096 toe (4.3 GJ) in Kiribati to 0.462 (20.7 GJ) in the Cook Islands.[6]

Renewable Energy
Providing 60–70% of total energy used in the South Pacific, biomass, mainly fuelwood for domestic cooking, is the single most important energy resource in most countries of the region, especially in rural areas. Consumption of indigenous renewable energy varies from 23% (Cook Islands) to 79% (Vanuatu) of total energy used.[7] There is a limited but significant potential for biomass use in industry, particularly in agricultural drying and related processes. Other applications of renewable energy include hydropower for electricity generation, various traditional and modern applications for solar energy — solar drying, water heating, pumping and photovoltaic electric lighting, wind for sailing and pumping, human and animal energy for small industry and transportation. There has been some interest in the production of ethanol as a motor fuel supplement ('gasahol'), and in combination with coconut oil ('cocohol'), although neither is presently economically viable, except in limited situations. There is considerable potential for the development of other small-scale renewable energy technologies for direct on-site use, especially of solar power and biomass and, in certain countries, of wind power. Wind energy has been used successfully in those countries with a sufficient wind energy profile, although problems of maintenance and hurricane damage have arisen.

Hydropower is the most currently used of 'commercial' scale renewable resources of energy, and has significant promise for future development. Hydropower provides 81% of total electicity generated in Fiji (Viti Levu; Monosavu dam, completed in 1983); 53% in Western Samoa (hydrosystems on Upolu, Savai'i and Asau); and 24% in PNG. Larger-scale hydropower is being developed in the Solomon Islands, and there is significant potential for smaller village stand-alone, run-of-the-river microhydro schemes in several other mountainous countries of the region. Small hydropower systems are expensive, however, and need software and training support.

Peri-urban and rural islanders consume from 0.7–1.5 kg of biomass per person per day (0.5 kg per day in urban areas). This factor alone should prompt serious reconsideration of the present importance and future potential of biomass fuel. The importance of biomass is often overlooked, however, given the focus of energy interests on other matters, especially the common equation of energy with electricity. It is interesting to speculate that if more (predominantly male) energy planners and experts experienced the lives of poorer rural islanders, especially as (predominantly female) cooks or wood gatherers, there may be more talk of energy crises in the region. Along with the need for improved energy use and technologies in such areas as wood stoves, the promotion of 'social forestry' through community fuelwood plantation is also important. (Studies have indicated that larger fuelwood plantations for commercial energy production are unlikely to be economically viable).[8]

The use of solar energy to generate electricity from panels of photovoltaic cells is a renewable energy resource of significant and increasing importance in the region. Photovoltaic electricity can be used directly to charge batteries for a DC supply (usually 12 volt), pump water or, with larger systems, conversion into 240 volts AC through an inverter. Photovoltaic systems require low maintenance and operating expenditure, although many systems have been found to be inoperative after 3–5 years, due mainly to technical problems deriving from poor user training, limited follow-up and spare parts support (particularly batteries), poor choice of technology and installation. The main problem for potential purchasers is that, although economically competitive with small diesel systems, photovoltaic systems have a high 'front-end loading' — a high initial cash outlay is required, compared to the small initial expenditure but continual running costs of kerosene and other forms of lighting. The solution to the problem of making photovoltaic systems more economically and technically user-friendly is partly economic and partly technical — requiring the organisation of financial assistance through credit schemes or revolving loan funds, and technical assistance through good equipment, service and spare parts support and user training.

Other renewables presently lack the promise often claimed for them. The production of burnable methane gas through biogas converters, whilst useful in detoxifying animal and human wastes, has not been very successful in the region. Biomass gasification produces a gas consisting mainly of poisonous carbon monoxide and explosive hydrogen that can be used as an engine fuel — although the technology is expensive and difficult to operate, and not without safety risks. The prospect for geothermal energy as a source for steam-powered electricity has been investigated, but the resources are distant from centres of habitation and the technology entails high costs and risks. Although a small prototype 'proof-of-concept' ocean thermal energy conversion (OTEC) plant has been successfully tested in Nauru, and a reciprocating column wave energy scheme proposed for Tonga, these systems essentially remain possible larger scale technologies of the future. Although some optimists observe that the combination of OTEC with fish-farming or mariculture doubles the chance of success, a more realistic view may be that the combination of novel technologies doubles the chance of failure.[9]

A problem for all larger commercial electricity-producing power systems is that they are very difficult to integrate into existing power grids at more than 10% of total input. This is due to the frequently fluctuating output of renewable energy sources and problems in connecting into the single-source power grids of most islands.

Some other projects purporting to be energy solutions require the highest caution. These include proposals for 'waste recycling and energy cogeneration' plants that have been touted around the region by various overseas entrepreneurs, whose main interest is the disposal of toxic waste. Such plants represent an essentially unproven and highly risky proposal to 'recycle' some of the heat used in the high temperature incineration of toxic waste. Apart from the risks of combining two novel technologies, the proposal presents a serious potential for major environmental pollution.

Imported Energy

Imports of liquid hydrocarbons to independent island countries increased from around 15,000 barrels per day in the early 1980s to nearly 25,000 in 1990, with around 50% going to PNG and 25% to Fiji.[10] Over the years 1980–86, the value of imported fuels as a percentage of total imports for the South Pacific as a whole averaged around 20%, ranging in individual countries from 10% in Vanuatu to 20% in Niue and the Solomon Islands and 23% in Fiji (not including re-exports). Energy imports represent around 20% of exports in larger island countries, 50–100% in middle-size and over

300% in smaller countries.[11] These data illustrate the significance of the energy sector as a major expender of foreign exchange and cause of trade deficits and balance of payments problems in many island countries.

Both electricity generation and transportation, consuming around 80% of imported energy used in the region in roughly equal measures, are very energy-intensive and concentrated in urban areas. Fuel consumption in the South Pacific is closely correlated to the degree of urbanisation, monetisation and GDP. Power generation and transportation are both highly monetised activities, and are conventionally regarded as the foundation of economic growth and development. As noted above, however, energy use may follow or accompany rather than lead economic development in the South Pacific, with initial increase in energy consumption being used mainly to enhance consumer quality of life, rather than for productive purposes.

Peri-urban and rural islanders consume 10–20 litres of kerosene per year (considerably more in urban households). Kerosene is mainly used for lighting, but increasingly for cooking. As populations increase, demand for biomass fuel exceeds supply, and deforestation and environmental problems increase. As household incomes increase, and for reasons of status, the main options of choice in situations of depleting biomass appear to be kerosene stoves or, if money and fuel supply permits, bottled LP gas or electric stoves. If this trend continues, imports of fuels and balance of payments problems stand to increase significantly — with important policy implications that few energy, development or environmental planners have seriously addressed. This factor alone should prompt serious reconsideration of the present importance and future potential of biomass fuel.

Although the possibilities for the use of alternative energy in the transportation sector are limited, there is some potential for the wind-power supplementation of diesel fuel used for inter-island shipping.

With the exception of hydropower in Fiji, PNG, Western Samoa and the Solomon Islands, and an as yet limited use of solar photovoltaics in rural areas, electricity generation is otherwise by diesel, typically produced by public power companies. Charges for electricity are generally subsidised, and vary greatly over the region. Because power stations represent significant national capital investments, there is some interest in privatisation. There are several constraints to privatisation, however, relating mainly to production and price. Because of the small size of markets and limited demand, power stations generally operate below optimum efficiency and load factors. To make privatisation attractive to investors, electricity charges would need increasing to around the level of the highest rates currently charged in the region — A$0.50 per kWhr (the top domestic rate charged by a French company contracted to supply electricity in Port Vila). Due to the importance of energy in development and the consequent desire to maintain price comparison with larger countries, there is an arguable need for subsidisation to support power generation in small countries. Privatisation of power production therefore seems unlikely for the present.

The price of petroleum products to the South Pacific is determined by the Singapore market (onto which transport costs are added). Australian refineries of transnational oil companies are the main fuel suppliers to the region, followed by Singapore, Indonesia and Hawaii. There has been little competition between suppliers within the South Pacific, due in part to trading patterns dating from colonial days and supposed limitations of small and isolated markets. Competition is increasing, however, mainly due to increasing market sizes, increasing use of competitive open-tender bidding by purchasing countries and the increasing regionalisation of energy supply, which benefits smaller countries.

Partly because of recent dissatisfaction with 'traditional' supply arrangements, national oil companies have been formed in Fiji and Kiribati to procure supplies at 'fairer' prices — activity in Fiji will be keenly observed, given the importance of Fiji in regional trade as a major re-exporter of petroleum products. Several countries have also introduced retail price controls. The national retail price of energy products is generally based on market conditions — so rural consumers pay higher prices. In Kiribati, price control equalises the cost of fuels in rural and urban areas, so that urban consumers effectively subsidise outer island consumers.

Country Profiles

To give a picture of national energy use, data from three countries is presented — PNG, Fiji and Kiribati. In PNG, 55% of energy imported in 1987 consisted of hydrocarbon fuels, of which 44% was used in electricity generation, 29% in transportation, 9% in agriculture, forestry and fishing, 7% in mining and industry, 4% for domestic cooking and lighting, 4% for shipping and 2% in manufacturing and services. Indigenous renewable energy resources accounted for 45% of total energy use — biomass 35%, hydropower 8% and solar energy 2%. 79% of biomass energy was used for domestic cooking, 18% for crop drying and 3% for electricity generation. 80% of solar energy was for domestic water heating and photovoltaic power, and 20% for solar drying. It is worth noting that less than 7% of the population had access to ELCOM electricity in 1986.[12]

In Fiji, approximately 50% of total energy used derives from indigenous sources, and 50% from imports. Indigenous energy sources include hydroelectric power and biomass — consisting of 71% bagasse (sugar mills are generally energy self-sufficient) and 29% fuelwood, of which 71% is used for domestic cooking. 32% of imported energy was used in power generation prior to hydropower from Monosavu, which has since dropped to around 10%. Around 80% of electricity is used in commerce and industry, and 20% for domestic purposes. In 1990, 39% of imported energy consisted of diesel fuels (mainly used for transportation), 26% aircraft fuels (mainly jet A1), 17% motor petrol, 7% bunker ship fuel, 6% kerosene and 3% LP gas. Reduction of the amount of imported fuels remains a major goal of energy planning, through better supply arrangements, conservation and the increased use of new and renewable energy, particularly small-scale hydropower, improved biomass usage (including improved cooking stoves) and solar energy. The prospects for wind, wood energy conversion, biogas, ocean and geothermal energy appear limited.[13]

In Kiribati, 69% of total energy consumed in 1987 consisted of indigenous biomass, primarily coconut biomass for cooking and oil for lighting (mainly on outer islands when supplies of kerosene and other fuels run out — a frequent occurrence). 79% of biomass was consumed on the outer islands of the Gilberts, Line and Phoenix groups. Biomass consumption on South Tarawa was restricted by population density, supply limitations and the greater availability of money and imported fuels. The fundamental importance of indigenous biomass fuel as a domestic fuel is expected to continue into the foreseeable future. Imports of petroleum fuels in 1985 accounted for 17% of total imports, of which 52% was automotive diesel oil (50% for power generation and 50% for transportation), 23% for petrol motor fuel, 10% for jet A1, 8% for avgas and 8% kerosene. 82% of imported petroleum was consumed on South Tarawa. Only South Tarawa has a reticulated electricity supply, where the tariff structure was designed to benefit low income domestic consumers. Some other population centres, government offices and church missions have generators. The use of efficient appliances and imported gas rather than electricity for cooking has been encouraged to conserve energy. More efficient use of biomass in improved cooking stoves and the investigation and use of various other new and renewable forms of energy, especially solar power, have also been promoted. The importance of economic, social and environmentally appropriate technology in these goals is fully acknowledged.[14]

Performance of Energy Technologies

Island governments will face increasing problems resulting from the trend towards depletion of indigenous resources of biomass and the increasing use of imported fuels, especially in terms of individual and national cost and the supply of energy to rural areas. The only viable options for planners are the efficient use and conservation of all energy resources, particularly energy imports, and the promotion of new and renewable sources of energy (NRSE). However, in the words of a senior regional energy specialist, 'Except for hydro projects, there is not a lot to show for the millions of dollars spent on NRSE technologies within the Pacific island countries'.[15]

Problems encountered with NRSE technologies relate mainly to interconnected social, organisational and technological factors. The sources of some of these problems, and hence the focus for their resolution, can be condensed into the following:

1. Projects should address genuine community needs, rather than needs perceived by outsiders who tend to see problems and solutions as technological; related to this, it is also important that assistance is timely — a recognised fuelwood shortage prompts the need for improved cooking stoves.

2. Projects must have the support, interest and involvement of recipients and energy agencies in all stages of project planning, implementation, operation, maintenance, necessary training and follow-up support.

3. Technology chosen needs to be basic, robust and reliable, with adequate and accessible technical support and spare parts service.

Energy Management, Policy and Planning

The oil price rises in the 1970s and 1980s, along with constraints of supply to the region, have encouraged Pacific island states to take an increasing interest in energy policy and planning. It is predicted that the demand for energy in the region, particularly in the sector of commercial electricity consumption, will overtake supply in the 1990s. Because of small market size and below-optimum operation, there is an overall need to use energy more efficiently in the region. Economies in energy use and petroleum imports will be best achieved through improved conservation and demand management, rather than increased supply to meet demand, through such mechanisms as the better matching of production to demand and the use of lower taxes to promote the installation and use of energy conserving technologies in the domestic, industrial and governmental sectors. Improvements in energy data collection, needs-monitoring, planning, management, information dissemination and promotion will be necessary to facilitate this.

National energy planning has a focus on energy imports and electrification, especially in urban areas, where most energy is used. There is limited interest regarding the development or importation of energy technology designed for the effective use of local energy resources, particularly in rural areas. There is, therefore, a dual need to increase the use of renewable energy in urban areas, and the promotion of interest and activities of effective energy use in rural areas, where most people live and most indigenous energy is used. Various renewable and new sources of energy seem promising, especially improvements in biomass use, micro-hydro and the development of solar energy for rural electricity and water heating. An increasing amount of attention regarding fuelwood plantation is also required.

There is, consequently, an increasing need for the local development, adaptation and marketing of energy technologies designed to use these resources. The key to the successful innovation of new and renewable small-scale energy technologies is the effective use of marketing through information dissemination and promotion using the popular media. These issues have often been treated separately. National energy agencies should encompass and integrate both areas of need in terms of management, policy and planning. There will be a continued need of support for human resource development at technical, policy and planning levels in the energy sector. International support and regional energy agencies will continue to have a significant role to play in these areas.

TECHNOLOGY AND DEVELOPMENT BANKING

LISIATE 'A. 'AKOLO

This chapter discusses the general criteria being used by smaller development banks (DBs) in the South Pacific to appraise loans involving technology and small industries development. The chapter also discusses how DBs in general relate to technology in such activities as the appraisal and monitoring of loans relating to technology, the training of bank staff in appraisal and monitoring of technological loans and the training of borrowers in technology management.

Development Banks in the South Pacific

Including the Agricultural Bank of Papua New Guinea, there are eight main DBs in the South Pacific (in Papua New Guinea, Solomon Islands, Vanuatu, Fiji, Western Samoa, Tonga, Cook Islands and Kiribati). South Pacific Development Banks (SPDBs) are normally established under statute, and enjoy a high degree of autonomy from their governments. In general, SPDBs are charged with the main functions of 'promoting economic growth and development in line with national policies, providing finance for primary production and for the establishment of commercial and industrial undertakings and providing assistance to new and on-going business ventures'.[1]

SPDBs vary in size and structure of share capital. The Agricultural Bank of Papua New Guinea had a paid up capital of K32.4m (A$48m) in 1988, and an outstanding loan portfolio of K66.4m (A$98m) in March 1989. The Fiji Development Bank had a paid up capital of F$35.6m (A$40m) in

1988, and an outstanding loan portfolio of F$116.5m (A$137m) in June 1989. At the bottom of the scale, the Kiribati Development Bank had a paid up capital of A$1.7m in 1987, and an outstanding loan portfolio of A$0.1m in the same year.

As SPDBs are small, they are involved in loans to both agricultural and industrial loan projects. Because there is a dearth of financial institutions or intermediaries that would normally provide credits for commercial purposes in the South Pacific, SPDBs are also involved in lending for commercial projects like wholesaling and retail shops, transport (including taxis) and so on. Providing loans for working capital is also common, especially for the financing of agricultural inputs, retail shop inventories, wages and basic raw materials. In 1989, 58% of total approval of the agricultural and commercial lendings of the Tonga Development Bank (TDB) was for working capital.

Development Objectives
SPDBs have had difficulties in achieving the development objectives expected of them. In a recent review of some SPDBs, it was reported that the main reasons for their inability to achieve development objectives have been lack of adequate staff training, resulting in poor loan appraisal and monitoring, causing consequent arrears problems; inexperienced senior management (in some cases); inadequate research and development activities to identify new and appropriate lending opportunities; and poor extension services by government technical departments.[2] Despite these problems, SPDBs have been important conduits for the transfer of funds and technologies to promoters of development projects. Regular reviews of the performance of SPDBs are conducted by their governments, international lending agencies such as the Asian Development Bank, International Fund for Agricultural Development, International Development Agency, European Investment Bank and aid donor governments, to ensure that their development functions and responsibilities are carried out.

Technology and National Development Policies
Like other development banks, SPDBs are a catalyst of development. They are expected therefore to be foremost in identifying, formulating and providing development finance for prioritised economic and social development projects that are incorporated in their governments' national development plans.

In helping choose the technology required by a project, SPDBs must consider the objectives of their national economic and social development policies. For instance, the Tonga Government Five-Year Development Plan for 1985–1990 stipulates a series of strategies for achievement of part of Tonga's national development objectives. These objectives include the following:

1. Procurement of the most appropriate and suitable technology that will in turn contribute to production efficiency and at the same time increase employment, especially in rural areas, by using local raw materials in processing and manufacturing.
2. Usage of labour intensive technologies to provide more opportunities for the employment and training of local people.
3. Effective contribution to broadening the base of local entrepreneurship and ownership.
4. Possession of potential for expanding exports or decreasing imports.
5. Lowering costs and improving the efficiency or standards of goods and services.
6. Increasing the incomes and living standards of people, particularly of those at the village or grassroots level.[3]

Indeed, the Development Plan distinctly states that a commitment must be given 'to the use of appropriate technology, whether this be high technology in the context of industrial development or intermediate technology in the promotion of the most efficient and effective uses of local national resources'.[4] The Plan also accepts the fact that 'development is a multifaceted process, where the balance needs to be struck between competing and often contradictory policy objectives and proposals — economic policies can run counter to the achievement of objectives in cultural and environmental conservation and all these in turn relate to an impact on the social changes which are an inevitable consequence of development'.[5]

The Tonga Plan therefore recognises that the TDB must be instrumental in initiating the use of technology for the achievement of economic development policies, but that, in the process, it could face contradictory policy objectives which could have adverse social and environmental effects. It is therefore one of the responsibilities of the TDB to identify an acceptable balance between complementary and contradictory policy objectives of government, and to maximise their contribution to Tonga's economic growth.

The SPDBs must ensure that proposed technologies will contribute to the advancement of the standard of living of the less advantaged people in their societies. The introduction of new technologies should benefit poorer disadvantaged people, rather than, as often happens, benefit those in the influential elite.[6]

A frequent problem regarding the application of the most appropriate technology results from the lack of dialogue between SPDBs and government ministries responsible for planning and implementing development policies. In Tonga, for instance, the implementation and monitoring of strategies devised to achieve the objectives of the Development Plan are largely the responsibility of the Central Planning Department and Ministry of Finance. The dialogue between these two agencies and the TDB has in the past been dismal. There is a need to establish closer cooperation between top officials of finance and planning agencies and SPDBs, through which a broadening of the scope and character of project appraisal to encompass the technology assessment approach is legitimated and operationalised. This constituency could be a valuable source of advice in establishing priorities for technology assessment.[7]

Technological Aspects of Project Appraisal

The smaller SPDBs do not always make in-depth appraisal of technological aspects of a loan project. This is because the size of projects is usually so small that adoption of new and advanced technology would be exorbitant and economically unwarranted, or because the nature of the project is similar to other existing projects, making it preferable to adopt technologies that are being used by other entrepreneurs. In any case, most loans by smaller SPDBs are for small industrial and agricultural projects that would not require new and sophisticated technologies. For instance, about 66% of the projects financed by the TDB in 1989 were for loans of less than T$1,000 (the T$ equates approximately with the A$). As most of these small loans were for working capital, the projects would not require in-depth technological appraisal. However, larger projects, even though they represent a small percentage of the total number, take a large percentage of the total loan for the year. The TDB loans above T$1,000 in 1989 comprised approximately 87% of the total approval of T$7.7m.[8] SPDBs must therefore undertake comprehensive technological appraisals of these larger projects.

Because of the small size of many projects, in SPDB project appraisals technical aspects of projects have tended to be considered as synonymous and interchangeable with technological aspects. In other words, a project that is considered technically sound is also considered technologically sound. Whilst this may not be strictly correct, and can in fact lead to practical misunderstandings (technical considerations may be interpreted as economic rather than technological, and assumed away or ignored), for convenience and convention, the practice is followed in the discussions below, with the proviso that technical and technological considerations may be combined into the same analysis.

Key Technical Information

The first thing a loan officer will look at when appraising a loan application is the key technical information about the project. This includes the following:

1. Description of the project, including the proposed method to implement, operate and maintain the project.
2. Location and site of the project, including proximity to markets and availability of major industrial infrastructure.
3. Magnitude and size of the project.
4. Plant and machinery involved in the project, including landed costs, manufacturing processes, capacity, layout and installation, supplies, availability of spare parts and maintenance facilities.
5. Buildings used by the project, including plans, size and layout.
6. Raw materials required by the project, including the sources of supply, quantity, quality and costs.

In assessing technological aspects, SPDBs will first consider the technological requirements of the project. For one reason, there is an integral relationship between the technological elements and financial and economical viability of the project. A project whose technology is not proven will encounter increased risks of failure. (Although higher risks can lead to higher returns, this is generally not the case in the South Pacific.) It would be better not to commit any loan approval for such a project until the soundness of its proposed technology is established.

Choice of Technology

Once the technology requirement is determined the choice of technology is the next task. Smaller SPDBs have found that the choice of technology is a complex undertaking. This complexity derives mainly from the fact that choice of technology should involve a systematic study of wider social, economic and environmental implications, particularly an evaluation of the effects on employment of introducing technology, the use of labour and the degree of dependence on external expertise and finance. The evaluation of technology is a multidisciplinary activity that is required to be conducted by various specialists who are not normally available in SPDBs.

Because SPDBs are not always familiar with the right type of technology, more so if the technology is being brought over from another environment, they must critically assess the following six factors: the existence of alternative technologies, the proven effectiveness of the proposed technology, the effect on employment of the introduction of new technology, the skills and expertise required to operate and maintain new technology, the supply and cost of raw materials and what infrastructural facilities and particular support or inputs the project may require, and whether these are available.[9]

Technological Alternatives

Is there a simple, less expensive and less sophisticated technology for the project? If so, who owns it? These questions are important because they cover a wide range of issues, from macro-level questioning of whether the technology contributes to the national economic and social development objectives of government, to micro-level questioning of whether the technology contributes to the viability of the project.

It is common that a project proposer chooses the technology before approaching the DB for finance. Project proposers generally adopt a technology that is being used by other entrepreneurs, or readily available from machinery suppliers, parent companies and, sometimes, technology information centres. It is the responsibility of SPDBs to ensure that the technology is appropriate and compatible with the national development objectives, but, at the same time, within the requirements and financial capability of the project. If the technology is unsuitable and incompatible, SPDBs should discourage the borrower or, alternatively, recommend the user adapt the proposed or adopt another technology that would better suit the requirements of the project.

On the other hand, the project proposer may not have chosen the technology before approaching the DB. In this case, the DB has the opportunity to discuss the choice of technology with the project proposer. The DB could even be influential in the choice of technology through imposing approval conditions on the project. The DB must however be absolutely confident about recommending a particular choice of technology to the project proposer (as the DB may then incur some moral or legal liability if the recommended technology encounters problems).

Scale

An important issue in this context is the scale or capacity of plant technology. Plant capacity is often discussed in terms of 'normal maximum capacity' and 'feasible normal capacity', with the former meaning the level of production that is technically possible, and the latter meaning what is technically feasible, but may not be humanly possible.[10] What should be noted is that the maximum capacity of a plant may not take into account such factors as maintenance and mechanical skills of the technical staff, availability of spare parts, staff turnover, working hours and so on. The capacity of the plant must not exceed the requirement of the market — apart from unwarranted wastage of resources, over-capacity can create excess production. This factor may in turn cause marketing difficulties, making the project unviable.

The question of excess production capacity is serious in the South Pacific. As noted by Marjoram, 'The application of modern technology tends to increase both the volume and rate of production. The technology from which choice is available has increasing minimum volume levels of production (technology gets bigger), and the increasing productivity of technology requires increased production to make operations economically viable (as technology gets more expensive). At the same time, the increasing volume of production is constrained by technological, social and economic factors of production and consumption, as production capacity may exceed current demands or needs in small countries. Problems of marketing and exporting then arise. These problems of increasing scale and productivity of technology, and marketing of products, have frequently led to project failure in the South Pacific, and are a direct consequence of the choice of technology'.[11]

Effectiveness of Proposed Technology
Has the technology been tried and tested in a similar environment, and on the same scale? For many fledgling borrowers in the South Pacific, the best recourse is to adopt a technology that is being used by people in similar industries. The technology is transferred from one process to another, or from one country to another, with the borrower adapting it to suit their needs and industrial environment.

At all times, SPDBs should be conscious of the fact that advanced technologies of Western countries may not be relevant to the South Pacific. Not only because the industrial and business environments are different, but also because technology originating in a technologically advanced developed country context may not fit the contexts of the South Pacific. As stated by the Secretariat of UNIDO, 'technological development has unfortunately been bracketed with the establishment of research and development institutes, institutes that are often insensitive to the requirements of industry and the production process. As a result, much money has been spent on developing skills without direct links to the actual work performed'.[12]

If the technology is new and has not been tried or tested in the South Pacific (or elsewhere), SPDBs must ensure that it will be used successfully and be compatible with the production and sales conditions of the project.[13] New technology may increase efficiency and production, but these improvements may only be within the limited framework of the narrow project base in which they are considered. As Menon states, 'beyond the terms of this narrow concept, there is the beginning of a realisation that technology has ramifications that go well beyond the product considered as merely a profit-centre in its own right. Many instances of this relate to the environment, others to social structure. Therefore, increasingly, questions arise whether a new technology should be looked at only in narrow terms of what is involved in an investment, or the product itself, its costs or quality'.[14] SPDBs must be cognisant of these factors, especially the possibility that the project may be short-lived precisely because of the wider unsuitability of the new technology.

Effect on Employment

How will the technology affect employment? This is a persisting issue of debate in developing countries, including those in the South Pacific. The small island economies of the South Pacific often see automated and capital-intensive technologies as antidotes for production inefficiency. This derives from the perspective that labour-intensive operations can only be economic in countries where population and poverty abound — which is not particularly the case in the South Pacific. The question is whether small South Pacific developing countries should put more emphasis on labour-intensive technology for employment reasons, or capital-intensive technology for efficiency and increased production.

Generally, developing countries' choice of technology is largely determined by the availability and relative proportion of the main factors of production — land, labour, capital, skills and natural resources. Because South Pacific countries have relatively limited capital, and small but available pools of labour resources, it seems preferable to choose a technology that uses more labour and less capital. There is justification then for greater emphasis on employing labour intensive technologies, so that labour can be fully and optimally utilised.[15] However, it should be noted that the choice of technology is influenced by factors other than employment, making the criteria for selection of technology differ according to different endowments, different objectives and different levels of development.

An article by Mena in the Second Asian Conference on Technology for Rural Development held in Kuala Lumpur in 1985 covered the main advantages of modern capital-intensive technology:

1. More efficient, closing the 'development gap' more quickly.
2. Provide economies of scale, resulting in capital saving (i.e. lower capital/output coefficients), providing surplus for more investment to further increase input.
3. Economise scarce managerial and technical skills.
4. Avoid relying on obsolete, labour-intensive technologies that would set back the developing countries into technological backwardness and stagnation.[16]

On the other hand, the main arguments for labour-intensive technologies are based on these points:

1. Technical efficiency is not necessarily economic efficiency, and what may be economically appropriate technology in one socio-economic setting may not be so in a different setting.

2. Modern technology is developed in industrialised societies, whose circumstances are much different from developing countries in terms of land, labour and capital availability, industry, enterprise and distribution structures, size of markets, consumer incomes and tastes and skill levels.

3. The problem is not so much the introduction of technology from developed, industrialised countries, but rather the price distortions within the local modern and traditional economy when this technology is sold 'off-the-shelf' to developing countries.

4. The high and increasing capital-intensity of Western technology, combined with the constraints that already exist on investment funds, means that only a small part of the labour force can benefit from the transfer of this technology.

The SPDBs should consider the relative merits of capital-intensive and labour-intensive technology. This is because SPDBs are often in a quandary — whilst their main objective is to promote projects that are economically and financially viable, justifying the adoption of capital-intensive technologies, they are also expected to promote projects that will provide additional employment, justifying the adoption of labour-intensive technologies. What course should SPDBs steer?

For example, should the TDB support a desiccated coconut factory that employs nearly 300 people, creates export earnings and generates spill-over or multiplier effects, yet runs at a financial loss due to high overhead largely resulting from the choice of relatively advanced, unproven and expensive technology? The support or subsidy given by the Tongan government to a factory that is not financially viable illustrates the fact that the lack of financial viability does not overwhelm other factors, leading to the closure of the factory (although this case is complicated — the factory was recommended in the early 1980s and built with Australian aid funds).

SPDBs have been permeated by this dilemma, resulting in losses to some of them. These losses are, however, partly vindicated by the argument that government is expected to subsidise such losses by allocations from its annual budget, or from purveyors of soft loans, and that through support of such projects governments are directly and indirectly stimulating the local economy and technological projects, and employment creation in the modern sector. The fact that the above project would not have taken place were it not for donor recommendation and finance is somewhat ironic, given the more recent trend toward 'economic rationalism' and avoidance of project subsidies among donor countries.

What is needed in the South Pacific is a 'technological dualism', whereby a satisfactory balance of the advantages of both labour-intensive and capital-intensive technologies is struck. A combination of labour-intensive and capital-intensive technologies that would suit the need and environment of the project should be identified. As observed by Marjoram, 'technologies that are most appropriate for use in the South Pacific are those which build upon rather than displace local technology (in terms of knowledge and hardware), combining new and low-cost ideas and materials to complement the old'.[17]

Operation of New Technology
Are the skills and expertise required by the project readily available in the country? If not, could they be easily acquired? The level of skills and expertise in the South Pacific is generally low. Invariably, there is a dearth of qualified civil, mechanical, electrical and electronic engineers; computer analysts, programmers and technicians; energy and power specialists; sectorial industrial and entrepreneurial specialists; science and technology specialists and other people with specialised skills that are in high demand in the South Pacific. This scarcity necessitates the in-depth assessment of the skills and expertise required by proposed projects, and poses questions about how the skills and expertise are going to be provided.

For most smaller industrial and agro-industrial projects, the skills and expertise possessed by local people is generally sufficient. These skills are however, restricted to projects based on or adapted from traditional or existing technologies, where processing or manufacturing technology is commonly known. In Tonga, such projects include handicrafts, cabinet-making and joinery, leatherwork, shoe and sandal manufacture, saw-milling, block-making, patchwork sewing and black coral jewellery.

Imported Skills and Expertise
There are at least five categories or sources of 'imported' skills and expertise available from overseas. These include:

1. Recruitment of a foreign expert with required skills to the staff of a project. While this source is common, it is rather expensive, and can pose problems of consistency and performance (experts are not always very expert). The contract of service would normally run for two to three years after which the contract may be renewed or terminated, at which time a new recruitment may be made if local counterparts have not acquired required skills. The replacement expert may then prefer to introduce different inputs or organisation, which may require new training and the change of project design, which can become very costly.

The recruitment of a foreign expert includes technical assistance consultants and advisors acquired through bilateral technical aid programmes. These technical assistance arrangements are normally available to government-owned organisations and statutory bodies. While this is often the cheapest method of acquiring expatriate skills, the confinement of such assistance to government-owned organisations and statutory bodies can restrict the spread of benefits to the private sector.

2. Hiring of special consultants or consultancy firms. This is normally expensive and generally used on a short-term basis. As with individual experts, the background of consultancy firms should be established before they are hired. Care must be taken, as consultancy firms who look impressive on paper may not be familiar with the local scene, and may transfer inappropriate technology. While consultancy firms play an important role in selecting and transferring technology, their activities and technology can undermine more appropriate technology and models of development in developing countries. The consultancy firm, often a turn-key contractor responsible for designing and erecting the machinery or equipment required by a project, may in their eagerness for the contract overlook considerations of appropriateness in small island countries.

3. Forming a joint-venture with an expatriate person or firm. The expatriate partner would normally provide skills or expertise as part of their contribution to the joint-venture. Once again, what the local partner must ascertain is that the skills and expertise of the expatriate partner are appropriate.

4. Attachment to overseas firms. The arrangement for training attachments or secondments can be made on a private basis, or through special government-sponsored industrial promotional programmes or industrial exposure visits, such as those provided by international agencies like the UNIDO, UNDP, Forum Secretariat and bilateral technical staffing programmes. It is important to ascertain that the training programme is relevant to government, company and Pacific island needs, and that the training or attachment agency is competent and relevant for those needs.

5. Procurement of technology (hardware and software) through patent and licence arrangements. As most Western technology is patented or copyright, the transfer of such technology can involve lengthy and costly negotiations regarding their use, and often necessitate the recruitment of an associated expert for the training of local staff.

The SPDBs must face the fact that if projects do not have the required skills or expertise, they have to import them. If this is the case, the question is whether projects can afford imported skills and expertise, and not just for a short periods of time, but for the entire period of requirement. SPDBs must ensure that a long-term training or study programme, even including attainment of proper technical and technological qualification at higher learning institutions like technical colleges and universities, be instituted and organised, and consistent with the long-term economic and commercial viability of the project.

Supply of Raw Materials

On the input side, SPDBs must ask what raw materials the project employs, how readily available and procurable these are, and at what cost. Most South Pacific countries are experiencing problems with availability of raw materials. Even if the basic raw materials are available, they may not be sufficient in quantity to meet demand. For example, the supply of coconuts in Tonga may not be sufficient to meet the demands of both existing and proposed coconut projects, including coconut oil, desiccated coconut, whole coconut exports, livestock meal, copra exports, coconut cream and coconut juice, not to mention routine household consumption. Where basic raw materials are not available in island countries, manufacturers import them. In Tonga, there are a number of processing industries that have relied almost exclusively on imported raw materials. These include factories producing knitwear, leather clothing and bags and a brewery. Several factories have collapsed due to high overhead and marketing costs that were mainly caused by the costs of imported raw materials. These include manufacturers of excavators, rugby and soccer balls, passionfruit juice, galvanised nails, livestock feeds, snackfood, leather and saddles and harnesses. SPDBs and assisted projects must be satisfied of acceptable availability and cost of raw materials.

Markets and Sales

On the output side, SPDBs must ask questions about actual and potential markets for produce, and sales to these markets. Many producers in the South Pacific encounter difficulties in identifying and ascertaining markets for their products. In the preparation, market research needs to be conducted to define and ascertain the existence and scale of target markets. This research should also seek to identify conditions relating to these markets, such as desired quality and problems in delivery. These considerations are particularly important regarding export markets.

Required Infrastructure and Support

Finally, SPDBs must ask various questions and ensure the required availability of necessary infrastructure and support. What major infrastructural facilities does the project require — for example power, water, transportation, telecommunications, waste disposal and effluent facilities and land for future expansion — and are these readily available? If these infrastructural facilities are not available, how much will it cost to build them? Would government, statutory bodies or other private organisations provide them? What is the time framework for building of these facilities? Are there government regulations that guide the construction of such facilities? What are the industrial rates being charged for electricity, water and other utilities? These questions are critical, and SPDBs must make accurate assessment of the costs involved. Underestimating these costs will affect the overall capital investment plans of the projects, and can easily tip the balance of financial viability.

More particularly, does the project require special facilities? Does the project need laboratory or treatment facilities? For example, within the different operations of the national marketing board in Tonga, there is a requirement for a food technology laboratory for the quality control testing of coconut oil, desiccated coconut and vanilla. These facilities necessitated the acquisition of special testing equipment and qualified laboratory technicians. As these items are costly, SPDBs must be careful to include such costs in the financial planning of projects.

Monitoring Functions of SPDBs

The monitoring of the performance of technology is an integral part of the overall monitoring of projects. It primarily consists of the inspection of technological processes and management to assess whether the technology is performing as planned, or not, and if not, to ask why.

There are two main types of monitoring evaluations — 'on-going' and 'ex-post'. In most SPDBs, on-going evaluation is commonly known as 'review'. On the other hand, ex-post evaluation involves assessments after the project is implemented, and in operation.

The review of technology is an assessment of the progress of the project, especially to ensure that designs, layout, installations, local utilities and other technological factors are in accordance with the original technological plan. It also involves a re-evaluation of the original assumptions on inputs being used for a specific quantum of output. If the expected output has not been reached, then an assessment of the changed circumstances that caused the shortfall should be made.

The technological review of projects is a method of monitoring signals of occurring or approaching danger to the investments of both the DB and the borrower. The procedure of review normally includes visits by the bank officers to the project. Such visits establish a rapport with the project, besides eliciting feedback on the existing circumstances and nourishing a favourable working relationship for anticipatory follow-up activities.

Technical Problems

There are three categories of technical problems usually confronted by projects: product-related (relating to quality, design and quantity); process-related (relating to appropriateness of the technology employed, type of machinery and equipment used) and input-related (relating to the quality and quantity of raw materials, labour and technical know-how).[18] The review must come out with explanations of these problems and provide proposals on how to overcome them.

An important part of the monitoring process is on-going systematic collection of production data. The data will be used in assessing the project's actual production output against the expected target. It is vital therefore that SPDBs have reliable and satisfactory production information systems, so that accurate evaluation of production efficiency, remedial actions and future needs of the project can be made. To be successful with their monitoring processes, SPDBs should have sound programmes for (a) training of monitoring officers and (b) training of borrowers.

Who Monitors?

An issue that often arises amongst SPDBs involves the question of who should conduct the technological (and other) reviews of the project. Should it be the task of the loan appraisal officers, or other operational officers such as loan rehabilitation or recovery officers? The TDB has established a Loan Rehabilitation and Recovery Division that does the review of major projects, especially 'non-performing' projects. It supports the view that there should be an independent assessment of the project, as officers who initially appraised the project might not be in a position to identify their own mistakes. By the same token, other SPDBs do not have separate rehabilitation or recovery divisions, contending that officers who originally made the appraisal would have had a better understanding of the project; and they should be responsible for correcting their own mistakes, or at least in a better position to correct them.

Another important question for SPDBs is how far should their staff be involved with the technological monitoring of the project. Should the staff be actively involved, or should they only do so in cases of delinquent projects?

The answer to the above is very much dependent on individual DBs and their respective industrial environments. The involvement of the staff will depend on such factors as type and quality of management and entrepreneurship, equipment, immediate goods and raw materials, government policies relating to taxes and duties on plant and equipment, pricing and so on. It is much easier to save the project before it falls into trouble, than to lift it out of trouble later on. In other words, SPDBs should get involved during the monitoring process to save the project from falling into trouble.

Monitor Training

The monitoring officer should devote particular attention to the following considerations:[19]

1. Evaluate consequential infrastructural problems. Have there been any changes in the project plan, statutory regulations or other factors that caused problems with power and electricity, water, drainage and effluent disposal, telecommunication, transport, dock and port-handling and so on?

2. Have there been any problems with the delivery of plant and machinery? If so, how does this affect production and sales targets? Has there been any problem with installation of this plant and machinery, especially in relation to environment and safety regulations? Has there been any technical omission or change required to plant and machinery due to oversight of the initial appraisal? Has there been any problem with supply of spare parts? Is there a short-term solution like providing alternative plant and machinery?

3. Have there been any problems with the supply of raw materials due to such events as natural calamities, labour unrest, trade blockades, shipping etc?

4. Have there been any problems with quality and inventory of the product? Has the quality of the product been irregular? Quality control is important not only in the sense that the end product is what was expected, but it should also avert production wastages and high rejection rate. Any sub-standard quality will delay the acceptability of the product by the market, thus affecting sales. It is necessary to correct problems at the initial, low production stage, gradually increasing to optimum production level when the market fully accepts the product.

5. Have there been any problems with obtaining technical clearances from statutory authorities and holders of patents, designs and copyrights?

6. Have there been any problems with recruitment of technical experts or technicians required by the project? Is the skill and expertise of the technical expert compatible with what was expected of him? Has there been any problem with labour required for plant and machinery? Has there been any change in technical personnel during the implementation of the project? The appraisal officer must be certain that the project has a skilful technical team. If technical personnel are away, a good back-up technical team is required to ensure continuous production efficiency and quality.

7. The monitoring officer must maintain strict confidentiality on technological information. The borrower at times finds it hard to disclose technological and technical information to the DB fearing that such information would be leaked out to competitors and other interested parties.

Borrower Training

The other important factor to consider is the borrower, who needs just as much training as the monitoring officer. Considerations regarding borrower training are listed below:

1. The borrower should follow the exact technological or technical specifications unless an adjustment is approved by a qualified authority, such as the designer or supplier of plant, qualified design or service engineer, patent holder, and similar technological experts. It is often the case that the borrower would make adjustments to the plant or machinery without any professional advice, resulting in rejection and 'self-exoneration' by suppliers or patent holders of any defect in manufacturing.

2. The borrower should pay special attention to the procurement arrangement. Because cost of plant and equipment is usually subject to price and exchange rate fluctuations, the borrower must ensure that sufficient contingency is provided. To minimise this problem, the borrower should follow these steps:[20]

   - establish the plans or designs of the plant or machinery required for the process.
   - select the best sources from which the plant or machinery may be procured.
   - invite suppliers to bid for the supply of the plant or machinery by a certain deadline.
   - compare the quotations, make sure that the bids are for the same types, qualities, specifications and properties.
   - award the contract to the best bidder, usually the bidder that meets the requirements at the lowest price.
   - prepare and sign formal procurement contract.
   - complete the necessary banking documentation and payments, once the plant or machinery is shipped according to schedule and agreement.

3. The borrower should understand that the DB has just as much interest in the stability and prosperity of the project as himself. There should therefore be a good rapport between the two parties. The monitoring officer should adopt a helpful attitude toward the project, the borrower on the other hand should appreciate this helpful attitude and have confidence in the advice of the monitoring officer. A concordant relationship between the DB and the borrower will embolden the flow of technological and technical information between them. The borrower should have no reservation in approaching the DB for assistance. There are times that plans do not happen as conceived; it is the responsibility of the borrower to consult and seek the assistance of the DB. The DB could provide assistance either from its own resources or outside sources. Even if the DB cannot directly assist

the project, at least it would understand the problem, making it easier to consider repayment holidays and such other flexibilities.

Women Can Do: Technology and Training for Women

Sue Fleming

Why women?

Why do we need to look at women, technology and development? New trends argue that writing about and working with women as a specific category only serves to marginalise women further. Why then continue to separate women from men, both on paper and in practice? This chapter explains some of the reasons why by looking at gender differences in the use, need and access to technology. It then goes on to describe a women-focussed initiative that set out to do something about the technology gender bias towards men — the Women's Development Training Programmme (WDTP), a project developed and subsequently based at and coordinated from the Institute of Rural Development (IRD) of the University of the South Pacific (USP).

The main rationale for women-focussed technology is based on the divisions of labour and responsibility between women and men throughout the Pacific. This results in differences in technology use — women's and men's tools and technology. In the Solomon Islands, for example, the hoe or digging stick is primarily a women's technology used for agricultural production, whereas the dugout canoe is primarily a men's technology, used for fishing and as a mode of transport. In Tonga women use tapa-beaters to make bark-cloth, and the men use long-handled 'spades' to dig holes for planting yams. In Kiribati the women use a careful arrangement of stones for cooking, and the men have special knives for tapping today.

The division of labour between women and men means that, although much technology is common to both women and men, certain technologies are used relatively exclusively by women and others by men. Women and men therefore have different interests regarding these technologies. Women need technology that specifically suits their needs and levels of skill and strength. For example, women do most of the firewood collection and cooking, are the main carriers generally, carriers and consumers of water and are generally the most important small farmers in the region — it is women rather than men who feed most families in the South Pacific. As such, women should have a major input into the improvement and choice of new types of technology as regards cooking stoves, water supply and sanitation and agricultural technology and techniques.

Although all islanders share in the general benefits of technology, it is women who benefit directly from improvements in technology that is mainly used by women. As women are the main decision-makers regarding the technology they will use, women should be more actively involved in the design, improvement, promotion, diffusion, choice and maintenance of this technology. Despite these comments, women are rarely in positions of official responsibility in these fields. Women are rarely found in Ministries of Energy working on woodstoves, in public health departments working on water supply and sanitation or working with agricultural technology.

The changes in the division of labour and the introduction of new technology resulting from development projects have also affected women and men differently. Women, for example, have been obliged to take over essential tasks in subsistence agriculture as men move into cash cropping, the focus of most agricultural development projects. Women are also often burdened with additional unpaid labour on these new 'male' crops. Increased competition for land from these cash crops also tends to push women onto more marginal land, increasing their required labour input, at the same time making firewood more distant and frequently more difficult to access. The result is an increase in women's work that could be helped with labour-saving technology.[1]

Whilst women and men share many common aspirations, women also have many particular aspirations of their own. Women, like men, also need new technologies to help realise their aspirations. Examples from the Pacific include the need for more sewing machines (and training in their maintenance and repair) for use in small-scale income generating projects, and the need for small trucks and canoes, either to support other income-generating activities or to facilitate the movement of goods and people through the establishment of small transportation and taxi businesses. The first is the extension of use of a traditional 'women's' technology; the second is an incursion into what many would regard as a traditional 'men's' technology.

Accessing Skills and Technologies

Although women and men have equal need for technology, these needs are not paralleled by equal access to technology. For example, water projects are usually implemented by male experts, both local and expatriate, who tend to work with men through male-dominated organisations and work-structures. The provision of village water supply projects in Vanuatu is an illustration of this. These projects were organised and implemented by expatriate technicians who were largely unaware of the relation between women and water in that country. They worked through meetings of village elders, who were almost exclusively male, and trained young men to maintain and repair the new water technology. It was only after considerable discussion that they recognised that the women were more motivated to improve water supply, carried out most of the construction and were likely to be more suited to maintaining the system than the young men chosen for the task (who may also have felt it was associated with 'women's work', of low status).

Agricultural advice and technology is another example of almost exclusive male-to-male contact, despite the role women play in that sector, particularly in subsistence agriculture in rural areas. In the South Pacific, agricultural extension workers are almost all male, and have difficulties in communicating with women agriculturalists and small farmers (suspicious husbands being one of the constraints). An attempt to train women as agricultural extensionists in Vanuatu illustrated some of the problems of integrating women into the existing organisations and structures, if corresponding and essential changes in the content and method of extension delivery are not made at the same time.

There is an obvious need for a focus on women in technology transfer that would ensure women's access to technology. But women's sections of both government and non-government organisations in the Pacific, as elsewhere, have tended to promote the 'domestic skills' of cooking, sewing and home-making, largely through the medium of women's clubs.[2] This work links back to the early social reform efforts of missionary wives, and the promotion of 'Englishwomen's skills'.[3] This history still exerts a strong influence on issues relating to women and development. The time women spend in production activities, such as fetching water and firewood, is generally undervalued or ignored, as are the technologies and techniques that could alleviate some of the burdens associated with this work, and the issue of the control women need to have over these resources.

Recognising Training and Resource Needs

The need for women-focussed technology has not gone unrecognised. In 1979 a conference, organised by the Economic and Social Commission for Asia and the Pacific (ESCAP) to formulate a regional programme of action for women in development, regarded appropriate technology and methods of technology transfer as a major priority area.[4] This concern was repeated at a further ESCAP meeting of Pacific women in 1980, where training in labour-saving technologies was emphasised, along with the parallel need for the development of leadership, political participation and economic management skills.[5]

Another meeting of Pacific women in 1981, organised through the South Pacific Commission, confirmed the need for technology training and resources for women. Recommendations included the call for women to be trained in all new agricultural techniques and technologies, and the need for equal access to all rural institutions, services, financial bodies, agricultural and other extension services of island countries and regional organisations.[6]

The need for research on new technologies for women's work was added to the agenda in 1981 by women delegates at a regional rural technology workshop organised by the Commonwealth Secretariat and Ministry of Agriculture in Fiji.[7] The need for increased awareness and training in technology for women were again accorded importance. The delegates elaborated on the types of technologies needed in priority areas of food processing and storage, domestic water supply, sanitation, and subsistence crop production. These recommendations were reiterated in 1984 at a subsequent workshop in Tonga.[8]

The importance given to issues involving women and technology by women at these various regional meetings does not necessarily imply a general understanding and acceptance of such issues and attitudes within individual island countries. These views were usually voiced by representatives of women's sections in government departments, who have little in the way of resources and skills to effect or implement significant change. Sectoral ministries, such as those of agriculture and health, often remained relatively unconcerned.

Changing Attitudes and Access to Technology

What then is the next step? What can be done about the relative ignorance and inactivity regarding issues relating to women, technology and development? It is clear that perceptions of legitimate arenas for women in development present a major constraint for issues relating to women and technology. Improving women's access to technology means recognising and restructuring attitudes in government departments, development agencies and NGOs. This should include the awareness-raising of decision-makers in fields such as water and agriculture as to the relevance of these areas to women and the importance of women in these areas. Further than that, it means convincing government ministries of the capacity and potential of women in deciding, managing and executing development projects in these fields, and involving local women in such projects.

The key structures in this process are women's organisations, both governmental and non-governmental, who have identified the problems of women's use of and access to technology. These organisations not only provide a forum for women to voice their concerns to policy-makers, they also provide a link between the resources of government and NGOs and the women in rural and urban areas. This link is both through direct membership of women's governmental and NGOs, and through the women community development workers of these organisations.

Going About Change — The Women's Development Training Programme

The Women's Development Training Programme was set up as a practical response to recognised needs regarding technology training and resource development noted above. On a more visible level, the Programme ran four to six week regional in-service workshops at the Institute of Rural Development, and provided resources for country-based follow-up workshops. Less visibly, the workshops were part of a wider development process that aimed to change attitudes towards women's development and issues relating to women and the choice of technology.

The process began by looking at the role, skills and training needs of rural women development and extension agents. There was much potential in their work — through women's organisations they could be a channel for new skills and resources, including needed technologies and techniques. They could put extension agents from other sectors in contact with the women with whom they work. Their experience of working with women's groups could also be built on to help women's confidence in identifying and using new technologies and skills. On the other hand, their potential was limited by the more traditional home economics training many had received. There were many significant skill-gaps and training needs to address.

Designing the required training was the next step, and this in itself proved a valuable development tool. The process of consultation and analysis began with women's organisations and rural women in participating countries. The consultations set guidelines that were used for further discussions with the relevant government departments in various sectors, and non-government organisations. Firstly, women gained confidence analysing the issues surrounding technology, and, secondly, technical specialists in the various sectors learnt, often for the first time, about gender analysis. Women's development became demystified, logical and supportable.

Women Can Do — the Workshops

The preparatory meetings for the workshops, finalised on a regional basis over the USP's satellite communication network, concluded with a curriculum for the short-term training of experienced women rural development workers. The technical areas to be included in the workshops were agriculture, food processing and preservation, energy, water supply and sanitation, each placed in the context of women's development issues, and complemented with applied research, planning, money-management and communication skills. From a practical point of view, workshop participants were to learn how to construct and teach others to build water tanks, pit latrines and cooking stoves. Follow-up was seen as a necessary component, to be carried out by participants in their rural working area, with a focus on specific technologies.

The workshop training was based on the regional experience of the participants, complemented by other resource people with relevant skills and experience in the region. The training placed a great value on local skills, offering the choice of alternative technological approaches where possible. The training was practical, following the simple philosophy that doing something is better than seeing something done, which is better than just reading or hearing about it. The focus was less on the technological hardware than on learning, analysing and construction skills; less on becoming a technician than on feeling confident about finding and adapting ideas and obtaining the right advice and resources.

The cultural and national differences throughout the South Pacific region provided a richness and variety of skills and technologies. This made it easier to build on ideas from within the region. For example, I-Kiribati women with some experience of building water tanks were able to help ni-Vanuatu women who wanted to learn such skills. The workshop also cut across a variety of gender definitions, giving improved recognition and development of concepts of the division of work and responsibilities between women, and between women and men. Solomon Islands women explained the importance of learning construction skills to Tongan women, and in the process they discussed how gender constrained what they felt able to do.

The workshops were recorded in words and photographs, and a video of one of the workshops was made and distributed around the region, generating great interest. This record not only acted as a reminder to participants, but also supplemented the materials and notes produced for and within the workshop. The reports and visual images also reinforced a new attitude and confidence about women's role and capability regarding technology. Yes, women can do it, they can work with ferro-cement, with hammers and saws, they can just as well build water tanks as embroider table cloths, and the photographs, video and words provide testament to this fact.

Visiting the South Pacific in June 1992, the author met participants and discussed the tangible results of the workshops. Women in Vanuatu were building and using community based ferro-cement water tanks, gaining much respect from the men in the process. Charcoal stoves were still being made in the Solomon Islands and sold through the Women's Interest Office along with charcoal made from offcuts at the sawmill (a stoves workshop organised and presented by Tony Marjoram for the WDTP was also held in Honiara in 1985). In Vava'u in Tonga, the banana and breadfruit chips were a huge success at fundraising events, and charcoal stoves were in great demand. The on-going presence in the Pacific of the technologies disseminated through the workshops lends support for a flexible longer-term view of how and in what way new technologies are absorbed and used.

Following Through — Working Towards Gender-Aware Technology and Policy

The Women's Development Training Programme had a specific focus — the in-service training of women rural field-workers. It also attempted to influence decision-makers' attitudes toward women, technology and development by promoting a differing set of gender images and an analysis of the role of women and technology. This promotion has encouraged the discussion of the effect of technology transfer on women's lives, and examination of the constraints regarding the contribution of women to technological change — criteria basic to a gender-aware approach.[9] But is an educational role such as that of the Programme enough? What else needs to be done?

Firstly, the provision of education and training and the improved access to skills have to be complemented with resources, particularly materials and finance to help support the trained and skilled rural field workers to achieve their goals of better using technology for community development. Credit and/or grant funding needs to be available, and structures for the support of increased community development activities have to be established or encouraged — the women's interest offices that channelled cloth and sewing threads to women's clubs have a role in providing cement and reinforcing wire, or at least advising women how to obtain these materials.

Secondly, it is not enough to deal only with access and skills — neither technology nor education is a unilateral solution to the problems of underdevelopment, or of women's continued and possibly increased marginalisation in processes of change. Wider aspects, including economic, environmental, institutional and ideological issues and relations need to be better understood and dealt with at micro, meso and macro levels.[10] Transformation must take place at a variety of levels: in the highest reaches of national political systems, and in political relations within the household.[11] Power relations in international spheres also form part of the macro context.[12]

In more practical terms, attention to the wider issues of technology and development will require a better understanding of the microcosms within which most men and women in the Pacific work — that is, the context of the family and/or small-scale labour-intensive enterprises. Most of the data treats labour as if it were a homogenous factor of production, and most of the research has ignored the special labour-market situation of workers in small and micro-enterprises, whether unpaid family labour, or poorly paid workers, such as apprentices and labourers.[13] The appropriateness of these foci have not been questioned, and there is an urgent need for more work on the appropriate organisational development and reform.[14]

Placing analysis in a wider context also means moving beyond the focus of the Programme on the small-scale subsistence sector, to include the estate sector and the urban economy. The focus of the Programme was justified in the short-term, as the overwhelming majority of women in the South Pacific live in rural areas, and work with subsistence agricultural production and processing. But it gives a blinkered analysis, and opens up the possibility of the increased association of women with appropriate technology solutions to development problems from mainstream technological changes, including the use of advanced technologies.[15]

The move from analysis to action means translating the wide range of factors relating to women, technology and development into policy. Historically, the promotion of appropriate technology has tended to focus on the micro-level, despite, or often because of, attitudes of ignorance or hostility within meso- and macro-level policy-making environments.[16] The Programme took one step beyond this in addressing the attitudes of policy-makers towards issues of women, technology and development, but this was not followed up in any systematic way by examining and detailing appropriate policy options.

There are useful starting points that can be built on. Recent work by Stewart and Ranis provides examples of policies affecting technology choice and change, with particular reference to organisational objectives, access to resources, available technologies, markets, organisations and institutions.[17] More interest and work needs to be focussed on defining, promoting and implementing appropriate policy incentives for technology and development in the South Pacific and appropriate means for the better integration of women into such initiatives and activities in the region.

TECHNOLOGY AND DEVELOPMENT PLANNING

DAVID F. ABBOTT

◆◆◆

Introduction — Development Planning

Development planning in the Pacific region has focussed primarily on the broad 'indicative' approach, rather than the more directive setting of specific quantitative targets for the principal macro-economic variables. Development planning is generally understood, in the narrow sense, as the process of producing plans and carrying out ex-post reviews of the performance of the economy, rather than in the broader, but more rigorous sense of macro-economic management of the economy.

There has been a general recognition that the factors at work in determining the success or otherwise of even these indicative plans cannot be easily predicted. The limited availability of reliable and timely statistical data in many of the Pacific nations, and the unforeseen impact of international economic developments, natural disasters or political events, beyond the ken or control of the planners, often play a critical role in determining the outcome of national development plans.

The lack of a quantitative macro-economic framework in many of the national plans is an illustration of the indicative nature of the planning process. Many plans purport to include projections for GDP growth, but these projections are generally not supported by detailed, reliable quantitative research. Data on GDP aggregates is not well developed — this is particularly true of the smaller island countries and those where the subsistence and informal sectors of the economy are large.

The indicative approach to national planning has, on the one hand, resulted in plans which have been little more than 'shopping lists' of public sector projects looking for external donor financing or, on the other, has produced documents of such generality that no sectoral investment programmes have been mentioned at all. The early plans of most of the countries fall into the former category, whilst the Solomon Islands plan for 1985–89 would be an example of the latter.

Within this broad and not very rigorous approach to development planning, the detailed consideration of the implications of technology policy, and indeed of any specific policy, has generally been treated in a relatively general fashion. In respect of technology policy, this is especially true at the macro level. Technology implications may be considered at the micro or sectoral level, but even in Fiji, where a report on Technology Policy was undertaken in 1983, no specific mention of this was made in the Ninth Development Plan, published in 1985.[1]

Objectives and Achievements

The stated objectives of development plans within the region do not vary to any significant extent. They all stress, in general terms, the need for greater self-reliance and the development of human resources, the broadening of the base of the individual economies and the need, wherever possible, to maximise the local value added from the exploitation of the available natural (and human) resources. Most also give priority to the development of rural areas and the preservation of cultural and social systems. These objectives are translated into a set of public or quasi-public (and occasionally private) sector policies, programmes and projects which seek to address the particular issues and lead to the attainment of the objectives.

There have, however, been wide variations in the level of achievement of the objectives and targets set in the various plans. These can only partly be blamed on varying natural resource endowments. The implementation of plans is often more influenced by human resource development issues, involving not only education but also motivation and commitment at the political level.

Technology

The implications of the use of 'appropriate' technologies is generally not considered as a major factor in the achievement of national objectives, although it is often recognised as an issue at the sectoral programme or project level, where the use of inappropriate technology can be an important factor in the failure of a particular project.

Whilst technology issues are implicit in all development and project planning activities, within the Pacific region there have been no serious efforts to incorporate or develop a true technology plan as a complement to development plans focussing mainly on economic issues. This chapter will seek to put the lack of a clear technology policy into the perspective of Pacific island nations. It will endeavour to show how consideration of technology issues can be incorporated into an existing framework for national planning, and within the human resource capacities of the countries.

Technology is only one of the many factors, albeit an important one, that have to be taken into account in the formulation of national plans and, at the micro level, individual development projects. Whilst it is undoubtedly an important issue, technology should not necessarily be singled out for special treatment if this same treatment cannot be afforded to other equally important issues, such as the environment, the role of women in development or the long term sustainability of development projects.

Technology Policy and Planning and National Development Plans

Planning Methodology

In considering the role and implications of technology in development planning it is first necessary to consider the nature and purpose of the planning mechanisms in the region. All the member countries of the South Pacific Forum have accepted some form of national development planning, generally regarded as 'indicative', and within this framework have produced a series of national development plans ranging from the very broad (Solomon Islands Fourth Development Plan 1985–89), to those detailed with specifically identified sectoral investment programmes. These constitutes the majority, and Fiji's DP9, for 1986–90, and Tonga's DP5, for 1986–90, would be typical.

Planning in the countries of the region has generally been of the Five-Year cycle type, with a major plan document produced at the beginning of each five-year period, with a mid-term review. Annual planning and review systems have been tried but have not been very successful, largely because of the lack of continuity in the staff of the planning offices and often simply the lack of staff to take on the extra work in both the sectoral ministries and the planning offices. There is a general consensus amongst planning officers themselves that the five-year cycle approach is too inflexible, and that a rolling plan or more strategic planning approach would be more appropriate in the present development context.[2] This change in approach has already occurred in Fiji over the last two to three years. Historically, Fiji has adhered to the five-year cycle, combined with a degree of rolling programmes through the budget formulation process. However, the DP9 was suspended after the political events of 1987, and there is now a more strategic approach to the planning function. This manifested itself at the 1989 National Economic Summit, and is reflected in the document detailing the Fiji government's policies and strategies for short and medium term.[3]

Formulation

The formulation of national development plans is coordinated through national planning offices, with the national objectives and strategies (and, if practical, the macro-economic framework) set either by cabinets or high level development coordination committees. The planning offices then liaise with the sectoral ministries and statutory bodies to set the various sectoral objectives, and to formulate the sectoral plans within the general national objectives and macro-economic framework. The sectoral ministries will at this stage be liaising downward to their own field and technical sections, so that there is participation in plan formulation at all levels.

In most early plans, as already noted, the emphasis was primarily on the public sector, with little private sector input or consideration of private sector needs. In the formulation of later, and most current plans there have been particular efforts to reverse this rather narrow approach, and to make special efforts to involve the private sector and NGOs more directly in the plan formulation process. This has involved the establishment of ad hoc task forces to review and revise each sectoral draft of the plan, and to provide the opportunity for private sector needs and opinions to be accommodated.

The task forces have been very useful in improving the plan formulation process, and have provided valuable inputs to make the plans truly 'national' in character, rather than purely public sector. Generally though, the work of the task forces has ceased once the plan document has been published, and they have not been reconvened until the next plan formulation period or perhaps at mid-term review stage. In Fiji, however, following the 1989 National Economic Summit, it was agreed to establish permanent sectoral consultative groups to provide an on-going dialogue between government and the private sector on development issues. This may be taken as a model for future such consultative processes and the success of the groups will be watched with interest.

Purpose of Planning

The purpose of national development planning is widely regarded by the governments, and many of the donors and other funding agencies, as being to provide a list of projects which can be presented to financing agencies and donors. The national plans, through the macro-economic and sectoral frameworks, provide the socio-economic and national justification for the projects.

In formulating plans and the projects therein, planners are always cognisant of the fact that funding is required in order to make any plan implementable. In the case of Fiji, the mobilisation of domestic resources and the balancing of these with generally non-concessionary project finance from the international agencies — such as the World Bank, Asian Development Bank and the European Investment Bank — contrast with the situation in most of the other countries, where external grants and concessionary loans are the primary sources of development finance.

This cannot be regarded as a very rigorous approach to planning, but the dependence of many of the countries on aid to finance a large proportion, if not all, the public sector capital investment programmes means that there is at least a degree of coordination and transparency in the programmes. The lack of up-to-date, comprehensive and reliable data on macro-economic balances also limits the quantitative planning capabilities of almost all the countries.

For the governments, the line ministries and indeed the planners themselves, it is not the final production of the glossy plan document that matters most. It is much more the planning process, by which the administrators in the ministries are required to put aside the daily paper-shuffling of their bureaucracies to focus on policy issues and the future directions of their respective ministries or agencies. It provides planning departments and ministries of finance with the opportunity to take a hard look at likely recurrent cost implications of the public sector investment programmes and to formulate appropriate medium-term budget strategies outside the regular annual budget negotiations, where time-frames and workloads are generally very tight.

Technology in National Development Plans

The full absorption of technology into the planning process, providing a counter to the introduction of inappropriate technology, would require there to be an explicit technology policy for each country and for each sector of the economy. No such policies exist, except as very broad statements in national plans. This means in effect that technology planning is done in an implicit manner and in a disaggregated way. In public sector projects, the choice of technology is very often determined by donor funding sources. This is particulary the case in the Pacific, where aid is the major source of finance for public sector investment programmes.

Perhaps the nearest that any of the current development plans comes to having an explicit policy for technology is that of one of the region's smallest and most isolated countries. In Tuvalu's Third

Development Plan, one of the objectives is, 'The continued improvement in the quality of life of all people of Tuvalu, recognising the importance of the subsistence sector and traditional social system that must be balanced against both the beneficial and harmful impact of an emerging cash economy. The government seeks to ensure an improvement in the quality of life for all people in Tuvalu, through the more effective delivery and accessibility of public services and the encouragement of income-generating activities across islands. At all times, the government will monitor and take remedial action, where possible, against any changes that unacceptably disrupt the traditional social system and subsistence activities upon which the majority of people will continue to rely. Greater recognition will be given to development which brings about improvements in subsistence and mixed-subsistence production and therefore, provide for a better quality of life for everyone'.[4]

The implication here is that the government of Tuvalu clearly recognises that the basis of the future lifestyle of people on the atolls of Tuvalu must remain in an improved but still subsistence environment. The introduction of inappropriate technology could seriously undermine the fragile nature of atoll living and falsely raise expectations amongst the people, not to mention place an unwanted burden on the government to service and maintain any such introduced technology.

Development in the Age of High Technology
This may be the clearest example of a government's recognition of a country's limited capacity to accept high technology in a subsistence based economy, with virtually no natural resources and only limited human resources for development within a harsh natural environment (which destroys electrical gadgets and circuits, and corrodes metal at an extraordinary rate — the body of a normal car rusts out in two to three years).

Notwithstanding this clearly implied preference for 'appropriate' technology which will be supportive of the subsistence way of life and the development of the domestic economy, no country can escape the introduction of increasingly complex technology in its international economic relations. External pressures make the introduction of high-technology, especially in telecommunications, difficult to decline.

Plans therefore pay lip service to new technology, whilst at the same time whisper the dangers of introducing technology that cannot be made to work effectively, or maintained properly in an essentially low-technology environment. In this respect, future recurrent operation and maintenance requirements and costs should be one of the most critical factors in determining the acceptability of technology in a specific project or activity.

Donor Technology

The source of much of the capital funding for projects involving technology comes from external aid donors, who often find it difficult to relate to low-technology and community development initiatives — an example of Western 'culture-shock' regarding small-scale grass-roots activities. Donors and funding agencies often prefer to implement a project utilising 'inappropriate' technology, but technology which they are promoting or with which they or their consultants are familiar in their own environment, rather than paying for the local community labour costs of a low-technology labour-intensive project.

An example of this might be a village coastal protection project, for which the donor might be prepared to pay several hundred thousand dollars for a contractor to build a seawall, but would not be prepared to pay for the local wages of a community effort where this could be shown to be just as effective. In many countries, the creation of rural employment through public sector capital investment programmes is an essential feature of government efforts to discourage urban drift.

Given that the economies of all the Pacific nations are very open and dependent on external assistance for their capital development programmes, these overseas influences can become major burdens for the national governments. Telecommunications, as mentioned, are a prime example of this. Internally, some countries still use morse code for inter-island domestic telegraphic traffic, whilst externally they are being thrust into the age of satellite technology as international HF circuits are phased out. This is not to say that the domestic networks have not benefited from technological progress. The modular printed circuits and solar-powered transceivers on the morse networks are a far cry from the old diesel-powered valve transmitters of a decade or so ago. This new technology is more robust and operator-proof, even in harsh atoll environments.

Technology in Development Policy, Planning and Project Formulation

The Fifth Development Plan for Tonga states that one of the aspects of the philosophy of development in Tonga is a 'commitment to the use of appropriate technology whether this be high technology in the context of industrial development, or intermediate technology in the promotion of the most efficient and effective uses of local natural resources'.[5] The Plan goes on to state that the government strategy is to 'encourage the use of appropriate technology, whether it be high, low or intermediate, so as to make the most effective and efficient use of natural and human resources'. This is closely followed by a commitment 'to raise the quantity and quality of professional, technical, administrative and trade skills amongst the people'. This is itself a clear recognition that no technology can be used effectively without trained and experienced operators.

Whilst technology is an important factor in considering national planning, in particular the public sector capital investment programme, it is by no means the only issue needing detailed consideration. Nor can it be considered in isolation. Issues of technology policy in planning tend to be linked, in particular, to environmental implications and, perhaps more importantly, to human resource development. No technology can be effectively and efficiently utilised without people who can both understand the technology and have some experience of using it to the best advantage. The lack of a clear technology policy framework within which national plans are formulated results in issues of technology being addressed at the sectoral or project level, where individual issues are appraised in the micro context.

A number of reasons have been cited for the lack of consideration of technology issues in national planning:[6]

1. There has not been enough awareness of or commitment to technology as an important strategic variable.

2. Sectoral plans are often formulated without taking cognisance of the technology involved and its cross-sectoral implications. In project and programme formulation the evaluation and appraisal procedures for projects do not generally give priority to issues of technology, except where the project itself is a technology choice project, for example, the choice of diesel as opposed to hydro-power. Other priorities — rates of return, employment or natural resource considerations — take precedence over technology.

3. Technology that has been transferred in various sectors has often not been fully or effectively utilised. The recipients have often lacked institutional mechanisms and the skilled human resources through which to utilise the components of imported technology in order to derive the maximum benefit from the particular application.

4. National technological goals, even if articulated in development plans, are often not incorporated during formulation, appraisal, monitoring and evaluation of projects.

5. In the absence of a technology plan or a deliberate policy for technological self-reliance, technology decision-making is influenced by the value system and personal preference of the diverse institutions and individuals who often must contend with the dominance of outsiders in foreign-assisted projects.

Technological Appropriateness

'Appropriate' technology will mean different things to different people in different circumstances. What may be 'appropriate' for urban Fiji may be entirely inappropriate for rural Fiji, Tuvalu or Kiribati.

The basic characteristics of an 'appropriate' technology are that it makes the most effective use of the available local resources, be they human, physical, natural or technical, towards the achievement of specific objectives. This definition implicitly recognises that, in the Pacific, the available resources may be extremely limited, and in some cases non-existent. As a result, much of the technology used will have a high external content. Appropriate technology must therefore be a mix of modern, intermediate and simple technologies.

Technology and Needs Assessment

In order to provide pointers regarding the 'appropriateness' of technology, it is necessary to assess new technology in relation to need and the capacity to absorb technology, prior to a more detailed appraisal. The following important elements need to be considered:

1. Regarding the needs addressed by the proposal:

    is the proposal dictated by national programmes (top down), or initiated by intended beneficiaries and their perceived needs (bottom up);

    do potential beneficiaries participate in the identification, design, implementation and operation of the project;

2. What are likely to be the real effects of introducing new technology, compared with intended objectives, in such areas as:

    the costs/resource utilisation of inputs, the efficiency and productivity of outputs, the redistribution of income or creation of employment, the economic opportunities and advantages presented by new or improved technology in the public, private and domestic sectors in such areas as utilities (water supply and sanitation, health services and electricity) and labour saving devices;

3. regarding absorptive capacity, what is the level of resource availability in terms of:

    local economic, social, cultural and institutional structures, human skills and manpower resources, physical conditions; location, climate, environmental, raw materials and other input availability,

    'riskiness' of the proposed technology in terms of applications in similar circumstances elsewhere.

Appropriate Technology can be 'High'

It must be acknowledged that following a path of 'appropriate' technology, at the expense of higher (as opposed to inappropriate) technology, can itself have an adverse impact on long-term costs and efficiency, especially in an industrial or commercial environment. In Fiji, for example, the recent policy reorientation towards deregulation and the free play of market forces in determining the allocation of resources requires that local industries compete with imports on an equal footing. This requires that local producers and manufacturers utilise 'appropriate' (high) technology in order to minimise production costs.

In some cases, the choice of technology may be finely balanced. For example, in power generation the choice may be between the relatively 'high' technology of hydropower, or the use of 'low' technology diesel generators. The former has a high capital cost, which requires high external inputs of technical assistance and human resources, but which makes use of indigenous natural resources. Whilst the latter, because the technology has been well established in the region for many years, requires lower levels of external technical inputs, but makes little use of local physical or natural resources and requires continued imports of fuel.

Choice of Appropriate Technology
The choice between the two must therefore be determined by the usual yardstick of a comparative cost/benefit analysis. The outcome may hinge not so much on the technology, but rather on the level of prices for intermediate inputs, the financing costs of the project and social, environmental and other 'external' considerations. In some sectors, notably telecommunications, there is very little choice in the use of technology. External factors determine the nature of the technology, and the country is forced to follow. Often such projects have to be supported by extensive inputs of technical assistance and training.

That national and international financing organisations play a decisive role in the evaluation of a project proposal submitted for funding is widely recognised (if not always accepted). This means that only a few technological alternatives are normally considered in the preparation of a project proposal. Sophisticated analytical techniques (for example, shadow pricing, sensitivity analysis and consideration of factor endowments) are used in evaluating the possible extent of funding for an identified project. However, no techniques are generally in use for the evaluation of technological alternatives which could enable a developing country to achieve, in the long run, more sustainable development on the basis of technology transfer in the international marketplace.

Consistency with the overall objectives of development plan documents, and the economic viability or cost effectiveness of individual proposals are generally the key factors in the present process of the economic appraisal of projects. The provision of a particular technology solution within the context of the national planning framework needs to be considered in the same way as other project inputs and outputs. Is there an effective demand for the particular technology? Effective demand for technology may be reduced by the lack of an explicit technology policy and the disaggregated nature of the planning process, lack of appropriate and effective fiscal incentives and structure of financial and trade systems, which often include constraints to the import and export of particular technologies.

The likely extent of the effective demand for a technology may be determined through the application of some standard assessment criteria:

1. The state of factor prices and other incentives relating to the technology.
2. Income distribution, which determines the effective market demand for various products and sectors.
3. The professional background and awareness of those who make decisions about technology to be used in projects.

The appropriateness and the extent of the effective demand for any technology application therefore relates to the developmental objectives, the socio-economic system and structure and to natural resource and factor endowments. It need not be related to the inherent 'quality' of the technology itself. Every country needs to assess what is appropriate or inappropriate in the context of its own development policies, strategies and capacity. This function could be achieved through some form of technology assessment unit or committee. The brief for such a function is discussed in the concluding remarks.

Technology and Project Appraisal

Every development project or programme, be it at the national or community level, and no matter which sector it may be in, may be regarded as being made up of three components:

- Inputs
- Outputs
- Conversion of inputs into outputs.

Conversion is brought about through the application of a 'technological process', or by the provision of physical facilities. It also requires the availability of the necessary human resource skills for effective operation and maintenance.

An essential part of the appraisal is the evaluation of the conversion process (not to be confused with the ex-post evaluation of the project's achievements in terms of its original objectives). This is to determine whether the project uses the most 'appropriate' technology, is the most cost effective, developmentally beneficial or yields the highest economic or financial internal rate of return of the various alternatives available. The evaluation should also include an assessment of the various assumptions that are made about the project and the conversion process.

In evaluating each of these issues the appraisal should also consider the various alternative strategies or options that may be available to achieve the same objectives. For almost all projects there will be at least one and often more alternative technologies or combinations of factor inputs and outputs available to achieve the same objectives. Whilst the appraisal may not be carried out by a technical expert in all aspects of the particular project it should be possible, in consultation with the originating agency, to determine whether or not the proposed solution is, in fact, the best available.

The approach that has been outlined allows the appraisal to follow a 'project logical framework' (or 'log-frame') which is shown in matrix form in Figure 1. This framework can be expanded with the complexity and scale of the project. In many cases it will be possible to make a fairly quick judgment as to whether the inputs, the technology proposed for converting inputs into outputs, and the 'effective demand' or marketing requirements for the output, are reasonable. If the framework is followed it should ensure that all the key issues in the project are addressed.

The project framework shows how the inputs to be provided under the project can be expected to achieve certain outputs, how it is hoped these outputs will lead to the achievement of certain objectives which in turn should contribute to wider sector and national objectives. It also shows how the achievement of project inputs, outputs and objectives is to be assessed, and the sources of data for measuring achievement. The final column shows the key assumptions on which the successful outcome of the project depends.

This logical framework approach (now used as a standard requirement for the appraisal of all projects for the European Development Fund) can be tailored to the specific assessment of technological aspects of either projects or programmes included within the framework of the national development plan or strategies.

Project appraisal is as much about assessing the practicalities of a project as determining its financial and economic rates of return. The ability of the appraiser to calculate these will in any event depend on the design of the project and the soundness of the underlying assumptions. The examination of the design and the assumptions thus forms the basis of the appraisal. Common sense and local knowledge can be vital tools in the appraisal process.

With large-scale and complex projects it is also most important that the inherent 'riskiness' of the project be given attention. This applies to the risks associated with all aspects of the inputs, outputs and the conversion process. Any delays in the supply of key inputs may impact on the timing of the outputs which in turn may adversely affect the long term viability of the project. It is not always easy to assess the risks in a quantitative manner but wherever possible this should be done through a sensitivity analysis in the appraisal.

Monitoring and Evaluation

The purpose of monitoring is to enable project managers, at each level of authority, to measure the progress of project implementation towards the achievement of the long term objectives. In the introduction and practical application of new technology, or indeed any project activity, it is important to have clear objectives and implementation targets against which progress can be monitored and results evaluated.

Monitoring the implementation of the technology and the ex-post evaluation of the project in meeting its objectives should be essential features of long term project management. This has not always, or indeed often, been the case in practice.

In developing a monitoring system it is therefore suggested that the following general principles be applied:

General Principle — Keep it Simple

Many project monitoring systems fail because they are too complex in their early stages. All systems should start with a simple framework. The capacity to include more information and variables to be monitored should be built in as the capability to provide the required information becomes available.

The availability of reliable and timely information and data is generally limited. There is therefore no point in demanding information that cannot be provided within the available manpower capacity.

Implementing agencies often do not realise the benefits to be gained from monitoring as, initially, it places an additional burden on them to prepare the required information and reports. In many cases they often get little feedback on their efforts. It is therefore important that the monitoring reports which are prepared are used in an action-oriented fashion. This will serve to demonstrate that good monitoring can result in better implementation and have a positive impact on the success of a project.

For monitoring systems to work, governments have to be prepared to commit resources, both human and financial, and be politically motivated to monitor projects.

This leads to the conclusion that a good monitoring system must start with the project formulation stage to ensure that a high standard is set in the way that projects are put together for consideration and implementation.

The schedule for project implementation should be set out in annual workplans or implementation schedules. In order to measure progress it is necessary to select a small number of key indicators from amongst all the project activities, which can be taken as representing the project as a whole.

A few well defined key indicators of performance will generally be the most effective means of providing monitoring information for management purposes. A large number of less important indicators may obscure the key issues and may involve considerable wasted effort.

Such key indicators regarding projects involving technology may be summarised in the following three categories:

- Is the technology acceptable to the recipients in the context of their local circumstances, knowledge and capabilities?
- Is the technology efficient in achieving the objectives and providing the required benefits to the target group?
- Are the complementary supporting inputs and services available to back up the implementation of the technology and make it sustainable in the long term?

Monitoring, being a management tool, is not an end in itself. The level of effort required to collect and analyse the monitoring information should not unduly burden the project managers, field staff or implementers to the detriment of implementation itself. The monitoring system should be an integral part of the management structure and of the day-to-day operational activities of project management. Introducing a system which highlights key activities, progress in implementation as well as constraints and problems, should lead to the successful achievement of objectives.

Monitoring as part of the management process requires effective decision making and two-way communication between managers and field staff. The two-way flow of information and feedback is a critical element in the process; no monitoring system can work effectively without it. The importance and position of monitoring in the project management decision process is illustrated in Figure 2.

Given the remoteness of many project areas, especially those involving the introduction of new technology into the rural areas, constraints to the successful implementation of technology activities may result from such basic requirements as lack of readily available spare parts, fuel and oil and the supply of other inputs, including technical knowledge.

An effective monitoring system need not be complex; indeed it should be simple to understand and to implement. Information and analysis should focus on a few key indicators of performance which can be used by management in a timely and effective manner. More complex issues, often involving evaluation rather than simple monitoring, should be the focus of specially designed periodic impact studies and surveys.

* * * *

Technology Assessment

For the full consideration of technology in the development process, it has been suggested above that there should be some special unit which would assess each proposal from a technological perspective. This may be performed in conjunction with issues related to the environment, the implications for women and wider macro-economic issues, such as those concerning import costs. Since such a specialist unit is likely to be beyond the resources of most, if not all, Pacific island governments, a realistic alternative needs to be identified. It is therefore suggested that such an alternative could be implemented through the 'development coordination committees' which exist, in one form or another, in almost all island countries.

These committees have the responsibility for overseeing the implementation of the development plans and policies of island governments, and are often chaired by ministers (for example the Prime Minister, in Tonga), permanent secretaries or directors of planning. These committees are already often responsible for assessing considerations of the environment and other issues which impinge on the choice of technology, and are the best informed and generally most effective arbiters of development in each country. In most cases, national planning offices serve as both advisers to and secretariats of the committees. They are therefore in a good position to provide the necessary impartial advice to such committees on technology-related issues, as they do for other development considerations.

Within the framework of either a fully fledged technology assessment unit, or the incorporation of such a function within an existing high-level committee, a number of broad responsibilities and functions can be identified. These may be summarised as follows:

1. To review all projects and assess their technological impact and adherence to the national technology policy if such exists or, if not, to general national policies and strategies for development.

2. To evaluate technology-oriented issues which should be included in the project profile, and in the appraisal and evaluation report submitted by the originating agency and the planning department.

3. Where necessary, to commission surveys to fill information gaps on the impact of new technology applications on target groups.

It is recognised that in developing a national plan or appraising an individual project proposal, the question of technology assessment cannot be considered in isolation. Whilst it may be difficult to quantify the exact questions that need to be asked in each situation, the general areas that need to be assessed are as discussed above, namely:

1. Is the proposed project technology 'appropriate' in relation to physical location and environment, financial affordability, local customs and socio-economic systems, land tenure and general economic viability and cost-effectiveness?

2. What are the linkages of the project and its technology with domestic agricultural, industrial and infrastructural support, and what further linkages would be necessary for the technology to be assimilated into the local economy?

3. Is there an effective demand for the technology?

4. Is there adequate provision for human resources development in the transfer of the technology to the local labour force?

Criteria for Technology Assessment

In order to carry out this assessment of technology, it is necessary to prepare a framework within which the "appropriateness" and desirability of the particular technology application can be examined, in the context of the national circumstances. A set of criteria needs to be developed by planning offices to be used in assessing each proposal. These criteria would cover issues including the social, economic, resource endowment, environmental and management capacities and capabilities of the country. The criteria would need to include consideration of the following issues:

*   state of development and scale of the economy
*   economic, financial and business viability (including marketing)
*   sustainability — financial, physical and operational
*   resource endowment and environmental impact
*   human resources development (management and operational skill levels relative to the proposed location and operating environment of the project)
*   energy management and conservation
*   social and cultural implications and impact (including implications for women).

These broad criteria will need to be reviewed over time and the 'weight' assigned to each adjusted as general economic and social systems change, and are changed, by the introduction of new technologies which they are being used to evaluate.

Often, in evaluating and assessing the technology for a particular project, the only available effective guidelines may be the broad national policies and strategies for the sector or the economy as a whole. It is therefore important for the officers carrying out technology evaluation tasks to have some knowledge of or familiarity with the technology and the relevant issues related to it. In particular, staff of planning departments should have access to independent advice on technology issues, or should be given the opportunity to gain experience and knowledge themselves through specialist training courses. It is to be hoped that through this training, and the encouragement of a particular interest in technology issues amongst planning officers, that the important role of technology in development will be given greater prominence in the formulation of national development plans and the appraisal of development projects.

Figure 5.1.1: Project Logical Framework for a Technologically Oriented Project (7)

Project Title: Date of Preparation of Framework:
Project Description:

PROJECT STRUCTURE	INDICATORS OF ACHIEVEMENT	HOW INDICATORS CAN BE QUANTIFIED OR ASSESSED	KEY ASSUMPTIONS
National or Sectoral (Longer Term) Objectives			
National or Sectoral technology objectives; identification of sustainable technology; objectives for technology transfer.	Quantitative or qualitative means of assessing if these objectives have been achieved by the use of the particular technology application.	Existing information sources or new sources which can be accessed or provided in a cost-effective manner. Monitoring and evaluation of project against National/Sectoral objectives.	External conditions necessary for Immediate Objectives to contribute to National/Sectoral objectives.
Immediate Objectives: Project Purpose			
Purpose for introducing particular technology. Intended immediate effects of technology on location, activity or target group. Expected benefits (or disbenefits) and beneficiaries, including technology transfer and skill training. Other changes resulting from the technology chosen: environmental, social, cultural.	Evidence that the technology has been used in accordance with the objectives: quantitative measures including internal rate of return or cost-effectiveness indicators; qualitative assessment of achievement and distribution of effects and benefits.	Information sources which already exist or can be provided in a cost-effective manner. Specific provisions for collection of required information as part of the Inputs and Outputs, impact assessments, surveys.	Adequate maintenance and operational support. Adequate operator training. Externalities and other factors outside the control of the project which can affect the progress from Outputs to the achievement of the Immediate Objectives.
Outputs			
Outputs (nature, quantity, quality and timing) to be produced by project/ technology to achieve the Immediate Objectives. Transfer of technology and skill training.	Equipment installed and operational to specification. Local operators trained. Arrangements in place for ongoing operation and maintenance.	Specific provisions for collection of required information, surveys, impact assessments, project monitoring reports. Training courses held.	Availability of operational support, spare parts etc. External factors critical to achieving timing of expected Outputs, timely availability of Inputs, Output demand conditions. Implementation risks.
Inputs			
Financial resources, materials and equipment, utilities and services, personnel. Provision on time and in required quantity and quality.	Quantitative measures, e.g. expenditure records, delivery according to project implementation schedule. Training programmes established.	Project implementation and progress reports.	Participation of target group/beneficiaries in project design/technology choice. Decisions and actions outside the control of the immediate project managers e.g. policy measure, externalities. Risks.

‹ure 5.1.2: Monitoring in the Project Management Decision Process

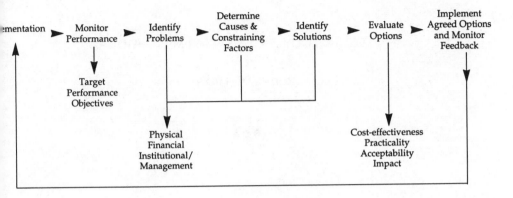

TECHNOLOGY AND DEVELOPMENT AID

RODNEY C. HILLS

Social and economic change seem inevitable, and governments of developing countries use aid as a significant factor influencing the rate and direction of change. Unfortunately, developing countries experience unattractive aspects of change as well as benefits. But, in many cases, we can minimise the less positive side-effects of change by encouraging sensible choices among technologies.

Projects are one way in which aid is administered and technology moved across international frontiers. Most aid projects, including those funded by Australia, are built around two key requirements of assisting economic growth and providing basic human needs. Both these factors help alleviate national and personal poverty, at least in general terms. While it seldom determines the choice of an aid project, technology is important: it is a design factor. However, once a project is identified and designed, the choice of technology will shape it, especially if the project is designed with an economic goal such as employment growth, which may be strongly influenced by technology choices.

While choices among technologies can be fairly simple, for example where a technology creates clear and explicit environmental hazards, more often choice is among shades of grey, in terms of cost and benefit. The choice of technology, and our capacity to manage the effects of the choice, fall squarely among the many risks to be managed in any project. Project designers cannot assume that technology is culturally neutral: such an approach ignores not only the obvious fact that technologies do have social effects, but also that any aid is intervention, and forces the speed and direction of change. While all donors agree aid should try to be socially neutral, it is expected to have demonstrable effects if it is to be judged successful; usually this will benefit the reputation of the recipient government. As a result, complete separation of technology and politics is impossible. Donor governments are sensitive to this fact in their choices of supportable activities.

Sectoral Review of Technology Transfer

It is useful to examine examples to illustrate the positive and negative ramifications of technology. In choosing these examples, a broad interpretation of the meaning of 'technology' has been used, in order to demonstrate its far-reaching effects. Technology can be software as well as hardware. The movement of ideas is an important aspect of technology transfer, and we need to be wary of confusing the transfer of useful ideas with a more negative cultural imperialism.

Agriculture

The agricultural sector has been the focus of much poverty- and production-focussed aid, since the rural-agricultural sector contains many of the poorest people. In addition, it has been a sector benefiting from significant technical advances which have spread quickly through the developing world. For example, plant breeding programmes at international agricultural research centres have produced the rices of IRRI (the International Rice Research Institute) and the wheats of CYMMIT (the International Centre for maize and wheat research in Mexico, now including other cereal crops). These varieties are particularly important agricultural technologies, capable of dramatically raising rural productivity through the efforts of agricultural extension services. As the seeds of new varieties are made available to farmers, along with improvements in cultivation techniques, it is impossible to predict the extent to which productivity gains will require continuing investment in research to maintain this productivity.

This became necessary in the 1970s, and was required to safeguard new varieties against the growing possibility that large stands of uniform crops could be quickly wiped out by invasions of pests and diseases. So far the management of risk flowing from the adoption of high-yielding varieties has been successful. This has been assisted by the long term view of research prevalent among donors who, early on, saw the need to defend the gains won by research. As a result, there have been significant advances in agricultural productivity around the world. The gains have far exceeded investment, and the harms of the change have been successfully contained, albeit by additional investment. It is an interesting example of how technology can produce a different kind of dependence — technological dependence.

There have been criticisms of technology transfer in terms of equity and distributional disbenefits. The most common criticism is that the technology specifically benefits larger farmers, who can afford the larger investments required. As a consequence, the technology also results in landholding consolidation and perhaps dispossession. This becomes a serious issue for the recipient government, which has to decide on the priority it assigns to agricultural productivity. It is hardly an area in which a donor agency can become involved.

Forestry

Similar questions may be asked in forestry, with the growing export of Australian tree species, particularly the eucalypts, which grow quickly and often to better quality trees outside Australia. In timber production the crop cycle is much longer than with agricultural crops. As a result, evidence for or against the technology will take much longer to be collected and assessed. Nonetheless, proponents of the planting programmes need to be watchful. In both field crops and forestry the technology is relatively simple and widely practised, but because the scale of operations is very large, the risks are commensurably great. It is arguable that the slower evolution of forestry practice allows a more comfortable social response. Certainly, experience with the Australian Nepal forestry project has shown how a technically oriented production process can be sensitively transformed into a useful community-based activity.

Some risks associated with agricultural technology come quickly to public notice, because they impinge on national politics. When this happens, if unemployment grows or there are landholding problems, the national political body must be responsive. This happened in the early stages of Indian agricultural reform, and the debate about the balance between economic benefit and social disbenefit still continues. Governments tend to want to press ahead with technical change because the economic benefits are substantial. In only a few cases is an alternative path chosen.

Health

In health care projects, technology choices are more widely known, perhaps because aid donors themselves are more aware of the high real costs associated with sophisticated technologies. Indeed, the health sector is one where technology cost has been widely debated throughout the international community for several years, and still remains a significant current debate in developed countries.

The design of appropriate health delivery arrangements has been part of the health care development debate over the last twenty years. In developing countries, this debate has largely been won by the advocates of low-cost preventive technology delivered through primary health care systems. As a result, the high cost of health care for the aged and terminally ill has been largely avoided in developing countries, partly because of this choice of policy and technology.

However, the aid–health–care debate usually has limited economic content, except for assumptions about greater economic productivity from a healthier population. The arguments tend to focus on quality of life or basic needs considerations. The additional costs of a longer-living older population are seldom addressed. Whether this issue will be picked up and considered under intergenerational equity in the growing debate on 'sustainability' remains to be seen. It may be too sensitive for both donors and recipients.

Education
In the education sector, a similar debate continues about the necessary institutional technologies to assist development. This is particularly true at the tertiary level. One aspect focusses on how specialised academic training for a relatively privileged few can be balanced against widely-based vocational training, particularly in manual skills, which can more effectively help raise personal incomes among the rural and poorer urban communities. More recently, concerns have focussed on the need to support primary rather than secondary or tertiary education. As elsewhere, the debate concerns the political choices about perceptions of future national directions and priorities. Educational technology has interesting aspects in the field of curriculum design. Both the content and the language of curriculum material can be localised. When this happens the technology is modified as it is transferred and made more appropriate. Without these adjustments curriculum aid is seldom culturally neutral.

Infrastructure
Compared with the political complexities of choices in the health and education sectors, technical choices in infrastructure aid seem relatively simple. For example, in bridge building, railway or road construction, technical choices revolve around issues of cost, efficiency and maintenance. The social and economic results of the total programme have usually been shown to be for the general good, and any immediate disbenefits to those nearby, perhaps displaced by the project or affected by environmental change, will be either overlooked of offset by other project activities at marginal cost. However, this rather simplistic approach will be difficult to sustain as donors and recipients respond more actively to environmental

concerns. Interestingly, it is in infrastructure that we frequently find activities which seem to get very close to the ideal of cultural neutrality. This perception is usually the result of adopting either a very restricted definition of technology, or a narrow project focus.

Two Australian infrastructure projects which have worked well have been the provision of marine navigational aids in Tonga and regional assistance in metrology. In the first case, modern technology, including solar power and low-maintenance signalling on marine markers, replaced manual and mechanical switching systems with a high rate of corrosion and breakdown. The second project helped countries maintain basic measurement standards which, in turn, helped manufacturers meet trade obligations, and domestic suppliers (including retailers) meet agreed standards of weights and measures. An important aspect in the near-neutrality achieved by both these projects is that there is no question of the need and practicality of the technology: all the new technology does is to provide the basic service in a more reliable and efficient way, with minimal social cost. It may be that the disbenefit will turn out in the long run to be greater dependency on foreign maintenance — a political problem rather than an economic or social one.

Management and Economics

Two areas of technology transfer which are often ignored are management methods and economic analysis. Many bureaucrats in developing countries have adopted attitudes to the allocation of resources and methods of corporate decision-making which they have learned during training in institutions in developed countries. For example, the bureaucratic structures which have been developed to produce and implement national plans often evolved in response to the requirements of the World Bank, or followed the example of the (previously) centrally-planned economies of Western Europe (mainly at a conceptual rather than practical level; lacking the ideological underpinning of the previously socialist economies). The degree of commitment towards planning and implementation varies between island nations. Some countries place little significance on either this form of planning, or on the criteria the planning process employs to reach decisions. In these cases technology may be adopted indiscriminately and, as a result, may be used inefficiently.

The technological software transferred to developing countries in management training carries significant, but usually hidden, cultural costs. While such transfers are usually justified on grounds of increased efficiency and improved judgment, this is in Western cultural terms, and reinforces a tendency not to recognise this intellectual material as technology transfer. The logjams which frustrate junior public servants in some developing country bureaucracies often result from a dysfunctional relationship with superiors who have to work in more traditional ways. The communication failures which result and the delays incurred must carry real financial costs to the taxpayers and donors concerned.

The Assessment of Technology

This brief and selective review demonstrates how widely issues of technology transfer can range. The breadth of review depends much upon the adopted definition and understanding of technology. In the West, we largely perceive economic benefits in terms of the efficiencies which are obtained from technical innovation. Technology innovation produces productivity gains and savings. This is the heart of why Western countries give aid, and the dominant form and type of aid given by the West is the transfer of Western technology.

From this sectoral review of technology transfer, we can postulate that issues concerning the value of technology transfer are better understood and more widely debated in those sectors where the cost is widely distributed (among taxpayers and donors), possibly coupled with a more focussed distribution of benefits or facilities, as in the health and education sectors. If the costs are restricted only to the sector concerned, the debate is limited.

From the donor perspective, we must be realistic in judging the resources which donor agencies can devote to assessing the effects of technology transfer. Donor agencies work under many different pressures and, among these, technology transfer issues are no more important than many others. Indeed, technology assessment would usually be a series of routine questions considered during aid project feasibility studies. These questions would include: Does it work? Is there a successful track record? Is it reliable? Can it be replaced or serviced? Later, the importance of new technology to the financial and economic success of a project, or to its social costs, would be considered as part of wider economic appraisal.

Sometimes feasibility questions will be very complicated because of the many connections development projects have with economic and social change, and the desire to press ahead with such projects. In these cases, the donor's judgment has to be about the will of recipient governments to push projects along in the face of possible domestic opposition, and perhaps also, the will of the donor governments to wear the criticism of lobby groups in the recipient and donor countries.

What realistic assessment of technology can therefore be expected from an aid donor, given that economic and financial criteria are at the heart of project appraisal? Perhaps a reasonable response at the institutional level is to provide a simple checklist which reminds aid officers of some cardinal points to consider when new technology is a significant part of a project. The assessment of technology cannot be much more than this because there are so many other imperatives in aid administration. Any mechanism which is too complicated, or which causes greater cost, because of delayed implementation, is not realistic. No institution responsible for spending a fixed budget can delay programmes irresponsibly, just as it is irresponsible to spend profligately. There is little point in either technologists, or sociologists, beating the drum too loudly on this issue. At the present time, the assessment of technology is no more significant in the decision-making process than other factors, such as women's issues or the environment.

The Appropriateness of Technology

No discussion of technology transfer in aid would be complete without reference to 'appropriate' technology. Unfortunately, the phrase is seldom used in a particularly meaningful way for the aid administrator, since almost any social appraisal process will tackle implicitly the issue of appropriateness. In addition, there is some danger that the term is used to argue special cases for technologies that are simple. 'Appropriateness' should mean no more than unobtrusive and useful: the real issue is whether a technology works more efficiently than any other, with no marginal cost. These are aspects of any technology which should be considered as part of appraisal. Of course technology choice takes on a different dimension when the issue is whether a government is being given something second-best, or out-of-date. When this happens political sensitivities become considerably more important than technical issues.

It is likely that, in the long and delicate process by which an aid programme is negotiated, questions of 'appropriateness' will be answered under other headings. To include this issue specifically will add little of consequence to an already difficult and sensitive process. Since, in the course of project negotiations, most decisions will be taken jointly, it is hardly practical or seemly for the donor to demand an explicit consideration of 'appropriateness'.

An interesting example is the Desiccated Coconut Factory in Tonga, funded by Australian aid, which effectively stopped production in 1989, and which has been roundly criticised because of poor engineering and design. It has been argued that it was quite inappropriate technology. With hindsight it seems unlikely that the project could have been much better appraised at the time it was requested, in the late 1970s. In a search for a more modern exporting economy, the Tongan government has pursued a small-scale industrialisation policy for several years, with some success. As a result, the government would probably have accepted the risk and may have been as willing as the Australian authorities to overlook possible social problems, even if a more thorough economic appraisal had been undertaken earlier (assuming that information would have been available to do that). Even after technical rectification, the factory did not work efficiently for a variety of mainly social reasons which were not foreseen. It is not clear whether the Tongan government were surprised by the social problems that appeared when the factory eventually came into production. Indeed, the project turned out to be useful in making explicit some of the very conservative Tongan attitudes to labour and shift work in agricultural processing. Tonga is, after all, sometimes viewed as one of the more progressive societies in Polynesia.

Construction of the factory was clearly in line with the Tongan government's desire to see Tonga become a wealthier society with a more modern economic base. In retrospect, it seems that neither donor nor recipient were aware of how conservative Tongan society would prove to be, despite the fact that the factory provided a way to increase personal incomes. The economic incentives may have been undermined by quite extraneous factors, including the relatively easy access families have to remittance funds from relations abroad. The factory has been criticised because it used modern technologies and assumed a sophisticated labour force. It would be fairer to present the case as a misjudgment of risk and strength of commitment, perhaps by both sides.

* * * *

The assessment of technology is conscientiously considered in the practical administration of most quality aid programmes. Although the process is not explicit, it receives considerable attention because it is a significant factor in all aid.

If Western nations had objectively studied each new technical development, and worried about social costs and appropriateness, they would never have accumulated the wealth and power they have today. So who are they to limit the technological choice of countries less wealthy than themselves?

Of course, some observers will argue that not all economic growth has been beneficial to the world as a whole, and that some aspects incur social and economic debt for present and future generations. The decisions which proceed from such an analysis are not ones that aid administrators are usually empowered or qualified to make. It is not comfortable to have to admit that every nation has the right to learn by its own mistakes. But the laws and conventions which govern relations between sovereign states have always allowed that to happen and, for the most part, still do.

Technology Policy and Management

Stephen Hill

Each of the island states of the Pacific region is unique in terms of geography, natural resources, economic base, cultural traditions, government infrastructure and national, social and economic priorities. These differences, and the layer of similarities that exist by virtue of being island states, are to some extent parallel with what can be found in island nations of the Caribbean and the Indian Ocean.

Similar to island states elsewhere, the Pacific islands have small populations dispersed often over large ocean areas, high proportions of population involved in subsistence agriculture, very limited natural resources, high commodity and geographic concentration of trade leading to considerable vulnerability to fluctuations in commodity prices, small domestic markets, yet high costs of transport both internally and to foreign markets. Many of the island states are heavily dependent on foreign aid and tourism, and have difficulty in shielding the effects on both economic and social development that follow from external interest in the nation's resources.

Whilst each nation of the South Pacific is unique in terms of the particular mix of these general development features, each nation does confront a problem of similar magnitude in balancing national cultural traditions and aspirations against the requirements of modernisation. In this sense, the South Pacific region is similar to the Caribbean and Indian Ocean regions. At the core of this problem of balancing culture against economic development is the often unintended impact of new technologies on national culture, and the unintended impact of technologies aimed at particular sectors on other economic and social sectors (some of the consequences of maintaining this balance were discussed in my previous chapter, in part one).

The Challenge of Developing Technology Policy within the South Pacific
Central to the effectiveness of South Pacific governments in balancing the various tensions that arise where their development intersects with the global economy is the ability to have some say over the way technology enters and affects their societies. In other words, technology policy and management is a very important dimension of national development strategies. The challenge in developing technology policies for small countries is, however, different from that confronting larger nations with substantial technological generating capacity. In smaller countries, such as in the Pacific, the task is less to do with developing the nation's own technologies and more to do with making sensible and conscious technological choices about what is imported and how it is adapted and used. In addition, the challenge is to integrate policy concerning technology across sectors, rather than to deal with each technology, such as those to do with agro-industries, energy, land use and telecommunications, as quite separate issues.

In developing such policies, small island states are in a similar position to most developing countries world-wide in that they are all in a disadvantaged position in their access to technical knowledge resources. These technical resources are almost exclusively controlled by large advanced industrialised nations, which do not necessarily have the interests of the developing nation at heart. Consequently, development must largely draw in technological capacities from elsewhere, largely from the rich and powerful nations.

The question for policy is: 'On what terms?'. It is quite unrealistic to imagine stopping technological entry and technologically-induced change. Foreign interests will therefore have a strong influence on the shape of development. As with a government customs search however, the technological baggage of these foreign interests needs to be opened up and searched. Many undesired and unintended impacts of technological change can be avoided: the use of imported technology can complement development plans well, but only if governments have some understanding of what is going on and exert some shaping influence on technological choices that the nation makes.

Often these choices are hidden in other areas of policy. National governments of the South Pacific region are now dealing with decisions that either imply or follow from technology-induced change. These include, for example, such areas as land use, rural and urban development, transport and communications, utilisation of marine resources, new industries, renewable and non-renewable resources and environmental protection. Also, whether governments decide anything or not about technology, individual farmers, fishermen and townspeople are presently making decisions that together imply a trajectory or direction of technological change within each nation. These include decisions about importing or using technologies and consumer products that come from overseas.

Each of these decisions — by government, by foreign interests and by individuals — creates an effect on the economic potential of the nation, as well as on the cultural practices that currently exist. Each of the decisions directly or indirectly implies technological choices. Equally, all these decisions are set in a framework of international influence. For example, international influence is felt through effects on wealth from variation in commodity prices, through effects on urban development and lifestyle from internationalised consumer products, through effects on economic potential from technologies that must be paid for in international currency and must be supported by international service and spare parts. In addition, many new technologies in areas such as port facilities, agro-industries, airline services and the like are directly introduced into national development through international aid programmes.

The role of government in controlling the development trajectory is therefore likely to be quite limited. However, this is no excuse for giving up, as the importance of having some say over national technological choices is too great. Instead, scarce decision-making resources have to be targeted as effectively as possible on shaping the core forces of technological change towards the social and economic goals the nation is seeking to achieve. The challenge is to plan strategically in terms of what can be influenced in full recognition of what cannot. There are lessons that can be learnt from other small developing countries, even though the particular context of the South Pacific must be always kept in mind.

Key Technology Policy Issues

A Preliminary Note of Caution
The South Pacific is unique as a region. Consequently, whilst the Caribbean is often pointed to as providing some useful technology development models, it should be recognised that the Caribbean as a region is further down the path towards a developed science and technology infrastructure than is generally the case in the South Pacific. Also, the basic dynamics of the economies and region are quite different to that of the island nations of

the South Pacific — in terms of, for example, considerably closer linkages in the Caribbean into both the legal and illegal American economy, the existence of a common language and more comparable national problems. Within the Caribbean the similarity in language and national situations forms a stronger basis for regional cooperation than is likely to be the case within the South Pacific.

Nations of the South Pacific are developing countries, and therefore share many of the 'development' conditions and concerns of, for example the Asian region. Again, however, whilst some larger Pacific island nations may be of similar size to smaller Asian nations, their cultures, economies and government infrastructures are generally quite different.[1]

So, whilst some useful lessons can be learnt from elsewhere, solutions that are appropriate for the South Pacific region are likely to be, at least to some extent, unique. Equally, it is likely that solutions for larger nations of the region will not necessarily be appropriate for smaller nations, or solutions for one culture appropriate for other cultures.

The challenge is to develop lines of action within each nation that draw on general lessons from other developing countries where these lessons are appropriate. However, at the same time, each nation needs to develop an understanding of where lessons appropriate to other nations are simply not applicable for their own particular national context. Given the scarcity of human resources, there may be some areas where the development of either sub-regional or regional management policies may be appropriate. But the final balance, the most appropriate action to develop some autonomy in the management of technological influences, must be appropriate for each nation's own unique situation.

Three General Themes

With the above qualification of uniqueness in mind, we can turn to some common themes about technology and technology management and policy that have emerged from small developing countries' experience elsewhere. Indeed, a great deal has been written about technology policy for developing countries, and within this summarised experience, three major themes have emerged over the last decade. These are:

1. The observation that national technological capability has an increasingly important place in trade and national welfare, compared with natural comparative advantage of the nation's resource base.

2. There is considerable debate about what is the best strategy for developing a national technological capability and, in particular, about the relative emphasis that should be placed on imported technology versus development of national technology and research resources.

3.   The observation that people are no longer as optimistic about the idea that acquiring Western technology would enable a rapid catching-up with the West. This optimism has given way to the recognition that the benefits derived from imported technology often come at considerable costs. These costs were felt as the benefits of imported technologies were often limited to the modern sector of national economies, and such economic advantages that ensued were often exported rather than remaining in the country. These costs were often severe and widely felt.

These three observations are arguably relevant to any developing country, because all are unequal partners in an international economic race where technological mastery has become the prime source of competitive advantage. The observations are therefore relevant to the situation of all nations of the South Pacific region.

Dealing with the Particular Situations of the South Pacific

Whilst a great deal has been written about development problems of the region, and about specific technologies, very little attention has been paid to general technology policy and management concerns of nations of the region.[2] From the evidence that can be put together however, the specific issues that arise do align with the three broad themes identified in other developing countries. The main issues that emerge include the following:[3]

Failure of technology choices

●   Many development projects fail or are less successful than anticipated. It appears that a major reason for these problems has been the poor choice of technology.

●   There are many cases where there has been very little assessment of technologies prior to decision-making. Such decisions have in some cases led to serious negative impacts on foreign exchange and unanticipated requirements for trained personnel.

Complexity of choice

South Pacific Island states face a growing requirement to select and incorporate technology into development goals. These are often complex choices requiring specialised expertise. Areas that involve difficult technology-related choice include, for example, shipping, air transport, communications, computing, industry, fishing, land use and energy.

Scarcity of human resources

There are few personnel with the training and experience to bring a technological perspective and assessment into economic and social planning. There are also few institutions established to support such assessments and their integration into overall planning. In many cases national development planners are the only human resource available for making decisions about technology.

The role of aid agencies

Aid agencies seek to respond to island state priorities, but also seek to ensure that the aid is used in ways that the agency (or its national government) considers will contribute to long-term development of the target country. There are also background considerations in aid ventures of donor country prestige or interest that may well orient the direction of development aid. Sometimes these objectives, of island state determination of priorities and donor government assessment, are in conflict. Sometimes the administrative requirements of aid programmes influence the assessment and choice of technologies that are introduced. This is the case for example in terms of minimum size of project that can be 'efficiently' administered, conditions of project management and in requirements that may be imposed on the purchase of donor country equipment and personnel services.

Dependence on the international economy

- Many of the technical systems that bring benefits in terms of closer linkage with the outside world, or linkage between islands, are complex and will increase dependence on foreign countries. This is the case particularly with, for example, civil aviation and telecommunications.
- More generally, integration with the world economy will inevitably bring with it pressure and stimuli for change, as international patterns of demand and supply shift, and as new wants and needs grow in the domestic economy in line with international fashion and changes.
- There have been many experiences where the technologies selected for import substitution or export-oriented industries have contributed to a far lower than expected flow of benefits, and a high level of ongoing costs through, for example, imported fuels, spare parts and the continuing need for foreign technicians.

Culture, economics and social structures

- There is a widespread concern that many of the changes generated by new activities associated with new technology will irreversibly displace traditional cultures.
- There is often not a clear national consensus in values and objectives both for individuals and social organisations, specifically, for example, concerning the relative balance between kinship obligation and professional responsibility.
- Organisation structures often involve an overlay of imported forms of organisation and procedure on traditional structures of decision-making and administration.

- There is some tension in the maintenance of traditional social structures and institutions between those who are seeking adaptation to changing requirements, and those who are seeking to defend tradition against foreign influence.
- Meanwhile, there is a widespread and strong desire to enjoy the benefits of modernisation, while still retaining national cultural traditions. It is recognised that this involves careful management of the development process in general, and of the inflow of foreign equipment and knowledge in particular.

Technology Policy and the Social Management of Technology

Constraints on Management

The problems and challenges outlined above underline the importance of enhancing the extent to which change in local technical, social and economic structures is managed. The extent to which 'social management' of change is possible is however limited. Governments are never in a position to control all of the forces that can inject quite radical change into the 'environment' of the national economy and culture. Practical constraints on 'social management' lie, for example, in:

- limited capacities to modify imported technology
- a diffuse pattern of technology imports that arises from the separate decisions of individuals or firms
- pressures that arise from aid donor agencies or foreign investors; and
- an uncertainty about what direction should be followed because of a lack of consensus within the society concerning national objectives.

In spite of these constraints, however, it would still seem that to the extent that national objectives are clear, the enhancement of 'social management' is a sensible strategy. With technology lying at the centre of core stimuli of change, 'social management' directly involves technology policy.

Explicit and Implicit Policy

Technology policies may be explicit, as in the case of national science and technology plans. Here, technology policy involves the assessment, choice, adaptation and development of technology, and, most importantly, the management of the interaction between technology choices and social and economic development.

Technology policies may also be implicit. Policies concerning education, foreign affairs, development, trade and so on, all have 'implicit' technology policy implications. Indeed, these implicit policies may be of far greater importance to the technological profile of the nation than any directly focussed science or technology policy that could be in existence.[4] This is the case in the South Pacific, as in other developing nations, where implicit science and technology policies are well established. In particular, implicit technology policies are likely to be subsumed under economic policy. Within the assumptions of economic planning, many social effects of technology choice remain unexamined. For example, technology transfer is generally seen as the same as capital investment, whilst choice of technique is seen as a choice between alternative capital/labour ratios.

The importance of considering implicit policy is that, as a nation embarks on designing an explicit technology policy capability, those involved need to pay attention first to each other area of government policy in terms of its implication for national technological choices.

The First Concern of Technology Policy
— Building Technological Capability

Most nations adopting explicit technological policies have identified their first concern as the building and strengthening of national technological capacities — the building of a human resource platform for generating and shaping technological change.

In many developing nations, this platform is identified with developing a scientific and research infrastructure. Within the South Pacific however, the human and financial resources are simply not available for developing anything like the scientific research, application and technical services structure that has come into existence in a number of the developing nations such as in Asia. This does not mean that the overall structure is irrelevant to the South Pacific. What it means is that nations of the South Pacific need, in the interests of developing an enhanced level of technological autonomy, to select those elements that are most important, and within the capabilities of very limited resources.

In making such a selection, what has been described about the technological functions of a range of institutions or systems in the Caribbean may provide some help.[5] The point is that building a technological capacity does not only mean building scientific institutions. Already in the South Pacific a range of institutions with the capacity to contribute to technological capacity exist: for example in primary and secondary education, manufacturing enterprises, specialist workshops and facilities, engineering firms, libraries and research institutions. It should be noted, though, that research institutions are often operating under the auspices of overseas aid agencies, and are therefore to some extent obeisant to the aid donor's interest.

At a regional level there is a greater wealth of resources that together comprise the institutions that contribute to the technological functions of the region. For example, university and higher education facilities, research laboratories and research experts, information systems, pilot plants and consultant firms.

Therefore, although there are severe constraints on available technological capabilities, resources do exist in the South Pacific. The first priority in technology policy would therefore seem to be to capture these resources strategically — perhaps paying particular attention to what can be shared on a regional basis in shaping existing technological capability towards individual national interests.

Filling-in the Technological Gaps

Within individual nations, the freedom of choice for technological planning is often very limited. There is, therefore, a need for resources of regional and international research and expertise. The question for planners concerned with building up an adequate technology decision-making capability is where to draw on outside resources, and where action simply must be taken at the national level. For every point where there is a gap in the overall structure at a national level is a point where unplanned international influence is likely to enter and take command over the process of technological decision-making.

In addition, technology capabilities can be developed nationally by capitalising on resources that presently exist, but which are not obviously a part of a technology policy or capability system.

For example, traditional societies usually have a wealth of technical knowledge that has allowed them for many years to produce and survive within a relatively stable ecological niche. This is a 'technical capability' that is quite often overlooked in the drive to introduce modern practices and technologies. Yet, traditional technical knowledge could be an asset rather than a 'resistant liability', to be excluded from the nation's overall technological capability. Indeed paying attention to traditional stocks of technical knowledge, and adapting introduced technologies accordingly, could well yield far more appropriate technological change.

Furthermore, through some training and re-orientation, it should be entirely feasible to use extension workers as researchers. Thus, in the field of agriculture, the better understanding of present social arrangements, practice and problems of agriculture, the conduct of limited field tests of new crop varieties and so on, could well be performed without building elaborate research institutions.

Similarly, through the provision of some forms of training for people presently involved in economic planning regarding the perspectives and techniques of technology policy and management, it could be possible to introduce a technology perspective into economic planning without any additional human resources. Given the development of accessible networks of overseas experts on specific technological issues, planners with a 'technology policy perspective' could then call on specific advice at the points where it was needed.

Creative solutions may be possible without stretching existing resources too far. But, to reinforce the point made above, the development of any degree of autonomy about what impact technology will have on a nation's economy and culture requires filling each element in the overall technological choice system in some way, either nationally or internationally.

Establishing Linkages

Inherent in the selection of what is most important for national development, and how best to fill recognised gaps in technological capability, is the choice of ways in which national efforts can be best integrated into international support systems. To be effective, technology policy needs to take advantage of international linkages.[6]

Therefore where, for example, it is quite unviable to build local research institutions, technology policy needs to be concerned with what technical information is critical to economic and social management, and how to build appropriate linkages to regional or international institutions from whence the information can be obtained. Particular areas include, for example, water and energy resources, and alternative industrial technologies that are appropriate to the particular island's situation.

Similarly, it may be appropriate for technology policy to set design parameters for technologies that are to be introduced — for example, concerning size, energy use, employment generation and so on. This may be undertaken, even though the technical design facilities and manufacturing capability may not yet exist within the nation.

The choice therefore could be one of selecting technologies that are already available but do not meet national design parameters, or to link with design and manufacturing capabilities elsewhere. Here it would be the task of technology policy to establish the parameters, to ensure that there are adequate linkages into regional or international sources of information about what alternatives may already be available (not just from commercial suppliers), and, if nothing meets critical design parameters, then to establish linkages with regional or international sources of design and manufacturing expertise.

In short, it is the fundamental task of technology policy makers to choose, and to recognise all the elements in the total process that provides autonomy in technology capability, and to establish linkages that will provide the missing elements of capability that the nation cannot afford to develop itself. In the South Pacific, paying attention to collective regional technology capabilities, for example regarding telecommunications, environment, marine resource exploitation and energy, is particularly important. Whilst national technological self-reliance at any level is unlikely, some level of regional technological self-reliance may well be possible, and could provide a critical bulwark against unwanted external economic and social intervention.

TECHNOLOGY POLICY INITIATIVES IN THE SOUTH PACIFIC

TONY MARJORAM

◆◆◆

The importance of technology in development, and the consequent need of technology policy to promote effective and sustainable development in the South Pacific has been mentioned in other chapters. The relative absence of explicit technology policy, generally combined with implicit policies that directly affect technology choice (policies may be conflicting as well as complementary) has also been noted, together with the need to examine and rationalise attitudes toward technology, and make implicit policy explicit, where possible.

Such goals complement the fairly widespread acknowledgement (for example, in development plans) of the importance of appropriate technology for 'grass-roots' development. The acknowledgement of the need for appropriate technology is often, unfortunately, accompanied by limited effective action. This is due to various reasons — differing policy interests, the general absence of explicit or implicit policy toward technology, constraints in translating what policy or statements there are regarding technology into practice, difficulties in actually defining what technology may be appropriate in various Pacific island contexts and, perhaps most importantly, the need for coherent and reinforcing links between policy makers, administrators and 'grass roots' extension workers. There is an overall need for policy formulation and implementation at the 'tree tops' to complement initiatives and activities at the grass roots.

Amid all the other demands and changes independent island governments face in the relatively recent post-independence period, however, interest in technology policy and planning in the South Pacific is increasing. Initiatives have been organised at the regional and national levels. These include two particular and 'explicit' national technology policy activities in Fiji and Papua New Guinea that are presented in this chapter as case studies. Both represent approaches to technology policy that serve as useful models to the smaller countries of the region.

Technology Policy

Interest in the role of science and technology in development, and hence in science and technology policy and planning, began in developed, industrialised countries in the post-war period of the later 1940s and 1950s. This followed the need for and success of wartime science and technology policy and planning, and the organised approach to post-war reconstruction in the Marshall Plan. A subsequent interest in the application, policy and planning of science and technology for development in developing countries began in the 1960s and 1970s. A milestone in this direction was the 1979 UN Conference on Science and Technology for Development (UNCSTD), which underlined important issues relating to the role of science and technology in development, and the problematic nature of the transfer of technology to developing countries.

Interest in science and technology policy in smaller and island developing countries began around this time, following the more general expansion of interest in economic development in developing island countries.[1] As with other 'island' issues, interest in science and technology in the developing island context arose almost simultaneously in the three main island areas — the Caribbean, Indian Ocean and South Pacific.[2] Although there are some similarities between these three areas, however, there are also significant differences regarding size and industrial development — as noted by Hill, 'whilst the Caribbean is often pointed to as providing some useful technology development models, it should be recognised that the Caribbean as a region is further down the path towards a developed science and technology infrastructure than is generally the case in the South Pacific. Also, the basic dynamics of the economies and other features of the Caribbean are quite different to that of the island nations of the South Pacific'.[3]

Technology Policy and the South Pacific

The first important examination of science, technology and development in the region was the production of the South Pacific Sub-Regional UNCSTD Paper in 1978. The draft UNCSTD paper was produced by Medford and Rothman, and a final version discussed, slightly amended and endorsed by representatives of thirteen countries, regional and international agencies.[4]

The UNCSTD paper examined the general role of science and technology in development, with a particular focus on constraints and opportunities for the South Pacific. The overall recognition in the paper was the need to improve the choice, transfer, management and assessment of technology for development in the region. The paper also observed a general need for better integration, utilisation and increased institutional support of indigenous and introduced science and technology, and improved regional and international cooperation in research and development.

At a national level, during production of Fiji's Eighth Development Plan (DP8, 1980–85) in 1980, science and technology policy was recognised as an important but neglected area of development policy and planning. A request for technical assistance led to a study of technology policy in Fiji in 1982–83 (this study forms the main basis for the following discussion of technology policy in Fiji). The importance of technology policy in Fiji was underlined in a World Bank study of the manufacturing industry in 1986. Apart from observing the general need to re-orient manufacturing from import-substitution to export-promotion, the study noted the importance of the capability to absorb and assimilate technology.[5] An interest in formulating a science and technology policy for Papua New Guinea was reflected and developed from the Waigani Seminar in 1984 — which had the theme of science and technology for development in PNG and the South Pacific.[6]

Ten years after the production of the UNCSTD paper, in response to limited activity regarding the paper and a renewed recognition of the need for science and technology policy and planning in the South Pacific, a High Level Regional Meeting on the 'Policy and Management of Science and Technology for Development in the South Pacific Region' was held in Apia in March 1987.[7] The meeting was attended by senior participants from island countries, regional and international organisations. The meeting examined and discussed the general topic of science, technology and development in the South Pacific through background reference documents, keynote papers, country technology profiles provided by participants and three working groups — focussing on technology and economic development, technology and social and cultural change and the impact of information technologies.

The main issues arising from the meeting included recommendations that science and technology considerations should be more closely integrated into national planning, and that national and regional capability regarding technology assessment, acquisition, adaptation, management (operation and maintenance) and monitoring should be supported and reinforced through improved communication, education and training. Particular follow-up action recommended at the meeting included the strengthening of regional capability to assess the impact of science and technology on development in the region. To further this goal, UNESCO was requested to prioritise the appointment of a science advisor at the regional UNESCO office in Apia (a science advisor was appointed in 1991). The main outcome regarding the strengthening of regional capability in the management of technology for development in the region was the UNESCO South Pacific Regional Technology for Development Workshop, held in Tonga in 1987.[8]

Technology Policy in Fiji and Papua New Guinea

Interest in science and technology policy, planning and management in the South Pacific increased through the 1980s. This interest culminated in the organisation of technology policy study documents in the two largest countries of the region — Fiji and Papua New Guinea.

Technology Policy in Fiji

As a result of the recognition that science and technology policy was an important but neglected area of development policy and planning, the ILO was requested to provide technical assistance to undertake a study of technology policy in Fiji. A consultant was provided, who also acted as a temporary technology advisor to the Central Planning Office, and the study was undertaken in two periods, January-October 1982, and April-May 1983. The study appeared as the Fiji 'Technology Policy Assessment' in 1985. The study was reported in two parts — as an overview Terminal Report, and in six volumes (of 500 pages) of Detailed Report.[9]

The Terminal Report outlines the objectives of the study in terms of anticipated and proposed outputs, activities, factors affecting performance of the study, a brief summary of findings, suggested follow-up activities, conclusions and recommendations. The Detailed Report contains an introduction to technology policy assessment, a profile of technology in Fiji, an outline of fiscal and trade policies, key development agencies and their attitude toward technology, rural technology policy, technology transfer and choice in Fiji, technical and managerial consultancy, supply and demand for scientific and technological expertise, conclusions and recommendations.

The immediate objectives of the study were to review implicit and explicit Fiji government policy toward technology, with specific emphasis on assessing the effectiveness of current procedures regarding the acquisition of imported technology, recommending policies for ensuring the best use of limited funds available for local R&D and improved alignment of policies towards technology with national development strategy (with special reference to guidelines for business and industrial development, Fiji Development Bank loan policy, technology information systems, the effectiveness of government and Fiji Sugar Corporation agricultural research and the capability and effectiveness of local consultancy firms).[10]

Longer term development objectives focussed on the role of technology policy in furthering the goals of Fiji's DP8, including strengthening and diversifying the national economic base, promoting more equitable distribution of the benefits of development, creating productive and rewarding employment opportunities and promoting increased self-reliance, a greater sense of national unity and regional and international cooperation. The consultant noted that each of these 'required more local capability to recognise, choose, bargain for, and use imported technologies, together with more effective local innovation'.

Anticipated outputs from the study included an analysis of Fiji's existing policies towards technology and the compatibility of these policies with long-term development objectives, guidelines for techniques and administrative changes necessary to facilitate effective bargaining for foreign technology, guidelines for establishing and operating a funding mechanism to encourage local innovation (should such seem desirable) and suggested means of improving local technical consultancy capability. Apart from the Terminal and Detailed Reports, other proposed outputs of the study included a special report on lending criteria of the Fiji Development Bank, a generalisation of the findings of the study to other Pacific island nations and a short Technology Policy Appraisal Manual.

Specific activities undertaken during the study included a survey of existing technology policies and analysis of compatibility with long-term development objectives; an assessment of the impact of Fiji government legislation and practices relating to imported technology and investment (including analyses of government procurement policy and technology in the foreign aid programme); a survey of technology use and the transfer process in manufacturing; an assessment of technology used in sugar cane harvesting and production, civil engineering, forestry and fisheries, and comparison with alternative technologies; an assessment of technical and management consultancy facilities and R&D capacity in Fiji and comments regarding future expertise requirements in science and technology, technology for 'basic needs' and a possible Technology Advisory Service.

The consultant listed various factors affecting the study. These included the observations that 'very little germane information or data were found to exist, and the number and range of interviews and contacts used to offset this deficiency was very much greater than had been anticipated', and that 'very little was known of technology policy in the Fiji Government Service, this reflecting the dearth of scientific and technological expertise in that Service. The inevitable consequence was that attitudes toward the Project in certain Departments were friendly but sceptical. This contrasted sharply with the attitude of public and private sector enterprise: most representatives of industry regarded the Project as a useful initiative which offered some prospect of a change in what they saw as unsatisfactory official policies and attitudes on technology-related matters'.

The main findings of the Fiji study were that:

1. A substantial number of explicit and implicit policies are operated, and sizeable sums of money are spent annually by government on scientific and technological activities.

2. Although most explicit policies are directed at increasing the labour-intensity of plant and machinery, very little has been achieved (with the exception of the policy to maintain labour-intensity in sugar cane harvesting, and the justification for choosing relatively advanced technology in forestry and civil engineering); economic development is relatively capital-intensive; explicit policy has generally failed because of ineffective or contradictory implementation.

3. Several implicit policies operate in favour of increasing capital intensity, particularly fiscal and wage policies, with tariff protection seeming unrelated to technology and broader development policy.

4. There is a general and increasing lack of scientific and technological expertise, particularly in Government administration and parastatal agencies such as the Fiji Development Bank and the Economic Development Board; this is partly due to the localisation programme, and reflects the need for basic technical training to dovetail into higher-level training overseas; the lack is an important source of inefficiency and poor technology decision-making.

5. Larger (often foreign-owned) companies experience little difficulty with technology transfer, whereas smaller indigenous firms frequently experience problems with the choice and performance of technology.

6. The rural technology programme of the government has proved ineffective, largely because of the fragmented and 'top-down' approach.

7. Fiji has a wide range of (mainly foreign-owned) technical and managerial consultancies, but with gaps in electronics and computing.

8. There is almost no R&D in manufacturing, although R&D in the sugar, timber and fisheries industries is evident.

The main recommendations of the Fiji study were that:

1. The role and importance of technology policy, within general development policy, should be better communicated and appreciated; this should be

acheived through clarifying the approach to planning and prioritising planning goals.

2. The strengthening of scientific and technological expertise, particularly in government and parastatal development agencies, is an important priority; more technical input is required in formulation of aid projects; the financial appraisal of projects involving technology needs to be improved; government procurement of technology and accounting regarding technology management should be rationalised and improved.

3. To facilitate the strengthening of scientific and technological expertise an Industrial Technology Unit, providing technology information and advice, would help to achieve this; a similar Rural Technology Unit would help support and coordinate activities in the rural sector.

4. Firms in the manufacturing sector face many problems (for example, of excess capacity); overseas consultants could be used to diagnose problems and local consultants carry out the implementation of recommended strategies; liberalised work permit regulations and slowing the pace of localisation should be considered.

5. Fiscal and wage policies should be made more neutral or biased toward labour-intensive technologies; tariff policy should be used as an instrument of technology and development policy; for example, import duty on repair and maintenance equipment should be dropped, and small exporters given extended import duty relief.

6. Investigations should be made regarding the possibility for some degree of mechanisation of sugar cane harvesting and, conversely, the increased use of labour-intensive technology in forestry and civil engineering.

7. R&D activity in fisheries, local timber use and sugar cane breeding should be encouraged (but not yet in process manufacturing).

Follow-up Activities

It was recommended that one or more officers in the Central Planning Office in Fiji receive training in technology policy, and that information on the approach and findings of the Fiji Technology Policy Assessment be disseminated in the region, with the suggested possibility of undertaking similar studies in other island countries.

Science and Technology Policy in Papua New Guinea

As a result of increased awareness of the importance of science and technology in development and a recognition of the consequent need for a coherent policy toward science and technology, a seminar, entitled the 'National Science and Technology Policy Workshop', was convened in Port Moresby on 4–6 September 1990. The seminar was attended by over 70 senior participants from government, parastatal and non-government agencies, organisations and institutions.

The main purpose of the seminar was to produce a National Science and Technology Policy discussion document for the PNG National Executive Council (the PNG Cabinet), which, when endorsed by the NEC, would form the basis for a National Science and Technology Policy, and allow establishment of the Papua New Guinea Science and Technology Council and Secretariat, as outlined below. The policy document was duly finalised, approved by the NEC and launched, the enabling legislation for the Council had been written and approved in the first reading in Parliament, a 1992 budget allocation made, duty statements drawn up and a draft work plan discussed.

The National Science and Technology Policy document (of 16 pages) began by recognising the role and importance of science and technology in development in PNG and the need for a National Science and Technology Policy.[11] The proposed policy derived from the PNG National Constitution, with the overall goal of 'optimising the quality of life of all Papua New Guineans through the sensible application of both traditional and modern science and technology for sustainable development in accordance with our National goals', and by 'gearing scientific and technological activities to the requirements of our people and providing coherent and practical advice to Government on policies, priorities and projects'. The policy document noted that the emphasis should be on 'coordination and cost-effective decision-making, rather than authority and control'.[12]

The policy document paid particular attention to 'traditional knowledge and practices, and to applying appropriate scientific and technological innovations in accordance with our systems of social and cultural values'. The importance of 'sustainable development and increased national self-sufficiency' were strongly emphasised.

An outline was presented for the effective management of science and technology for development in the PNG context, regarding both various sectoral priorities and overall human resource development. The main overall initiative was the establishment of a PNG Science and Technology Council, to be accountable to the NEC, for the 'intelligent and cost-effective implementation of the policy'. Suggested activities included a Science and Technology Year, with the theme of 'Science and technology for the people of PNG'; a Wokabaut Science and Technology Museum; national science and technology prizes; a Public Sector Information Technology Strategy; workshops on 'Information Technology for the Benefit of the People', and 'Management of Technology for Development'. Other suggested science and technology initiatives related to library and information services, extension agencies and officers, primary, secondary and tertiary education, professional associations and consultancy services.

Strong support for the early establishment of the National Institute of Standardisation and Industrial Technology was also indicated.

Following an executive summary the policy document included a preamble on the importance of science and technology in development in PNG and the need for a coherent, practical and effective science and technology policy. A statement of the overall goal of the policy setting was established regarding the National Goals and Directive Principles of the PNG Constitution in terms of human development, equality and participation, national sovereignty and self-reliance, conservation and sustainable development in accordance with the customs and cultures of PNG. The connection and consistency of a policy for technology with policies in other areas (such as economic development, education and training, industry, environment, localisation, youth and standards) was noted, and the support a technology policy would give to the existing institutional framework.

The overall objectives of the policy would be to:

1. Establish a process wherein scientific and technological activities are encouraged, supported, geared to the requirements of our people, and evaluated in terms of the practical consequences to their wellbeing and fulfillment.

2. Set up effective guidelines and mechanisms for the provision of coherent, practical advice to government on policies, priorities and projects in the broad field of science and technology, based upon our people's best interests.

3. Achieve coordinated and cost-effective decision-making, resource allocation, curriculum development, teaching, research and its practical applications, information exchange and evaluation across all sectors in relation to science and technology.

4. Ensure that traditional knowledge and practices are understood and strengthened, and that appropriate scientific and technological innovations are applied in accordance with our systems of social and cultural values.

5. Promote sustainable development and the application of scientific and technological activities in ways that conserve and enhance the physical, biological and social environment.

6. Foster national self-sufficiency and the advancement of Papua New Guinea as a partner in the regional and international scientific activity, rather than being unduly dependent upon imported technology and non-citizen experts.

The strategies for implementation of the science and technology policy were grouped into the categories of the management of scientific and technological activity; science and technology in PNG context; sustainable development; sectoral priorities; human resource development; coordination and communication.

PNG Science and Technology Council

As noted above, the major practical outcome of the science and technology policy is the establishment of the PNG Science and Technology Council (PNGSTC). The main role of the Council would be to encourage, support and provide practical, coherent advice, information and evaluation relating to decision-making, education, research and development in science and technology. The Council would promote this role to further national goals, in accordance with social and cultural values, in the public and private sectors. The Council would achieve this through coordination, consultation and facilitation, involving existing agencies where they are already active, and enhancing national and international linkages in science and technology.

The functions of the Council would include:

1. Information gathering, analysis and consultation regarding actvities in science and technology, to determine positive and negative implications and optimum courses of action.
2. Liaison with government and non-government agencies and institutions to ensure cross-sectoral consideration of scientific and technological issues.
3. Advising National Executive Council, central agencies, other government departments and appropriate bodies of the merit, implications and relative priorities of resource requirements and the best use of current resources regarding science and technology.
4. Reviewing and coordinating overseas aid in the field of science and technology.
5. Facilitating effective national and international linkages of science and technology information and specialists between universities, research institutes, government, parastatal, non-government agencies and the private sector.
6. Conduct technology assessments to determine positive and negative effects of transfer and development of projects involving science and technology on society, culture and economy.
7. Establish working groups and sub-committees of the Council to encourage and promote such activities as research grants, scholarships, prizes, visits, exchanges, exhibitions, conferences, directories, publications, information dissemination and similar activities in the fields of science and technology.

It was suggested that the chairperson of the Council function as the senior officer of the Council Secretariat, and also be recognised as the chief scientific advisor to government, appointed on contract by the National Executive Council. It was suggested that the Council consist of representatives of government departments, the private sector, universities, professional associations, the churches and NGOs. It was recommended that the council members have backgrounds in science, technology, policy and planning, and include members reflecting the wider society and culture of PNG.

The Secretariat serving the Council was suggested to comprise a small specialist team consisting of the chairperson/chief science and technology advisor, an executive officer, three policy advisors, three research officers and an information/publications officer. It was recommended that all but two of the policy advisors should be Papua New Guinean, and that a priority would be the training of the research officers, preferably recent graduates from the sciences, social sciences and humanities, to act as counterparts to the policy advisors. It was proposed that the interim PNGSTC Secretariat be responsible to the Secretary of the NEC (the Deputy PM), and that, following approval by the NEC and passing of support legislation, the Council be responsible directly to the NEC. The anticipated annual recurrent cost of implementing the National Science and Technology Policy would be around K225,000 (A$320,000), with an estimated annual project budget of around K400,000 (A$570,000).

Evaluation of Practical Outcomes in Relation to Policy Objectives
The policy document noted the importance of conducting an independent evaluation of the implementation and performance of policy around the third year after commencement of activities. The evaluation would assess progress toward the overall policy goal. Particular questions included:

1. Has a process been established wherein scientific and technological activities are encouraged, supported and geared to the requirements of the people?
2. Are effective guidelines and mechanisms in existence and in use for the provision of coherent, practical advice to government on policies, priorities and projects in the broad field of science and technology?
3. Is there coordinated and cost-effective decision-making, resource allocation, curriculum development, teaching, research, applications, information exchange and evaluation across all sectors in relation to science and technology?
4. Are traditional knowledge and practices being understood and preserved, and are appropriate scientific and technological innovations being applied in accordance with our systems of social and cultural values?
5. Is Papua New Guinea engaged in sustainable development and the application of scientific and technological activities in ways that preserve and enhance the physical, biological and social environment?

6.   Are science and technology contributing to increased national self-sufficiency and has Papua New Guinea become a partner in regional and international scientific activity, rather than being unduly dependent upon imported technology and non-citizen experts?

* * * *

Fiji and PNG have many differences, but face many similar problems relating to technology and development. It is interesting to examine and compare the approach and analysis of the two technology policy documents. They do not have identical frames of reference, but both address the question of the management of technology for development. Although there are differences of approach and analysis, there is some overlap and similarity in that both documents tell a similar story, but from different perspectives. In this sense, the documents are complementary.

The Fiji Technology Policy Assessment has a particular technology focus, and is the result of an in-depth study, coordinated and largely conducted by an outside consultant. The Fiji policy document is detailed and decriptive. The Fiji study noted the widespread problems caused by the shortage of indigenous technological expertise, associated difficulties in implementing projects with a technological component. Despite the absence of an actual, coherent explicit technology policy, the Fiji study also noted the number of explicit and implicit policies directly relating to technology, drawing attention to the general problems of such explicit policies, and the ineffective and sometimes contradictory nature of implicit policies. In some ways, it is not hard to see why certain Fiji government servants may have been 'friendly but sceptical' about the study.

The PNG National Science and Technology Policy addressed issues of science and technology policy, although the emphasis was on technology. The PNG policy document was produced in a seminar by group of local specialists drawn from the public and private sectors, with interests in science technology, policy, planning and general development. The PNG policy document is brief, and focusses on implementation. The Fiji policy document was not used as background material for the PNG seminar, although, because of the similarities of problems faced, many of the findings and recommendations of the Fiji study were almost tacitly subsumed by the seminar participants.

Both documents note the overall importance of technology policy and planning, the need to strengthen expertise in terms of technical specialists, management, policy-making and planning and the need for increased coherence in policy and planning relating to technology. To achieve these goals, the Fiji study suggested industrial and rural technology units, and the PNG seminar recommended a similar but more powerful

Science and Technology Council. The Fiji study suggested the use of fiscal policy to complement technology and development policy, for example in a general bias toward labour-intensive technology. Whilst the PNG document does not discuss such detail, such an attitude was implicit at the seminar. The seminar document also offers many useful suggestions regarding the function, initiatives and activities connected with the implementation and evaluation of technology policy and planning.

TECHNOLOGY, DEVELOPMENT AND ISLAND FUTURES

TONY MARJORAM

As observed, the Pacific islands are increasingly dependent upon and impacted by Western technology — the overwhelming prospect of the greenhouse effect and sea level rise, unsustainable fishing practices, toxic waste disposal, nuclear testing and transportation and problems associated with mining at Bougainville and elsewhere. Internal impacts of Western technology are of equal if not greater significance. The expanding transfer of Western technology in imports and aid is causing increasing technological dependence and problems of assimiliation.

Despite the concern with the external and internal effects and impacts of Western technology, there has been little 'futures' thinking regarding technology and development in the island Pacific. This is unfortunate, as sophisticated techniques are not essential for futures study in the region. What is more useful is an analysis of trends of change, particularly future technological trends in the West, and an assessment of their likely impacts and implications in the islands. These are the goals of this chapter.

The chapter is not intended as a rigorous piece of technology forecasting and impact assessment — small island futures are so uncertain and dependent on external change that such a goal would be pointless. Rather, the chapter is intended to present an overview of possible island futures, and a discussion of how islands may maximise benefits and minimise impacts of change.

Some people question why the Pacific islands cannot remain relatively isolated from the rest of world. Islanders, however, like people elsewhere, have long developed a taste for outside goods and services, which consist essentially of technology. The islands are therefore increasingly and inextricably linked to the outside world. In this situation, it is considered better to attempt to foresee and plan for the future, rather than approach it unprepared.

Island Realities, Technology and Future Trends

There are numerous problems and constraints of smallness and isolation for the Pacific islands, and few opportunities or 'comparative advantages'. Human and many physical resources (except for some primary products) are limited, and social and physical environments are sensitive to change. Productive capacities and markets are small. General and technological infrastructures are limited — services, goods and spare parts are expensive to procure, install and maintain. Industrial processes and equipment are often no longer available to 'fit' such a diminutive scale — what is now small by world standards is large in the islands. There are increasing problems of dependence and assimilation in the region, particularly as regards technology. Gone are the days (if there ever were any) of 'subsistence affluence' — the islands are 'beautiful, but no place to live'.[1]

Pacific island populations include the highest growth rates in the world, and populations are young. Population density varies widely. In many countries (particularly in Polynesia) there is high internal rural-urban drift and external 'out-migration' (mainly to New Zealand and Australia). Migration is facilitated by modern air transport and telecommunications — 'technological change in transport and greater involvement with the market economy have increasingly marginalised the smaller island countries in relation to Pacific rim countries'.[2] One consequence of this is that migrant islanders face huge overseas telephone bills — in 1987, Tonga was second only to America in per capita expenditure on international telephone calls, mostly collect calls paid by metropolitan relatives. Problems of welfare, health and nutrition are increasing — the displacement of traditional foodstuffs by imported Western food and consequent 'food dependency' is similar to the situation for technology. Lifestyle changes have lead to a consequent rise in 'Western' diseases, particularly among the wealthier islanders.

Economic development is funded by aid, tourism, income from exports and government revenue. In some countries, remittances from migrant workers are a valuable source of direct income for many islanders and the main national income. Supposed opportunities or Ricardian 'comparative advantages' of the Pacific islands include tourism, remittances, access to donor-funded concessionary produce and manufactures export schemes, a strategic geopolitical position and aid. From their dependence on migration, remittances, and aid-supported bureaucracy and government, Pacific islands have been identified as 'MIRAB' or 'MIRAGE' economies — the latter reflecting what Brookfield sees as an illusion of development in the region.[3]

Aid has become a permanent feature of development in the region and could be considered a factor of production (alongside capital, labour and technology), rather than an externality.[4] Almost the total development budget in many island countries derives from aid, particularly bilateral aid. Development projects also have significant implications for future recurrent budgets, mainly funded by government revenue. Aid to the region is frequently 'tied' to donor countries and is provided for political-diplomatic, commercial as well as perceived developmental reasons by donor countries. Island states benefit from a 'small country bias' in many donor programmes — as the Jackson Report review of Australian aid commented, 'small states carry the same voting weight in the UN as large, so the strategic and political imperatives of aid tend to favour small countries'. The Jackson Report also observed that 'the faster development takes place the better Australian strategic and economic interests will be served' and, somewhat contentiously, 'as development programs succeed, the need for aid will decline and ultimately disappear'.[5]

Aid donors prefer projects which appear large by island standards because they are easier and less proportionately expensive to administer, although relatively large projects are not always the most appropriate form of assistance. Because of the small size of island countries, aid flows also appear high in per capita terms, although it is misleading to think of aid in individual terms, as most is spent on large infrastructure projects. Relatively high levels of aid also bring problems of assimilation and dependence.

Viewed from within, small islands may not be as beautiful as they appear to outsiders, and many islanders would not share this roseate view of the success of development projects, or of the declining need of development aid. As Western Samoan Albert Wendt laments, 'Over half our annual budget is from foreign aid. Like most other Pacific countries, we've become a permanent welfare case. I can't see us ever getting out of the hole. Many of our leaders don't want to: foreign aid is now built into their view of development, into their way of life. It is also in the interest of foreign powers (our supposed benefactors) to keep us hooked on their aid'.[6]

Technology and Industrial Development

Pacific islands are 'dual economies', consisting of modern/urban and traditional/rural spheres, mainly comprising of the public and private economic sectors, and the 'non-economic' rural sector. Larger industry is focussed on or export-oriented primary production, with smaller industry focussed on import substitution. The larger private sector is mainly foreign owned — 'the foreign sector is the economy'.[7] There is limited overlap between the two spheres, and little potential for technology transfer from the modern/urban to the traditional/rural sphere. Much economic activity takes place in the 'traditional' sector, although it is often ignored in statistical data. The public sector provides many services and industries not otherwise available.

Many industries receive support from government and donors through various grants and loans, fiscal incentives and concessionary schemes, with the aim of promoting overseas investment, industry, technology transfer, infrastructure and human resource development. Trade and economic development schemes intended to favour the islands include SPARTECA, PIIDS, DIFF and STABEX.[8] Although certain industries may be preferred through a process of 'industrialisation by invitation', limited overseas interest, similar national strategies and competition between island nations has led to a largely 'open door' atmosphere, where few economically 'sound' proposals are declined. As in the Caribbean, the other major island region, where 'the two key elements of the Caribbean development stategy, import substitution and industrialisation by invitation, have both failed to develop the economies of the region'.[9]

Rural areas, where most islanders live, are becoming increasingly marginalised as a consequence of increasing urban drift and socio-cultural dislocation, despite the recognised need for rural development activities. Rural areas also account for much of the technology transfer to the region in the form of small consumer and producer goods. Such 'durables' have a brief life-span, however, due to the generally harsher operating conditions and more limited support facilities in rural areas.

Planning and Development in the Small Island Context

The problems of smallness and isolation in the islands have exercised the minds of many outside experts. The South Pacific is a development planner's paradise — development planning is essentially synonymous with economic development, and nearly all planners are economists. The islands have been seen as 'laboratories' for alternative development strategies, and various development models — 'cures for under-development' — have been applied throughout the region in a 'passing parade of paradigms'.[10] Technology is regarded by many planners in the region (in the Western 'tradition') as an aspect of capital, alongside the other inputs or factors of production — labour and land/raw materials. Non-economic aspects of development — such as technology — are treated by many planner/economists in the South Pacific as non-problematic.

The national development plans of most islands are mainly 'shopping-lists' prepared for aid donors, often written by expatriate planners provided by aid donors. Within the five-year horizon of most plans there is generally little futures thinking, partly because of the time-scale and 'shopping-list' nature of the plans, their general micro-economic project orientation and the fact that the future for such small countries is so uncertain. Although there has not been much 'futures' thinking at national level in the South Pacific, concern for sea-level rise, nuclear testing and toxic waste disposal illustrate considerable disquiet regarding technology and environmental issues at the regional level. This concern at the regional level could usefully be expanded at the national level.

Industrialisation and industry-led development in the islands are problematic. To UNCTAD, 'in a small country with no free trade, industrial growth may be inefficient; however, with free trade, a small country may experience no growth at all, and may in fact deindustrialise'.[11] On the other hand, another observer recommends that 'the expansion of manufacturing capacity should be encouraged . . . the guide should probably be the successful experience of East Asian countries which had adopted outward-looking, export-oriented rather than import-substitution industrial-isation'.[12]

It is curious but not altogether surprising that the newly-industrialised countries' model of industry-led development and other ideas such as economic rationalism (with the ideological focus of promoting the free market over the state) have been encouraged in the island Pacific. Given the constraints of size and consequent need for many services only island governments can properly provide, however, such approaches illustrate the problems and frequent inappropriateness of applying Western models to the island Pacific. Small island states face distinct difficulties with industrialisation, and it is debatable how much genuine viable and sustainable development industrialisation has achieved in the small, isolated, traditional and agriculturally-oriented Pacific islands.

Technologically-oriented industries introduced to the region have encountered a whole range of constraints and problems relating to technical, social, economic, marketing and environmental factors in terms of operation and maintenance, skills training and high labour turnover, high capital and unanticipated operating costs and consequent cash-flow shortfalls. Problems of technology in the provision of services abound —

relating to constraints of smallness, isolation, tropical island conditions and limited technological infrastructure. It is difficult to maintain complex technology, such as an X-ray machine, and often easier to obtain new equipment through aid.

The failure of many aid projects (donors, however, never speak publicly of failure, only 'limited success') indicates that aid agencies have yet to thoroughly adjust their minds to Pacific realities. Indeed, conditions have prompted some outsiders to observe that smaller Pacific islands are not 'viable', and that migration is the only answer — 'for those countries with very poor prospects for self-sustaining development and poor standards of living, opening-up of migration policy may be an essential adjunct to aid'. Such comments completely overlook the close identity most islanders feel to their land. More realistically, other observers note that consideration of island problems 'have overturned the classical theories of economic development'.[13]

Technology Transfer Differentials in the South Pacific

Technology futures in the Pacific islands reflect (through a distorted mirror) past and present innovation and trends in the 'heartland' Western countries of the main donors and suppliers of technology. Technology transfer to the islands is not uniform, it is different in different sectors, there are lags or 'technology transfer differentials' between the islands and overseas. Technology differentials — 'technology gaps' — illustrate the unevenness of technological change between countries, and are most distinct between developed and developing countries. This is particularly evident in small developing countries such as those of the South Pacific. There will be an increasing 'crisis of structural adjustment' in developing countries in coming to terms with technological change in developed, industrialised countries.

Catch-22s of Technology and Development

The 'Catch-22' of technology and development arises in the South Pacific because of the limited technological infrastructures and the undoubted need for outside technology in the islands. Imported technology and technological advice is often insensitive and inappropriate to local conditions and customs, however, and requires local appraisal, in which islands are deficient. A similar Catch-22 also occurs in many aid donor agencies, due to the paucity of technological expertise and the predominance of economists and 'content-free' administrators. These Catch-22s are a major background reason for many failed development projects in the South Pacific, and will increase with technological change in the West, unless support is given to the development of technological infrastructures, policy and planning in island nations.

Technology, Economic Development and the Future

Economic interest in the role of technology in development has grown since the late 1970s. This reflects two concerns — the first regarding the deficiencies of the Keynesian model of demand-management in stimulating economic growth, the second focussing on the technological 'blind spot' of neo-classical economics, where technological change and associated issues such as technology policy, planning, choice and decision-making are often neglected or ignored. The main interest in technology has arisen from the perspective of 'supply-side' economics, based partly on recognising the importance of radically innovatory 'heartland technologies' that create 'waves' of economic development. Technology is regarded as the central and revolutionary motivator or engine of economic growth, and the main focus is on restructuring the role of the state to facilitate technological change and economic growth. Microelectronics is identified as a major current heartland technology.[14]

Changes in heartland technologies occasion changes in technological-economic models or 'paradigms' in the West. The 'old' energy- and materials-intensive techno-economic paradigm, for example, is changing to a new information intensive paradigm. This brings associated changes in 'technological trajectories' — technological development within the paradigm, indicated by changes in modes of production and division of labour, and a 'cultural revolution' in firms and industries.[15] Perceptions of change vary from those who believe that present changes are part of underlying, unidirectional but accelerating long-run trends and the 'steady accumulation of scientific knowledge and technical know-how', to those who are 'convinced that we are indeed witnessing a major transition in the industrialisation era'.[16] Kaplinsky notes historic changes from handicraft production to manufacture, 'machinofacture' and 'systemofacture'. Although perceptions of change vary, outcomes are similar.

Changes in the technology paradigm occur unevenly across sectors and reduce sectoral differences, for example between primary production, industrial manufacturing and tertiary services. Services are becoming industrialised — in telecommunications, banking, transport and health services, and industries are becoming 'servicised' or 'tertiarised' — by software, producer services and value-added manufacturing. Radical innovation creates new needs for new skills, information and the use of 'intelligent' capital that itself embodies and is used to take advantage of new knowledge.[17]

Technology Change in the West and its Impact on Developing Countries

Few observers have reflected on the consequences and impacts of change in Western technology and technology paradigms upon developing countries

— change in technology leads to change in the structure and culture of countries as well as companies. The change in technology paradigm is particularly uneven between developed and developing countries, and between different sectors in developing countries — especially between modern and traditional sectors.

Analyses of the significance and impact of new technology for less-developed countries are ambivalent. The increased productivity of new technology in the West could negate the 'comparative advantage' of low labour costs in developing countries, and relocate formerly labour-intensive industries back to the West, increasing the technology-gap between developed and developing countries (assuming that developing countries could not take advantage of such technology). At the same time, however, technological discontinuities could allow developing countries the possible advantage of 'technological leap-frogging' (assuming that developing countries could take advantage of new technology). Kaplinsky argues that changes in modes of production and divisions of labour occasioned by new technology may create certain advantages for developing countries.[18] Most observers agree on the increasing scientific content of technology, and how this mainly acts to the disadvantage of developing countries. Crucial factors are the location and ability of developing countries to acquire and assimilate new technology into production processes — which depend essentially on their technological infrastructures and associated policy and planning.

Island Futures, Internal and External Change

As Pacific island populations grow, so will the exposure and aspiration to Western values, lifestyle and goods. Urban-rural drift will most probably continue, with the increasing marginalisation of rural areas. Problems of providing education and employment for young people will increase, accompanied by increasing dependency, social dislocation and frustration. Migration will continue to be restricted. This will limit remittances, which also tend to decline over time as migrants settle, loosen ties with home and increase their own financial commitments.

There are few signs that 'development' in the islands has reduced the need for aid since the Jackson Report. On the contrary, countries are becoming more dependent on aid. Technological infrastructures are expanding, but technological dependence is increasing rather than decreasing. Technology transfer differentials between the West and the developing countries of the South Pacific will increase with technological change in the West. Imports of manufactured goods will most probably increase. Exports of primary and processed goods are likely to decrease as populations grow, and with few industries enjoying conspicuous success.

Whilst many island countries are looking to tourism in the short and longer term, expansion of the tourist industry is not without problems, and longer term costs in terms of forgone opportunities of more economically and environmentally sustainable development.

The consequences of the change to a new information intensive paradigm in the West is less ambivalent for the island states of the South Pacific than for larger developing countries. The Pacific islands are particularly disadvantaged as regards technology futures — they are small and isolated, do not have particularly low labour costs (relative to productivity), have very limited technological infrastructures and capabilities, and significant technology transfer differentials. The Pacific islands could not take advantage of technological leap-frogging. It is therefore likely that the technology-gap and 'comparative technological disadvantage' of the islands will increase. The increasing science-base to Western technology, industrialisation of services (such as health, telecommunications, transport and banking), and 'tertiarisation' of industries (such as software and producer services) will create particular transfer problems for small developing nations, where it is difficult not to 'go with the flow' of donor neighbours.

These considerations have negative implications for strategies of import substitution and especially export promotion in the region. The products of many island industries could generally become less competitive with overseas products in the overseas and home markets, requiring a rethink of policies regarding small industry promotion, especially for export.

There are several implications of the above observations for island policy-makers regarding technology, industry and development. The dominant development model promoting industry and the private sector can be seen to have serious drawbacks in the South Pacific. There is little opportunity for industry-led economic development or a roll-back of government to make way for private sector development, and the likelihood, as UNCTAD observe, that open markets could even cause de-industrialisation in the islands. Already, where moves have been made to privatise government services, it is apparent that the private sector cannot often properly fill the gap (as in the case of government stores, supplying a variety of goods and services, for example).

Planning for the Future
If the above issues are not addressed, development in the region will become increasingly uneven or 'skewed'. The Pacific islands could become increasingly marginalised and dependent — used increasingly for military testing, toxic weapons and waste disposal and dumping, the fishing basin

and tourist playground of the Western world. As Ward chillingly concludes, 'perhaps a hundred years hence . . . almost all of the descendants of today's Polynesian or Micronesian islanders will live in Auckland, Sydney, San Francisco and Salt Lake City. Occasionally they may recall that their ancestors once lived on tiny Pacific islands. Even more occasionally they may visit the resorts which, catering for scuba divers, academic researchers or gamblers may provide the only permanent human activities on lonely Pacific islands, set in an empty ocean'.[19]

Islands are, however, able to structure their internal response to external change. The most important ways in which the internal response to external technology change and transfer could be improved include reinforcing the technological infrastructures and local technology policy, planning and management capabilities. This would ensure that islands are better able to mesh with, assimilate and take advantage of external technological change at the 'trailing edge' of 'leading edge' companies and countries. The emphasis on value-added industrial export promotion and import substitution requires review, so that the real benefits of concessionary schemes such as SPARTECA, PIIDS, DIFF and STABEX can be identified and maximised. The greater possibility of adding value through increased agricultural production and processing warrants particular interest — as Lipton advises, 'if you wish for industrialisation, prepare to develop agriculture'.[20]

In the context of the foregoing comments, size factors mean that restructuring nations along Schumpeterian lines to facilitate technological change and growth is somewhat irrelevant in the South Pacific. It is however very relevant to recognise and acknowledge technological change in Western developed countries, reduce where possible and work within the constraints imposed by technology differentials and the 'Catch-22s' of technology and development. This can be addressed through the reinforcement of technological infrastructures and the development of technology management, policy and planning skills in the region, and among aid donors — 'partners in development'.

At a more practical level, there is a general need for the improved identification and innovation of 'appropriate' technology around the region. New technology should ideally consist of incremental improvements upon traditional technology, materials, skills and knowledge, rather that 'radical' innovation, although this should not exclude more radical technology. The task is to 'modernise the traditional, and traditionalise the modern'. There is a related need for more local technology and local technologists at all levels, including 'barefoot technicians'.

There is a particular need for the development of national and regional South Pacific capability for technology management in the areas of technology policy-making, planning, technology choice, adaptation and operation. This can be achieved by a wider recognition of issues of technology and development, and the training of personnel to act as technology advisors in development planning offices, development banks and other relevant agencies.

NOTES AND REFERENCES

INTRODUCTION

1. The notion that external agents of change impact upon and displace traditional social and cultural forms remains relatively common. The idea of the articulation of traditional society and culture with agents of change derives from the work of Meillassoux and, applied to PNG, of Fitzpatrick. (See Meillassoux, C., *Maidens, Meal and Money*, Cambridge, 1981, and Fitzpatrick, P., *Law and State in Papua New Guinea*, Academic Press, London, 1980.)

2. Medford D., and Rothman, H., *The South Pacific Sub-Regional UNCSTD Paper*, Centre for Applied Studies in Development, University of the South Pacific for United Nations Conference on Science and Technology for Development (UNCSTD), 1978; Swamy, A., Durutalo, S., and Sanday, R., 1981, *Technology Decision-Making in the Public Service: A Study of Fiji and Kiribati*, Centre for Applied Studies in Development, University of the South Pacific for the Commonwealth Secretariat, 1978.

1.1 TECHNOLOGY, DEVELOPMENT AND THE SOUTH PACIFIC

1. Nelson, R., and Winter, S., 'In Search of a Useful Theory of Innovation', *Research Policy*, 6, 1, 1977, pp. 36–76.

2. See Marjoram, Tony, *Toys? Boys? Technology and 'Development' in the Island South Pacific*, Seminar on Technology for Community Development in Australia, SE Asia and the Pacific, Alice Springs, Proceedings of the Seminar, Development Technologies Unit, Faculty of Engineering, University of Melbourne, July 1990.

3. Stewart, F., 'Technology Transfer for Development', in Evenson, R. E., and Ranis, G., *Science and Technology: Lessons for Development Policy*, Westview, Boulder, 1990, p. 306.

4. Wood, R. E., *From Marshall Plan to Debt Crisis: Foreign Aid and Development Choices in the World Economy*, University of California, Berkeley, 1986.

5. Most of the data in the Tables represent conditions up to the mid-1980s and is drawn from various editions of *South Pacific Economies: Statistical Summary* (SPESS) of the South Pacific Commission (SPC), supplied by the member countries of SPC. Some caution in interpretation and comparison is necessary, due to dissimilar collection methodologies, and incomplete, estimated or otherwise imprecise national statistics. Gender disaggregated data is not available from the above sources; GDP and other economic data are difficult to estimate accurately, particularly because of subsistence activity, which may not be adequately included.

6. Literacy rates epitomise many of the problems of collection, interpretation and the significance of such data, and should be viewed with caution. Literacy rates also reflect access to education, cultural and linguistic diversity.

7. To counter the dominance of economic data in statistics used by many to determine national development, the UNDP produced a 'Human Development Report' in 1990. The Report combines existing data such as life expectancy, adult literacy and effective purchasing power (reflecting life, knowledge and access to resources) to present a 'Human Development Index' for each country. See United Nations Development Programme, *Human Development Report*, UNDP and Oxford UP, New York, 1990.

8. For the importance of 'progressing with the past' in terms of agricultural technology and the general importance of traditional knowlege, see Clarke, W. C., 'Progressing with the Past: Environmentally Sustainable Modifications to Traditional Agricultural Systems', in Fisk, E. K., ed., *The Adaptation of Traditional Agriculture: Socioeconomic Problems of Urbanisation*, Monograph, Development Studies Centre, Australian National University, Canberra, 1978. See also Clarke, W. C., 'Looking to the Past for a Sustainable Future', in Rollason, R., ed., *Development — A Green Issue: Environment and Development in SE Asia and the Pacific*, Development Dossier No. 30, Australian Council for Overseas Aid, Canberra, 1991.

9. See Schumacher, F., *Small is Beautiful: A Study of Economics as if People Mattered*, first published by Blond and Briggs, London, 1973; and Illich, I., *Tools for Conviviality*, Harper, New York, 1987.

10. Cox, E., and Sahumlal, J., *Gender Bias in Technologies for Urban and Rural Development in Papua New Guinea*, paper presented to the 17th Pacific Science Congress, Honolulu, 1991; see also chapter by Elizabeth Cox in this volume.

11. Fairbairn, Te'o Ian, *Island Economies: Studies from the South Pacific*, UNESCO/University of the South Pacific, Suva, 1985, pp. 70–2.

12. See Marjoram, Tony, *Thinking Technology: Technology and Development in the South Pacific*, UNESCO, 1989.

13. On need for technological self-reliance, see *Solomon Islands National Development Plan; 1985–1989*, Ministry of Economic Planning, Honiara, 1985.

1.2 TECHNOLOGY TRANSFER

1. Brown, L. A., *Innovation Diffusion: A New Perspective*, Methuen, London, 1981.

2. Stewart, F., 'Technology Transfer for Development', in Evenson, R. E., and Ranis, G., eds, *Science and Technology: Lessons for Development Policy*, Westview, Boulder, 1990, pp. 301–24.

3. Marjoram, Tony, 'Small Is Beautiful? Technology Futures in the Small Island Pacific', *Futures*, May 1991.

4. Padgett, B., 'Technological Mobility and Cultural Constraints', in Chatterji, M., ed., *Technology Transfer in the Developing Countries*, Macmillan, London, 1990, pp. 129–39.

5. Stewart, op. cit.

6. Marjoram, Tony, *Toys? Boys? Technology and Development in the Island South Pacific*, Seminar on Technology for Community Development in Australia, SE Asia and the Pacific, Alice Springs, July 1990.

7. See Basu, P., 'Technology Transfer and Rural-Urban Dualism', in Chatterji, M., ed., *Technology Transfer in the Developing Countries*, Macmillan, London, 1990, pp. 140–51.

8. Marjoram, Tony, 'Technology Transfer and Choice in the South Pacific: A Policy Perspective from Tonga', paper presented to the Waigani Seminar, Port Moresby, August 1984.

9. 'Technological' imports are those defined according to the Standard International Trade Classification (SITC) as categories 3, 5 and 7 — mineral fuels, chemicals, machinery and transport equipment. The main source of the

data is the *South Pacific Economic and Social Statistics*, South Pacific Commission, Noumea, various years. The Pacific islands export of technological goods in SITC categories 3, 5 and 7 is negligible, apart from some re-exports from Fiji to smaller island countries.

10. See Marjoram, op. cit.
11. Vernon, R., 'Trade and Technology in the Developing Countries', in Evenson, R. E., and Ranis, G., eds, op. cit., pp. 255–70.
12. Stewart, op. cit.
13. Although no country is totally representative of the South Pacific (and Tonga has relatively high per capita aid, migration and remittance income), it is hoped that the use of a country case study can help to provide a better picture of the region than the presentation of rather dry trade and aid data alone. Most of the data is drawn from Central Planning Department, 'Fourth Five Year Development Plan, 1980–1985', Nuku'alofa, Tonga, October 1981.
14. Marjoram, Tony, *Report of the Workshop: UNESCO South Pacific Technology and Development Workshop*, Nuku'alofa, Tonga, 1987.
15. See Rosenberg, Nathan, *Perspectives on Technology*, Cambridge University Press, Cambridge, 1976.

1.3 TECHNOLOGY AND ECONOMIC DEVELOPMENT

1 See Benjamin Higgins, editor, Regional Development in Small Island Nations, special issue, *Regional Development Dialogue*, UN Centre for Regional Development, Nagoya, 1982; see particularly Barry Shaw, 'Smallness, Remoteness and Resources: An Analytical Framework', pp. 95–109.
2 In economic theory, technology is considered a variable. Such a variable can be estimated in an equation or model against other variables. How close this estimation corresponds to actuality can be indicated by a coefficient from 0 to 1 — a zero coefficient indicates no correspondence, unity indicates perfect correspondence. A coefficient that is close to being fixed indicates that the variable itself is almost fixed — in this case that there is almost no choice of technology.
3 See Margaret Mead, *New Lives for Old: Cultural Transformation in Manus, 1928-53*, Gollancz, London, 1956.
4 On the economics of appropriate technology, see Benjamin Higgins, 'Appropriate Technology: Does it Exist?', *Regional Development Dialogue*, vol. 3, no. 1, Spring 1982, pp. 158–86.
5 R. G. Crocombe, *Land Tenure and Agricultural Development in the Pacific Islands*, Extension Bulletin no. 187, Taipei Food and Fertiliser Centre, April 1983, p. 2.

1.4 BALANCING TECHNOLOGY, DEVELOPMENT AND CULTURE

1. Linton, Ralph, *The Study of Man*, Appleton, New York, 1936.
2. Kluckholn, Clyde, 'The Concept of Culture', in Lerner, D., and Lasswell, H. D., *The Policy Sciences*, Stanford University Press, Stanford, 1951.
3. Kroeber, A. L., and Kluckholn, Clyde, *Culture — A Critical Review of Concepts and Definitions*, Random House (Vintage Books), New York, 1963.
4. Biersack, A., 'Introduction: History and Theory in Anthropology', in Biersack, ed., *Clio in Oceania: Toward a Historical Anthropology*, Smithsonian Institution Press, Washington, 1991, p. 9.
5. Berger, Peter L., and Luckmann, Thomas, *The Social Construction of Reality*, Anchor Press, Garden City, New York, 1967.
6. Fisk, E. K., *The Economic Independence of Kiribati*, Australian National University, Canberra, 1985.

7. Tonkinson, Robert, 'Melanesia: Technology in Tradition and Change', paper presented to the 17th Pacific Science Congress, Section 4, Technological and Cultural Change in the Pacific; Pacific Science Congress, Hawaii, June 1991, p. 17.
8. Linton, Ralph, *The Tree of Culture*, Knopf, New York, 1955, p. 45.
9. Hogbin, Ian, *Social Change*, Watts, London, 1958.
10. Geertz, Clifford, 'Ethos, World View and the Analysis of Sacred Symbol', in Dantes, Alan, ed., *Every Man His Way*, Prentice Hall, Englewood Cliffs, NJ, 1968, p. 314.
11. The dimensions of this cultural force, identified from analyses of technological change across a range of historical and contemporary societies, are outlined in Hill, Stephen, *The Tragedy of Technology — Human Liberation vs Domination in the Late 20th Century*, Pluto Press, London, 1988.
12. Hill, Stephen, 'Eighteen Cases of Technology Transfer to Asia/Pacific Countries', *Science and Public Policy*, 13, 3, pp. 162–9.
13. Standingford, J. R. K., *Outer Island Development Policy*, Australian Development Assistance Bureau, Canberra, 1985.
14. Standingford, J. R. K., 'How Appropriate is "Appropriate Technology"?', First International Conference on Technology for Development, Canberra, 1970, p. 77.
15. ibid.

1.5 TECHNOLOGY, DEVELOPMENT AND THE ENVIRONMENT

For general reference, see Hufschmidt, M. M., et al, *Environment, Natural Systems and Development: An Economic Valuation Guide*, Johns Hopkins, Baltimore & London 1983; and de Pury, P., *People's Technologies and People's Participation*, Commission on Churches' Participation in Development, World Council of Churches, Geneva, 1983.

1. Dahl, A. L., *Regional Ecosystems Survey of the South Pacific Area*, Technical Paper No. 179, South Pacific Commission, Noumea, New Caledonia, 1980.
2. International Union for the Conservation of Nature (IUCN) and United Nations Environment Program (UNEP), *Review of the Protected Areas System in Oceania*, IUCN Conservation Monitoring Centre, Cambridge, 1986.
3. Gomez E. D., et al, 'Other Fishing Methods Destructive to Coral', in Salvat, B., ed., *Human Impacts on Coral Reefs: Facts and Recommendations*, Antenne Museum, French Polynesia, 1987, p. 67–76.
4. Randall, J. E., 'Collecting Reef Fishes For Aquaria', in Salvat, B., ed., 1987, Human Impacts on Coral Reefs: Facts and Recommendations, op. cit., pp. 29–40.
5. Waldbott, G. L., *Health Effects of Environmental Pollutants*, Mosby, Saint Louis, USA, 1973.

2.1 APPROPRIATE TECHNOLOGY: AN OVERVIEW

1. For conventional development indicators, see *World Development Report, 1990*, Oxford UP for the World Bank, Oxford, 1990; for more 'human' indicators of development, see *Human Development Report, 1990*, Oxford UP for UNDP, Oxford, 1990.
2. Francis, A. J. and Mansell, D. S., *Appropriate Engineering Technology for Developing Countries*, Research Publications, Melbourne, 1988, p. 2; see also Stewart, Frances, *Technology and Underdevelopment*, Macmillan, London, 1977.
3. Although cross-cultural metaphors are often misleading, that of the cuckoo is particularly pertinent. Cuckoos lay their eggs in the nests of smaller birds, therefore having no role in rearing their young. After hatching, cuckoo chicks

instinctively push the eggs or chicks of their 'adoptive' parent birds out of the nest, consuming ever-increasing amounts of food as they outgrow their 'parents'. The transfer of Western technology is analogous to the activities of the cuckoo — Western technology tends to displace indigenous technology, consuming more and more resources.

4. Even the present Australian government, during a period notable for dramatic reductions in regulation, in order to permit the 'fittest' enterprises to survive in world-competitive condition, felt obliged to intervene in the affairs of a very large multinational company (Kodak) by providing assistance in order to induce the overseas parent to keep the plant in Melbourne operating. This illustrates the importance of attracting and retaining overseas industry and technology.

5. See Francis and Mansell, op. cit., p. 24.

6. See Mansell, D. S., and Stewart, D. F., eds, *Barriers to Change and Technical Implications of the Provision of Shelter for the Homeless by the Year 2000*, UNESCO Regional Seminar, University of Melbourne, 1987; and Bob Fuller, *Beware the Research Bias: Lessons from a Solar Drying Project*, paper presented at UNESCO Regional Seminar on Technology for Community Development in Australia, SE Asia and the Pacific, Alice Springs, July 1990.

7. Jequier, N., ed., *Appropriate Technology: Problems and Promises*, Organisation for Economic Cooperation and Development, Paris, 1976.

2.2 IF IT'S NOT APPROPRIATE FOR WOMEN . . .

The title of this chapter derives from a poster produced by Anne Walker at the International Women's Tribune Centre, New York, for the 'Tech and Tools' Forum on Appropriate Technology, held in Nairobi in 1985.

1. *Women and New Technologies: An Organising Manual*, report of the Women and New Technologies Workshop, organised by the Energy, Environment and Appropriate Technology Programme of the World YWCA, Fiji, held in the Netherlands, September 1989; for a report of the Workshop, see *International Women's Tribune Centre Newsletter* no. 44 and *Women and Development Quarterly*, IWTC, New York, March 1990.

2. See the World YWCA *Handbook of Resolutions and Recommendations* from WYWCA meetings held since 1894, WYWCA, Geneva.

3. *Women and Children First*, symposium organised in preparation for the UN Conference on Environment and Development (UNCED, held in Brazil in 1992), May 1991.

4. Personal communication with Elizabeth Cox, rural development worker with the University of Papua New Guinea (at the time of writing with the Australian Freedom from Hunger Foundation).

5. Video on Indo-Fijian women, Shaista Shameen, Department of Sociology, University of Waikato, Hamilton, New Zealand.

6. See *Sisters of Invention*, report of the workshop on Asia and Pacific Women's Small Technologies and Business Forum, Manila, 1983.

7. 'The Kinds of Technologies We Would Feature', see *Sisters of Invention*, op. cit.

8. 'Tech and Tools Fair', organised by the International Women's Tribune Centre, the World YWCA and the Kenya Appropriate Technology Committee, Nairobi, 1985.

9. From 'Tech and Tools Fair', ibid.

2.3 TECHNOLOGY INFORMATION AND COMMUNICATION

1. The pile of old batteries was seen by the author next to a large radio-cassette player in a non-electrified village in Fiji. The buried truck is reported in the chapter by Stuart Kingan and Tony Utanga, and also mentioned in Stephen Hill, *The Tragedy of Technology*, Pluto, Sydney, 1988.

2. For example, see the video and accompanying poster series promoting women's participation in vocational and trade-training produced by the International Labour Organisation and South Pacific Commission, *Pacific Women in Trades*, funded by AIDAB and UNIFEM, ILO Office for the South Pacific and South Pacific Commission Regional Media Centre, Suva, 1990.

3. A regional energy network once made successful use of this facility, until the satellite faltered and USPNET went into temporary abeyance; see Tony Marjoram, *Stoves Development and Information Dissemination in the South Pacific*, Institute of Rural Development, University of the South Pacific, February, 1984; paper presented for satellite discussion, Asia and Pacific Regional Information Network (APRIN), August 1985.

4. The leaflet, 'Making a Smokeless Wood-Burning Stove', leaflet number 4 in the series *Transfer of Appropriate Technology*, was produced by the present author, whilst working as the Technology Specialist of IRD/USP. Other leaflets in the 'Making' series relate to Fish Smoker, Charcoal, Low Cost Solar Water Heater, Charcoal Stove, Cement from Coral, Ferro-cement Water Tank, Low-Cost Village Forge, School Stove, Solar Drier, Improved Earth Oven, Ventilated Improved Pit Toilet.

2.4 COMMUNICATION TECHNOLOGY: IN WHOSE INTERESTS?

1. Takeuchi, F., 'Screen Power-Cinema in the Pacific Islands', *Pacific Perspective*, vol. 10, no. 1, 1981, p. 3.

2. IPDC (International Programme for Development Communication, UNESCO), 1984, PACBROAD Regional Project Submission to IPDC, p. 2.

3. Johnstone, I., 'From Closed to Open Television — A Long Term Project for the South Pacific', *Asian Broadcasting Union Newsletter*, no. 95, May 1973, p. 7.

4. Molnar, H., *Pacific Islands Broadcasting Association Annual Meeting, Port Vila, Vanuatu, August 7–10, 1990*, Report for the Australian National Commission for UNESCO, Canberra, December 1990, p. 12.

5. Horsfield, B., Cook, P., and Stewart, J., 'Television and Culture in the Pacific Islands: Outline of a Research Programme', paper presented at the IAMCR Conference, Bled, Yugoslavia, August 1990, p. 9.

6. Hamelink, C., *Cultural Autonomy in Global Communications*, Longman, New York, 1983; Katz, E., and Wedell, *Broadcasting in the Third World*, Harvard University Press, Cambridge, (USA), 1977.

7. Fell, Liz, 'International Communication: Australia & the South Pacific', a paper for the First Canberra Conference on International Communication, December 1986; Horsfield, B., 'The Pacific Regional Television Meeting, 27 November – 1 December 1989, Suva', *Report for the Australian National Commission for UNESCO*, Canberra.

8. PACBROAD, 1987, *Third General Meeting of Leading Representatives of National Radio Networks in the Region of the Pacific*, 30 November to 2 December, Tonga, p. 39.

9. Bussiek, H., *Some Suggestions for a Programme Structure in a South-Pacific Radio Station*, Apia, April 1986, p. 3.

10. Thomas, Pamela, 'Communication and Health in the Pacific', *UNESCO Review*, May 1987, p. 6.

11   Layton, Suzanna, 'The Pacific Island Press: Diversity, Change and Continuity', *Australian Journalism Review*, vol. 11, 1989, pp 17–18; Robie, David, 'Pacific Media Ownership: The Mega Voice of Neo-colonialism', *Pacific Eyes*, International Federation of Journalists in association with the Australian Journalists Association, Sydney, 1990, pp. 6–10.

12.   Waqavonovono, M. 'Who Manipulates Pacific Media? Influences on Newspapers and Television', *Pacific Perspective*, vol. 10, no. 1, 1981, p. 16.

13.   Krogh, T., and Fusimalohi, T., '*Mission Report — Pacific Journalism Training and Development of the Printed Media (PACJOURN)*', UNESCO, Paris, 1986.

14.   Horsfield, J., 'Broadcast Television in Papua New Guinea', paper presented at the International Communications Association Conference, San Fransisco, 1989.

15.   Horsfield, ibid.

16.   Barney, R., 'Pacific Islands', in Lent, J., ed., 1978 (see below), p. 302.

17.   Horsfield, ibid.

18.   Horsfield, et al, 1990, p. 1.

19.   Molnar, 1990, p. 12.

20.   Horsfield, et al, 1990, p. 9.

21.   Molnar, 1990, p. 12.

22.   Mattelart, A., *Transnationals and the Third World*, Bergin and Garvey, Boston, 1983; Michaels, E., *The Aboriginal Invention of Television in Central Australia, 1982–1986*, Australian Institute of Aboriginal Studies, Canberra, 1986; Molnar, H., 'Remote Aboriginal Community Broadcasting in Australia — Developments and Priorities', *Report for the UNESCO Global Study on Alternative Media*, Paris, 1991.

2.5 TECHNOLOGY AND MARINE RESOURCE DEVELOPMENT

The authors would like to thank Dr Dave Doulman for his useful comments on an earlier draft of this chapter.

1.   Wright, A. and Kurtama, Y. Y., 'Man in Papua New Guinea's Coastal Zone', in Ruddle, K., Morgan, W. B., and Pfafflin. J. R., eds., *The Coastal Zone: Man's Response to Change*, Harwood Academic, Christchurch, 1988, pp. 411–46.

2.   Wright, A. and Preston, G., *Issues in South Pacific Development and Management in the 1990s*, paper prepared for the ACP/EC Joint Assembly Meeting, 19–20 March 1990, Port Moresby, Papua New Guinea, 1990 [mimeo].

3.   See Wright and Preston, op. cit.

4.   Doulman, D. J., 'An Overview of the Tuna Fishery and Industry in the Pacific Islands Region', in Buchholz, ed., *New Approaches to Development Cooperation in South Pacific Countries*, Papers of the Institute of International Relations, Verlag Brietenbach, Saarbrucken, 1987, pp. 149–61.

5.   See Wright and Preston, op. cit.

6.   See Green, R. C., 'New Sites with Lapita Pottery and Their Implications for the Settlement of the Western Pacific', *Working Papers in Anthropology*, No. 51, Dept. Archaeology, University of Auckland, Auckland, 1978, p. 24; see also Johannes, R. E., *Words of the Lagoon: Fishing and Marine Lore in the Palau District of Micronesia*, University of California, Berkeley, 1981.

7.   Wright, A., 'Marine Resource Use in Papua New Guinea: Can Traditional Concepts and Contemporary Development Be Integrated?', in Ruddle, K. and Johannes, R. E., eds, *The Traditional Knowledge and Management of Coastal Systems in Asia and the Pacific*, UNESCO, Jakarta, 1985, pp. 79–99.

8.   See South Pacific Commission, *Regional Tuna Bulletin*, First Quarter, 1989; Tuna and Billfish Assessment Programme, South Pacific Commission, Noumea; and Doulman, D. J., 'Fisheries Management in the South Pacific: The Role of the

Forum Fisheries Agency', Proceedings of the Otago Foreign Policy School, University of Otago, Dunedin, 1990 (in press).

9. Doulman, D. J., 'Fisheries Joint Ventures Revisited; Are They the Answer?', *Infofish Marketing Digest*, March 1990, pp. 12–16.

10. Doulman, D.J., 1990, 'Fisheries Management . . . ', op. cit.

11. Whitmarsh, D., 'Technological Change and Marine Fisheries Development', *Marine Policy*, January 1990, pp. 15–22.

12. Doulman, D. J., and Terawasi, P., 'The South Pacific Regional Register of Foreign Fishing Vessels', *Marine Policy*, in press.

2.6 SOCIAL AND POLITICAL CONSTRAINTS ON APPROPRIATE TECHNOLOGY

1. *LikLik Buk: A Sourcebook for Development Workers in Papua New Guinea*, LikLik Buk Information Centre, Appropriate Technology Development Institute, Unitech, Lae, Papua New Guinea, 1976 (original Pidgin edition), 1977 (original English edition), 1986 (updated English edition) and 1988 (updated Pidgin edition). See also chapter by David Williams in part four.

2.7 EDUCATION AND TRAINING FOR TECHNOLOGY AND DEVELOPMENT

1. Education in developing countries reflects policy and practice of colonial powers. An example is the streaming of secondary education into academic 'grammar' and vocational 'secondary-modern' schools, introduced in the 1945 Education Act in England. This was based on the research (later found to be falsified) of psychologist Cyril Burt who followed the belief that intelligence was mainly inherited and reflected in educational ability, which was fully developed at age 11 and measurable by test. (The English educational system was reorganised in 1965.)

2. Tim Simkins, *Non-Formal Education and Development*, Manchester Monographs, 8, Department of Adult and Higher Education, University of Manchester, 1977, p. 20.

3. Seers, D., 'What Are We Trying to Measure?', in Baster, N., ed., *Measuring Development*, Frank Cass, London, 1972.

4. From Simkins, op. cit., quoting ILO, *Matching Employment Opportunities and Expectations: A Programme of Action for Ceylon*, ILO, Geneva, 1971.

5. Coombs, P. H., *The World Educational Crisis: A Systems Analysis*, Oxford, 1968, p. 126.

6. Dore, R., *The Diploma Disease: Education, Qualification and Development*, Allen and Unwin, London, 1976, p. 11.

7. Colclough, C., 'Basic Education: Samson or Delilah?', *Convergence*, vol. 6, no. 2, 1976, p. 54.

8. Rado, E., 'The Explosive Model', *Manpower and Unemployment Research in Africa*, vol. 6, no. 2, 1973.

9. Three models of education are the 'structuralist' model — the 1960s model of economic planning and labour-needs forecasting noted above; the 'functionalist' model — referring to 'real' educational needs (after Coombs and Ahmed, see below); and the 'status-conflict' model — education systems are considered as fields in which individuals and social groups compete for qualifications and, hence, social status. See Coombs, P. H. and Ahmed, M., *Attacking Rural Poverty: How Non-Formal Education Can Help*, Johns Hopkins and IBRD, Washington, 1974; and Dore, R., *The Diploma Disease: Education, Qualification and Development*, Allen and Unwin, London, 1976. Dore observes that the 'status-conflict' model is particularly relevant to countries that are late developers, such as the Pacific islands.

10. Reimer, E., *School is Dead: An Essay on Alternatives in Education*, Penguin, London, 1971, p. 89; see also Illich, I., *Deschooling Society*, Calder and Boyars, London, 1971.
11. These data, representing conditions in the mid-1980s, are drawn from South Pacific Commission, *South Pacific Economies: Statistical Summary*, for 1987 (pub. 1989). Data for tertiary education are difficult to obtain, and have not been included.
12. Moromoro, M., and Le Grys, G. A., *Appraisal of the Current State of Science and Technology in Papua New Guinea: Options for Action*, paper presented at the Workshop for the Preparation of a National Science and Technology Policy for Papua New Guinea, Port Moresby, 4–6 September 1990, p. 2.
13. Central Planning Office, *Fiji's Ninth Development Plan, 1986–1990*, Suva, p. 136. This comment illustrates the likely presence of the 'status-conflict' model.
14. Bamford, G., *Training the Majority: Guidelines for the Rural Pacific*, Institute of Pacific Studies, University of the South Pacific, Suva, 1986, p. 129.
15. Ibid., pp. 2–6.
16. Moromoro, M., and Le Grys, G. A., op. cit.
17. More narrowly defined marine and agricultural training schools have not been included in this 'technological' listing. See Tony Marjoram, *Directory of Technology for Development in the South Pacific*, Development Technologies Unit, University of Melbourne, for UNESCO, 1990.
18. Bamford, op. cit., p. 128.
19. Ibid, p. xvii.
20. Ibid, p. xviii.
21. See *Thinking Technology: Manual for Technology and Development in the South Pacific*, Tony Marjoram, Development Technologies Unit, University of Melbourne.
22. Court, D., 'Dilemmas of Development: The Village Polytechnic Movement as a Shadow System of Education in Kenya', in Court, D., and Ghai, D., eds, *Education, Society and Development: New Perspectives from Kenya*, Oxford, 1974.

3.1 TECHNOLOGY IN AGRICULTURE: AN OVERVIEW

1. Strictly speaking, gathering and hunting are not production; for the purpose of this chapter, subsistence production is taken to mean the organised sowing and harvesting of crops or production of livestock.
2. The one input which often cannot be supplied in the Pacific is irrigation, due to a lack of available water resources.
3. *A Review of the Banana Export Industry in the Kingdom of Tonga*, Ministry of Agriculture, Forests and Fisheries, Nuku'alofa, Tonga, 1979.

3.2 AGRICULTURAL MECHANISATION . . . TONGA

1. Yen, D. E., 'Pacific Production Systems', in Ward, R. G., and Proctor, A., *Pacific Agriculture: Choices and Constraints*, ANU, Canberra, 1979.
2. Beaglehole J. C., ed., *The Journals of Captain James Cook*, 3 vols, Hakluyt Society, Cambridge, 1967.
3. Brookfield, H. C., 'Local Study and Comparative Method: An Example from Central New Guinea', *Annals of the Association of the American Geographers*, 52, 1962, pp. 242–54.
4. *Third Five-Year Development Plan, 1976–80*, Kingdom of Tonga, Nuku'alofa, 1976.
5. Moengangongo, T. H., *The Economics of Running the MAFF Machinery Pool*, unpublished manuscript, Nuku'alofa, 1981.

6. Moengangongo, T. H. and Fonua, I. L., *Evaluation of Tractor Performance*, unpublished manuscript, Nuku'alofa, 1980.
7. Ibid.
8. *Tonga Agricultural Census*, Statistics Department, Government of Tonga, Nuku'alofa, 1985.

3.3 Technology, Food and Food Processing

1. Ravuvu, A., *Class and Culture in the South Pacific*, Centre for Pacific Studies (Auckland) and Institute of Pacific Studies (Suva), 1987, p. 37.
2. Coyne, T., *The Effects of Urbanisation and Western Diet on the Health of Pacific Populations*, Technical Paper 186, South Pacific Commission, Noumea, 1984, pp. 1–175.
3. Moengangongo, S., 'Indigenous Food Storage Systems', *Alafua Agricultural Bulletin*, 8, 1983, pp. 101–4.
4. Parkinson, S., *The Preservation and Preparation of Root Crops and Some Other Traditional Foods in the South Pacific*, FAO RAS/83/001 Field Document, 1984, pp. 1–31.
5. Murai, M., Pen, F., and Miller, C. D., *Some Tropical South Pacific Island Foods*, University of Hawaii Press, Honolulu, 1958, pp. 1–155.
6. Holmes, S., *Nutrition Survey in the Gilbert Islands*, South Pacific Health Service Report, Suva, 1953.
7. Aalbersberg, W. G. L., Lovelace, C. E. H., Madhoji, K., Parkinson, S., and Davuke, S. V., 'The Traditional Fijian Method of Pit Preservation of Staple Carbohydrate Foods', *Ecology of Food and Nutrition*, vol. 21, 1988, pp. 171–80.
8. CIAT Centro Internacional de Agricultura Tropical, *Fresh Cassava Conservation Goes Commercial*, vol. 1, no. 7, 1988, p. 9.
9. Sivan, P., 'Post Harvest Durability of Fresh Roots of Cassava Varieties in Fiji and Storage of Roots in Moist Sawdust', *Fiji Agricultural Journal*, no. 41, 1979, pp. 95–102.
10. Crabtree, T., Kramer, E. C., and Baldry, T., 'The Breadmaking Potential of Cassava as a Partial Replacement for Wheat Flour', *Journal of Food Technology*, 13, 1978, pp. 397–407.
11. Aalbersberg, W. G. L., Parkinson, S. V., and Prasad, I., 'Use of Traditional South Pacific Fermentation of Staple Carbohydrate Foods in the Production of Wheat Flour Substitutes', in *Trends in Food Biotechnology*, Been, N., Lim, H., and Wong, K. eds, *Proceedings 7th World Congress Food Science and Technology*, Singapore, 1987, pp. 319–27.
12. Carpenter, T. R., and Steinke, W. E., 'Taro — a Review of *Colocasia esculenta* and its Potentials', in *Animal Feed*, Wang, T., University of Hawaii Press, Honolulu, 1983, pp. 269–300.
13. Mattei, R., *Sun Drying Cassava for Animal Feed: A Processing System for Fiji*, FAO RAS/83/001 Field Document 3, 1984, pp. 1–25.

3.4 Affordable Housing and Development Training in Kiribati

1. For information on existing fibre-reinforced corrugated sheet and curved tile systems, see Parry, J. P. M., 'Intermediate Technology Building', *Appropriate Technology*, vol. 2, no. 3, November 1975.
2. A hip roof is a sloping roof that is supported by the side walls of the building, there is no central ridge and no roof truss is required (for smaller buildings). A gable roof has a central raised ridge, normally supported by a roof truss or triangulated framework.
3. Various technical terms in the table may need explanation: the headlap is the overlap at the top of the tile; battens are the horizontal strips that support and

onto which the tile are fixed; rafters support the battens, and run from wall to ridge (for gable roofs), or lower to higher wall (hip roofs); the pitch of a roof is the angle of the roof from horizontal. The price of a 40kg bag of cement is around A$13 in Kiribati (compared to A$8 retail in Australia), the cost of aluminium roofing is over $17/sq.m in Kiribati (A$10 in Australia) and the commercial rate to buy coconut thatch in Kiribati is approximately $2/sq.m.

4. A band-saw is so called because the blade is actually a band with teeth on one edge, driven between two pulleys.

3.5 TELECOMMUNICATIONS: POTENTIAL AND PROBLEMS FOR NEW TECHNOLOGY

1. South Pacific Bureau for Economic Cooperation, *Rural Telecommunications Study of the South Pacific*, Suva, 1982; the telecommunications experts included two from Australia (one from Telecom, one from the Overseas Telecommunications Corporation, OTC), and one from New Zealand (NZ Post Office).
2. South Pacific Bureau for Economic Cooperation, *South Pacific Telecommunications Development Programme — Planning Report*, Suva, April 1986.

3.6 PIPES AND PITS: WATER SUPPLY AND SANITATION

1. For an overview of issues, see Simpson, A., 'Pacific Island Countries and Water Resources Management', in *Regional Consultation on Water Supply and Sanitation: Beyond the Decade*, Regional World Health Organisation Office for the Western Pacific, Manila, June 1990; for groundwater resources, see Department of Technical Cooperation for Development, UN, *Ground Water in the Pacific Region*, United Nations, New York, 1983. For a practical approach to water supply and sanitation in the South Pacific, see Fleming, S., *Basic Water Supply and Sanitation*, Women's Development Training Programme, Institute of Rural Development, University of the South Pacific, June 1987; and Marjoram, T., *Pipes and Pits Under the Palms: Water Supply and Sanitation in the South Pacific*, Waterlines, vol. 2, no. 1, July 1983, pp. 14–17. See also Swiss Centre for Appropriate Technology (SKAT), *Manual for Rural Water Supply*, SKAT, St Gallen, 1980; Wagner, E. and Lanoix, J., *Water Supply for Rural Areas and Small Communities*, World Health Organisation, Geneva, 1971; World Bank, *Appropriate Technology for Water Supply and Sanitation*, Volumes 1–12, World Bank Series and separate publishers, Washington DC, 1982.
2. World Health Organisation, *The Decade for International Drinking Water Supply and Sanitation: Review of Mid Decade Progress*, WHO, Geneva, 1985. These figures include the most recent comparative data for the region. The South Pacific island countries covered in the report are Cook Islands, Niue, Papua New Guinea, Tonga, Tuvalu, Vanuatu and Western Samoa. There are certain problems with the definition and determination of adequate water supply and sanitation facilities.
3. Belz, L., *The Fresh Water Lens*, unpublished paper, World Health Organisation, Tonga, 1985.
4. Marjoram, T., *Rural Water Supply in the South Pacific*, paper presented at the Third International Conference on Rain Water Cistern Systems, Khon Kaen, Thailand, January 1987.
5. Watt, S. B., *Ferrocement Water Tanks and Their Construction*, Intermediate Technology Publications, London, 1978.
6. Ferro-cement tanks should not require any maintenance or repair if they are properly constructed. If a leak does occur, however, and provided the structure is not seriously damaged, repairs can be facilitated by reinforcement and re-plastering, draining the tank as necessary. Small leaks can be repaired

by filling the tank and stirring in around two-cupfuls of cement powder into the water. The tank should then be left for a week, in which time the cement will then find its way into and hydraulically seal the leak. Intransigent leaks may require two such applications. The treatment has been found to work wonders with leaking or porous tanks. Corrugated steel tanks may also be repaired by converting them into ferro-cement tanks by covering the inside and outside with chicken wire and then plastering with a mortar as if constructing a ferro-cement tank, with the old tank acting as its own formwork.

7. Marjoram, T., and Fleming, S., *Building a Ferrocement Water Tank*, Institute of Rural Development and Women's Development Training Programme, University of the South Pacific, Tonga, 1986; see also Marjoram, T., and Fleming, S., *Making a Ferrocement Water Tank Without Formwork*, demonstration video tape, Institute of Rural Development, University of the South Pacific, 1986.
8. Marjoram, T., and Fleming, S., *Making a Ventilated Improved Pit Toilet*, op cit.
9. Marjoram, T., *'Making a Village Water Pump'*, Institute of Rural Development, University of the South Pacific, Tonga, 1986.
10. Australian International Development Assistance Bureau, *AIDAB and Water Development*, AIDAB Evaluation Series No. 8, Australian Government Publishing Service, Canberra, 1990.

3.7 INTER-ISLAND SHIPPING AND MARINE TRANSPORT

1. Gini, Paul, 'Domestic Shipping in the South Pacific', in Kissling, C. C., ed., *Transport and Communications for Pacific Microstates*, Institute of Pacific Studies, University of the South Pacific, Suva, 1984, p. 137.
2. Ibid., p. 136.
3. Finch, A. W., *Consultancy on Inter-Island Shipping Services in the Republic of the Marshall Islands*, for South Pacific Bureau for Economic Cooperation (SPEC), 1989, pp. 24, 33–5.
4. Dunbar-Nobes, Anne C., *Vanuatu: Domestic Shipping Services in a Newly Independent State*, in Kissling, C. C., ed., op. cit., pp. 151–5.
5. It is understood that improved safety standards have now been introduced in Tonga, and that the situation is somewhat improved.
6. Haden, David, 'Inter-Island Shipping's New Face', *Pacific Islands Monthly*, April/May 1989, pp. 36–7.
7. The loss of life that occurred in the capsize of a Lutheran Mission vessel off the north coast of PNG in August 1991, was reported to be the result of a freak wave, and not connected to the design or operation of the vessel.

3.8 LAND TRANSPORT: ON WHEEL AND FOOT

1. Barwell, I., Edmonds, G. A., Howe, J. D. G. F., and de Veen, J., *Rural Transport in Developing Countries*, Intermediate Technology (for International Labour Organisation), London, 1985, pp. 127–8.
2. Ibid., p. 138.
3. Francis, A. J., and Mansell, D. S., *Appropriate Engineering Technology for Developing Countries*, Research Publications, Blackburn, Victoria, Australia, 1988.
4. *Towards Safer Roads in Developing Countries: A Guide for Engineers and Planners*, prepared by Ross Silcock Partnership for the Overseas Unit of the Transport and Road Research Laboratory and the Overseas Development Administration, UK, HMSO, London, 1991. See various Overseas Road Notes produced by the Overseas Unit, Transport and Road Research Laboratory,

Crowthorne, UK, 1991, including *Maintenance Management for District Engineers*, Overseas Road Note No. 1, *Maintenance Techniques for District Engineers*, Note No. 2, *A Guide to Road Project Appraisal*, Note No. 5, *A Guide to Geometric Design*, Note No. 6. For abstracts of publications covering all aspects of roads in developing countries, see *Road Documentation for Developing Countries*, Overseas Unit, Transport and Road Research Laboratory for International Road Research Documentation Scheme (IRRD), OECD, Crowthorne, UK, 1989.

5. Edmonds, G. A., and Howe, J. D. G. F., eds, *Roads and Resources: Appropriate Technology in Road Construction in Developing Countries*, Intermediate Technology (for International Labour Organisation), London, 1980.

6. *Road Monitoring for Maintenance Management*, Manual and Damage Catalogue for Developing Countries (2 Volumes), OECD and World Bank, Paris, 1990.

7. UNIDO, *The Manufacture of Low-Cost Vehicles in Developing Countries*, Development and Transfer of Technology Series, United Nations Industrial Development Organisation, Vienna, 1978, p. 8.

8. *Fiji's Ninth Development Plan, 1986–1990: Policies, Strategies and Programmes for National Development*, (DP9), Central Planning Office, Suva, 1985, p. 108.

9. UNIDO, op. cit., p. 8.

10. Fiji DP9, op. cit., p. 103.

11. Ibid., p. 104.

12. Barwell et al, op. cit., p. 65.

13. Ibid., p. 66.

14. UNIDO, op. cit., p. 23.

15. Barwell et al, op. cit., pp. 40–1.

16. UNIDO, 1978, op. cit., p. 8.

17. Barwell et al, op. cit., p. 138.

3.9 AVIATION

1. For an interesting descriptive and pictorial record of this, see James Sinclair, *Wings of Gold: How the Aeroplane Developed New Guinea*, Pacific Publishers, Sydney, 1978.

2. Annual survey of aviation in the South Pacific, *Islands Business*, November 1989, p. 41.

3. Christopher C. Kissling, *Air Transport, Tourism and Economic Development in South Paciific Microstates*, paper prepared for the ISLANDS 88 Conference, Hobart, 1988; see also Christopher C. Kissling, ed., *Transport and Communication for Pacific Microstates: Issues in Organisation and Management*, Institute of Pacific Studies, University of the South Pacific, 1984. Kissling is one of the major academic observers of Pacific island aviation.

4. Kissling, 1984, op. cit., p. 3.

5. Kissling, 1988, op. cit., p. 9.

6. Gideon Zoloveke, Manager of Solomon Airlines, *Islands Business*, November 1989, p. 41. See also the annual aviation survey in *Islands Business*, November 1990.

7. From *Islands Business*, November 1989, p. 32.

8. See Kissling, 1984, op. cit.; as Kissling notes, this pattern of analysis owes much to Benson, J. K., 'The Interorganizational Network as Political Economy', *Administrative Science Quarterly*, 20, 1975, pp. 229–49.

9. On dependency theory, see Amin, S., *Accumulation on a World Scale: A Critique of the Theory of Underdevelopment*, Monthly Review Press, New York, 1974, and Frank, A. G., *Latin America: Underdevelopment or Revolution?*, Monthly Review Press, New York, 1969. For a look at dependency theory and the South Pacific,

see Richard Peet, 'The Conscious Dimension of Fiji's Integration into World Capitalism', *Pacific Viewpoint*, 21 (2), 1980, pp. 91–115.
10. Kissling, 1984, op. cit., p. 9.
11. The report is an unpublished *Regional Aviation Study* undertaken for SPEC/UNDP by Alistair Tucker, Murray, Halcrow and Associates, London, January 1985. The comments are from John King, an Ansett executive closely involved with the development of Ansett joint ventures in the South Pacific, Director of Air Vanuatu and Polynesian Airlines, and Ansett delegate to International Air Transport Association (IATA) in untitled and undated exerpts from a report to SPEC. See Kissling, 1984, op. cit.
12. There are six 'Freedoms of the Air', these are:
    1. Right of transit without landing (overflight);
    2. Right of non-traffic stop (technical stop for refuelling etc);
    3. Right to set down traffic from home state in foreign state;
    4. Right to pick up traffic from foreign state bound for home state;
    5. Right to pick up and put down traffic in (different) foreign states;
    6. Right to pick up and put down traffic in foreign states and home state (combining rights 5 and 3).
    'Cabotage' is an additional right. 'Cabotage' is the right to pick up and put down traffic in the same foreign state. Aviation traffic rights in the Pacific are based on the 1944 Chicago Convention.
13. For a fuller exposition, see Kissling, 1984, op. cit., pp. 91–5.
14. Ibid., p. 7.
15. Ibid., p. viii.
16. *Islands Business*, November 1989, p. 41.
17. Kissling, 1984, op. cit., p. 81.
18. Dennis Hoskin, Acting General Manager, Friendly Island Airways, in *Islands Business*, November 1989, p. 37.
19. Quoted in *Islands Business*, November 1989, p. 39.
20. Kissling, 1984, op. cit., p. 87.
21. For many of these examples, see *Islands Business*, November 1989, p. 37.
22. Kissling, 1984, op. cit., p. 106.

3.10 MINING: EL DORADO OR FOOL'S GOLD

1. This chapter focusses on mining for precious and commercial metals such as gold and copper, rather than mining and quarrying for local use. Throughout the South Pacific stone and sand is mined for construction and road building, coral has been mined for cement manufacture in Fiji and limestone for glass and lime manufacture in Papua New Guinea. These are low-cost materials which cannot stand the cost of transport. They must be mined close to where they are used.
2. See for example: Cobbe, J. H., *Governments and Mining Companies in Developing Countries*, Westview, Boulder, Colorado, 1979; Emerson, C., 'Mining Enclaves and Taxation', *World Development*, 10, 1982, pp. 561–71; O'Faircheallaigh, C., *Mining and Development*, Croom Helm, Sydney, 1984; Stewart, D. F., 'Small-scale Mining and Development: The Case of Papua New Guinea', *Natural Resources Forum*, 11, 1987, pp. 219–27; Stewart, D. F., 'Large-scale v Small-scale Mining: Meeting the Needs of Developing Countries', *Natural Resources Forum*, 13, 1989, pp. 44–52.
3. Nelson, Hank, *Black White and Gold*, Australian National University Press, Canberra, 1976.

4. Carruthers, D. S. (Chariman of Bougainville Copper Ltd), Submission to the Australian Senate Joint Committee on Foreign Affairs and Trade, 26 September 1990.
5. Reported by Panguna priest Fr Bob Wiley and quoted in Dorney, Sean, *Papua New Guinea*, Random House, Sydney, 1990, p. 118.
6. Dove, Miriung and Togolo, 1974; quoted in Quodling, P. W., *Bougainville Copper Limited — A History*, April 1990.

4.1 TECHNOLOGY MANAGEMENT AND THE DEVELOPMENT OF SMALL INDUSTRIES

1. The interview was conducted by Ian Wood of Radio Australia. The transcript of the interview has been restructured and edited by Tony Marjoram.
2. For details of earlier work on small micro-hydro turbines (or mini-hydro), see Inversin, A. R., *A Pelton Micro-Hydro Prototype Design*, Appropriate Technology Development Unit (now Institute), PNG University of Technology, 1980.
3. The wokabaut somil was developed by the Village Equipment Supplies division of the South Pacific Appropriate Technology Foundation of Port Moresby. Other reference is made to the wokabaut somil in this volume.
4. See also the next chapter, by David Williams, 'LikLik Buk Revisited'.
5. See the chapter by Don Stewart in part three. Don Stewart is also active in researching and developing improved sluice boxes at the International Development Technologies Centre, University of Melbourne. On small-scale gold mining in Papua New Guinea, see Stewart, D. F., 'Small-scale Mining and Development: The Case of Gold Mining in Papua New Guinea', *Natural Resources Forum*, United Nations, New York, 1987, pp. 219–27.
6. See Blowers, M., *Handbook of Small-Scale Gold Mining for Papua New Guinea*, Pacific Resource Publications, Christchurch, New Zealand, 1988.

4.2 LIK LIK BOOK REVISITED . . . VILLAGE DEVELOPMENT

1. Quoted from the internal cover of *LikLik Buk: A Rural Development Handbook Catalogue for Papua New Guinea*, LikLik Buk Information Centre, Lae, PNG, 1977 edition.
2. Quote from Amanda Twohig, editor of the 1986 edition of *LikLik Buk*, Lae, 1986.

4.3 THE DEVELOPMENT OF APPROPRIATE TECHNOLOGY IN PNG

1. See the chapter by Lukis Romaso.
2. See the chapter by David Williams.
3. The level of utilisation and acceptability of these stoves in Fiji was later found to be somewhat overestimated.

4.4 ENERGY SUPPLY AND MANAGEMENT

1. Peter C. Johnston, *Outlook for the Utilisation of New and Renewable Energy in the Pacific and the Tasks for Cooperation*, UNDP/ESCAP Pacific Energy Development Programme, Suva; paper prepared for the 4th Symposium on Pacific Energy Cooperation, SPEC 4, Tokyo, January 1990. The author would like to acknowledge the assistance and data provided by Peter Johnston, formerly Project Manager of the Pacific Energy Development Programme.
2. Jim Rizer and Jim Hansen, *Energy in the Pacific Islands: Issues and Statistics*, Resources Programmes, East-West Center, Honolulu, 1990; the Appendices of this report, drawn from the diverse data on the Pacific region, have provided valuable background information for this chapter.

3. See, for example, Anthony Burgess, *The Seven Sisters: The Great Oil Companies and the World They Made*, Viking, New York, 1975.
4. Johnston, op. cit.
5. Personal communication, Chris Harwood (CSIRO Forestry Division, Canberra, Australia; previously with PEDP).
6. Rizer and Hansen, op. cit.; 1 toe = 44.8 GJ.
7. Johnston, op. cit. Some caution regarding indigenous energy use is required owing to the difficulty in collecting such data, especially in rural areas.
8. Personal communication, Chris Harwood.
9. Tony Marjoram, 'Pipe Dreams in the Pacific', (review of potential for OTEC) *New Scientist*, 12 August 1982; Tony Marjoram, *Wave Power in Tonga — A Second Wind?*, paper presented at the Pacific Congress on Marine Technology, Honolulu, March 1986.
10. Personal communication, Chris Harwood; see also Liebenthal, A., *Pacific Regional Energy Assessment Issues Background and Objectives*, Pacific Household and Rural Energy Seminar, organised by UNDP, World Bank and PEDP, Port Vila, November 1990.
11. Tony Marjoram, *Science and Technology Policy in the Small Island States of the South Pacific*, paper presented at 17 ANZAAS Congress, Hobart, February 1990. Expressing energy imports as a percentage of total imports or exports in countries of low per capita energy use is obviously relative, and may be distorted by the presence or absence of large import and export industries.
12. UN Pacific Energy Development Programme, *Regional Seminar on the Reduction of Electric Power System Losses in the Pacific Islands and Papua New Guinea*, Suva, June 1990; it should be noted that, while the data for imported fuels are relatively accurate, data for indigenous energy use are at best good estimates based on limited surveying and informed 'guesstimation'.
13. *Fiji's Ninth Development Plan 1986–1990: Policies, Strategies and Programmes for National Development*, Central Planning Office, Suva, 1985; see also Rizer and Hansen, op. cit.
14. *Kiribati: Sixth National Development Plan, 1987–1991*, National Planning Office, Ministry of Finance, Kiribati, 1988.
15. Johnston, op. cit., p. 7.

4.5 TECHNOLOGY AND DEVELOPMENT BANKING

1. For information on development banks, see Cole, R., *South Pacific Development Banks; Key Issues in Their Future*, Pacific Islands Development Program, East West Centre, Honolulu, Hawaii, February 1990, p. 1; for related publications, see 'Akolo, L. A., 'Mobilizing Development Funds in Small Economies: The Tonga Experience', *Review*, vol. 11, no. 18, University of the South Pacific, May 1990; and Diamond W., and Raghavan, U. W., *Aspects of Development Bank Management*, Johns Hopkins, New York, 1982.
2. Cole, op. cit., p. 2.
3. Kingdom of Tonga, *Fifth Five-Year Development Plan 1986–1990*, Central Planning Department, Nuku'alofa, December 1987, p. 38.
4. Ibid., p. 3.
5. Ibid., p. 4.
6. Menon, M. G. K., 'Technology Assessment for Development', in *Technology Assessment for Development*, Report of the United Nations Seminar on Technology Assessment for Development, Bangalore, 1978, p. 32.
7. Klaus-Heinrich Standke, 'Assessing Technology for Technological Choice', in *Technology Assessment for Development*, Report of the United Nations Seminar on Technology Assessment for Development, Bangalore, 1978, p. 37.

8. Tonga Development Bank, *Quarterly Report*, Nuku'alofa, March 1990.
9. Some of these points are discussed in a paper by Reynold Feria, *Technical Aspects of Appraisal — Industrial Projects*, ADB-TDB Program on Development Banking for the South Pacific Region, Tonga Development Bank, Nuku'alofa, 1985.
10. *A Manual on Project Planning for Small Economies*, Project Planning Centre for Developing Countries, University of Bradford for Commonwealth Secretariat, 1982, p. 10.
11. Tony Marjoram, *Technology Choice and Development in the South Pacific — Preliminary Report*, Institute of Rural Development, University of the South Pacific, Tonga, November 1985, p. 3.
12. 'Technological Choices and Information Sources For Development Banks', printed in *Development Banking in the 1980s*, UNIDO, New York, 1980, p. 72.
13. Tony Marjoram, *Small is Beaut in the South Pacific*, Institute of Rural Development, University of the South Pacific, Tonga, 1985, p. 8.
14. Menon, op. cit., p. 32.
15. Mathur, O. P., *Project Analysis for Local Development*, Westview Press, Boulder & London, 1985, p. 37.
16. Mena, M. M., 'Development of Appropriate Technology for the Rural Sector in the Developing Countries of Asia', *Proceedings of the Second Asian Conference on Technology for Rural Development*, Kuala Lumpur, Malaysia 4–7 December 1985; proceedings also appear as Radhakrishna, S., Mohinder Singh, M., and John, C. K., eds, *Proceedings of the Second Asian Conference on Technology for Rural Development*, World Scientific, Singapore, 1988, p. 156.
17. Marjoram, *Small is Beaut in the South Pacific*, op. cit., p. 8.
18. Chandrasekharan, K., *Tonga Development Bank, Staff Training Manual*, Tonga Development Bank, Nuku'alofa, 1990, p. 88.
19. Some of these points are discussed in an article by Venkatadas, S.J., 'Follow-up of SSI Advances — Role of Technical Officers,' in *Technical Aspects in Project Appraisal*, IDBI, 1981, p. 107.
20. Some of these points are discussed in *Appraisal Manual for Industrial Credit Projects*, China Investment Bank, Beijing, vol. 1, 1985, p. 5.

4.6 WOMEN CAN DO: TECHNOLOGY AND TRAINING FOR WOMEN

1. Griffen, V., ed., *Knowing and Knowing How: A Self-Help Manual on Technology for Women in the Pacific*, Centre for Applied Studies in Development, University of the South Pacific, Suva, 1981; see also Carr, M., *Blacksmith, Baker, Roofing-sheet Maker: Employment for Rural Women in Developing Countries*, Intermediate Technology, London, 1984.
2. Rogers, Barbara, *The Domestication of Women: Discrimination in Developing Societies*, St Martin's, London, 1980.
3. Schoeffel, P., *The Rice Pudding Syndrome: Women's Advancement and Home Economics Training in the South Pacific*, paper submitted to the conference on 'Women and Food: Feminist Perspectives', Sydney, 1982.
4. Economic and Social Commission for Asia and the Pacific, *Women in Development — A Regional Program of Action*, ESCAP, Bangkok, 1979.
5. Economic and Social Commission for Asia and the Pacific, *Report of the Subregional Follow-up Meeting for Pacific Women on the World Conference of the United Nations Decade for Women*, Suva, Fiji, 29 October–3 November 1980.
6. South Pacific Commission, *Seminar of South Pacific Women*, Papeete, Tahiti, 20–24 July 1981, Report of Meeting, South Pacific Commission, Noumea, 1981, p 22.

7. Commonwealth Secretariat and Ministry of Agriculture, Government of Fiji, *South Pacific Rural Technology Workshop*, Suva, Fiji, 1981.
8. Commonwealth Secretariat and Institute of Rural Development, University of the South Pacific, *South Pacific Rural Technology Workshop*, Nuku'alofa, 1984.
9. Bourke, S. C., and Warren, K. B., 'Access is Not Enough: Gender Perspectives on Technology and Education', in Tinker, I., ed., *Persistent Inequalities: Women and World Development*, Oxford, New York, 1990.
10. Tinker, op. cit.
11. Bourke and Warren, op. cit.
12. Tinker, op. cit.
13. Thomas, H., 'Dilemmas for Research', in *The Other Policy: The Influence of Policies on Technology Choice and Small Enterprise Development*, Stewart, F., Thomas, H., and de Wilde, T., eds, IT Publications, London, 1990.
14. Stewart, F., and Ranis, G., 'Macro-policies for Appropriate Technology: A Synthesis of Findings', in Stewart, Thomas and de Wilde, eds, op. cit.
15. Bourke and Warren, op. cit.
16. Stewart and Ranis, op. cit.
17. Ibid.

5.1 TECHNOLOGY AND DEVELOPMENT PLANNING

1. Forsyth, D., *Technology Policy Assessment for Fiji*, International Labour Organisation, Geneva, 1983.
2. See, for example, *Conclusions of the Second Regional Conference of Development Planners*, South Pacific Bureau for Economic Cooperation and South Pacific Commission, November 1989.
3. See 'Policies and Strategies for Short and Medium Term', in *Challenges for Development: Towards the Year 2000*, National Economic Summit, Government of Fiji, Suva, 1989.
4. *Third Development Plan, 1989–1992*, Government of Tuvalu, Funafuti, 1989.
5. See *Fifth Five-Year Development Plan, 1986–90*, Central Planning Department, Nuku'alofa, December 1987.
6. Drawn from *Technology for Development: Study by the ESCAP Secretariat for the 40th Session of the Commission*, Economic and Social Commission for Asia and the Pacific (ESCAP), Tokyo, 1984.
7. Adapted from McCulloch, M., *Project Frameworks — A Logical Development for More Effective Aid*, Overseas Development Administration, London, 1986.

Further references not cited in text:

Asian Development Bank, *Guidelines for Economic Analysis of Projects*, Manila, 1987.

Beenhakker, A., *A System for Development Planning and Budgeting*, Gower, New York, 1980.

Bridger, G. A. and Winpenny, J.T., *Planning Development Projects: A Practical Guide to the Choice and Appraisal of Public Sector Investments*, HMSO, London, 1987.

Casley, D. J., and Kumar Krishna, *Project Monitoring and Evaluation in Agriculture*, World Bank, Washington, 1987.

Crown Agents, *Practical Problems in Economic Development — Practical Appraisal Manual — Essays on Problems and Methodology*, London, 1988.

Little, I. M. D. and Mirlees, J. A., *Project Appraisal and Planning for Developing Countries*, Heinemann, 1974.

Little, I. M. D., *Economic Development: Theory, Policy and International Relations*, Basic Books, New York, 1982.

Meier, G. M., *Leading Issues in Economic Development*, Oxford University Press, 1970.

Overseas Development Administration, *Economic Analysis of Development Projects*, HMSO, London, 1983.

Rondinelli, D. A., *Development Projects as Policy Experiments*, Routledge, London, 1990.

Squire, L. and van der Tak, H., *Economic Analysis of Projects*, John Hopkins University Press for World Bank, Washington, 1975.

United Nations Department of Technical Cooperation for Development, *Guidelines for Development Planning: Procedures, Methods and Techniques*, E.87.II.H.1., New York, 1987.

United Nations, *Planning for Economic Development*, E.64.II.B.3., New York, 1963.

5.3 TECHNOLOGY POLICY AND MANAGEMENT

1. See, for example, Rahman, A., and Hill, S., *Science, Technology and Development in Asia and the Pacific*, SC/82/CASTASIA II REF 1, UNESCO, Paris, 1982; also Hill, Stephen, 'Basic Design Principles for National Research in Developing Countries', *Technology in Society*, 9, 1, 1987, pp. 63–73.

2. See, however, Jalan, B., ed., *Problems and Policies in Small Economies*, Croom Helm, London, 1985; Cole, R.V., and Parry, T.G., *Selected Issues in Pacific Island Development*, National Centre for Development Studies, Canberra, 1986; Fairbairn, Te'o I.J., *Island Economies: Studies from the South Pacific*, Institute of Pacific Studies, University of the South Pacific, Suva, 1985. For work with an explicit technology policy focus, see Forsyth, David, J.C., *Assessment of National Technology Policy in Fiji*, World Employment Programme, Technology and Development Branch, International Labour Organisation, Geneva, 1985; Marjoram, Tony, *Technology Transfer and Choice in the South Pacific: A Policy Perspective from Tonga*, Institute of Rural Development, University of the South Pacific, paper prepared for the Waigani Seminar, Papua New Guinea, 1981.

3. This analysis was developed for the UNESCO/SPEC sponsored 'High Level Regional Meeting on Policy and Management of Science and Technology for Development in the South Pacific Region', Apia, March 1987. It was based on an analysis of the literature written about technological application, development and the South Pacific, and from a survey of key consultants across all technological areas who were working in the South Pacific. See Hill, Stephen, and Scott-Kemmis, Don, *Technology Policy and Management — Issues for the South Pacific Region, Sectoral Issues and Workshop Questions*, Meeting Document No. STP 8, Centre for Technology and Social Change, Wollongong, 1987.

4. David Forsyth, in an analysis of Fiji's technological policies, demonstrates the pervasive context for the formulation of technology policy that is cast by implicit policies. He notes that where the implications of implicit policy for explicit technology policy have yet to be clearly identified, a level of conflict may exist between the various broad arms of explicit and implicit policy. See Forsyth, op. cit.

5. Girvan, Norman, 'The Approaches to Technology Policy Studies', *Social and Economic Studies*, 28, 1, March 1989, Special Issue: Essays on Science and Technology Policy in the Caribbean.

6. This is a point that is particularly made by the Commonwealth Secretariat in their analysis of small island states and their policy needs. See Commonwealth Secretariat, *Technological Change: Enhancing the Benefits*, Commonwealth Secretariat, London, 1986.

5.4 TECHNOLOGY POLICY INITIATIVES IN THE SOUTH PACIFIC

1. For technology and development in island development, see Hill, S., and Rahman, A., *CASTASIA II: Science, Technology and Development in Asia and the Pacific, Progress Report, 1968–1980*, Second Conference of Ministers Responsible for the Application of Science and Technology to Development and those Responsible for Economic Planning in Asia and the Pacific, UNESCO and ESCAP, Manila, March 1982; *Technology for Development*, Study by the ESCAP Secretariat for the 40th Session of the Commission, Economic and Social Commission for Asia and the Pacific, Tokyo, 1984.

2. See, for example, Dellimore, J. W., *Guidelines for Integrating Scientific and Technological Considerations and Activities with Development Planning in Small Island States*, UNESCO, Paris, March 1990; and Forsyth, David J.C., *Appropriate National Technology Policies: A Manual for their Assessment*, International Labour Office (with financial support from the UN Fund for Science and Technology for Development), Geneva, 1989.

3. Hill, Stephen, 'Technology Policy and Management', this volume.

4. Medford, D., and Rothman, H., *The South Pacific Sub-Regional UNCSTD Paper*, United Nations Conference on Science and Technology for Development, funded by UNESCO and undertaken at the Centre for Applied Studies in Development, University of the South Pacific, 1978.

5. World Bank, *Fiji: A Transition in Manufacturing*, World Bank, Washington, November 1986.

6. *Science and Technology for Development in the South Pacific*, Waigani Seminar, Port Moresby, August 1984.

7. *Policy and Management of Science and Technology for Development in the South Pacific Region*, UNESCO-SPEC High Level Regional Meeting, sponsored by UNESCO, the South Pacific Bureau for Economic Cooperation (SPEC, now the Forum Secretariat), the Australian Development Assistance Bureau and the Foundation for International Training (Canada), Apia, 16–19 March 1987.

8. Marjoram, Tony, Report of the UNESCO Regional Workshop, 'The Management of Technology for Development in the South Pacific', Nuku'alofa, 1987.

9. Forsyth, David J.C., *Technology Policy Assessment*, Terminal Report, FIJ/TOI/81, International Labour Office, Geneva, 1985.

10. Annotated points (with some paraphrasing) and quotations are drawn from Forsyth, 1985.

11. *National Science and Technology Policy*, National Science and Technology Workshop for Government of Papua New Guinea, draft policy document, Port Moresby, 1990.

12. Similar to the Fiji document, annotated points (with some paraphrasing) and quotations are drawn from the PNG *National Science and Technology Policy*, 1990.

5.5 TECHNOLOGY, DEVELOPMENT AND ISLAND FUTURES

1. See Fisk, E.K., 'Subsistence Affluence and Development Policy', *Regional Development Dialogue*, 1982; and F. Sevele, quoted by Bedford, R.D., 'Demographic Process in Small Islands: The Case of Internal Migration', in Brookfield, H.C., ed., *Population-Environment Relations in Tropical Islands: The Case of Eastern Fiji*, UNESCO, Paris, 1980, p. 57.

2. See Ward, R.G., 'Earth's Empty Quarter? The Pacific Islands in a Pacific Century', *Geographical Journal*, 155, 2, July 1989, pp. 235–46.

3. Bertram, I.G., and Watters, R.F., 'The MIRAB Economy in South Pacific Microstates', *Pacific Viewpoint*, 26, 1985, p. 499; and Brookfield, H.C., quoted in Bertram and Watters, p. 497.

4. Personal communication Kevin Makin, economist and planning officer at Central Planning Department, Tonga, 1986.

5. *Report of the Committee to Review the Australian Overseas Aid Program* (the Jackson Report), Australian Government Publishing Service, Canberra, 1984.

6. Wendt, A., 'Western Samoa 25 Years After: Celebrating What?', *Pacific Islands Monthly*, 58, June 1987, p. 15.

7. Dommen, E., and Hein, P., 'Foreign Trade in Goods and Services: the Dominant Activity of Small Island Economies', in Dommen and Hein, eds, *States, Microstates and Islands*, Croom Helm, London, 1985.

8. SPARTECA is the South Pacific Regional Trade and Economic Agreement of the South Pacific Forum; PIIDS is the Pacific Island Industrial Development Scheme, introduced by New Zealand to help NZ companies establish in the region in a process of 'abetting, not aiding' (see Richardson, J., 'Abetting, Not Aiding', *Islands Business*, 8, November 1982); DIFF is the Development Import Finance Facility of Australia, similar to PIIDS; STABEX is the European Community scheme for commodity purchase, at premium rates, and price stabilisation.

9. Barry, T., Wood, B., and Preusch, D., *The Other Side of Paradise: Foreign Control in the Caribbean*, Grove Press, New York, 1984, p. 73.

10. See Dolman, A.J., 'Paradise Lost? The Past Performance and Future Prospects of Small Island Developing Countries', in Dommen and Hein, op. cit., p. 58; Fisk, E.K., 'Traditional Agriculture and Urbanisation: Policy and Practice', in Fisk, ed., *The Adaptation of Traditional Agriculture: Socioeconomic Problems of Urbanisation*, Monograph 11, Development Studies Centre, Australian National University, Canberra, 1978, p. 371; and Baker, R., review of Lipton, M., 'Why Poor People Stay Poor', *Journal of Modern African Studies*, 13, 1979, p. 167.

11. UNCTAD, *Least Developed Countries Report*, UNCTAD, New York, 1985, p. 25.

12. Charle, E.V., 'Foreign Trade Patterns and Economic Development in the South Pacific', *Journal of Pacific Studies*, 12, 1986, p. 26.

13. See Australian International Development Assistance Bureau (AIDAB), *Australia's Relations with the South Pacific*, Australian Government Publishing Service, Canberra, 1987, and Connell, J., Keynote Address to Commonwealth Geographic Conference on Small Island Development, Valletta, Malta, March 1990.

14. This analysis is based on the work of Schumpeter, J.A.; see Cooper, C., and Kaplinsky, R., eds, 'Technology and Development in the Third Industrial Revolution', *European Journal of Development Research*, 1, 1, June 1989, pp. 1–3.

15. Dosi, G., 'Technology Paradigms and Technology Trajectories', *Research Policy*, 11, 3, 1982, pp. 147–62.

16. See Dore, R., 'Latecomers' Problems', *European Journal of Development Research*, 1, 1, June 1989, pp. 100–7; and Kaplinsky, R., 'Technological Revolution' and the International Division of Labour in Manufacturing: A Place for the Third World?', *European Journal of Development Research*, 1, 1, June 1989, pp. 5–37.

17. Vaitsos, C.V., 'Radical Technological Changes and the New 'Order' in the World Economy', *European Journal of Development Research*, 1, 1, June 1989, pp. 60–84.

18. Kaplinsky, op. cit.

19. Ward, op. cit.

20. Lipton, M., *Why Poor People Stay Poor*, Temple Smith, London, 1977, p. 24.

BIBLIOGRAPHY

Aalbersberg, W. G. L., Parkinson, S. V. and Prasad, I., 'Use of Traditional South Pacific Fermentation of Staple Carbohydrate Foods in the Production of Wheat Flour Substitutes', in Been, Lim and Wong, 1987.

Aalbersberg, W. G. L., Lovelace, C. E. H., Madhoji, K., Parkinson, S. and Davuke, S. V., 'The Traditional Fijian Method of Pit Preservation of Staple Carbohydrate Foods', *Ecology of Food and Nutrition*, vol. 21, 1988.

'Akolo, L. 'A., 'Mobilizing Development Funds in Small Economies: The Tonga Experience', *Review*, vol. 11, no. 18, University of the South Pacific, May 1990.

Amin, S., *Accumulation on a World Scale: A Critique of the Theory of Underdevelopment*, Monthly Review Press, New York, 1974.

Asia and Pacific Women's Small Technologies and Business Forum, *Sisters of Invention*, Report of the Workshop, Manila, 1983.

Asian Development Bank, *Guidelines for Economic Analysis of Projects*, Manila, 1987.

Australian International Development Assistance Bureau (AIDAB), *Australia's Relations with the South Pacific*, Australian Government Publishing Service, Canberra, 1987.

Australian International Development Assistance Bureau, *AIDAB and Water Development*, AIDAB Evaluation Series no. 8, Australian Government Publishing Service, Canberra, 1990.

Baker, R., review of Lipton, M., 'Why Poor People Stay Poor', *Journal of Modern African Studies*, 13, 1979.

Bamford, G., *Training the Majority: Guidelines for the Rural Pacific*, Institute of Pacific Studies, University of the South Pacific, Suva, 1986.

Barry, T., Wood, B., and Preusch, D., *The Other Side of Paradise: Foreign Control in the Caribbean*, Grove Press, New York, 1984.

Barwell, I., Edmonds, G. A., Howe, J. D. G. F., and de Veen, J., eds, *Rural Transport in Developing Countries*, Intermediate Technology (for International Labour Organisation), London, 1985.

Basu, P., 'Technology Transfer and Rural-Urban Dualism', in Chatterji, M., 1990.

Beaglehole, J. C., ed., *The Journals of Captain James Cook*, 3 vols, Hakluyt Society, Cambridge, 1967.

Bedford, R. D., 'Demographic Process in Small Islands: The Case of Internal Migration', in Brookfield, H. C., ed., *Population-Environment Relations in Tropical Islands: The Case of Eastern Fiji*, UNESCO, Paris, 1980.

Been, N., Lim, H., and Wong, K., eds, 'Trends in Food Biotechnology', *Proceedings 7th World Congress Food Science and Technology*, Singapore, 1987.

Beenhakker, A., *A System for Development Planning and Budgeting*, Gower, New York, 1980.

Belz, L., 'The Fresh Water Lens', unpublished paper, World Health Organisation, Tonga, 1985.

Benson, J. K., 'The Interorganizational Network as Political Economy', *Administrative Science Quarterly*, 20, 1975, pp. 229–49.

Berger, P. L., and Luckmann, T., *The Social Construction of Reality*, Anchor Press, Garden City, New York, 1967.

Bertram, I. G., and Watters, R. F., 'The MIRAB Economy in South Pacific Microstates', *Pacific Viewpoint*, 26, 1985.

Biersack, A., ed., *Clio in Oceania: Toward a Historical Anthropology*, Smithsonian Institution Press, Washington, 1991.

Biersack, A., 'Introduction: History and Theory in Anthropology', in Biersack, 1991.

Blowers, M., *Handbook of Small-Scale Gold Mining for Papua New Guinea*, Pacific Resource Publications, Christchurch, New Zealand, 1988.

Bourke, S. C., and Warren, K. B., 'Access is Not Enough: Gender Perspectives on Technology and Education', in Tinker, I., 1990.

Bridger, G. A., and Winpenny, J. T., *Planning Development Projects: A Practical Guide to the Choice and Appraisal of Public Sector Investments*, HMSO, London, 1987.

Brookfield, H. C., 'Local Study and Comparative Method: An Example from Central New Guinea', *Annals of the Association of the American Geographers*, 52, 1962.

Brown, L. A., *Innovation Diffusion: A New Perspective*, Methuen, London, 1981.

Buchholz, ed., *New Approaches to Development Cooperation in South Pacific Countries*, Papers of the Institute of International Relations, Verlag Brietenbach, Saarbrucken, 1987, pp. 149–61.

Burgess, A., *The Seven Sisters: The Great Oil Companies and the World They Made*, Viking, New York, 1975.

Carpenter, T. R., and Steinke, W. E., 'Taro — a Review of *Colocasia Esculenta* and its Potentials', in Wang, T., *Animal Feed*, University of Hawaii Press, Honolulu, 1983.

Carr, M., *Blacksmith, Baker, Roofing-sheet Maker: Employment for Rural Women in Developing Countries*, Intermediate Technology, London, 1984.

Carruthers, D. S., *Submission to the Australian Senate Joint Committee on Foreign Affairs and Trade*, 26 September 1990.

Casley, D. J., and Kumar Krishna, *Project Monitoring and Evaluation in Agriculture*, World Bank, Washington, 1987.

Central Planning Department, Government of Tonga, *Fourth Five-Year Development Plan, 1980–1985*, Nuku'alofa, 1981.

Central Planning Office, Government of Fiji, *Fiji's Ninth Development Plan, 1986–1990: Policies, Strategies and Programmes for National Development* (DP9), Central Planning Office, Suva, 1985.

Chandrasekharan, K., *Tonga Development Bank, Staff Training Manual*, Tonga Development Bank, Nuku'alofa, 1990.

Charle, E. V., 'Foreign Trade Patterns and Economic Development in the South Pacific', *Journal of Pacific Studies*, 12, 1986.

Chatterji, M., ed., *Technology Transfer in the Developing Countries*, Macmillan, London, 1990.

China Investment Bank, *Appraisal Manual for Industrial Credit Projects*, vol. 1, Beijing, 1985.

CIAT (Centro Internacional de Agricultura Tropical), *Fresh Cassava Conservation Goes Commercial*, vol. 1, no. 7, 1988.

Clarke, W. C., 'Looking to the Past for a Sustainable Future', *Development — A Green Issue: Environment and Development in SE Asia and the Pacific*, in Rollason, 1991.

Clarke, W. C., 'Progressing With the Past: Environmentally Sustainable Modifications to Traditional Agricultural Systems', in Fisk, 1978.

Cobbe, J. H., *Governments and Mining Companies in Developing Countries*, Westview, Boulder, Colorado, 1979.

Colclough, C., 'Basic Education: Samson or Delilah?', *Convergence*, vol. 6, no. 2, 1976.

Cole, R. V., *South Pacific Development Banks; Key Issues in their Future*, Pacific Islands Development Program, East West Centre, Honolulu, Hawaii, February 1990.

Cole, R. V., and Parry, T. G., *Selected Issues in Pacific Island Development*, National Centre for Development Studies, Canberra, 1986.

Commonwealth Secretariat and Institute of Rural Development, University of the South Pacific, *South Pacific Rural Technology Workshop*, Nuku'alofa, 1984.

Commonwealth Secretariat and Ministry of Agriculture, Government of Fiji, *South Pacific Rural Technology Workshop*, Suva, 1981.

Commonwealth Secretariat, *Technological Change: Enhancing the Benefits*, London, 1986.

Connell, J., Keynote address to Commonwealth Geographic Conference on Small Island Development, Valletta, Malta, March 1990.

Coombs, P. H., *The World Educational Crisis: A Systems Analysis*, Oxford, 1968.

Coombs, P. H., and Ahmed, M., *Attacking Rural Poverty: How Non-Formal Education Can Help*, Johns Hopkins and IBRD, Washington, 1974.

Cooper, C., and Kaplinsky, R., eds, 'Technology and Development in the Third Industrial Revolution', *European Journal of Development Research*, 1, 1, June 1989, pp. 1–3.

Court, D., 'Dilemmas of Development: the Village Polytechnic Movement as a Shadow System of Education in Kenya', in Court and Ghai, 1974.

Court, D., and Ghai, D., eds, *Education, Society and Development: New Perspectives from Kenya*, Oxford, 1974.

Cox, E., and Sahumlal, J., 'Gender Bias in Technologies for Urban and Rural Development in Papua New Guinea', paper presented to the 17th Pacific Science Congress, Honolulu, 1991.

Coyne, T., *The Effects of Urbanisation and Western Diet on the Health of Pacific Populations*, Technical Paper 186, South Pacific Commission, Noumea, 1984.

Crabtree, T., Kramer, E. C., and Baldry, T., 'The Breadmaking Potential of Cassava as a Partial Replacement for Wheat Flour', *Journal of Food Technology*, 13, 1978.

Crocombe, R. G., *Land Tenure and Agricultural Development in the Pacific Islands*, Extension Bulletin no. 187, Taipei Food and Fertiliser Centre, April 1983.

Crown Agents, *Practical Problems in Economic Development — Practical Appraisal Manual — Essays on Problems and Methodology*, London, 1988.

Dahl, A. L., *Regional Ecosystems Survey of the South Pacific Area*, Technical Paper no. 179, South Pacific Commission, Noumea, 1980.

Dantes, A., ed., *Every Man His Way*, Prentice Hall, New Jersey, 1968.

de Pury, P., *People's Technologies and People's Participation*, Commission on Churches' Participation in Development, World Council of Churches, Geneva, 1983.

Dellimore, J. W., *Guidelines for Integrating Scientific and Technological Considerations and Activities with Development Planning in Small Island States*, UNESCO, Paris, March 1990.

Diamond, W., and Raghavan, U. W., *Aspects of Development Bank Management*, Johns Hopkins, New York, 1982.

Dolman, A. J., 'Paradise Lost? The Past Performance and Future Prospects of Small Island Developing Countries', in Dommen and Hein, 1985.

Dommen, E., and Hein, P., eds, *States, Microstates and Islands*, Croom Helm, London, 1985.

Dommen, E., and Hein, P., 'Foreign Trade in Goods and Services: the Dominant Activity of Small Island Economies', in Dommen and Hein, 1985.

Dore, R., 'Latecomers' Problems', *European Journal of Development Research*, 1, 1, June 1989, pp. 100–7.

Dore, R., *The Diploma Disease: Education, Qualification and Development*, Allen and Unwin, London, 1976.

Dorney, S., *Papua New Guinea*, Random House, Sydney, 1990.

Dosi, G., 'Technology Paradigms and Technology Trajectories', *Research Policy*, 11, 3, 1982, pp. 147–62.

Doulman, D. J., 'Fisheries Joint Ventures Revisited; Are They the Answer?', *Infofish Marketing Digest*, March 1990.

Doulman, D. J., 'An Overview of the Tuna Fishery and Industry in the Pacific Islands Region', in Buchholz, 1987.

Doulman, D. J., 'Fisheries Management in the South Pacific: The Role of the Forum Fisheries Agency', *Proceedings of the Otago Foreign Policy School*, University of Otago, Dunedin, 1990 (in press).

Doulman, D. J. and Terawasi, P., 'The South Pacific Regional Register of Foreign Fishing Vessels', *Marine Policy*, forthcoming.

Dunbar-Nobes, A. C., 'Vanuatu: Domestic Shipping Services in a Newly Independent State', in Kissling, 1984.

Economic and Social Commission for Asia and the Pacific, *Women in Development — A Regional Program of Action*, ESCAP, Bangkok, 1979.

Economic and Social Commission for Asia and the Pacific, *Report of the Subregional Follow-up Meeting for Pacific Women on the World Conference of the United National Decade for Women*, Suva, Fiji, 29 October–3 November 1980.

Economic and Social Commission for Asia and the Pacific, *Technology for Development: Study by the ESCAP Secretariat for the 40th Session of the Commission*, ESCAP, Tokyo, 1984.

Edmonds, G. A., and Howe, J. D. G. F., eds, *Roads and Resources: Appropriate Technology in Road Construction in Developing Countries*, Intermediate Technology for the International Labour Office, London, 1980.

Emerson, C., 'Mining Enclaves and Taxation', *World Development*, 10, 1982, pp. 561–71.

Evenson, R. E., and Ranis, G., eds, *Science and Technology: Lessons for Development Policy*, Westview, Boulder, 1990.

Fairbairn, Te'o I. J., *Island Economies: Studies from the South Pacific*, UNESCO and Institute of Pacific Studies, University of the South Pacific, Suva, 1985.

Feria, R., *Technical Aspects of Appraisal — Industrial Projects*, ADB-TDB Program on Development Banking for the South Pacific Region, Tonga Development Bank, Nuku'alofa, 1985.

Finch, A. W., *Consultancy on Inter-Island Shipping Services in the Republic of the Marshall Islands*, for South Pacific Bureau for Economic Cooperation, 1989.

Fisk, E. K., 'Subsistence Affluence and Development Policy', *Regional Development Dialogue*, special issue, 1982, pp. 1–13.

Fisk, E. K., ed., *The Adaptation of Traditional Agriculture: Socioeconomic Problems of Urbanisation*, Monograph 11, Development Studies Centre, Australian National University, Canberra, 1978.

Fisk, E. K., *The Economic Independence of Kiribati*, Australian National University, Canberra, 1985.

Fisk, E. K., 'Traditional Agriculture and Urbanisation: Policy and Practice', in Fisk, 1978.

Fitzpatrick, P., *Law and State in Papua New Guinea*, Academic Press, London, 1980.

Fleming, S., *Basic Water Supply and Sanitation*, Women's Development Training Programme, Institute of Rural Development, University of the South Pacific, Suva, June 1987.

Forsyth, D. J. C., *Technology Policy Assessment*, Terminal Report, FIJ/TOI/81, International Labour Office, Geneva, 1985.

Forsyth, D. J. C., *Appropriate National Technology Policies: A Manual for Their Assessment*, International Labour Office (with financial support from the UN Fund for Science and Technology for Development), Geneva, 1989.

Forsyth, D. J. C., *Technology Policy Assessment for Fiji*, International Labour Organisation, Geneva, 1983.

Forsyth, D. J. C., *Assessment of National Technology Policy in Fiji*, World Employment Programme, Technology and Development Branch, International Labour Organisation, Geneva, 1985.

Francis, A. J., and Mansell, D. S., *Appropriate Engineering Technology for Developing Countries*, Research Publications, Melbourne, 1988.

Frank, A. G., *Latin America: Underdevelopment or Revolution?*, Monthly Review Press, New York, 1969.

Fuller, R., 'Beware the Research Bias: Lessons from a Solar Drying Project', paper presented at UNESCO Regional Seminar on Technology for Community Development in Australia, SE Asia and the Pacific, Alice Springs, July 1990.

Geertz, C., 'Ethos, World View and the Analysis of Sacred Symbol', in Dantes, 1968.

Gini, P., 'Domestic Shipping in the South Pacific', in Kissling, 1984.

Girvan, N., 'The Approaches to Technology Policy Studies', *Social and Economic Studies*, 28, 1, Special Issue: Essays on Science and Technology Policy in the Caribbean, March 1989.

Gomez, E. D., et al, 'Other Fishing Methods Destructive To Coral', in Salvat, 1987.

Government of Fiji, *Fiji's Ninth Development Plan, 1986–1990*, Central Planning Office, Suva.

Government of Fiji, 'Policies and Strategies for Short and Medium Term', *Challenges for Development: Towards the Year 2000*, National Economic Summit, Government of Fiji, Suva, 1989.

Government of Papua New Guinea, *National Science and Technology Policy*, National Science and Technology Workshop, draft policy document, Port Moresby, 1990.

Government of the Kingdom of Tonga, *Fifth Five-Year Development Plan 1986–1990*, Central Planning Department, Nuku'alofa, December 1987.

Government of the Kingdom of Tonga, *Third Five-Year Development Plan, 1976–80*, Central Planning Department, Nuku'alofa, 1976.

Government of the Kingdom of Tonga, *Tonga Agricultural Census*, Statistics Department, Nuku'alofa, 1985.

Government of Tuvalu, *Third Development Plan, 1989–92*, Funafuti, 1989.

Green, R. C., 'New Sites with Lapita Pottery and Their Implications for the Settlement of the Western Pacific', *Working Papers in Anthropology*, no. 51, Dept. of Archaeology, University of Auckland, Auckland, 1978.

Griffen, V., ed., *Knowing and Knowing How: A Self-Help Manual on Technology for Women in the Pacific*, Centre for Applied Studies in Development, University of the South Pacific, Suva, 1981.

Haden, D., 'Inter-Island Shipping's New Face', *Pacific Islands Monthly*, April/May 1989.

Higgins, B., 'Appropriate Technology: Does It Exist?', *Regional Development Dialogue*, vol. 3, no. 1, Spring, 1982, pp. 158–86.

Hill, S., 'Basic Design Principles for National Research in Developing Countries', *Technology in Society*, 9, 1, 1987, pp. 63–73.

Hill, S., *The Tragedy of Technology — Human Liberation vs Domination in the Late 20th Century*, Pluto Press, London and Sydney, 1988.

Hill, S., 'Eighteen Cases of Technology Transfer to Asia/Pacific Countries', *Science and Public Policy*, 13, 3, pp. 162—9.

Hill, S., and Rahman, A., *CASTASIA II: Science, Technology and Development in Asia and the Pacific, Progress Report, 1968–1980*, Second Conference of Ministers Responsible for the Application of Science and Technology to Development and Those Responsible for Economic Planning in Asia and the Pacific, UNESCO and ESCAP, Manila, March 1982.

Hill, S., and Scott-Kemmis, D., *Technology Policy and Management — Issues for the South Pacific Region, Sectoral Issues and Workshop Questions*, Meeting Document no. STP 8, Centre for Technology and Social Change, Wollongong, 1987.

Hogbin, Ian, *Social Change*, Watts, London, 1958.

Holmes, S., *Nutrition Survey in the Gilbert Islands*, South Pacific Health Service Report, Suva, 1953.

Hufschmidt, M. M., et al, *Environment, Natural Systems and Development: An Economic Valuation Guide*, Johns Hopkins, Baltimore and London, 1983.

Illich, I., *Tools for Conviviality*, Harper, New York, 1987.

Illich, I., *Deschooling Society*, Calder and Boyars, London, 1971.

International Labour Organisation and South Pacific Commission, *Pacific Women in Trades*, ILO Office for the South Pacific and South Pacific Commission Regional Media Centre, Suva, 1990.

International Labour Organisation, *Matching Employment Opportunities and Expectations: A Programme of Action for Ceylon*, ILO, Geneva, 1971.

International Women's Tribune Centre, *Women and Development Quarterly*, IWTC, New York, March 1990.

International Women's Tribune Centre, *International Women's Tribune Centre Newsletter*, no. 44, 1990.

International Women's Tribune Centre, World YWCA and Kenya Appropriate Technology Committee, *Tech and Tools Fair*, Nairobi, 1985.

International Union for the Conservation of Nature (IUCN) and United Nations Environment Program (UNEP), *Review of the Protected Areas System in Oceania*, IUCN Conservation Monitoring Centre, Cambridge, 1986.

Inversin, A. R., *A Pelton Micro-Hydro Prototype Design*, Appropriate Technology Development Unit (now Institute), PNG University of Technology, 1980.

Jackson Report, *Report of the Committee to Review the Australian Overseas Aid Program*, Australian Government Publishing Service, Canberra, 1984.

Jalan, B., ed., *Problems and Policies in Small Economies*, Croom Helm, London, 1985.

Jequier, N., ed., *Appropriate Technology: Problems and Promises*, Organisation for Economic Cooperation and Development, Paris, 1976.

Johannes, R. E., *Words of the Lagoon: Fishing and Marine Lore in the Palau District of Micronesia*, University of California, Berkeley, 1981.

Johnston, P. C., 'Outlook for the Utilisation of New and Renewable Energy in the Pacific and the Tasks for Cooperation', paper prepared for the 4th Symposium on Pacific Energy Cooperation (SPEC 4), Tokyo, January 1990.

Kaplinsky, R., '"Technological Revolution" and the International Division of Labour in Manufacturing: A Place for the Third World?', *European Journal of Development Research*, 1, 1, June 1989, pp. 5–37.

Kissling, C. C., ed., *Transport and Communications for Pacific Microstates*, Institute of Pacific Studies, University of the South Pacific, Suva, 1984.

Kissling, C. C., 'Air Transport, Tourism and Economic Development in South Pacific Microstates', paper prepared for the ISLANDS 88 Conference, Hobart, 1988.

Kluckholn, C., 'The Concept of Culture', in Lerner and Lasswell, 1951.

Kroeber, A. L. and Kluckholn, C., *Culture — A Critical Review of Concepts and Definitions*, Random House (Vintage Books), New York, 1963.

Lerner, D. and Lasswell, H. D., *The Policy Sciences*, Stanford University Press, Stanford, 1951.

Liebenthal, A., *Pacific Regional Energy Assessment Issues Background and Objectives*, Pacific Household and Rural Energy Seminar, organised by UNDP, World Bank and PEDP, Port Vila, November 1990.

LikLik Buk Information Centre, *LikLik Buk: A Sourcebook for Development Workers in Papua New Guinea*, Appropriate Technology Development Institute, UniTech, Lae, Papua New Guinea, 1976 (original Pidgin edition), 1977 (original English edition), 1986 (updated English edition), 1988 (updated Pidgin edition).

Linton, R., *The Study of Man*, Appleton, New York, 1936.

Linton, R., *The Tree of Culture*, Knopf, New York, 1955.

Lipton, M., *Why Poor People Stay Poor*, Temple Smith, London, 1977.

Little, I. M. D., *Economic Development: Theory, Policy and International Relations*, Basic Books, New York, 1982.

Little, I. M. D., and Mirlees, J. A., *Project Appraisal and Planning for Developing Countries*, Heinemann, 1974.

Mansell, D. S., and Stewart, D. F., eds, *Barriers to Change and Technical Implications of the Provision of Shelter for the Homeless by the Year 2000*, UNESCO Regional Seminar, University of Melbourne, 1987.

Marjoram, T., *Directory of Technology for Development in the South Pacific*, Development Technologies Unit, University of Melbourne for UNESCO, 1990.

Marjoram, T., *Making a Village Water Pump*, Institute of Rural Development, University of the South Pacific, Tonga, 1986.

Marjoram, T., *Thinking Technology: Manual for Technology and Development in the South Pacific*, Development Technologies Unit, University of Melbourne, 1989.

Marjoram, T., *Rural Water Supply in the South Pacific*, paper presented at the Third International Conference on Rain Water Cistern Systems, Khon Kaen, Thailand, January 1987.

Marjoram, T., 'Small Is Beautiful? Technology Futures in the Small Island Pacific', *Futures*, May 1991.

Marjoram, T., *Toys? Boys? Technology and 'Development' in the Island South Pacific*, paper presented at Seminar on Technology for Community Development in Australia, SE Asia and the Pacific, Alice Springs, July 1990; International Development Technologies Centre, Faculty of Engineering, University of Melbourne.

Marjoram, T., *Technology Transfer and Choice in the South Pacific: A Policy Perspective from Tonga*, paper presented at the Waigani Seminar, Port Moresby, August 1984; Institute of Rural Development, University of the South Pacific.

Marjoram, T., *Technology Choice and Development in the South Pacific — Preliminary Report*, Institute of Rural Development, University of the South Pacific, Tonga, November 1985.

Marjoram, T., *Report of the Workshop: UNESCO South Pacific Technology and Development Workshop*, Nuku'alofa, Tonga, 1987.

Marjoram, T., *Stoves Development and Information Dissemination in the South Pacific*, Institute of Rural Development, University of the South Pacific, 1984.

Marjoram, T., 'Pipes and Pits under the Palms: Water Supply and Sanitation in the South Pacific', *Waterlines*, vol. 2, no. 1, July 1983, pp. 14–17.

Marjoram, T., *Small is Beaut in the South Pacific*, Institute of Rural Development, University of the South Pacific, Tonga, 1985.

Marjoram, T., 'Pipe Dreams in the Pacific' (review of potential for OTEC), *New Scientist*, 12 August 1982.

Marjoram, T., *Making a Smokeless Wood-Burning Stove*, leaflet number 4, Transfer of Appropriate Technology, Institute of Rural Development, University of the South Pacific, 1983.

Marjoram, T., 'Science and Technology Policy in the Small Island States of the South Pacific', paper presented at 17 ANZAAS Congress, Hobart, February 1990.

Marjoram, T., 'Wave Power in Tonga — A Second Wind?', paper presented at the Pacific Congress on Marine Technology, Honolulu, March 1986.

Marjoram, T., and Fleming, S., *Making a Ventilated Improved Pit Toilet*, Institute of Rural Development and Women's Development Training Programme, University of the South Pacific, Tonga, 1986.

Marjoram, T., and Fleming, S., *Building a Ferrocement Water Tank*, Institute of Rural Development and Women's Development Training Programme, University of the South Pacific, Tonga, 1986.

Marjoram, T. and Fleming, S., *Making a Ferrocement Water Tank Without Formwork* (demonstration video tape), Institute of Rural Development, University of the South Pacific, 1986.

Mathur, O. P., *Project Analysis for Local Development*, Westview Press, Boulder and London, 1985.

Mattei, R., *Sun Drying Cassava for Animal Feed: A Processing System for Fiji*, FAO RAS/83/001 Field Document 3, 1984.

McCulloch, M., *Project Frameworks — A Logical Development for More Effective Aid*, Overseas Development Administration, London, 1986.

Mead, M., *New Lives for Old: Cultural Transformation in Manus, 1928–53*, Gollancz, London, 1956.

Medford, D., and Rothman, H., *The South Pacific Sub-Regional UNCSTD Paper*, United Nations Conference on Science and Technology for Development, funded by UNESCO and undertaken at the Centre for Applied Studies in Development, University of the South Pacific, Suva, 1978.

Meier, G. M., *Leading Issues in Economic Development*, Oxford University Press, 1970.

Meillassoux, C., *Maidens, Meal and Money*, Cambridge, 1981.

Mena, M. M., 'Development of Appropriate Technology for the Rural Sector in the Developing Countries of Asia', *Proceedings of the Second Asian Conference on Technology for Rural Development*, Kuala Lumpur, Malaysia 4–7 December 1985; also in Radhakrishna, Mohinder Singh and John, 1988.

Menon, M. G. K., 'Technology Assessment For Development', in *Technology Assessment for Development*, Report of the United Nations Seminar on Technology Assessment for Development, Bangalore, 1978.

Ministry of Economic Planning, Government of the Solomon Islands, *Solomon Islands National Development Plan; 1985–89*, Ministry of Economic Planning, Honiara, 1985.

Ministry of Agriculture, Forests and Fisheries, Kingdom of Tonga, *A Review of the Banana Export Industry in the Kingdom of Tonga*, Nuku'alofa, 1979.

Moengangongo, S., 'Indigenous Food Storage Systems', *Alafua Agricultural Bulletin*, 8, 1983.

Moengangongo, T. H., and Fonua, I. L., 'Evaluation of Tractor Performance', unpublished manuscript, Nuku'alofa, 1980.

Moengangongo, T. H., 'The Economics of Running the MAFF Machinery Pool', unpublished manuscript, Nuku'alofa, 1981.

Moromoro, M., and Le Grys, G. A., 'Appraisal of the Current State of Science and Technology in Papua New Guinea: Options for Action', paper presented at the Workshop for the Preparation of a National Science and Technology Policy for Papua New Guinea, Port Moresby, 4–6 September 1990.

Murai, M., Pen, F., and Miller, C. D., *Some Tropical South Pacific Island Foods*, University of Hawaii Press, Honolulu, 1958.

National Planning Office, Government of Kiribati, *Kiribati: Sixth National Development Plan, 1987–91*, National Planning Office, Ministry of Finance, Kiribati, 1988.

Nelson, H., *Black White and Gold*, Australian National University Press, Canberra, 1976.

Nelson, R., and Winter, S., 'In Search of a Useful Theory of Innovation', *Research Policy*, 6, 1, 1977, pp. 36–76.

O'Faircheallaigh, C., *Mining and Development*, Croom Helm, Sydney, 1984.

Organisation for Economic Cooperation and Development and World Bank, *Road Monitoring for Maintenance Management: Manual and Damage Catalogue for Developing Countries* (2 vols), OECD, Paris, 1990.

Overseas Development Administration, *Economic Analysis of Development Projects*, HMSO, London, 1983.

Padgett, B., *Technological Mobility and Cultural Constraints*, in Chatterji, M., 1990.

Parkinson, S., *The Preservation and Preparation of Root Crops and Some Other Traditional Foods in the South Pacific*, FAO RAS/83/001 Field Document, 1984.

Parry, J. P. M., 'Intermediate Technology Building', *Appropriate Technology*, vol. 2, no. 3, November 1975.

Peet, R., 'The Conscious Dimension of Fiji's Integration into World Capitalism', *Pacific Viewpoint*, 21 (2), 1980, pp. 91–115.

Project Planning Centre for Developing Countries, *A Manual on Project Planning for Small Economies*, University of Bradford for Commonwealth Secretariat, 1982.

Quodling, P. W., *Bougainville Copper Limited — A History*, April 1990.

Radhakrishna, S., Mohinder Singh, M., and John, C. K., eds, *Proceedings of the Second Asian Conference on Technology for Rural Development*, World Scientific, Singapore, 1988.

Rado, E., 'The Explosive Model', *Manpower and Unemployment Research in Africa*, vol. 6, no. 2, 1973.

Rahman, A., and Hill, S., *Science, Technology and Development in Asia and the Pacific*, SC/82/CASTASIA II REF 1, UNESCO, Paris, 1982.

Randall, J. E., 'Collecting Reef Fishes for Aquaria', in Salvat, 1987.

Ravuvu, A., *Class and Culture in the South Pacific*, Centre for Pacific Studies (Auckland) and Institute of Pacific Studies, Suva, 1987.

Regional Development Dialogue, Regional Development in Small Island Nations, special issue, UN Centre for Regional Development, Nagoya, 1982.

Reimer, E., *School is Dead: An Essay on Alternatives in Education*, Penguin, London, 1971.

Richardson, J., 'Abetting, Not Aiding', *Islands Business*, 8, November 1982.

Rizer, J., and Hansen, J., *Energy in the Pacific Islands: Issues and Statistics*, Resources Programmes, East-West Center, Honolulu, 1990.